The Annual

of the
Society of Christian Ethics

2001

Volume 21

Contents

Religion and Liberalism Revisited

Panel on Theology Beyond the Liberal Paradigm: Civil Society and its Discontents

Critiques and New Directions in Catholic Moral Theology

Historical Studies in Christian Ethics

Judaism and Bioethics

Panel: Is There a Unique Jewish Bioethics?

Ethics in International Context

PREFACE

With this volume we conclude our five-year term as co-editors of *The Annual*. We do so with the hope that we have met the expectations of the Society as shaped by the work of those editors who preceded us. The editorship of this journal is a trust in at least two senses of the term. First, as editors, we have had the responsibility of maintaining and publishing the "bank" of scholarship represented by the membership's work. Second, being assigned this responsibility is an act of trust on the part of the society which we have deeply appreciated and striven to respect. We thank all those authors, peer-reviewers, editorial board members, and Society officers and staff with whom we have had the pleasure of working in this Society-wide collaborative endeavor. *The Annual* is truly a product of the many, not just a chosen few. We end our term secure in the knowledge that the Society has chosen two new editors well able to continue leading this collective work of the Society in a manner that may expand ever further its contribution to the scholarly fields which it incorporates.

As with past Presidential addresses published at the beginning of *The Annual*'s volumes, this issue reflects the special interests and angle of vision of the current President Harlan Beckley—in his case concern over the ethics of poverty. Beckley himself addresses poverty in the industrialized world by focusing special attention on distinguishing and criticizing three approaches to justifying the welfare state: rights-based, reciprocity-based, and agency-based justifications. After exploring the strengths and weaknesses of these justifications, Beckley then mounts a provocative case for the proposition that taking seriously a Christian notion of common grace may well correct their deficiencies, although he leaves the fuller task of constructing an alternative justificatory account for another venue.

Beckley's vision for revitalizing concern for the ethics of poverty is continued in the section on poverty, welfare, and inequality. Here we begin by publishing the plenary address of Mary Jo Bane and the remarks of her respondent Emilie Townes, both of which were specially commissioned by Beckley. Banes' address proposes to submit both public policy analysis and Christian ethics to the discipline of democratic politics, particularly by inviting religious discussion into public debates about domestic policy and welfare issues. While agreeing with the overall tenor of Banes' call, Townes cautions that the proponents of public policies are often unaware of contestable religiously-formed values at the root of such policies, and argues the latter must be self-consciously guided by norms of relational justice and the ethics of care if they are to be truly beneficial for the poor and marginalized. The papers by Christine Hinze and Douglas Hicks, respectively, both deepen and broaden this vision of relational justice in economic affairs. Hinze uses recent anthropological work on purity and pollution codes to examine cultural attitudes and practices surrounding the devaluation of "dirty" work which undergirds much economic and social inequality of marginalized groups in American and more broadly Western society. She argues that Christian ethics ought to work to bring to light and then dismantle these powerful, often unconscious, but nonetheless destructive ideological supports of injustice in household and public economies. Hicks sets his sights on poverty and inequality in the context of globalization, arguing that a social-relational anthropology informed by a preferential option for the poor should help us to understand and address global inequality and deprivation: giving moral priority to the needs of the poor and marginalized, while also recognizing the humanity of the affluent and criticizing those practices by which the latter separate themselves from the public life of their societies.

The papers in the section on religion and liberalism function to deepen, expand, and explore Banes' call for bringing religious arguments and actors into the square of public debate about economic (and other) policies. The papers from the panel on theology beyond the liberal paradigm focus on the potential role of the churches in civil society and political debate. John Bowlin notes the similarities between Christian churches and other intermediate associations (see his vivid example of Oklahoman gamecock clubs) and then uses Aquinas' treatment of justice and religion to demonstrate their character as natural societies which yield morally ambiguous mixtures of virtue and vice. William Cavanaugh contrasts and criticizes two models for Christian involvement in civil society--one informed by the public theology of John Courtney Murray, and the other by the grassroots citizen activism of Harry Boyte—arguing that both models finally fail to appreciate the depth of interpenetration of state and civil society, an interpenetration which threatens to reduce the church to mundane public terms and to subjugate its values and ends to those of self-interest. Cavanaugh calls for a more sophisticated and robust disciplineship—in contrast to citizenship— predicated on the notion of "church as public space," which thinks differently (and more justly) about economic policies. Charles Mathewes explores how agonistic political thought—in contrast to liberal political theory—offers an opportunity for Christian thinkers to interpret and approach political conflict and debate as a struggle about "our loves" which can be tutored by the conviction that such struggle need not be construed as a zero-sum game. Jean Bethke Elshtain then concludes the panel of papers by raising pointed questions and puzzles about each which we would all do well to ponder. Although it was not part of this panel, Eric Gregory's paper on Augustine and Arendt fits well into this section because it presents and criticizes Arendt's reading of Augustine in order to move beyond liberal reciprocity toward a version of Augustinian liberalism that does not sentimentalize or privatize love but rather uses it to construct a more viable liberalism less open to destructive individualism, commercialism, and narrow rationalism. In his emphasis on "good citizenship as good loving," Gregory's essay may share some common ground with Mathewes' proposal.

The papers in the next section are united in their concern for Catholic moral theology, but they take this concern in different directions. Aline Kalbian's paper analyzes Pope John Paul II's 2000 Jubilee public confessions for the church's past sins, especially toward the Jews, by exploring the uses of two distinctive metaphors that appear to problematize these acts of contrition—namely, the metaphor of church as mother sorrowing over the sins of her children (problematizing just whose sins are at issue) and the metaphor of repentance as purification of memory (raising the problem of whether and how memories of sins should be treated). In the context of an era of truth commissions and public repentance, Kalbian's discussion of these metaphors and their implications for notions of collective responsibility is indeed timely. William McDonough's paper moves in a somewhat different direction, taking up the Catholic Church's approach to homosexuality and same-sex partnerships. Using the recent work of Alasdair MacIntyre on dependence and human flourishing, McDonough argues that a genuine natural law of care should recognize the sanctity and worth of same-sex life-partnerships and that such a development would—contrary to its present view—be more consistent with the Church's recent thinking about authentic love and marriage. Todd Whitmore's paper comparing the economic thought of John Paul II with that of Michael Novak explores the strength of the Catholic Church's social justice teachings, especially in their affirmation of economic rights, in contrast to the limitations of Novak's economic theory and moral theology. Despite claims that Novak's thought has influenced the thinking of John Paul II on such matters, Whitmore argues quite convincingly on the basis of close textual comparisons that not only are these claims not true but also they could not be true in light of the considerable divergence of Novak's thought from Catholic social teaching on economic justice. In the final paper of this section, Christopher Steck, using the thought of Iris Murdoch among others, examines the theme of tragedy in the aesthetic dimension of von Balthasar's theology, suggesting that this theme and dimension can be usefully deployed to show how the perception of Christ's life illumines the tragic quality of the Christian moral life as well as its concomitant character as "hopeful fidelity."

The papers by Jennifer Herdt and Jean Porter in the following section represent in a robust manner the Society's ongoing commitment to the work of historical retrieval and reinterpretation of past Christian thinkers. Against recent critics who have charged seventeenth century British theologians with domesticating divine transcendence, Herdt reclaims the work of some of these theologians—notably Benjamin Whitcote—to show that such blanket criticisms are not only misguided but also overlook potentially strong connections between seventeenth century conceptions of divinity and notions of transformative justice. Jean Porter's paper on notions of natural equality in Bonaventure and Aquinas reaches even further back to the late medieval period, offering a careful contextual and comparative analysis that educes certain surprising similarities on the ideal of equality between these two thinkers, even amid important differences. As is often the case with Porter's work, she concludes her historical reconstruction by drawing out some normative implications for how we understand equality in our contemporary context.

The section of Judaism and bioethics is a panel of papers solicited by past President Ronald Green in conformity with his vision that the Society needs to engage more explicitly in dialogue with the moral traditions of other religions, especially Judaism. This panel is noteworthy for its attempt to identify the distinctiveness of Jewish ethics generally and Jewish bioethics in particular. The papers are marked by their efforts to clarify that tradition's distinctive methodology, as well as the values it shares with other traditions. One comes away from these papers with an appreciation of how ethicists in the Jewish tradition use legal and historical precedent to construct critical positions in response to changing contemporary circumstances and developments in biomedical technology.

The final section on ethics in international context seems to capture aspects of the visions of past Presidents Ronald Green and Charles Reynolds in their calls for more comparative ethics in the Society's work as well as more moral dialogue with other religious traditions. Jack Hill's paper explicitly engages the discipline of comparative ethics by deploying an ethnographic and narrative approach to the ethics of the Pacific Islanders of Fiji and Atiu. This study is done with careful attention to cultural, social, and historical context, and Hill concludes by drawing provocative lessons for future work in cross-cultural moral inquiry. The final paper by Neville Richardson is also comparative in nature, since it uses the leitmotif of "keeping theological ethics theological" from the American context (e.g., Hauerwas) to organize its approach to analyzing developments in Christian ethics in post-apartheid South Africa. The result is provocative for the manner in which it draws forth the reader's appreciation that Christian ethics in South Africa and the United States share a common concern for the problem of how the church can most effectively engage in political debate and the reconstruction of civil society without losing its distinctive theological character. In this respect, Richardson's paper returns us to the subject of earlier papers in the volume.

As usual, we have many people to thank for the collaborative work of this volume—the authors, published and unpublished; the peer-reviewers from the general membership; the members of the editorial board; the leadership and staff of the Society; and our editorial assistants and office staff at our universities. Special thanks are due to our editorial assistant Garry Crites, who has worked with us for all the five volumes we have edited. His has been a yeoman's task which he has borne with intelligence, competence, grace, and goodwill under sometimes trying circumstances. We will miss working with him.

John Kelsay
Sumner B. Twiss
Co-Editors

PRESIDENTIAL ADDRESS

Forty-second Annual Meeting
The Society of Christian Ethics

2001

Presidential Address:
Moral Justifications for the Welfare State[1]

Harlan Beckley

The subject matter of this address, apropos of its theological content, has come to my attention through events beyond my control. Three and one-half years ago, my university appointed me to direct a program for the Interdisciplinary Study of Poverty. As this appointment altered the direction of my scholarship, I soon noticed how little focused attention theological and religious ethicists have given to poverty. We never fully participated in the surge of poverty studies that developed in the wake of Lyndon Johnson's War on Poverty. Several of us have written on economic justice. Some of these writings address the issue of poverty—for example, Darryl Trimiew's informative and thorough book on economic rights—but very few concentrate on poverty.[2] Rare exceptions exist. Warren Copeland's *Ethics of Poverty in the United States* comes readily to mind.[3] More recently, Elizabeth Bounds, Pamela Brubaker, and Mary Hobgood have edited a valuable collection of essays on feminist critiques of welfare policy.[4] These books should not be so conspicuous for their attention to poverty. Our Society can support a broader discussion of poverty across a spectrum of theological, ethical, and political views.

I hope this essay stimulates and contributes to that discussion. I will first consider three highly influential arguments regarding the welfare state and follow with a theological response to ethical shortcomings in these arguments. I propose to identify crucial matters that have been neglected in current moral justifications for the welfare state.

We begin with two distinct justifications for the modern welfare state, the first by British moral philosopher and public intellectual Raymond Plant and the second by U.S. philosopher J. Donald Moon.

Annual of the Society of Christian Ethics, 21 (2001): 3-22

Plant's Rights-Based Justification

Plant gained considerable notoriety for his rights-based defense of the welfare state in the face of British Conservative attempts to dismantle it. He rests his case for welfare rights on society's obligation to preserve each person's freedom to exercise her capacity for "rational, autonomous agency."[5] Rational autonomy designates a capacity to choose and pursue moral ends. Plant makes the familiar claim that freedom is both positive and negative. Positive freedom entails the resources necessary for human agents to pursue a moral life. Negative freedom prohibits interventions that could hinder this pursuit. Humans have the same claim to social and economic resources requisite for pursuing their moral ends as they have to protection from interference that obstructs their pursuit of these ends. We have a right to whatever welfare assistance is required for the positive freedom to exercise our rational, autonomous agency.

Neither the right to assistance nor the right to non-intervention is unlimited. Plant restricts rights to basic needs, that is, needs that must be satisfied in order to pursue any moral ends whatsoever. No right exists to non-basic needs, that is, goods or protections indispensable for a particular life plan that an individual happens to choose. Humans have a right to needs requisite for any life plan whatsoever but no right to what is needed to execute the particular life plan they have chosen.[6] His distinction between basic and non-basic needs enables Plant, so he contends, to establish universal rights to welfare assistance. These rights are not contingent on the values, customs, and institutions of a particular society or the specific life plan or behavior of the rights holder. If he could support these claims, Plant would have achieved a rights-based claim to welfare independent of the particularities of any society and of the behavior of welfare recipients. However, neither his claim to universal welfare rights nor his claim to welfare rights independent of recipient behavior withstands scrutiny.

As he shifts from explaining why both positive and negative freedoms are indispensable for exercising rational autonomy to demarcating basic from non-basic needs in order to distinguish rights from demands for a just share of society's resources, Plant alters his criterion for justifying rights. Plant correctly contends that persons require both positive and negative freedoms to pursue any possible moral end, presumably some form of moral excellence. He also rightly points out that not all positive or negative freedoms are rights, only those which he designates as basic needs. However, what he calls basic needs are determined by whatever is required to pursue a conception of the good or well being. This shift from moral excellence to well being undermines Plant's justification for welfare rights. The positive freedom needed for moral excellence is minimal. It requires only subsistence and a meager education in order to know right from wrong. It does not constitute a claim for income assistance, a living wage, job training, or other support associated with a modern welfare state. We all know, or we can visualize, morally excellent persons living a meager existence.[7] The means required for well being are more substantial and entail aspects of welfare support, but they are not necessary for rational autonomy as Plant understands it.[8] Plant's rights-based argument might justify a universal right to subsistence and the most elemental education, but it does not justify a universal right to what we call welfare.[9]

Rejecting Plant's rights-based claim to welfare does not deny welfare assistance as a social right.[10] However, a social right to welfare such as Donald Moon proposes, depends on a substantial, though still partial, conception of the good and the circumstances in a particular society. It cannot be a universal right in the sense that Plant claims for welfare rights.

Plant's effort to immunize welfare rights from recipient behavior—what he calls "right[s] of unreciprocated recipience"[11]—fares no better than his claim that they are universal. The purposes behind this effort are laudable. Plant seeks to distinguish society's strict duty to distribute the basic needs of welfare from a charitable, but not required, grant to meet citizens' non-basic needs. Even more important, welfare rights unconditioned by recipient behavior avoid the stigma of welfare.[12] Plant correctly claims that welfare ought to be an obligation of society bearing no stigma for the recipient. He, however, makes no distinction between income and material support without any expectation from the recipient, on the one hand, and welfare assistance that encourages, expects, and even enforces reciprocal behavior, such as work in the labor market, on the other. Plant charges that capitalist societies attach a stigma to all transfers of resources that occur outside of the market.[13] His claim may be empirically valid. Unfortunately, some citizens do malign all recipients of public assistance. Some astute observers of the welfare system contend that public assistance contingent on behavior necessarily stigmatizes all recipients.[14] It is theoretically possible, however, to discriminate between unresponsive recipients of assistance and those who comply with reasonable standards of reciprocity appropriate to the market economy. According to Donald Moon, in modern market economies, welfare does not entail moral opprobrium if it is linked to conditions of reciprocity required for self-respect. If Moon is correct, welfare rights depend in part on behavioral expectations of particular societies.

Both the achievements and failures of Plant's rights-based justification of welfare are instructive. First, he shows us that the freedom to pursue ends, whether moral ends or well-being, is positive as well as negative. It requires provision for resources that enable action as well as restraint from interfering with individual liberty. Plant reveals the folly of opposing welfare assistance because citizens have less claim for positive assistance than to forbearance from interfering with pursuit of their ends.[15] Second, welfare rights, if they exist, are not easily derived from universal human rights. They cannot be derived from an abstract concept of the moral end of rational persons. The basic needs indispensable to rational autonomy do not necessitate the array of assistance associated with the welfare state. Third, in order to specify welfare assistance to which citizens are entitled, we will need to appeal to the values and resources of particular cultures and societies. Fourth, welfare assistance without stigma does not require assistance independent of reasonable demands on the recipient.

The Welfare State as a Condition for Self-Respect

Donald Moon's justification for welfare as a condition for self-respect in a modern market economy responds to these deficiencies in Plant's rights-based justification.[16]

Moon also seeks to defend welfare as a right rather than an act of charity. Moon, however, contends that rights-based justifications for welfare—Plant is his immediate target—neglect "the norms that specify what one has to be and to do to attain self-respect" in a modern market economy.[17] Moon's welfare rights depend on a perceived linkage between self-respect (as an appropriate sense of satisfaction with one's own moral achievements) and the good of economic independence or self-sufficiency in a modern market economy. The welfare rights Moon defends are partially contingent on distinctive moral traditions and societal and economic circumstances within the modern market economy.

Moon argues that rights-based justifications for welfare conflict with the "self-understandings" of the citizens of welfare states.[18] He turns to the Friedrich Hegel for this self-understanding. Moon believes that Hegel observed correctly that modern market economies struggle with a deep moral contradiction. Such economies promise citizens opportunities to provide for themselves materially and to exercise considerable control over their own lives. Yet these economies inevitably violate this promise by producing poverty alongside of wealth. This poverty exiles some citizens from the market's institutional promise and robs these citizens of "the possibility of maintaining their well-being and dignity."[19] This persistent breach of promise justifies a demand for extra-market policies as a means to overcome the moral contradiction.

Overcoming the breach must be consistent, however, with the self-understanding of citizens within these market economies. The economies offer material well-being and self-control in return for reciprocity. Reciprocity, as Moon understands it, demands that citizens gain economic independence through their own labors. For citizens who have internalized this morality of reciprocity—and most, including welfare recipients, themselves, have—self-respect depends on realizing economic self-sufficiency through participation in the market. Citizens exiled from the market are, through no fault of their own, impeded from attaining self-respect. They will feel themselves moral failures unless they can either gain economic independence through reciprocity or claim and eventually obtain rights to public assistance that makes this reciprocal behavior possible.[20]

Accordingly, welfare must be contingent on recipient participation in the economy. Moon, citing Hegel, contends that for citizens to receive public assistance "directly, not by means of their work, . . . violate[s] the principle of civil society and the feeling of individual independence and self-respect."[21] Hence, a right to basic material needs, which Plant advocates, cannot repair the moral dilemma of a modern economy. Mere provision for needs violates the expectations of society. Citizens of modern welfare states will stigmatize forms of public assistance that do not demand participation in the economy. Moreover, they are justified in doing insofar as the market's promise of economic independence through reciprocal labor is morally justified.

Moon's conceptions of reciprocity and self-respect preclude universal welfare rights but retain social or citizen welfare rights to three sets of policies. First, he calls for "macroeconomic management" that advances opportunities for economic independence through expanding employment. Second, he advocates "universal services," such as education, that assure citizens the necessary means to participate in the economy. Third, he insists on "social insurance" that protects against contingencies beyond the control of self-respecting citizens. Moon has in mind mandatory insurance programs such as workmen's compensation and unemployment insurance to protect citizens against unfortunate circumstances, for example, structural unemployment. The managed economy that also provides for universal education can foresee but cannot prevent these contingencies. From Moon's perspective, one could plausibly argue that healthcare should be either a universal service or subject to a mandatory insurance program, as on-the-job injuries are. Healthcare could hardly be left to the market alone, as it has been for too many citizens in the United States, leaving them vulnerable to exclusion from the promises of the market system. Finally, the cash and in-kind assistance that we typically call welfare could be viewed as a mandatory social insurance program. However, it can be viewed as insurance only as long as citizens perceive themselves and others equally vulnerable to temporary destitution from which they could recover after short-term assistance.[22]

Moon's interpretation of reciprocity precludes several other forms of public assistance. Cash transfers that guarantee a minimum level of income and government provision for employment would leave persons in a permanent position of dependence that undermines self-respect. Provision for services (e.g., education, healthcare, or childcare) that target the poor violate the principle of reciprocity. Unlike universal services or mandatory social insurance, which are funded by all citizens to benefit all citizens, these means-tested programs do not require reciprocity. Moon is more ambivalent about income supplements for those who work. But if reciprocity demands economic independence through participation in the market, as Moon asserts, minimum wage legislation, earned income tax credits, and other forms of compensation supplements for the working poor would seem to undercut self-respect.[23]

The incompatibility between these forms of welfare assistance and self-respect leaves Moon with a dilemma. Although he believes that justified welfare policies can do much more than they have, especially in the United States, to diminish the Hegelian contradiction in the market economy, he concedes that the norms and practices of the market economy will continue to exile some citizens from its promises. Despite his frustration with this prospect and admirable honesty in describing it, Moon proffers no realistic alternative.

Whatever dissatisfaction we may register with Moon's argument and proposal, we should agree that he corrects deficiencies in Plant's. First, he reconciles welfare rights with a principle of reciprocity endemic to market economies, a principle which, appropriately revised, is morally defensible. Second, Moon's welfare program treats poverty as a barrier to participation in the economy, not merely as material deprivation. Poverty is more than income deprivation. Persons whose basic needs are met, yet who are denied the self-respect that comes through participation in the economy, remain impoverished. They have no opportunity for a decent life in a market society.

Despite these contributions, Moon's justification remains inadequate. First, he wrongly insists that reciprocity entails economic independence, provision for oneself and one's family through participation in the market. Even though many persons presume that reciprocal labor commands economic self-sufficiency, it is neither the regnant view nor intrinsic to a market economy. Reciprocity requires giving something proportionate to what one receives. In this instance, the proportionate giving should be substantial participation in the labor market, which for most adults is nearly full-time work. That proportionate effort need not produce economic self-sufficiency from the vagaries of an often capricious labor market. Supplements to the market through wage regulation, refundable tax credits for hours worked, and other means-tested compensation need not undermine self-respect.[24]

Second, Moon assumes that all physically and mentally unimpaired persons possess the full capacities of human agency, the capacity to perform duties commensurate with self-respect. He ignores the possibility that persons' capacities may be wounded by the residues of previous injustice, persistent misfortunate, or habitual irresponsibility. Consequently, his justification for the welfare state considers only policies that construct opportunities for persons who already control their capacity for self-respect. Moon ignores policies aimed at restoring capacities for reciprocity and self-respect such as remedial education, job training, and therapy. He rejects employment programs that enforce and foster work behavior.

Competence Cannot Be Assumed But Can Be Enforced

Lawrence M. Mead, a neo-conservative political scientist influential in shaping welfare reform in the United States, challenges Moon, Plant, and others—both proponents and opponents of the welfare state—who assume the moral autonomy of the non-working poor.[25] Mead contends that most of the long-term, non-working poor—approximately 5-7% of the U.S. population by his account—lack what he unfortunately and misleadingly calls competence.[26] They are bound in poverty by a psychological incapacity to pursue their rational self-interests. He characterizes these persons as having an inconsistent commitment to work and other patterns of behavior required by their own economic goals and the principle of reciprocity.

Since the publication of *Beyond Entitlement* in 1986 and his concomitant support for a version of welfare reform, Mead has been mistakenly lumped with Charles Murray and others who believe that public assistance offers an incentive to avoid work.[27] Mead argues that the long-term, non-working poor are unable to respond to economic incentives. They are unable even to perceive the opportunities available to them because they feel defeated. They lack what psychologists call a sense of self-efficacy. Mead's evidence for this claim is primarily negative. The increase, beginning in the early 1970s, of the percentage of the poor who do not work or work only sporadically, cannot be explained, Mead claims, by structural barriers to work. Economic hard times, low wages for unskilled workers, lack of jobs, racial discrimination, inadequate childcare support, and the absence of decent, low-cost transportation explain, according to Mead's evidence, only a small fraction of non-work.[28] The principal explanation, he concludes, must be the inability of these persons to recognize the jobs available to them. These persons depend on assistance, not because it offers them a good life without work but because it sustains their inertia.

Mead offers no definitive explanation for this lack of what he calls competence. He considers some plausible causes such as psychological damage due to a history of injustice, which he believes may explain patterns of work and family behavior among some African Americans.[29] His description of lack of competence—he never calls it incompetence—also fits with other explanations: habits formed by accumulated willful refusals to claim educational or job opportunities, loss of self-efficacy due to persistent misfortune, or internalizing sub-cultural norms detrimental to achieving one's professed economic goals. Mead explicitly denies any connection between lack of competence and innate inabilities, whether due to genetic defects or to physical and mental illnesses. Moreover, he distinguishes lack of competence from rejecting values endemic to the modern market economy. Countercultural behavior would be rational, Mead maintains, but the non-working poor "fail to do what they themselves desire."[30]

Mead's explanation for this significant slice of American poverty shifts the focus away from disputes about conceptions of justice and rights or about opportunities in the economic structure. It concentrates on the agency of the non-working poor. While libertarians protest the injustice of taxation for the sake of public assistance, Mead writes sparingly about justice. Moreover, his views pertinent to economic justice are most decidedly not libertarian. He does not oppose big government. Although Mead would undoubtedly object to Plant's rights theory for failing to tie welfare assistance to work, his implicit understanding of justice roughly approximates Moon's principles of economic opportunity and reciprocity.[31] Contrary to Moon, however, Mead assumes that economic opportunities are substantially available and prescinds from a discussion of justice. The crucial issue, Mead insists, is agency, not principles or structures. He is dismayed that most economists and philosophers examining poverty assume the rational autonomy of poor persons.

Mead does not propose to dissolve the welfare state. Indeed, government plays a significant role in his anti-poverty policy. He proposes to use the established system of public assistance to address the competency problem by making work a condition for assistance.[32] Government and powerful institutions should exercise their authority to sanction expectations for reciprocity among the poor. Assistance should not be discontinued but should be contingent on behavior, primarily work. Government best serves the long-term poor by expecting work in return for assistance. Mead's most recent writings combine this work enforcement with job training programs that simultaneously nourish and demand skills development and good habits, a policy he calls "help and hassle."[33]

Mead's misguided patronizing language describing the non-working poor should not obfuscate his challenge to justifications for welfare that ignore the issue of agency. By ignoring the problem of consistent motivation, these justifications neglect possible benefits work enforcement policies may have for both society and poor persons. As long as reciprocity remains a consensus principle for the economic system, justifications for welfare that do not enforce it discredit arguments for public assistance and also demean those excepted from this standard. Such justifications undermine recipients' opportunities for self-respect. Moreover, justifications for welfare that avert attention from the distinctive problems of agency among poor persons are incapable of addressing the need for remedial and therapeutic programs whose concurrent care for and demands on clients are indispensable for regenerating impaired rational autonomy.

We can learn from Mead without endorsing his derogatory portrayal of the non-working, long-term poor. I will register five objections to his account, all of which should inform a justification for the welfare state.

First, Mead's evidence for a defeatist attitude is inconclusive. Defeatism probably explains less joblessness than he asserts. The evidence that available jobs go unfilled is substantial, but the reasons for this phenomenon are unclear.

Rebecca M. Blank, economist and Dean of the School of Public Policy at the University of Michigan, argues that decreasing demand and real wages for undereducated workers over the past two decades best explain the failure of unskilled workers to increase their work effort. Inadequate labor-market incentives, Blank contends, explain most non-work. Low-skilled adults are perfectly rational in reducing their work effort. When the incentives are increased, low-skilled workers will take jobs.[34]

This dispute over whether inconsistent motivation or a rational response to incentives best explains joblessness cannot be resolved on the available evidence. What reciprocal benefits must jobs offer in order to make it irrational not to seek them? Mead contends that persons who reject low-paying jobs act contrary to their rational interests, even if the compensation leaves them below the poverty line, itself a dubious measure of a decent livelihood.[35] Mead even interprets resistance to work out of "moral revulsion rather than calculations of self-interest" as irrational. "[T]he motive," he says, "is to save . . . self-respect or make a political point."[36] If so, the person is not defeated but actively asserting her self-respect. Recall Moon's view that protesting against an economic system that denies economic self-sufficiency in return for one's productive labor may be a rational affirmation of self-respect. Mead unwittingly affirms Moon's observation. Resisting jobs that fail to reciprocate for labor may be the only available rational means for some persons to affirm their self-respect. The substantial and increasing number of working poor in our economy indicates that many poor persons may be justified in resisting work.

On the other hand, justifications for behavior do not explain motivations. Even if rejecting low-paid work is rational, many non-working poor persons may not be motivated by a desire to affirm their long-term, rational interests. Their work effort may be hindered by an inconsistent motivation. Indeed, cumulative evidence from Mead and others lends far more credibility to his explanation for non-work than radicals, liberals, or libertarians admit. My second objection obtains, however, even if Mead's explanation for non-work is substantially accurate.

Reciprocity demands that work in the labor market command the compensation needed for a decent life, whether or not this compensation induces most poor persons to work. Those who work deserve just compensation. Those not working should expect it if they do work. Mead offers no reason for disagreeing. He does not object to a higher minimum wage, earned income tax credits, healthcare, childcare, and other benefits for the working poor. Indeed, these policies are compatible with the little Mead says about justice. Unlike Moon, he associates reciprocity and self-respect with work effort, not with gaining economic independence. Nevertheless, Mead's focus on behavior and agency crowds the issue of a just wage off his moral and political agenda. He observes, almost insouciantly, that the American public will become more agitated about fair wages for low-skilled adults once they go to work.[37] Better conditions for the working poor would render Mead's own policies more coherent. Justifications for enforcing work through conditional public assistance depend on just compensation for work.[38]

My third criticism concerns Mead's failure to distinguish what he calls a lack of competence from what Amartya Sen calls deficient capabilities.[39] Debilitating addictions and psychological traumas can render persons incapable of work, at least in the short term. These disabilities are not amenable to the "help and hassle" of job-enforcement programs that can remedy the inconsistent motivation Mead describes. Persons so encumbered, whether or not they are partially or fully responsible for their condition, cannot take responsibility for their current work effort. Their hope for self-respect through participation in the economy depends on long-term therapy. The admitted difficulty in discriminating between uncertain motivation, subject to correction by authoritative sanctions and support, and deficient capabilities does not abrogate the injustice of demanding behavior persons cannot achieve. Rebecca Blank perceptively argues that public assistance should accommodate persons for whom work is not a short-term option due to a variety of addictions and psychological problems.[40] A justification for welfare need not embrace permanent material assistance, with no expectations or demands, for temporarily disabled persons. But such persons require therapy and prolonged material assistance rather than immediate work enforcement.

Fourth, Mead uncritically links reciprocity through a minimal amount of paid labor with integrating poor persons into the mainstream of the economy.[41] This unexamined linkage, coupled with his self-professed paternalism[42] that "seeks openly to manage behavior,"[43] raises the specter of using public assistance to limit liberties and enforce mainstream values.[44] We must distinguish reciprocity, requiring a decent minimum of paid labor, from full integration into dominant values of society. Specifications of the amount and types of appropriate work, of family, sexual, and reproductive behavior, and of consumption patterns are unjustified unless they are required by reciprocity. The balance between unpaid caregiving work and paid labor by single parents may be the most difficult and sensitive issue in distinguishing what reciprocity requires from what liberty permits.[45] Without resolving this and other nettlesome issues, we can caution against public assistance that confuses enforcement of reciprocity with enforcement of regnant values and lifestyles.

Fifth and most significant, I object to Mead's depiction of the non-working poor as other, "alien," and "undeserving."[46] This characterization begins with using "lack of competence" to describe the poor who fail to recognize opportunities in their best rational interest. Mead portrays poor persons as utterly different from the rest of us. If accurate, this depiction would doom justifications for all welfare assistance to the non-working poor. Even enforcing work could no longer be conceived and administered as an authoritative expectation for reciprocity, as Mead advocates. Properly executed, programs for work enforcement with high expectations for behavior reveal greater respect for the capacities of poor persons than the right to unconditional assistance. If poor persons are viewed as utterly different, enforcement becomes punishment or a program for behavioral modification, spurning the conditions for self-respect. Mead's caricature of the agency problem he identifies undercuts even his own anti-poverty policies.

We need not flinch at acknowledging and describing differences between the non-working poor and working citizens, as some welfare liberals do.[47] Mead is probably correct, even if exaggerated, in claiming that many of the non-working poor are "different in some way."[48] Barring a severe and unexpected physical or mental disability or a catastrophic economic downturn, most long-term working citizens will not become part of the non-working poor. It is fantastical to preach to them that only an adverse economic event separates them from the non-working poor. They differ from many of the non-working poor in their capacity to participate in the economy. The crucial question then becomes: can an accurate description of this difference allow us to view poor persons as equal citizens, requiring society's support for their distinctive needs?

Defenders of the welfare state who assume the rational autonomy of the non-working poor ignore this question. Mead hints at an answer in an article Stanley Carlson-Thies and James Skillen invited him to write on Christian perspectives on welfare. Drawing on little-known Methodist theologian Paul Tournier, Mead writes that working citizens who "accept dependents as fellow sinners, yet also demand that they take command of their lives . . . can accept weakness, and yet go on to expect effort and excellence."[49] This brief theological intrusion in Mead's writings on poverty, ostensibly incompatible with his social scientific portrayal of the non-working poor, suggests an answer to our question informed by a doctrine of grace. I shall follow this cue.

United by Grace

Christian doctrines of grace focus, as Mead does, on agency. Also similar to Mead, grace assumes differences in the skills and virtues requisite for human well-being and the moral life. Unlike Mead, these differences are not grounds for labeling some persons as other or undeserving of public assistance. Moreover, understanding human agency in the light of grace informs what justice requires. By acknowledging conditions that enable the exercise of rational autonomy, grace lends support to aspects of Plant's demand to advance positive freedoms and Moon's concern to establish the enabling conditions for self-respect in the market economy.

Not all doctrines of grace are identical or equal. The understanding of common grace in the theology of James M. Gustafson deployed here draws heavily on John Calvin and the Reformed tradition. Common grace refers to gifts of divine beneficence that enhance the distinctive possibilities for persons without saving them from sin and death. Calvin understood common grace as unevenly distributed among humans. It explained, Calvin believed, why Camillus was more virtuous than Cataline, even though neither was saved.[50] Calvin did not restrict common grace to the blessings endowing a human life in general. Calvin allowed for special common grace that transforms a life in process. He observed, for example, that when God wished to make Saul king, God "formed him as a new man."[51]

Gustafson also distinguishes among kinds of grace. "Grace in creation" refers to God's creating and sustaining beneficence, while "special grace" refers to new possibilities that redeem persons, but only partially, from sin and finitude.[52] For Calvin, saving grace alone redeems from sin and death. For Gustafson, who jettisons a doctrine of total salvation, grace in creation and special redeeming grace are both common grace.[53] He offers no doctrine of saving grace. All humans, as Gustafson understands us, depend on common grace for the skills and virtues we develop over a lifetime and for incremental redemption from our distinctive faults and limitations.

Although one may embrace doctrines of saving and common grace simultaneously, as Calvin did, common grace fits well with the topic at hand. First, it applies to all persons, the saved and the unsaved. Second, as Gustafson understands common grace, it applies to a broad range of human skills, virtues, and acts, not merely to a person's standing before God. It redeems from limitations for which we are not responsible—for example, a loss of self-efficacy due to the ravages of previous injustice—as well as from seemingly insurmountable failures for which we are responsible—for example, habituated indolence or addiction to drugs. The diminished autonomy of the non-working poor, like those who are not poor, often results from a combination of finitude and sin. Third, common grace and many of its insights into welfare policy are credible to persons who do not consider themselves Christians or even theists. Gustafson claims that a belief in common grace may be evoked by ordinary experiences and confirmed by social science.[54] More surprising perhaps, Calvin cites Homer as supporting the view that humans excel through the daily sustaining benefits bestowed by Jupiter.[55]

I will identify three pertinent insights from Gustafson's understanding of common grace followed by three implications for justifications of the welfare state.

First, human agents are dependent on and interdependent with nature, the culture in which they live, their history, their society, and even the selves that they have become.[56] Divine beneficence is mediated through these five spheres of human life. To the extent that persons are rational, free, and able to live according to their values and principles, they have reason to consider themselves beneficiaries of grace. Not surprisingly, Gustafson has much more modest expectations of human agents than either Plant or Moon. Plant and Moon understand, of course, that free and rational agency requires natural capacities for functioning, and they are much more attuned than libertarians to how the structures of society can limit and augment human freedom. Moon also considers how the culture of market economies shapes possibilities and expectations for citizens. However, neither Plant nor Moon consider, as Mead does, how histories of injustice and personal misfortune, sub-cultural norms and social organization in communities of concentrated poverty, or habits of the formed-self influence motivational resolve to participate in the economy. Mead and others—most notably developmental psychologists—attempt to offer social scientific explanations for motivations and behavior. The precise influences and resulting capacities of different persons and communities can be *partially*—but only partially—uncovered by social scientific examination of how all five of these spheres enable and restrict agential capacities.

Second, these social scientific inquiries and sensitive observers will necessarily reveal different agential capacities between groups, for example, between the non-working poor and other citizens. The uneven distribution of common grace affirms that such differences occur. Grace, however, impels us to view these differences within a common context: shared gratitude for what we are enabled to do and mutual acknowledgment of faults and limitations. Calvin, characteristically vivid, said that we all share an inclination to "abominations" apart from grace.[57] Gustafson's muted description more closely approximates the truth. Despite differences, we are all flawed, in need of grace. We should gratefully recognize our dependence on grace, taking only "limited credit for such virtues as [we] have."[58] From this perspective, we can admit real differences in fundamental abilities and even in moral capacities without separating humans into the deserving and undeserving.[59] For one thing, where inconsistent motivation exists among the non-working poor, it emanates, at least in part, from an uneven distribution of common grace through their distinctive histories, sub-cultures, and interactions with society. Moreover, recognizing universal moral fault enables citizens to name others' specific faults while remaining open to learning of their own faults through a process of mutual correction. My students returning from summer internships with impoverished people invariably report a more acute awareness of their own faults. They confess to a sense of unwarranted pride, self-centeredness, materialism, and complacency about injustice as they encounter the humility, generosity, suffering, and courage of persons with whom they work. A perspective from grace reproves our tendency to cast as morally inferior those whose faults and virtues differ from our own. Yet it need not cause us to shrink from examining the behavior and motives of the non-working poor for fear that our findings will demean victims.

The third insight disposes us to see the possibilities special grace creates for renewed and new agential capacities. It generates hope that persons are often liberated from the residual effects of sin and from finitude.[60] The possibilities come in both negative and positive forms.

The negative form assumes recipients of grace are subject to judgment that can be redemptive. Calvin understood God's judgment as altering motives to change behavior for the sake of advancing God's good, but it did not make persons more virtuous, even incrementally.[61] Gustafson, in this instance more sanguine than Calvin, believes judgments may provoke reconsideration of previous actions, enabling an enlarged and more virtuous perception of relationships.[62] Viewed from this perspective, Mead's proposals to enforce work can, if administered correctly, enable new possibilities for the non-working poor. Moreover, events that compel greater consciousness of the material suffering of the working poor and the isolation of the non-working poor can enable non-poor citizens to perceive new obligations to alleviate poverty. In religious language, judgments can be a means of redemptive grace.

Calvin calls the positive form of grace a special blessing of God. God, for example, may endow with heroic qualities a person destined to lead.[63] Gustafson refers to more specific media of God's grace. He writes of legislative and judicial actions, medical inventions, and community charity. These and other human interventions can be construed as grace liberating persons from some constraints of apparent fatedness. He observes that forgiveness for persons who have failed can heal breaches and enable them to fulfill their duties.[64]

Interventions in the economy that enable these negative and positive possibilities for partial redemption from both finitude and moral failure are not merely for the rational, autonomous citizens assumed by Plant and Moon. They are also for persons constrained by what Mead calls a lack of competence and Sen calls deficient capability. This belief in possibilities is insufficient to justify specific welfare policies, but it demands policies designed to restore and augment agential capacities.

How May Justifications Proceed?

These lessons from common grace contain three implications for justifying the welfare state. The first two address the scope and content of welfare assistance. When, in Gustafson's words, "the exercise of agency is dependent upon and limited by biological, social, cultural, and other conditions, respect only for autonomy [is] denigrating." "[W]hat is respected [must be] amplified beyond 'rational autonomy.'"[65] Respect for persons must include efforts to overcome internal impediments to their autonomy. Hence, welfare policies that do no more than offer "basic needs" or opportunities in the economic structure are insufficient. Welfare should be constructed to foster the restoration of damaged autonomy. To the extent that Mead's description of the non-working poor is accurate, welfare policy should incorporate sanctions and supports that augment the capacity of this group to participate in the economy. Second, sensitivity to the gratuitous sources of talents and skills and how they are rewarded in the sometimes volatile labor market reinforces justifications for guaranteed employment and a decent compensation package for those committed to full-time work. In this case, the perspective from common grace corrects Moon's unjustified assumption that reciprocity requires attaining economic self-sufficiency from an unfettered labor market.

A third implication concerns the disposition of the general populace toward poor persons as well as reasons to support public assistance. Citizens who recognize that their own capacities for reciprocity depend on enabling forces beyond their control will be disposed differently toward the non-working poor. They will acknowledge obstacles confronting those who possess less substantial gifts for this specific achievement. Moreover, a belief that we are uneven beneficiaries of general and special grace gives reason to back policies that might effectively augment the capacities and opportunities of the non-working poor, including those culpable for their present condition.

An understanding of common grace does not justify the modern welfare state, and I have offered no complete justification. I contend, however, that something like this understanding of grace is indispensable for correcting deficiencies in most justifications for the welfare state. We need this kind of assessment of the differences and commonalities between the poor and non-poor to justify a welfare state that encompasses the full gamut of policies required to alleviate poverty in all of its dimensions. These policies must include: opportunities for work that is rewarded with compensation requisite for a decent livelihood; provision for the education and healthcare needed to participate in the economy; social insurance and public assistance for contingencies that cause temporary setbacks or permanent disabilities; enforcement of minimal reciprocity in economic relations; and opportunities to renew lost capacities or develop new capacities, regardless of what caused the incapacity. Common grace, rightly understood, informs and demands each of these dimensions of the welfare state.

NOTES

[1] I wish to thank Kelly Brotzman, Daniel Finn, James Gustafson, Lawrence Mead, Douglas Schuurman, Charles Swezey, Leah C. Schaefer, and Matthew Petrusek for comments on various drafts of this essay. Lawrence Mead alerted me to the work of Amy Wax and a recent article by Stuart White. I am also grateful to students and colleagues at Washington and Lee University who listened and responded to an earlier version of this address.

[2] See Darryl M. Trimiew, *God Bless The Child That's Got Its Own: The Economic Rights Debate* (Atlanta: Scholars Press, 1997).

[3] Warren Copeland, *And The Poor Get Welfare: The Ethics of Poverty in the United States* (Nashville, Abingdon Press, 1994).

[4] Elizabeth M. Bounds, Pamela K. Brubaker, & Mary E. Hobgood, *Welfare Policy: Feminist Critiques* (Cleveland, Pilgrim Press, 1999).

[5] Raymond Plant, "A Defence of Welfare Rights," in *Economic, Social and Cultural Rights: Progress and Achievement*, ed. Ralph Beddard and Dilys M. Hill (New York: St. Martin's Press, 1992) 25. All humans potentially capable of this autonomous agency possess

rights claims (30), but rights claims are inapplicable to genetic human beings who do not possess this capacity (23). "A Defence of Welfare Rights" is virtually a reprint of "Needs, Agency, and Welfare Rights," in *Responsibility, Rights, and Welfare: The Theory of the Welfare State* (Boulder, CO: Westview Press, 1988). See also chapters two and four in *Political philosophy and social welfare: Essays on the normative basis of welfare provision* by Plant, Harry Lesser, and Peter Taylor-Gooby (London: Routledge & Kegan Paul, 1980) for another principal source regarding Plant's justifications for the welfare state.

[6] Plant, "A Defence of Welfare Rights," 29. See also Plant, Lesser, and Taylor-Gooby, *Political philosophy and social welfare*, 244-46.

[7] We would not, for example, claim that a hungry person or an illiterate person lacks the positive freedom for moral autonomy.

[8] I do not oppose exploring a basis other than moral autonomy, e.g., human dignity, to justify positive freedom for a decent level of well-being. Indeed, I believe this type of argument must be employed to justify a welfare state. This argument, however, encounters problems with distinguishing needs that constitute rights from what Plant calls non-basic needs and is also bound to particular cultures in ways that Plant's justification of universal rights rejects.

[9] Henry Shue, *Basic Rights: Subsistence, Affluence and U. S. Foreign Policy*, 2nd ed. (Princeton, NJ: Princeton University Press, 1996) offers a different kind of argument for universal basic subsistence rights (viz., to "unpolluted air, unpolluted water, adequate food, adequate clothing, adequate shelter, and minimal preventive public health care" (23)). Shue argues, correctly I believe, that if any rights to liberty exist, there must also be basic subsistence rights because they are indispensable to the worth of liberty. Although Shue and Plant agree on the necessary complementarity of positive and negative rights, Shue does not ground his rights argument in a universal foundational concept like autonomy nor do basic subsistence rights constitute anything approaching the substantive assistance in the modern welfare state.

[10] See Stuart Gordon White, "Basic Income and Beyond: An Essay on the Rights of Social Citizenship," (Ph.D. diss., Princeton University, 1996) for a comprehensive and excellent, although still inadequate, justification for welfare assistance as a social right. Social right, as used here, refers to rights of citizenship dependent, in part, on principles and values in particular moral traditions (e.g., the principle of reciprocity in modern market economies) and the circumstances of particular societies (e.g., levels of education required for participation in the economy and society).

[11] See Plant, Lesser, & Taylor-Gooby, *Political philosophy and social welfare*, 53.

[12] Ibid., 71.

[13] Ibid., 53.

[14] Joel T. Handler and Yeheskel Hasenfeld, in *We the Poor People: Work, Poverty, & Welfare* (New Haven: Yale University Press, 1997), claim that mandatory work programs for public assistance are always counterproductive. They contend that these programs inherently undercut the social-service provider's disposition to serve and breakdown trust between the provider and his client (85-93). Mandatory programs are inconsistent with viewing the client as a moral agent, "worthy of trust and support" (146). Handler's and Hasenfeld's claim, if correct, renders my conclusions here unfeasible. See, on the other hand, Amy L. Wax, "Rethinking Welfare Rights: Reciprocity Norms, Reactive Attitudes, and the Political Economy of Welfare Reform," *Law and Contemporary Problems* 63/1&2 (Winter/Spring 2000) for evidence that social service offices are able to exercise moral discrimination in administering reciprocal requirements for work. Wax is arguing against conservatives who claim that bureaucratic discretion inevitably tends to excessive leniency. She, nonetheless, defends the claim that welfare requirements can be consistent with respecting clients as moral agents (284-85).

[15] Darryl Timiew, *God Bless The Child That's Got Its Own*, rests his argument for economic rights on the compatibility, equal importance, equal practicality, and necessary complementarity of positive economic rights and negative political and civil rights.

[16] I juxtapose Moon and Plant because their contrasting justifications for the modern welfare state offer sophisticated versions of two important and commonly held views. We can learn a great deal from a critical examination of their arguments.

[17]Donald Moon, "The Moral Basis of the Democratic Welfare State," in *Democracy and the Welfare State*, ed. Amy Gutmann (Princeton, Princeton University Press, 1988) 28.

[18]Moon, "The Moral Basis of the Democratic Welfare State," 32, 28.

[19]Ibid., 28-30. See also Moon, *Constructing Community*, 128-29, 135.

[20]Moon, *Constructing Community*, 130-32, and "The Moral Basis of the Democratic Welfare State," 33-34. Moon's concept of self-respect clearly differs from Kant's. Moon assumes that most citizens of modern market economies internalize (perhaps by consent after deliberation) the standard of reciprocity embedded in the institutions of their societies, ostensibly a heteronomous morality. On the other hand, Moon acknowledges that a few citizens may reject this moral self-understanding and the principle of reciprocity intrinsic to the market economy. These more independent, if not truly autonomous by Kant's definition, citizens may maintain self-respect by rejecting the moral premises of the modern economy. Others, barred from complying with the principle of reciprocity, which they do internalize, may, in the short-term, retain self-respect by resisting economic structures that deny them the support requisite for satisfying the demands of reciprocity. In this case, society fails to fulfill its reciprocal obligation according to the regnant self-understanding. We shall see that this rational alternative to participation in an unjust labor market eludes Lawrence Mead in his brief comments on self-respect. Notwithstanding these alternatives for attaining self-respect, Moon, probably correctly, believes that most citizens will have to achieve self-respect through paid labor.

[21]Moon, *Constructing Community*, 132.

[22]Moon, "The Moral Basis of the Welfare State," 44-46, and *Constructing Community*, 133-35. Moon's support for insurance demonstrates that reciprocity, as he understands it, permits some interdependence and means-tested assistance. The key seems to be whether the recipients of this welfare contribute to these programs over time through work and taxes and whether their needs are due to contingencies beyond the control of a typically rational economic agent.

[23]Moon, "The Moral Basis for the Welfare State," 47-49, and *Constructing Community*, 135-39.

[24]Stuart White, in *Basic Income and Beyond*, bases welfare assistance on a principle of reciprocity explicitly severed from self-sufficiency (103) and from economic contributions proportionate to those received from the market (51-53). White defines reciprocity through work as a "socially-defined decent minimum of paid labour" (207). He contends, arguing directly against Moon, that society is obligated to guarantee employment (251-65). White also argues for constant access to job training and education, minimum wage laws, and income supplements for low-skilled workers (215-17). White, like Moon, contends that reciprocity and self-respect require work, not mere cash or material assistance, but White considers assistance to those working in light of mutual dependence, not individual or familial self-sufficiency. See also chapters on reciprocity (52-94) and welfare (271-306) in *Democracy and Disagreement* by Amy Gutmann and Dennis Thompson (Cambridge, MA: Harvard University Press, 1996). White (Gutmann's student) informs their application of reciprocity to welfare and work (402, n. 3).

[25]Mead's principal works are *Beyond Entitlement: The Social Obligations of Citizenship* (New York: The Free Press, 1986), *The New Politics of Poverty: The Nonworking Poor in America* (New York: BasicBooks, 1992), and *The New Paternalism: Supervisory Approaches to Poverty* (Washington, DC: Brookings Institution Press, 1997). Readers of this journal will be especially interested in "The Poverty Debate and Human Nature" in *Welfare in America: Christian Perspectives on a Policy in Crisis*, ed. Stanley W. Carlson-Theis & James W. Skillen (Grand Rapids, MI: 1996) 209-42. Mead assumes government financed public assistance and supports a form of it, but he proffers no justification for it. His work, nevertheless, informs this essay on justifications for the welfare state because his distinctive and insightful, albeit distorted, view of the agency of poor citizens corrects naive assumptions about agency among many ethicists, including Plant and Moon.

[26]See *Beyond Entitlement*, 21-25, 34-41, and 76-82; *The New Politics of Poverty*, 27-30, 131-45, 157-58; and "The Poverty Debate and Human Nature," 210—16, 222-29 for various renditions of what Mead calls the problem of functioning or competence and of the scope and

explanation for this problem. The most recent writings reduce the percentage of the population he believes is affected by this problem and softens his view on the extent to which poor persons are responsible and blameworthy for their behavior.

[27]See Mead, *The New Politics of Poverty*, 136, 157, for his disagreement with libertarians who charge that the non-working poor are rational maximizers choosing public assistance and leisure over earned income.

[28]See ibid., chaps. 4-6, 66-132, for Mead's account of why these structural barriers do not explain non-work.

[29]Ibid., 148-49; Mead, "The Poverty Debate and Human Nature," 214-15; and Mead, *The New Paternalism*, 22-23. Lest we too quickly dismiss Mead's sometimes unrefined and tendentious analysis as racist, we should consider that he denies that non-work can be explained by inferior endowments and asserts that a similar psychological defeatism is operative in rural white communities (*The New Politics of Poverty*, 137-39). Mead also concedes that race discrimination may still explain wage inequality between whites and minorities, although not non-work and poverty (ibid. 113). He also implies that most psychologically defeated persons are non-culpable victims of previous, although not current, injustice and misfortune.

[30]Mead, *The New Paternalism*, 28. See also Mead, *The New Politics of Poverty*, 139-40.

[31]Ironically, Mead implicitly corrects deficiencies in Moon's conception of reciprocity. Inasmuch as Mead favors continued public assistance for persons who work, he does not insist, as Moon does, that reciprocity entails economic independence. See *Beyond Entitlement*, 244.

[32]See *Beyond Entitlement*, 82-88, 241-44; *The New Politics of Poverty*, 171-75, 183-84; and "The Poverty Debate and Human Nature," 238.

[33]Mead, *The New Paternalism*, 57-63.

[34]Rebecca Blank, *It Takes a Nation: A New Agenda for Fighting Poverty* (Princeton, NJ: Princeton University Press, 1997) 51-75. "Work effort" refers to number of hours worked over a specified period of time, not to the effort put into work or into a job search.

[35]See Kathryn Edin and Laura Lein, *Making Ends Meet: How Single Mothers Survive Welfare and Low-Wage Work* (New York: Russell Sage Foundation, 1997) for a detailed and revealing account of how revenues and expenses for low-skilled working, single mothers leave their families in slightly greater hardship than welfare-reliant mothers. Edin and Lein conclude that the women they interviewed "usually behaved in ways that reflected reasoned calculations of which alternatives would be likely to expose their children to the least harm" (221). Mead believes that breaking into the labor market with its prospects for advancement is still rational for the long run.

[36]Mead, *The New Politics of Poverty*, 142.

[37]Ibid., 57-61. At one point, Mead implies that the behavior of the poor is a prerequisite to justice for the poor: "When competence is no longer at issue, then justice can be" (239).

[38]Here again a correct rendering and application of the principle of reciprocity is crucial. Amy Gutmann and Dennis Thompson show how the reciprocity that justifies work requirements also demands that society provide opportunities for work and to receive the basic income needed while working. *Democracy and Disagreement*, 291-301. Stuart White argues that work requirements without provision for reciprocal conditions of fairness for workers is exploitive. *Basic Income and Beyond*, (108-20, 207-29). White refers specifically to Mead in n. 26, pp. 228, 245. See also "Review Article: Social Rights and the Social Contract—Political Theory and the New Welfare Politics," *British Journal of Political Science* 30 (July 2000): 507-32 for a more accessible account of White's insistence that the moral legitimacy of behavioral conditions for public assistance depends on "fair reciprocity." White's interpretation of Mead's conception of competence (225-27) differs significantly from my interpretation in this essay.

[39]Sen developed his conception of capabilities (i.e., a person's freedom to choose and developing a set of functionings, including work in the labor market) to aid in the examination of inequality and poverty. His most comprehensive treatment of this conception appears in *Inequality Reexamined* (Cambridge, MA: Harvard University Press, 1992). In a manuscript, "Capability as Opportunity: How Amartya Sen Revises Equal Opportunity," *Journal of*

Religious Ethics (forthcoming), I argue that Sen himself fails to apply his conception of capabilities to psychological impediments persons develop through their life histories.

[40]Blank, *It Takes a Nation*, 254-60. This accommodation to psychological disabilities appears to contradict Blank's argument that low-skilled poor adults will respond rationally to work incentives. However, both claims may accurately explain the behavior of different groups among the non-working poor. In order to allay any doubts, I should note that Mead exempts from full work requirements—some would say grudgingly—persons who are permanently disabled. See, for example, *The New Politics of Poverty*, 125-27.

[41]See, for example, "The Poverty Debate and Human Nature," 236. In *The New Paternalism* , Mead writes about correcting the "lifestyle problems of the poor" (30).

[42]Describing the policies he advocates as paternalistic gains Mead attention, but, like the word competence, paternalism obscures more than it reveals. Insofar as Mead intends to advocate "help and hassle" to assist persons in achieving goals they themselves profess and to enforce reciprocity through a decent minimum of socially useful labor, his policies could be more accurately described as ensuring basic opportunities and reciprocity.

[43]Mead, *The New Politics of Poverty*, 181.

[44]Stuart White, "Social Rights and the Social Contract," infers an imposition of "materialism" from one reading of Mead's conceptions of paternalism and competence (526).

[45]Several of the essays in *Welfare Policy,* ed. Bounds, Brubaker, and Hobgood raise the issue of welfare policy enforcing paid labor at the expense of caregiving labor for one's own children. Carol Robb, "Rational Man and Feminist Economists on Welfare Reform," 77-91, focuses usefully on rational behavior in caregiving and how economic policy can respect that rational choice. Like Robb, I would not propose direct subsidies for caregiving labor but favor policies permitting those who care for dependents some latitude in hours worked for paid labor without sacrificing a minimally decent income for their families. See Gutmann and Thompson, *Democracy and Disagreement*, 297-98, and White, *Basic Income and Beyond*, 131-37, 161, for discussions of caregiving labor in relation to policies that enforce paid labor based on a principle of reciprocity.

[46]See, for example, *The New Politics of Poverty*, 28-30. Mead might fairly claim that as a political scientist he describes the attitudes and values of citizens that do not reflect his own views. Moreover, he may accurately characterize the majority of citizens as perceiving the non-working poor as other and alien. If Mead accurately depicts the attitudes of U.S. citizens toward the non-working poor, accepting the implications of common grace discussed below becomes all the more urgent for changing the cultural ethos. Even granting Mead's descriptive purpose, he cannot be excused for failing to correct this distortion when he uses this characterization of the non-working poor as a principal justification for policies that he clearly advocates.

[47]Herbert J. Gans, *The War Against the Poor: The Underclass and AntiPoverty Policy* (New York: BasicBooks, 1995) comes very close to dismissing all social scientific study of poor persons as agents for fear that "labeling" the poor will brand them undeserving and undermine efforts to diminish the real causes of poverty.

[48]Mead, *The New Paternalism*, 33. Susan E. Mayer, *What Money Can't Buy: Family Income and Children's Life Chances* (Cambridge, MA: Harvard University Press, 1997) offers a social scientific attempt to demonstrate and identify an aspect of that difference. Mayer, a self-described liberal, ignores Gan's admonition to social scientists. Her findings, although debatable in their specifics, severely challenged what she calls "the common liberal claim that 'the poor are just like everyone else except that they have less money'" (3).

[49]Mead, "The Poverty and Human Nature," 241.

[50]John Calvin, *The Institutes of Christian Religion*, II,iii,4. All citations to the *Institutes* are from The Library of Christian Classics, vol. XX, ed. John T. McNeill, trans. Ford Lewis Battles (Philadelphia: Westminister Press, 1960).

[51]Ibid., II,iii,4; see also II,ii,17.

[52]James M. Gustafson, *Ethics from a Theocentric Perspective: Theology and Ethics*, vol. 1 (Chicago: University of Chicago Press, 1981) 247-51.

[53]See ibid., 109-10, 268 for Gustafson's comments on traditional doctrines of salvation. He does not employ the term common grace, but he limits grace to what the Reformed tradition has called common grace.

[54]Ibid., 133, 207-225, 250-51. Skeptics who immunize themselves from the insights of all religious language because it rests on the authority of a particular tradition would do well to consider the descriptions and explanations for agency from the perspective of grace. Do they measure up to common criteria of adequacy less well than Mead's conception of competence or the conception of autonomy that Plant and Moon assume? The tendency to insulate religious or Christian language from the language of social science, philosophy, or other religious traditions exists among proponents of common grace as well. Cornelius Van Til, in his favorable commentary on common grace, insists that this doctrine cannot be taken seriously outside the Reformed tradition. See Cornelius Van Til, *Common Grace* (Philadelphia, Presbyterian and Reformed Publishing Company, 1947) 12.

[55]Calvin, *Institutes*, II,ii,17.

[56]Gustafson, *Ethics from a Theocentric Perspective*, vol. 1, 282-84.

[57]Calvin, *Institutes*, II,iii,3. In his commentary on I Peter 4.10, Calvin even suggested that inequalities in the distribution of common grace form a bond for "retaining friendship" among humans who "cannot live without mutual assistance," a "bond of unity" that even the "heathens" notice and observe. See *Commentaries on The Catholic Epistles* in *Calvin's Commentaries*, vol. 22, reprint (Grand Rapids, MI: Baker Book House, 1981) 130-31. Herman Kuiper cites this passage in *Calvin on Common Grace* (Grand Rapids. MI: Smitter Book Company, 1928) 174. Calvin may have been referring to differences in skills only, but we can extend the complementarity that he recognizes to include mutual correction among those with different virtues and vices.

[58]James M. Gustafson, *Ethics from a Theocentric Perspective*, vol. 2 (Chicago: University of Chicago Press, 1984), 287.

[59]Admittedly, the doctrine of common grace has not always functioned to unite. It has been used by the self-proclaimed recipients of grace to claim that God's favor has made them alone virtuous and deserving of society's benefits. Reinhold Niebuhr, who himself employs the notion of "grace inherent in common sense," observes that the Puritans gradually shifted from gratitude for God's favor to the U.S. to a view that God favored this nation and bestowed unique virtue on it. See Reinhold Niebuhr, *The Irony of American History* (New York: Charles Scribner's Sons, 1952) 75, 70. Calvin was subject to using the doctrine of common grace to affirm God's favored. He saw in common grace God's purpose to raise some above the common lot in order "to keep the rest obedient to them" (*Institutes*, II,iii,3).

[60]Gustafson, *Ethics from a Theocentric Perspective*, vol. 1, 133, 248.

[61]God's judgment induces "shame" or "fear of the law" that "bridles the perversity of nature," but the judgment "does not purge within" (*Institutes*, II,iii,3).

[62]Characteristically cautious about exaggerating enabling possibilities, Gustafson also follows Calvin in observing that judgment may sometimes realize only the more modest result of redirecting destructive behavior. See Gustafson, *Ethics from a Theocentric Perspective*, vol. 1, 246-47, 307-08.

[63]Calvin, *Institutes*, II,iii,4.

[64]Gustafson, *Ethics from a Theocentric Perspective*, vol. 1, 248-50. Once again Gustafson is the optimist. Whereas Calvin understands the positive effects of common grace as merely instrumental to God's purposes for the good of society, Gustafson also allows for common grace to serve the recipient's virtue and well-being.

[65]Ibid., 291.

POVERTY, WELFARE, AND INEQUALITY

Social Science, Christian Ethics
and Democratic Politics:
Issues of Poverty and Welfare

Mary Jo Bane

Two narratives.

Narrative #1:

> A new analysis of Census data finds that . . . the Earned Income Tax
> Credit—a tax credit for low income working families—now lifts more
> children out of poverty than any other government program . . . .

> Government benefits lift from poverty more than four of every five
> elderly people who otherwise would be poor, the study found, but fewer
> than one in three children who otherwise would be poor. In 1996,
> government benefit programs lowered the child poverty rate from 23.6
> percent before receipt of government benefits to 16.1 percent after
> receipt of benefits.

> The Earned Income Tax Credit, expanded under Presidents Reagan,
> Bush and Clinton, emerged in 1996 as the single program removing the
> largest number of children from poverty, the study reported. The EITC,
> which offsets some or all of federal income and payroll taxes and, in
> many cases, also provides a wage supplement to low-income working
> families, lifted 4.6 million people—including 2.4 million children—
> from poverty in 1996 . . . .

> Since the EITC is available only to working families, its effects on
> children in those families are especially strong, the study found. Among
> working families, the EITC has a larger effect than any other program or
> category of programs both in reducing the number of poor children and
> in reducing the severity of poverty among those who remain poor.

> Center on Budget and Policy Priorities
> "Government Benefit Programs Cut Poverty
> Nearly in Half, Analysis Finds"
> March 9, 1998

Narrative #2:

> There was a rich man who was dressed in purple and fine linen and who feasted sumptuously every day.
>
> And at his gate lay a poor man named Lazarus, covered with sores, who longed to satisfy his hunger with what fell from the rich man's table; even the dogs would come and lick his sores.
>
> The poor man died and was carried away by the angels to be with Abraham. The rich man also died and was buried.
>
> In Hades, where he was being tormented, he looked up and saw Abraham far away with Lazarus by his side.
>
> He called out, "Father Abraham, have mercy on me, and send Lazarus to dip the tip of his finger in water and cool my tongue, for I am in agony in these flames."
>
> But Abraham said, "Child, remember that during your lifetime you received your good things, and Lazarus in like manner evil things, but now he is comforted here, and you are in agony. Besides all this, between you and us a great chasm has been fixed, so that those who might want to pass from here to you cannot do so, and no one can cross from there to us."
>
> Luke 16: 19-26 (NRSV)

At the risk of appearing post-modern, let me refer to both of these as "stories." Both stories are relevant to public life and to the life of discipleship. Both can be starting points for analysis of and recommendations for concrete personal, political, or policy action, though usually in different settings. (I have never begun congressional testimony with Luke; nor do I begin scriptural reflections with statistics.)

Both stories require exegesis, analysis, and interpretation. Both are vulnerable to, pardon the expression, proof-texting or lying with statistics. Both can generate constructive intellectual debate. Neither leads deductively or definitively to single conclusions about either personal action or public policy.

I contend that both stories have a place in democratic deliberation and decision making about social policy—in conversations among citizens, in legislative debates, in regulation and implementation within public agencies, in voting; in short, in the arenas and the methodologies we have invented for doing public work in a democracy.[1] Since neither methodology leads inevitably to right answers, I assert that both policy analysis and Christian ethics ought to practice the virtue of humility and submit to the discipline of democratic politics while we live this side of the kingdom. That is the argument I want to make here.

Let me start with social science/policy analysis, since I have considerably more standing in this arena. It may be interesting for us to think about the policy analysis methodology, both about what it can do and what it cannot (or should not) do in shaping public policy. We teach our Kennedy School students a policy analysis framework, which is similar to the frameworks that guide the work of government analysts, budget-makers and advocates. Eugene Bardach, of the public policy school at Berkeley, in an elegant little book written for his students,[2] advocates an "eightfold path" for doing policy analysis: Define the problem; Assemble some evidence; Construct the alternatives; Select the criteria; Project the outcomes; Confront the tradeoffs; Decide!; Tell your story.

For example, we might look at the problem of the working poor—families that work full time or close to it but have family incomes below the government defined poverty line. We can assemble facts about families that show a relatively large number of such families, and can also show that their low incomes result from low wages. Policy alternatives that come to mind include raising the minimum wage, providing education and training, enacting a negative income tax (NIT), or supplementing wages or earnings. In evaluating these alternatives we might examine the effects on employment of a minimum wage increase; the long time horizon, high cost, and uncertain impact of education and training strategies; the employment incentive effects of NIT (mostly negative) and wage or earnings supplements (mostly positive); and the poverty-reducing potential of all the alternatives. This kind of analysis has led to near unanimity among policy wonks that an earnings supplement like the Earned Income Tax Credit (EITC) is the approach with the fewest negative effects, and has led groups like the Center for Budget and Policy Priorities to put a good deal of effort into telling the story and making the case for expansion of the credit.

It will not surprise you to learn that this mode of analysis is attractive to public policy students and their faculties, and to the rational analysis school of policy analysis. And it has real strengths. It makes very clear that good intentions are not enough to justify policy; that outcomes and tradeoffs must be examined; that policies often have unexpected side-effects and always have costs that need to be assessed. It brings the tools of empirical research and logical argument to public topics. But it will also not surprise you to learn that there is often controversy at each step of the process, and that analysis does not always carry the day in legislative voting. Returning to the EITC example, there are empirical disagreements about the magnitude of the credit's effects on work and on marriage, and on how important these are. Although the policy has wide support, arguments continue about its structure, about how generous it should be and about how much government money should be directed to the EITC rather than to more general tax cuts or other purposes.

Disagreement with the conclusions of policy analysis sometimes occurs because legislators are venal and/or stupid, a favorite explanation of some of my students. But that is not in fact usually the case. Much of the time there are uncertainties about the facts, greater uncertainties about predictions of causes, effects and costs, or genuine disagreements about the importance of different criteria used to assess the facts. Even those who operate within the roughly utilitarian framework that underlies policy analysis seldom use or advocate a strict "net benefits" choice test. People disagree about what benefits are important, whose benefits are important, what costs are reasonably borne by whom and so on.

As an example of the complexity, we can look at the 1996 welfare reform bill, about which people of good will genuinely could and did disagree. Some disagreements were at the level of fact and prediction; the evidence was not exactly rock solid on either side. For example, there was and remains uncertainty about what proportion of the welfare caseload experienced serious barriers to work, whether personal barriers or labor market constraints, rather than simply being unwilling to work at available jobs. There was uncertainty about the potential long term benefits of education and training program as compared with much less time consuming "work first" programs that evaluations had shown to be cost effective. There was uncertainty about the effects on children of requiring work by parents as a condition of welfare receipt. There was uncertainty about the extent to which the existence and generosity (or lack thereof) of welfare benefits influenced decisions about work and family formation.

Social science had (and has) something to say about these, both ways of gathering, analyzing, and assessing empirical information and also methodologies for dealing with risk and uncertainty. But the methodologies require assumptions about probabilities and the values placed on alternative outcomes, which are themselves often uncertain. In few cases are the results of policy analysis even as clear as they are with respect to the EITC. In the welfare arena, the range of empirical uncertainty is wide enough to encompass a wide range of policy alternatives. For example, the desirability or lack thereof of work requirements depends crucially for many people on empirical effects on the supervision and development of children; empirical evidence and analytic methods are, however, unable to answer this question.

And of course disagreements are not only about empirical facts and predictions. Some of the disagreements that made the welfare debates so contentious, for example, were about the definition of the problem: was it lack of money, lack of opportunity, lack of self-discipline or something else; and about the appropriate locus of responsibility for the poor: did major responsibility lie with the person, the family, the community, the church, state government, federal government? And if the answer to that question was "all of the above", how should responsibility be allocated? Other disagreements were about the categories of people for whom the public had responsibility: for example, immigrants;

people in other states; people with barriers to work that to some extent result from personal behavior—substance abuse, pregnancy, dropping out of school; children of parents who for whatever good or bad reason did not work. And in a world of empirical uncertainty, questions arose on how to decide—in whose or in what direction should one err?

Bardach's fourth step of his eight-fold path is "select the criteria." Policy analysis, reflecting the general stance of economists, tends to implicitly or explicitly assume a utilitarian ethic: policy should maximize utility as defined by individuals. Stokey and Zeckhauser, in their 1978 *Primer for Policy Analysis*,[3] are unabashedly explicit about using this criterion (as well as about the principle that government should defer to the private market except in cases of market failure), which they describe as "widely accepted." Bardach generally follow this approach as well, arguing that policy analysts rightly stress the criterion of efficiency. Individuals express their preferences through voting or public opinion polling. Knowing (or guessing, or making up) aggregate preferences, policy analysts can use cost benefit analysis or its analogues to approximate the "best" policy.

Now there is little evidence that either the public or public officials actually arrive at policy prescriptions in this calculating utilitarian manner. Almost everyone recognizes that judgments are involved in selecting criteria, and most everyone recognizes that "efficiency" cannot be the final answer. Bardach, for example, notes that in addition to efficiency, policy analysis might consider criteria of equality, equity, fairness, justice, freedom, community, and "other ideas." Philosophically trained ethicists articulate ethical systems derived from constructions of what reasonable people would or should agree to. Ordinary people behave in many ways that give the lie to a purely self-interested construction of reality. Americans also appear to judge the quality of politics and policy on moral and altruistic criteria, not just those of short-term self-interest.

It seems relevant to all this that large proportions of Americans show up for weekly worship (nationally, 40 percent in the 1998 Gallup survey reported attending church or synagogue within the last seven days), most of them in Christian churches. Americans tell pollsters in overwhelming numbers that they believe in God (95 percent believe in God or a Higher Power) and an afterlife (67 percent), and that religion is very important in their lives (67 percent, plus 27 percent who report that it is fairly important). 89 percent want their children religiously educated. 56 percent of polled adults believe that their "life belongs to God or a higher power" (with 20 percent reporting that their life belongs to their family and 20 percent that their life belongs to themselves.) 65 percent reported that they "believe that religion can answer all or most of today's problems," with only 20 percent saying that, in contrast, "religion is largely old fashioned and out of date." When polled about expectations for the year 2025, 62 percent reported that they expect moral values to be worse then than they are now. 36 percent thought church or religious leaders were now doing a good job of raising moral and ethical standards (the highest ranking of any institution) and 68 percent said they thought religious leaders could have a great deal of influence.[4] Even my students often admit that religious motivations have guided their choice of a career, of problems to work on, and of goals they hope to achieve.

The religious affiliations of Americans have undergone a "restructuring" over the last few decades, as many sociologists and historians of religion have noted.[5] Membership in mainline Protestant denominations has declined, while membership in evangelical and "enthusiastic" churches have increased. Independent "mega-churches" are also part of this restructuring. The growing denominations and churches appear to be, to put it very simplistically, more biblical, more morally traditional, more demanding of time and commitment, and more emotionally compelling than those that are declining.[6]

The widespread church going of Americans suggests that much of the "ethics talk" they hear has religious roots. When Americans attend worship services, most listen to scripture readings and hear preaching that by and large tries to draw from scripture lessons for daily life. In my own Roman Catholic tradition, and in Protestant traditions that also use a lectionary, set scripture readings are part of worship services every Sunday, and homilies typically attempt to draw lessons for daily life—ethical lessons—from the assigned scripture readings. (Or at least that seems to be the advice that homilists are given.[7] I have looked for but not found a real study of what preachers actually say.) Donald Miller's study of mega-churches also describes preaching firmly rooted in scripture but practical in application.[8]

Denominations and individual preachers vary in the extent to which they consider it necessary or even appropriate to draw political or policy conclusions as part of their reflections. Congregations also vary in the extent to which they approve of (and presumably pay attention to) talk of policy and politics from the pulpit, and in what they perceive as political. African American congregations, for example, tend to be quite political. Catholics report (in a Notre Dame study[9] and in Anna Greenberg's research[10]) that at least some issues, like poverty and hunger, are and ought to be discussed by the clergy. Many of the respondents in sociologist Alan Wolfe's study of middle class morality (about which more in a minute),[11] however, seem to consider religious faith quite private, and consider political talk an unwarranted intrusion into other people's right to lead their own lives.

At the same time, the religious teachings that most Americans at some level accept are relevant for community and public life as well as for the interior life and individual moral choices of believers. Biblically based religious traditions are covenantal and communal. Scripture readings and preaching based on the bible cannot help but deal, on occasion, with issues of poverty and riches, justice and charity, and obligations to "the least of these brothers and sisters."[12] I suspect most Americans, including public officials, have considerably more exposure to and familiarity with the story of Lazarus than with statistics about poverty, and perhaps consider it more relevant to their own lives and the public life of their country. Religious stories can hardly help but influence the judgments people make about policy, whether or not their influence is explicitly identified. The Lazarus story, for example, does not lead in and of itself to a conclusion that an earnings related tax credit, or indeed any public action, is the best response to the mandate to attend to and care for the poor. But that there is a mandate is hard to deny, much more powerfully presented than in statistics. Taking the mandate seriously requires considering both private charitable responses and collective public action.

The question I now want to raise is whether and in what ways it is appropriate to introduce religiously grounded ethical teachings, as such, into public policy deliberations. I am especially concerned here with scripturally based ethics, the moral lessons derived from revealed texts. This topic is interesting because I strongly suspect that much of the ethics talk that Americans hear and have internalized comes from sacred texts and from scripture-based preaching.

The issue of religious language in public deliberation generates lively debate, with many students of politics and ethics making the case that religious arguments for public decisions should always be excluded from debate or admitted only in limited ways.[13] I do not find their arguments persuasive, but it seems useful to try to lay them out. One line of argument arises from the fact that America is a religiously pluralist nation and that our constitution rightly both protects the free exercise of religion (or no religion) and proscribes the establishment of religion. The establishment provision means that government cannot favor one religion over another or over no religion, and cannot impose religious belief, practice or values. The prohibition is explicitly meant to limit majority rule: even if a majority of the population or legislature wished to incorporate a religious value into law it should not and constitutionally could not do so. Instead, they argue, the grounds for coercive public action must be grounds to which all citizens, at least in principle, would consent.

Thus, for example, Michael Perry,[14] who is quite sympathetic to religion and religious arguments, argues that there must be a convincing secular argument for a political choice about the morality of human conduct (for example, about abortion or homosexuality) to legitimate the use of coercive state authority. Presumably (I have not seen these arguments made as lucidly as Perry makes his) similar arguments would apply to virtue and civic obligation: there must be a convincing secular argument for imposing virtuous behavior, for example, charity (in contrast to justice), through taxation and government action.

Another argument is that religious differences are inherently (or at least historically) divisive and fractious. The polity is more stable and the society more harmonious if religious arguments are excluded from political life. History and contemporary experience suggest the dangers to human freedom that can arise when strong faith is coupled with state power; liberal democracies must be ever vigilant to curb these divisions. Kent Greenawalt presents and explore these arguments for restraint thoroughly and thoughtfully.[15]

Though these worries are not trivial, it seems to me that there are good arguments for bringing faith grounded ethics, indeed scripturally grounded ethics, as such, into public policy deliberation. Note that I am assuming here that religiously based ethical arguments, when they come into the public debate, are subject to examination and discussion. Believers cannot and should not assume that their assertions about policy issues will simply be validated on the basis of respecting religious belief, any more than policy analysts should assume that their conclusions will be deferred to on the basis of respecting technical expertise. Believers, or policy analysts, or indeed anyone, can choose not to enter the public discussion and not to subject their beliefs and interpretations to public scrutiny. Public debate, however, requires a willingness not simply to express positions but to listen and be open to accommodating to the arguments of others.[16]

For me (betraying my biases as an applied social scientist) the best reason for inviting religious discussion into public debate is that it is already there, but implicit and unexamined; better to have it in the open and contestable. For many Americans, faith and ethics exist together and are hard to separate. For serious believers, separation would be impossible and wrong. When religious arguments are excluded, people simply devise secular rationales, thus removing from public knowledge and examination the real reasons for their positions. Religious ethics, as you know much better than I, can be done well or poorly, with more or less sophistication and more or less appreciation of its own power and its own limits, as can policy analysis. I do not want to get too far out of my depth here, which will happen very quickly, but I have learned enough I think, to know that theological argument is not simply dueling scriptural texts. (I like Luke 16; you like John 5; let's fight.)[17] Some constructions of the scripture are obviously more adequate than others in terms of fidelity to the most reliable texts, to the whole body of teachings, important themes, etc. And of course other sources—tradition, reason, and experience, in one formulation—can be used well or poorly in aid of learning and application from scripture.[18] Many of you, I assume, earn your living in this activity. Some of you, perhaps, engage, or are willing to engage, the important issues in public, not just in peer-reviewed journals. Since Americans, it can be assumed, hear a lot of scripture based ethics and presumably believe and follow at least some of it, it might well be salutary to have some public examination of the quality of the arguments. For example, I would love to see an inter-religious discussion, in religious language, of whether personal charity to those we immediately encounter is indeed the only requirement implicit in the Lazarus and Good Samaritan stories and their analogues.

A second consideration complements and qualifies the first. Although for many Americans religion influences morality and politics, it does not, it appears, do so as strongly as one might have expected. Implicit certainly in Christian faith and worship, and in other world religions as well, are ethical norms that guide human relationships and daily practice as well as teachings that structure beliefs. But Alan Wolfe's study of the middle class (in *One Nation, After All*) suggests that its morality is modest and pragmatic, constructed from a variety of sources including bible stories, constitutional principles and memories of childhood teachings.[19] Wolfe found middle class Americans to be remarkably non-judgmental and tolerant, reluctant, by and large, to draw from their religious faith moral precepts that ought to guide the behavior of other people.

Wolfe's study also suggests that middle class morality is "morality writ small," unwilling to judge or impose, and largely limited to the realm of personal relationships and obligations. Although Americans express a general sense of obligation toward the genuinely needy, they seem to feel that when government or other large and impersonal institutions attempt to help, they get it wrong, and as often as not make things worse. The best that can be done is for individuals to take personal responsibility for themselves and their families, to perform individual acts of charity toward those they encounter who truly need it, and to influence others to do the same through personal example, not through law, policy, or even strong arguments.[20]

In this world, it can at least be argued that the bigger danger is from not enough serious commitment rather than from too much. In the complicated world we live in, the needs of the poor and the vulnerable, especially those in countries other than our own, simply cannot be adequately addressed by personal virtue and individual acts of charity. Some sort of ethics writ larger, ethics both personal and public, is badly needed. Religiously-grounded ethics are candidates for providing a richer, more demanding morality than at least Alan Wolfe's middle-class respondents articulate. The social teachings of my own Catholic tradition, which emphasize "faithful citizenship" and the preferential option for the poor, are a strong, though not the only, example.

It is worth noting that some secular moral arguments, like Rawls' difference principle[21] or Peter Singer's utilitarian arguments for sharing wealth[22] are more demanding than most allegedly Christian ethics. But religious morality can be more compelling and attractive than secular formulations; it can also be more accessible and more honest. (I think here of the difficulties many people, including myself, have in connecting with the arguments of John Rawls[23] or Thomas Scanlon.[24]) The bible stories, for example, speak to many people's hearts and imaginations in ways that Rawls' original position cannot. And people hear the bible stories when they go to church; they do not hear about the difference principle or the utilitarian calculus.

A final counter to the arguments of those who would exclude religious arguments is that the costs of excluding them are underestimated and the dangers of including them overestimated. One potential cost is that of continuing ethical flabbiness, as noted above. Another potential cost is that of unfairness to serious believers, especially theological conservatives. If one believes that the most important questions for both life and politics involve the tension between God-centered lives and secular materialism, then excluding religion from the argument gives away the contest. Moreover, if obedience to God is the basic tenant of life, then engagement in a purely secular dialogue would be either dishonest or sinful, and those who believe this tenet would be unfairly excluded from public life if they were precluded from making religious arguments. (Both Greenawalt and Perry take this argument, presented by David Smolin, quite seriously.[25])

Looking at the potential dangers, it is at least arguable that individualistic materialism and ethical non-judgmentalism are more dangerous than religious zealotry to the stability and harmony of the polity. The United States seems irreversibly pluralist; no sect has or is likely to have the power to impose its views; and even committed religious conservatives accept the principle of religious freedom. Wade Clark Roof's study of religion and spirituality among the baby boomers finds a broad middle range of opinions across both born-again and mainline Christians, with little evidence of a culture war.[26] Christian Smith's study of Christian America finds that most evangelicals, even those who would like to see America more Christian, are remarkably tolerant.[27] (For some, indeed, Christian America means freedom from religious coercion.) Like Alan Wolfe's middle class respondents, the evangelicals interviewed by Smith by and large preferred to spread the good news through personal example and eschewed coercion of all sorts. Though one can never be certain that intolerance will never again rear its ugly head, and though a pluralist society needs to be vigilant in this respect, at least at this point the dangers seem modest.

These arguments suggest, at least to me, that our twenty-first-century American polity ought to welcome and indeed invite religiously-grounded and religiously-articulated deliberation. This seems to me especially important as we move toward a new round of debate on domestic poverty and welfare issues, not to mention the question of aid to developing countries. The 1996 welfare reform bill must be reauthorized in 2002. More broadly, the country is, or ought to be, focused on the plight of the working poor and others left behind by the prosperity of the 1990s. The American public appears to be troubled by the persistence of poverty and constrained opportunity for so many in the midst of plenty, even as they remain skeptical of government's ability to do much about it. This debate needs both good empirically based policy analysis and serious ethical argument to translate that concern into a public mandate and effective public action. A more comprehensive and inclusive debate on these issues, a debate that takes seriously the ethical imperatives of our professed religious faiths, would almost surely be a better debate and might even lead to policies more protective of the vulnerable than we have experienced in the recent past.

My most vivid memories from the 1996 welfare debates are of moments of startling ugliness. During the Congressional debates on the final welfare bill, one Republican member held up a picture of a warning sign from the Florida everglades with a picture of an alligator and the admonition "Do Not Feed;" the not particularly subtle analogy was to welfare recipients being "fed" by the welfare system. A Democratic member responded by likening the Republicans to Nazis and accusing them of genocide.

The welfare bill that was signed into law by the President contained some provisions that are best described as gratuitously punitive, a number of them added as amendments during the final debate. Both the provocative rhetoric and the specifically punitive policies were clearly driven by electoral calculations. In campaign after campaign before the 1996 elections, Senators and members of Congress bragged about their toughness on welfare.

Back at the White House, advisor Dick Morris was conducting daily polls and focus groups for the President's reelection campaign. Morris reported that his polling results indicated that the president would drop 15 points in his approval ratings and risk defeat in the real polls if he vetoed the welfare bill; this finding, he says, strongly influenced the president's decision to sign the bill against the nearly unanimous advice of his cabinet.[28] Both Congress and President appeared to be responding to a voting public that was angry about welfare, impatient for change, and ready to punish any politician that got in the way.[29]

The provisions of the welfare bill that was passed and signed, however, were in many respects more draconian than the public told the poll-takers they supported. The public, indeed, registered support for proposals more like those of the early Clinton administration or, interestingly, of the National Conference of Catholic Bishops and other religious groups. By and large the religious lobbyists were listened to politely by members of Congress, but not treated with the attention or fear that might be expected if the religious groups were indeed representing tens of millions of members; and there was in fact little evidence of grass-roots support for their positions. I do not know what might have happened had discussions about poverty and welfare taken place in the hundreds of thousands of congregations across the country, or if representatives of these congregations had brought their thinking, in religious language, to their elected representatives, but I believe that at least the tone of the debate, if not its specific outcomes, would have been better. It is hard to imagine that it would have been more divisive.

Let me close by briefly switching perspectives and speaking as a Christian. I have argued here that it would be good for the polity if believers brought their faith-inspired ethics and commitments into the public debate, specifically into the debate about poverty and welfare. But the point of religion is not improvement in the quality of public debate. I can already hear people mumbling that the church subverts its transcendent mission if it enters into political deliberation, and especially if it subjects revealed truths to questioning and challenge.

To that argument I would respond with the proposition that discipleship requires faithful citizenship. The Roman Catholic tradition is quite clear in its social teachings that the mission of the church encompasses both salvation and liberation in this world and the next, that faith requires a "preferential option" for the poor and the vulnerable, that "structural sin" exists and requires collective action, and that Christians are called to participate in civic and political activity to promote justice and protect life.[30] My own tradition has been less strongly consistent in embracing the virtues and the constraints of democratic politics, but has been led by its commitment to the inherent equality of every human person to teach the theological importance of religious freedom and open participatory government. The clear implication of these religious teachings is that participation in democratic politics in pursuit of peace, justice and care for the vulnerable is not simply permitted but indeed required by faith.

In a modest attempt to practice what I have been preaching here, I put that explicitly faith grounded proposition forward, for your deliberation.

NOTES

[1] I reserve judgment here on the appropriateness of religious argument in judicial decision making; I am inclined to agree with those who argue that this is different, but I have not worked through the issue. And it's less relevant to poverty and welfare issues.

[2] Eugene Bardach, *A Practical Guide for Policy Analysis: The Eightfold Path to More Effective Problem Solving* (New York: Chatham House Publishers, 2000).

[3] Edith Stokey and Richard Zeckhauser, *A Primer for Policy Analysis* (New York: Wm. Norton, 1978).

[4] All poll data from the 1998 Gallup poll, as reported in George Gallup, Jr. and D. Michael Lindsay, *Surveying the Religious Landscape* (Harrisburg, PA: Morehouse Publishing, 1999).

[5] See, for example, Wade Clark Roof, *Spiritual Marketplace: Baby Boomers and the Remaking of American Religion* (Princeton: Princeton University Press, 1999); Rodney Stark and Roger Finke, *Acts of Faith: Explaining the Human Side of Religion* (Berkeley: University of California Press, 2000); Robert William Fogel, *The Fourth Great Awakening and the Future of Egalitarianism* (Chicago: University of Chicago Press, 2000); and Robert Wuthnow, *The Restructuring of American Religion: Society and Faith Since World War II* (Princeton: Princeton University Press, 1988).

[6] Most analysts believe that the differential growth of different denominations is not so much due to switching or conversion as to differential natural growth rates.

[7] For a study that I have been doing of Catholic congregations I looked at homiletic advice provided by a variety of sources, including the St. Anthony "homily helpers" which outline a homily based on the weekly lectionary readings.

[8] Donald E. Miller, *Reinventing American Protestantism: Christianity in the new Millennium* (Berkeley: University of California Press, 1997).

[9] Jim Castelli and Joseph Gremillion, *The Emerging Parish: The Notre Dame Study of Catholic Life Since Vatican II* (San Francisco: Harper and Row, 1987).

[10] Anna Greenberg, *Divine Inspiration: Faith, Congregations and American Politics*, forthcoming.

[11] Alan Wolfe, *One Nation, After All* (New York: Viking Penguin, 1998).

[12] Evangelical Ron Sider makes this point very graphically in some of his speeches. He carries with him a copy of the Bible from which he has removed all the references to poverty and wealth. The book is completely tattered.

[13] See, for example, John Rawls, *Political Liberalism* (New York: Columbia University Press, 1993); Amy Gutmann and Dennis Thompson, *Democracy and Disagreement* (Cambridge MA: Harvard University Press, 1996); Kent Greenawalt, *Private Consciences and Public Reasons* (New York: Oxford University Press, 1995); and Michael J. Perry, *Religion in Politics: Constitutional and Moral Perspectives* (New York: Oxford University Press, 1997). For a different kind of argument, see Stephen. L. Carter, *The Culture of Disbelief* (New York: BasicBooks, 1993).

[14] Perry, *Religion in Politics*.

[15] Greenawalt, *Private Consciences and Public Reasons*.

[16] Ronald F. Thiemann explains this position very well in his *Religion and Public Life: A Dilemma for Democracy* (Washington DC: Georgetown University Press, 1996).

[17] I have been personally influenced by the work of Richard B. Hays (*The Moral Vision of the New Testament: A Contemporary Introduction to New Testament Ethics* [San Francisco: HarperSanFrancisco, 1996]), Frank Matera (*New Testament Ethics: The Legacies of Jesus and Paul* [Louisville KY: Westminster John Knox Press, 1996]), and William C. Spohn (*Go and Do Likewise: Jesus and Ethics* [NY: Continuum Publishing, 1999]).

[18] The Catholic bishops' letter on the economy is for me an excellent example of combining theology with more secular ethics and policy analysis. National Conference of Catholic Bishops, *Economic Justice for All: Pastoral Letter on Catholic Social Teaching and the U.S. Economy*, Washington DC: NCCB, 1986.

[19] Wolfe, *One Nation, After All*, 209.

[20] Robert Wuthnow reports poll data that corroborate Wolfe's findings. Asked about whether various approaches to helping the needy would actually help, 50 percent of respondents said people giving a few hours a week to doing volunteer work would help a lot, whereas only 24 percent said spending more money on government services would help a lot. See his *God and Mammon in America* (NY: The Free Press, 1994).

[21] John Rawls, *A Theory of Justice* (Cambridge MA: Harvard University Press, 1971).

[22] Singer, Peter, *Writings on an Ethical Life* (ECCO Press, Harper Collins, 2000).

[23] Rawls, *A Theory of Justice*; Rawls, *Political Liberalism*.

[24] T. M. Scanlon, *What We Owe to Each Other* (Cambridge MA: Harvard University Press, 1998).

[25] Greenwalt, *Private Consciences and Public Reasons*; Perry, *Religion in Politics*.

[26] Roof, *Spiritual Marketplace*.

[27] Christian Smith, Christian, *Christian America? What Evangelicals Really Want* (Berkeley: University of California Press, 2000).

[28] Dick Morris, *Behind the Oval Office* (New York: Random House, 1997), 298-305

[29] An excellent discussion of the politics of welfare is found in R. Kent Weaver's *Ending Welfare As We Know It* (Washington DC: Brookings Institution Press, 2000).

[30] NCCB, *Economic Justice for All*.

Response to "Social Science, Christian Ethics and Democratic Politics: Issues of Poverty and Wealth" by Mary Jo Bane

Emilie M. Townes

As a social ethicist who uses an interdisciplinary framework as part of my method, I see that all epistemologies lead us to ethical issues, because knowing is, itself, an act that has consequences for the knowing subject and for the community. This ethics of knowing has extraordinary relevance as we unfold ourselves into a troubling twenty-first century, with contested political races, massive voter registration drives now being countered with massive disenfranchisement, and a pliant public and press who often seem interested only in who will win the game rather than discuss the morality of its existence. The sad part is that this is nothing new for poor communities or colored peoples (no, these are not always the same) in this country. It is just that this time it was national, it was public—and the same damned thing happened in broad daylight that usually takes place in some misbegotten metaphorical or actual backwoods.

The act of knowing is always contextual, always fraught with our best and worst impulses. It is never objective. It is never disinterested, no matter how many rational proofs we come up with to argue to the contrary. It would seem that the same can be said of policy analysis as Bane's succinct analysis of Eugene Bardach's model and public policy analysis in general suggest. I agree deeply with Bane's assertion that religious viewpoints are present but implicit and unexamined in public policy debates. Where I want to trouble the waters a bit more is in our assumptions about the nature of the individual, the state, the church, and the poor, for these are *very* contested terrains within religious disciplines generally and within Christian ethics in particular.

Annual of the Society of Christian Ethics, 21 (2001): 39-43

So my remaining remarks are not so much about the particulars of Bane's paper as they are about a key issue I find implicit in her paper: Just who are we as religious folk when we enter discussions of public policy?

I.

We human beings are prone to radicalizing certain behaviors: we can turn initially positive knowledge into negative values, and we can make good things emerge from disastrous quagmires. But just as epistemologies are contextual, so are all our other reference points for living, and we become dangerous when we fail to recognize this about ourselves and then suffer the temptation of absolutizing our knowledge. For instance, it is ironic to this American Baptist that the modern day Protestant work ethic has moved so far from John Calvin's ideal. Calvin's ethic is one of grateful obedience that leads to self-denial: He held together love of God and love of neighbor which extends charity to our neighbor and shares with that person our blessings. However, there is a tension in Calvin's moral command to pursue one's vocation in the world with vigor because it is a sign of being chosen by God *and* Calvin's moral injunction against ostentation and spending. Weber's point is that a religious ethic can legitimate a socioeconomic form that is not a part of its original intent.

My point is that Weber's thesis leads to public policies that are often unaware of the kind of religious values that form their roots, and the makers of these policies are ill-equipped to critique their assumptions because they cannot remember what they never knew.[1] For many, if not most, Protestants, a major part of who we are religiously in the United States stems from an enlightenment conception of the self in which there are natural inherent rights for all people, and each person is an independent unit who is an autonomous, self-determining ego. Key here is the notion of autonomy; in Protestant religious understanding, such autonomy represents a concern for principles of authentic belief and practice. It is validated by an appeal to human experience and reason, and has unleashed a rampant individualism in many of our private and public beliefs and practices, stressing personal responsibility and despising any hint of dependency. Stressing personal responsibility while detesting dependency encourages conceiving society as a necessary evil and monitoring it so that it does not inhibit personal freedom. Society should not get in the way of our individuality or our ability—often seen as God-given if not ordained by God—to use reason and personal experience to justify all manners of private behavior and public policy, especially those that enhance life and respect the dignity and worth of all persons and those that see difference and attention to context as anathema.

Stressing personal responsibility while detesting dependency often wedges the diversity of humanness into a stultifying and in some cases death-dealing homogeneity that is only healthy for a precious (and elite) few. So as Protestant

Christianity has defended the autonomy of the individual in order to stress the value of every human being, our freedom, and the great respect owed to each and every one of us, we have come to radicalize this notion so much that we are now reaping a bitter harvest from the unrestrained exercise of our passion for possessing, for self-assertion, and for power as individuals, as a nation, and in our social institutions.

But not so ironically, the Protestant work ethic helped build large segments of our culture and society, and it carved out enormous national wealth based on a capitalist economy. It has often been one of the engines fueling some movements for social change such as the civil rights movement; recent movements in public housing complexes, often led by women, to take back and define their living spaces; and economic empowerment in which churches set up independent corporations to address community problems and issues. These movements rest, to varying degrees, on the values of hard work and thrift.

The difference between these movements and an understanding of society as a necessary evil is in their very understanding of society. In many, if not most, segments of dispossessed communities, the notion of uninhibited personal freedom remains a utopian folly. Advancing public policies that see society as a necessary evil has truncated the lives of the poor; many black folk see current public policies as forms of genocide. This is even more deadly when we consider those public policies that have a direct impact on the lives of black women and children: welfare, health care, reproductive health, childcare, domestic and sexual violence, and the prison industrial complex. In effect, women and children are at the mercy of public policies that stress equality and personal liberty, but the religious values that are at the core of these policies—an appeal to the person as an independent unit, the autonomous, self-determining ego, stress on personal responsibility, the abhorrence of dependency—belie a basic inability or unwillingness to recognize structural sins and/or inequities that demand public policies which move beyond the notion that government must work through individuals who care about themselves first and foremost.

We need public policies that are more complex than the incremental conversion of individual souls; far too much of our current public policy debates concentrate on individual morality. Public policy reflects the working out of our national value judgments. As Bane notes, it is rare that the specific moral and civil religious implications of such judgments are made explicit. Some religious values emphasize personal or private moral norms, other religious values emphasize public morality such as social justice, poverty, corporate responsibility, working conditions, health care, and war.

II.

To return to Calvin, if we value and respect our neighbors, then we must take seriously a sense of accountability to and for one another—not only as individuals, but as a society. One of the earliest words I learned in church was love; I also learned that to love without justice is asking for trouble. Justice is the notion that each of us has worth, that each of us has the right to have that worth recognized and respected. Justice lets us know that we owe one another respect and the right to our dignity. Justice can lead to public policies that claim rights as a part of the assertion of our dignity and well being. Justice is relational, not autonomous: it leads to a sense of caring that is actualized in accessible and affordable health care and childcare and the development of an urban and rural development policy that is systemic rather than episodic. It recognizes the actuality of our interdependence.

So as we engage with notions of democracy and public policy within conscious religious frameworks, it is crucial that we make explicit our conception of the good—not in terms of how the state sees it, but in terms of how we understand it from our various religious worldviews—and realize that we will not always agree. Most importantly, for those of us who are middle class Christians, we need to bring the poor to the center of our questions, our options, and our decision-making—not theoretically, but concretely. We have a maddening tendency to be troubled by poverty and constrained opportunity, but we rarely do more than listen to those who must endure and survive inequities. Perhaps one of the reasons we remain skeptical about the government's ability to do much about poverty is that our theological worldviews do not offer us much of an alternative, either.

If we keep the unrestrained autonomous self on our collective eyeball, if we refuse to yoke our individual selves and concerns with the matrix of life with others, we will never be able to engage truly in democratic politics with a spirit of justice or peace. Our traditional religious discourses will take us away from our daily needs. We will be even more complicit with the dominant political powers, for religious folk and religious discourse—and religion itself—will no longer be the "sigh of the oppressed" or "the heart of the world without a heart" as Feuerbach said so well. We will not be able to offer any genuine alternative to the way public policy has been formed, because we have become absorbed by the consumer market. We will lose our essence, our salvific power. We, as people of faith, will end up with no heart.

III.

As we enter analysis, policy formation, and articulation now in more conscious ways as people of faith and faithlessness, we must begin with a consideration of the good and wrestle with this, sometimes even with twisted hips. But begin we must, for it is my hunch that, in teasing out a conception of the good that is not bounded by our individual skin but that is within a collective ethos of individuals, groups, cultures and the like, we can discover what faithful citizenship truly means.

NOTE

[1] Katie Geneva Cannon, "Remembering What We Never Knew," *The Journal of Women and Religion* 16 (1998):167-177.

Dirt and Economic Inequality:
A Christian-Ethical Peek Under the Rug

Christine Firer Hinze

Abstract

This essay argues that cultural practices surrounding body-related dirt form a crucial axis along which racial-ethnic, class, and gender disparities are illumined, and ideological supports for inequities in household and public economies exposed. Late-modern technological, information-based societies valorize nearly-disembodied freedom and demand high degrees of bodily control, while denying or scorning bodies' limits, messiness, and incorrigibility. This leads to subtle but powerful prejudices concerning bodily dirt, dirty work, and those who perform it. A contemporary concatenation of dualistic leanings and purity rules fuels these prejudices, which in turn help legitimate otherwise patently unacceptable social and economic inequities. Effective Christian analyses of economic inequality, therefore, will uncover and challenge distorted cultural assumptions concerning bodily-related dirt, and develop strategies for renovating them.

"We live in a sweep-under-the-rug culture: we make messes, and then we ignore them. Or we hope no one finds out about them. Or we bury the mess in the Nevada desert—and then hope the bucket doesn't leak. We expect that somehow, someone else will take care of everything— and that someone is too often regarded as somebody whose life isn't worth as much as ours."[1]

At the sporadic moments when dirt has been even visible in recent Christian ethical discussions, it has most often been feminists who have pointed it out. Twenty five years ago, Rosemary Radford Ruether's first contribution to *Theological Studies* departed from her scholarly specialization in the history of Christian thought to focus on housework.[2] In 1982, Daniel Maguire entitled his presidential address to the Society of Christian Ethics, "The Feminization of God and Ethics." In a memorable line, Maguire averred that no one should be allowed to do Christian ethics "who hasn't had baby shit under his fingernails."[3] And in a 1993 essay, Barbara Hilkert Andolsen warned against ignoring "the sometimes difficult, unpleasant physical work involved in care for the frail elderly," insisting that "we need to be attentive to the profound moral significance of the work of those who deal reliably and gently with mucous, urine, and feces."[4] In different ways, Ruether, Maguire, and Andolsen each attempted to train a spotlight on, to send up a flare locating, the subject of this essay: dirt, more specifically the dirt produced by human bodies, and the work of contending with it.

Though usually left beyond the pale of Christian moral analysis, bodily-related dirt is an unavoidable component of daily experience. What is more, this humble and easily-overlooked reality lies at the very heart of the challenges confronting progress toward social and economic justice in the twenty-first century. Examining cultural attitudes and practices surrounding dirt, cleanliness, and dirty work opens important perspectives on racial-ethnic, class, and gender disparities, and exposes powerful ideological supports for inequities in household and public economies. Inattention to dirt and dirty work thus constitutes a serious lacuna in standard Christian-ethical discussions of economic inequality. In an effort to begin to redress this gap, this essay metaphorically peeks under the rug for a sustained look at the dirt middle-class North Americans usually are at pains to keep swept out of sight, and at the work performed by those—most often, unpaid women, or poorly-paid racial-ethnic women—whose job it is to manage, conceal, or remove it.

A good deal of social-scientific and cultural-historical literature has appeared on the provision of bodily-related labor in home and workplace since Ruether, Maguire, and Andolsen identified household and bodily dirt as moral, theological, and feminist issues. With the aid of these literatures I hope to uncover some of the reasons why this topic has remained on the margins of mainstream discussions of economic ethics. As we will see, questionable patterns surrounding bodily dirt have contributed to difficulties that continue to vex movements for economic justice, locally and globally. Remedying this situation will require norms, practices, and policies that incorporate more honest and responsible ways of acknowledging, delegating, and rewarding body-related dirty work.

The essay proceeds as follows. First, I describe what is meant by dirt and dirty work, and the particular sorts of it focused on here. Next, I lift up some aspects of the work of Mary Douglas and her interpreters on cultural purity codes, and explore how such codes may continue to circulate in contemporary U.S. culture around the subject of dirt and dirty work. In addition, I argue, middle-class attitudes toward cleanliness and dirt, and the ethos that demands that one repress or conceal bodily dirt and associated bodily functions, are influenced by a dualistic impulse to deny or flee from the strictures of the body, a tendency to which Westerners and Christians have historically been vulnerable. Turning to dirty work in contemporary domestic and waged economies, I then consider how purity and dualist dynamics embedded in constructions of gender, class, and race-ethnicity conspire to assure that the most devalued and scorned dirty work is performed by members of the most devalued and scorned groups, quintessentially, poor women of color. The concluding section deduces implications for Christian economic ethics, pointing out ways in which an adequate Christian perspective exposes, challenges, and may help transform distorted ways of dealing with dirt.

My major thesis is this: *In a cultural milieu that systematically degrades and devalues (while seeking to deny and conceal) bodily-related dirt and dirty work, the entire apparatus of economic and social inequality finds one of its most potent foundations.* Christians, therefore, need to make the re-evaluation of dirt and dirty work an integral aspect of their agendas for economic justice.

Dirt and Dirty Work in Contemporary Cultural Experience

What is dirty work? In contemporary North American culture, "dirty work" denotes work particularly linked to the physical body and the earth, labor that brings one into contact with what is considered dirt, and toil that soils one's own body. Some work, for example, mining, construction, and certain factory work, is considered dirty because of the dirt it leaves on the bodies performing it, or because of the physical toil and wear it exacts. Other work, such as collecting garbage, cleaning toilets, or emptying bedpans, is regarded as dirty because of the contact it involves with soiled, frail, or physically-needy bodies or the physical detritus that bodies produce.[5] Dirty work may be unpaid or paid work performed in households, or paid work in the formal economy. Such work encompasses a spectrum of activities ranging from toilsome, economically "productive" labor such as farming, mining, and construction work, to toilsome, ostensibly "nonproductive" (but more accurately called socially reproductive) labor in areas such as cleaning, food preparation, care for children or the infirm, and personal service of all sorts.

Besides these denotations, dirty work carries connotations of work deemed distasteful, repugnant, and hence to be avoided whenever one has a choice in the matter. The less mediated by technology, by formal training and certification (hence social legitimation and status), or by controlled distance between the worker and others' bodily functions, fluids, and excreta, the more undesirable and dirty the work is apt to be considered. Comparing the work of a chef, professor, or surgeon on the one hand, to that of a dishwasher, custodian, or nurse's aide on the other illustrates the point. These connotations give dirtiness an affective load, evoking feelings of aversion among those who manage to avoid dirty work, and often among those who do not. People performing work deemed dirty may find the repugnance dirt elicits rubbing off on them, rendering their social status and self-esteem at least threatened, and often harmed. Sociologist Lillian Rubin's widowed mother, for instance, made it clear to her young daughter that her job in a coat factory was "dirty," and compared unfavorably to "clean work." "Her aspirations weren't high," explains Rubin:

> "[C]lean work" meant some kind of an office job. But it wasn't just that the factory was dirty and the office clean. The dirty-clean divide was a metaphor for something more, a way of expressing her understanding of the disdain with which she, who worked with her hands, was regarded, and therefore regarded herself.[6]

Those who perform dirty work do so for varied reasons. Some do it because they have no choice; they are coerced. At the extreme, one thinks of work gangs composed of convicts, laboring to pick up trash on the sides of roads; less graphic but still coercive are situations in which persons accept jobs regarded as undesirably dirty because they see no other realistic options.[7] Others do it motivated by economic reward, very often coupled with the hope that their willingness to perform such jobs as domestic cleaning or factory work will pave the way for a future in which their children will be able to escape it. "My mother," Rubin recalls, "would admonish me to prepare myself for something better. 'I do dirty work; you'll do clean work,' was the mandate of those years."[8] In households, unpaid bodily-related dirty work is taken on as a frank necessity— someone has to do it—and often, simultaneously, as a "labor of love." Historically, certain people have been regarded as especially suited for dirty work. They may be deemed so either because of some groups' natural talents or inclinations, as when women are considered better than men at dealing with laundry or messy babies, or their inherent limitations, as when menial jobs are assumed to be "naturally" fitting for members of groups considered inferior.

When we consider the different sorts and sites of dirty work, a gendered hierarchy in the ways that such work is typically distributed and rewarded is easily identifiable. Dirt and work associated with the earth and the outdoors has been more frequently the domain of men's labor and the formal wage economy. Dirt and work associated with bodies, especially work that involves contact with bodily fluids or waste products, has been the domain of women and more often located in the unpaid domestic household. Class position and status are keyed for both men and women to whether one's paid job is a dirtier, "blue or pink" collar, or a cleaner, "white collar" position.[9] But within the working class, labor associated with "manly" dirt (e.g., the soil, mines, farming, fishing, construction) is more socially respectable and consistently garners a greater economic return than the female-keyed dirty work associated with the household and the body. For working-class men, coming home dirty can be a badge of a hard day's work. Working-class women who toil as home health aides or domestic cleaners are far more likely to change their clothes and tidy themselves up before traveling back to their own households.[10]

In this essay I am particularly concerned with the perception and valuation of the bodily-related dirty work involved in the multifaceted tasks of social reproduction. As described by Evelyn Nakano Glenn, social reproduction refers to "the array of activities and relationships involved in maintaining people both on a daily basis and intergenerationally. Reproductive labor includes activities such as purchasing household goods, preparing and serving food, laundering and repairing clothing, socializing children, providing care and emotional support for adults, and maintaining kin and community ties."[11] Not all reproductive labor is dirty work; but much bodily-related dirty work falls under the aegis of reproductive labor. In the waged economy, this particular sort of dirty work tends to be the least desired and most poorly remunerated. In households, this is the unpaid work that women usually perform and that affluent women often seek to delegate to servants. I contend that the persistent cultural devaluation of this sort of work is at the root of much social and economic inequality.

In developing this claim, an important complication must be kept in mind. Unlike the dirty work conventionally ascribed to men, much of the unpaid or poorly-paid bodily-related work women have traditionally performed involves intimate, personal service. Because of this, its dirtiness is accompanied, and at times can be mitigated, by opportunities for genuine personal expressions and relations of care. Yet their intimate links to the freedom and personhood of the giver and receiver make certain elements of the *care* that is mediated and expressed through the performance of bodily-related dirty work intrinsically non-commodifiable.[12] For those who depend on low-wage dirty work to support their own families, this feature of domestic, child care, or health aide-type labor can be highly ambiguous, for it frequently casts workers into roles and relationships they experience as manipulative or hypocritical.[13] On the other hand, when freely given in just circumstances, the personal elements constitutive of genuine care can suffuse bodily-related dirty work, and, without eliminating its toil, transform it into something akin to love's labor.[14]

With transformative potential, however, comes a further set of economic and moral ambiguities. Feminist scholars have argued that popular interpretations of this "redeeming" dimension of women's labors, ironically, have impeded the struggle to gain it its proper economic and social status. By highlighting and praising the care delivered with the labor, nineteenth- through twentieth-century middle-class culture frequently bathed women's dirty work in an idealized, sentimental light. Such sentimentality functions ideologically to conceal the economic contributions and value, as well as the drudgery, of women's toil.[15] Lavish accolades are heaped on homemakers, mothers, care-givers, and nurses, while the economic return and status accorded such labor in both households and workplaces has remained remarkably low. As we move now to consider how purity, dualism, and racial-ethnic classifications cluster around the devaluation of bodily-related dirty work, the delicacy of the tasks involved in dismantling oppressive economic and cultural arrangements, while preserving or reconstructing avenues for providing needed and caring bodily-related labor under just circumstances, will continue to be evident.

Purity and Dirt:
Dirt's Symbolic Power to Identify and Separate Social Groups

We have noticed already that when it comes to dirt and dirty work, some dirty work seems dirtier than others—that is, there attaches to some experiences of dirt a greater feeling of distaste or revulsion. Work involving this kind of dirt is the most strenuously avoided; it often involves the lowest status and poorest remuneration. I have suggested that in our culture, the kind of dirt and dirty work that fits this description is that which involves direct contact with bodily dirt or dirty bodies.

Contemporary forms of aversion to bodily dirt reflect historical developments that span the last century. Since the late 1800s, middle-class U.S. standards for household and especially bodily cleanliness have risen to unprecedented levels.[16] There is absolutely no doubt that a major impulse for what Juliet Schor calls "America's love affair with the immaculate" has been public concern for hygiene and disease prevention. The health benefits of clean water, sanitary toilet facilities, municipal systems of waste disposal, and regular personal hygiene are indisputable. But intertwined with legitimate concerns for health has been another social-psychological dynamic, one that amounts to a modern form of an ancient cultural pattern Mary Douglas has identified as the "purity code." Douglas, William Countryman, and others argue that more or less elaborate forms of purity codes are nearly universal among cultures.[17] Such codes entail socially-learned, affective/visceral reactions toward what is considered in that culture "clean" and what "dirty." Clean identifies people, things, and actions that are acceptable, and therefore belong within, that culture. People, actions, or things deemed dirty are experienced as "abject:"[18] disgusting, contaminating matter that must be kept apart from or pushed out of the physical or social body.

In traditional purity codes, the body serves as a social metaphor for communal identity, coherence, and order. Keeping clean and repelling or expelling what is designated as dirt are necessary for the body's health, safety, and proper functioning. Although what is designated as dirty (and thus a bearer of disorder, pollution, and danger) varies among different cultures, what passes the boundaries of the body—"foods, waste products, shed blood, menstrual blood, sexual emissions, sexual acts, birth, death"—is always of special concern.[19] Group members are inculcated with a variety of purity rules surrounding these body-boundary issues. Such rules influence behavior not through abstract standards, but by commonly shared reactions of acceptability or revulsion "dictated by our scarcely conscious laws of clean and unclean . . . ."[20] Purity codes, then, both reflect and protect personal and social identity. In situations where identity and its boundaries are threatened or come into question, purity dynamics are more likely to come to the fore.

Douglas's investigation of purity codes focuses on ancient and traditional cultures. Intriguingly, however, despite its cherished individualism and freedom, middle-class North American culture also incorporates a set of emphatic interdictions concerning bodily representation and comportment, which demand the careful containment of the body's capacity to produce dirt in the form of excrement, perspiration, the emission of blood, nasal mucus, saliva, and so forth. As Lisa Cahill has noted, the bodily comportment expected in contemporary individualist cultures "reflects a quite strong social ethos, including an internal classification system."[21] All of this is strongly, if informally, policed. I am fit to be seen in public only to the extent that bodily dirt is removed, concealed, or controlled. Those who fall short of accepted purity standards are subject to loss of status, of credibility, or in the extreme, of membership in the group. In short, one's relative ability to put distance between oneself and the bodily dirt produced by one's own body, and that produced by the bodies of others, constitutes an important marker of status, power, and belonging. During the twentieth century, business and advertising helped extend cleanliness's cachet far beyond basic hygiene into overtones that bespoke the very credentials of belonging. Etched into communal consciousness, and reinforced by purity-related feelings, was this message: to be fully enfranchised, economically respectable, and socially accepted—truly American—one must also be clean. But, since dirty work persists, it feels fitting that such work be relegated to those who cannot afford to be clean, or whose "naturally" (in fact socially-constructed) marginalized condition makes them dirty already.

Socially reproductive tasks, by their nature, often require close and labor-intensive contact with bodies and their dirt. Technological advances over the past century notwithstanding, toilsome, body-serving effort and its associated dirt continue to mark household work and much lower-paid service work today. As in the past, such vaguely polluting work is disproportionately performed by people from groups which themselves have been branded, subtly or blatantly, as less than acceptably clean. As far as we may be from a traditional world of religious purity laws, in the modern West four groups—women, persons of color, non-native born persons, and the poor—continue to be linked, symbolically and literally, to marginalizing dirt.

Women's symbolic association with bodily dirt and its "impurities" is rooted in what is perhaps the archetype of bodily-related dirty work, labor and birth.[22] As feminist scholarship has amply demonstrated, complicated identifications of women with the body and sex, and with sin and evil, have undergirded historical associations of women with dirtiness. Contemporary purity dynamics, which demand that the body's boundaries be strictly policed and bodily dirt controlled, concealed, and removed, target women on two levels: women are more sharply subject to pressures to conform their own bodies to these demands, and they are consistently expected to be chief agents in controlling, concealing, and removing the dirt of others.[23] Race-ethnicity as a social construct that pits "cleaner," lighter-skinned dominants over against "dirtier," darker-skinned subordinates also employs purity dynamics as one of its cultural weapons. As analyzed by David Theo Goldberg, in racist discourse corporeal properties furnish the metaphorical media for "distinguishing the pure from the impure, the diseased from the clean and acceptable, the included from the excluded." Classification of purported racial differences determines order and establishes hierarchy on the basis of racially-defined values of purity.[24] At every point in U.S. history, foreigners and recent immigrants have been perceived and derided as dirty. Dirty Micks, dirty Wops, dirty Polacks—such appellations, with related slurs and jokes, could form a litany of the succeeding immigrant groups arriving on the Golden Shores over the past century. And the association of poverty with physical and metaphorical dirtiness is even more entrenched.[25]

At least four social consequences flow from contemporary Western purity rules concerning dirt and cleanliness. First, a cultural calculus of "clean" and "dirty" operates on a literal and conscious, but also on a symbolic and subconscious level to both teach and legitimate social identifications and separations. Second, strict conditions concerning bodily cleanliness, behavior, and comportment with respect to dirt are set for those who would belong to the dominant culture. Third, perceived dirtiness or cleanliness serves to determine who enjoys full membership in "respectable" middle-class circles, who is on the margins, and who is foreign or other. And fourth, those whose work involves direct contact with what is considered dirty are to some degree contaminated and stigmatized by their work, further entrenching the marginalized status of group members (women, foreigners, people of color, the poor) already likely to be labeled as dirty.

Dualism and Dirt:
The Denial of the Body and the Dream of Disembodied Freedom

Coming to terms with the duality-yet-interdependence between body and spirit in human experience has been a perennial vexation of Western culture. Western philosophy and religion have exhibited recurring tendencies toward dualism, whereby body and spirit are deemed radically separate, and the bodily rejected in favor of the spiritual. As scholars have amply demonstrated, Christianity over the centuries has not infrequently fallen prey to these same tendencies. Yet time and again the Christian tradition has ultimately rejected anthropological dualism, insisting that the human consists of a unity-in-distinction of body and spirit.

Accompanying the boundary-maintaining and status-defining functions that contemporary purity rules attach to bodily-related dirt and the work associated with it, I want to further suggest, is a version of the ancient dualist dream of fleeing the body and attaining a state of freedom unencumbered by material limitations. The world's elites now communicate, invent, and trade instantaneously across the globe in a disembodied virtual world. The entertainment, information, and connectivity available through telecommunications break down boundaries of space and time. Technological society, swiftly moving from a toil-based to a "knowledge-based" economy, appears to hold out the promise of a world wherein not only dirt but also bodies that produce dirt no longer need to hold anyone down or back from freedom and fulfillment. A popular icon of this appealing fantasy is the characterization of a scientized future in such television series as *Star Trek*, where all traces of bodily-related dirt have been magically eliminated, complete with uniforms in which it is impossible to imagine going to the bathroom.

Other contemporary attitudes and practices surrounding bodily-related dirt and dirty work bolster the impression that dualism is in play. When bodily-related dirt is treated as an enemy to be conquered; when dirt is deemed irrelevant and not a significant or legitimate topic for public or scholarly scrutiny; when dirt is ignored as someone else's problem and responsibility—in each case one detects a whiff of dualism. To the degree that privileged Westerners are either bewitched by this fantasy of escaping the body's limits, or ignore its effects, we implicate ourselves in patterns and structures that tend to marginalize and exploit certain groups of workers and certain kinds of work, as the body-related toil that still must get done is increasingly relegated to the hidden backrooms of public workplaces, to remote corners of the global market, and, significantly, to the edges of consciousness of affluent householders and their children.

Barbara Ehrenreich, following a stint working as a domestic, focuses on the way this problem insinuates itself into households:

> There is another lesson that the servant economy teaches its beneficiaries, and most troublingly the children among them. To be cleaned up after is to achieve a certain magical weightlessness and immateriality. Almost everyone complains about violent video games, but paid housecleaning has the same consequence-abolishing effect: you blast the villain into a mist of blood droplets and move right along; you drop the socks knowing they will eventually levitate, laundered and folded, back to their normal dwelling place. The result is a kind of virtual existence, in which the trail of litter that follows you seems to evaporate all by itself . . . . A servant economy breeds callousness and

solipsism in the served . . . . In an ever more economically unequal culture, where so many of the affluent devote their lives to such ghostly pursuits as stock-trading, image-making, and opinion-polling, real work . . . labor that engages hand as well as eye, that tires the body and directly alters the physical world—tends to vanish from sight.[26]

Besides being self-deceptive, inaccurate, and religiously unacceptable, this gnostic way of construing reality breeds the precise conditions necessary to assure elite collusion in the exploitation of those other human beings whose bodily labor must feather (and change, and launder) the beds wherein the privileged enjoy their sweet dreams.

The racial and class exploitation built into dualistic attempts—by those with economic means—to break free of the constraints of bodily-related dirt is reflected and illustrated in the social history of U.S. households over the past century. That history discloses intricate and morally-troubling alliances and skirmishes across racial, class, and gender boundaries amid shifting standards and circumstances concerning cleanliness and dirt. Prominent in this story, documented by Phyllis Palmer, Suellen Hoy, Juliet Schor and others, is an escalating middle class assault on dirt, coupled by a retreat from the actual performance of dirty work by the middle class.[27] Among other things, this retreat has reflected more-advantaged housewives' attempt to escape the stigma and status threat accompanying women's historically intimate connections to dirty household work and to bodily labor connected with sex, childbearing, and care for the ill or frail. But throughout this period, their efforts to put aside dirty work *in a patriarchal context where the work continues to be simultaneously designated as women's domain, and socially and economically devalued,* have implicated white, middle class women and men in problematic, frequently exploitative relationships with those who fill the ranks of low-pay, low-status domestic and "service" jobs that specialize in the bodily labor that the middle class seeks to avoid.

As dominant mores concerning the middle-class household and women's role within it continued to evolve, economically-advantaged housewives sought to live up to what Palmer notes was a contradictory ideal. On the one hand, housewives as guardians of domesticity were expected to create a warm, clean, and attractive home for husbands and children. This expectation "required hard labor and meant contending with dirt." On the other hand, middle-class women were expected to embody feminine virtue, defined in terms of purity: "spirituality, refinement, and denial of the physical body." Additionally by the 1920s and 1930s, there emerged a new ideal of the modern wife as an intelligent and attractive companion. The solution, for those who could afford it, was to transfer the heavy and unsavory parts of household work to paid help. Thus within middle class households, white and racial-ethnic women played out master-servant relationships that implicated them as both victims and agents of the devaluation of dirty work.[28]

Glenn charts the stresses and contradictions faced by female domestic workers, whose toil enabled white middle class women to pursue domesticity and "pure womanhood" at the cost of that same opportunity for their servants. Along with Palmer and Romero, Glenn notes the pattern of denial practiced by white women in this regard. This pattern was abetted by two fundamental elements consistently found in the construction of racial-ethnic womanhood by middle-class whites: "the notion of inherent traits that suit the [racial-ethnic] woman for service," and "the denial of these women's identities as wives and mothers." With the help of such racist and classist assumptions, "the exploitation of racial-ethnic women's physical, emotional, and mental work for the benefit of white households could thus be *rendered invisible* in consciousness, if not in reality.[29] This sort of cover-up enabled elites to ignore—and perpetuate with undisturbed consciences—the cruel ironies emblemized in the Rev. Jesse Jackson's recollections of his single mother's absence, year after year, from her own family on Christmases and other holidays, while she spent the day toiling in the home of her white employers.

As Ehrenreich illustrates and Glenn documents, the more recent trend toward replacing independent domestics by cleaning services has scarcely altered the work's poor pay and low status, nor the high numbers of poor women of color who fill the ranks of Merry Maids and similar concerns across the country today. As more reproductive labor shifted into the wage economy over the course of the twentieth century, much of the dirtiest bodily-related work continued to be performed by poorer, racial-ethnic women: Hispanic Americans in the Southwest, Asian Americans in the West, African Americans in the Northeast. In the first half of the twentieth century, Glenn observes, "racial-ethnic women were employed as servants to perform reproductive labor in white households, relieving white middle-class women of dirty and onerous aspects of that work." In the second half of the century, with the expansion of commodified services, that is, services turned into commercial products or activities, "racial-ethnic women are disproportionately employed as service workers in institutional settings to carry out lower-level, dirtier and supposedly less-skilled reproductive labor, while 'cleaner' white-collar supervisory and lower professional positions are filled by white women."[30]

Like purity codes, the perpetuation among affluent elites of dualist or semi-dualist illusions both reflects and promotes animosity toward, and the attempt to escape from, the physical realities and limits of humans' embodied, mammalian nature. In this most advanced economy and culture, the mutually-reinforcing dynamics of purity and dualism that we have traced contribute significantly to cultural practices that manifest what would otherwise be surprisingly primitive reactions, and obviously distorted relations, to bodily-related dirt and dirty work. The consequences of these questionable responses to dirt are systemic, and serve to reinforce social and economic inequalities as well as the unjust treatment of workers who contend directly with dirt. They are therefore matters of profound concern to Christians, and for Christian social ethics.

Implications for Christian Ethics

I have been arguing that a cultural milieu that systematically degrades and devalues (while seeking to deny and conceal) bodily-related dirt and dirty work furnishes the contemporary apparatus of economic and social inequality with one of its most important supports. Christian ethicists, therefore, need to place the re-evaluation of dirt and dirty work at the center of their agenda for economic justice. Probing and challenging dirt-related attitudes and practices is necessary not only for addressing justice issues pertaining to those who perform dirty work in households and local workplaces. This same cultural complex acts to innure elites to the suffering and misery of those unseen "Two-Thirds World" workers whose toil provides many of our products and conveniences. And this pattern of oblivion and denial is deeply implicated in collective inattention, especially among the economically advantaged, to the earth's ecological plight.[31] For Christians and others seeking to understand and combat entrenched structural injustice, grasping and seeking ways to transform this potent "memetic pattern" are therefore of crucial significance.[32]

To accomplish this transformation, I propose that Christian treatments of economic inequality broaden to incorporate three interrelated tasks.

First, Christians and Christian ethicists ought to bring to light, question, and resist or seek to dismantle physical purity codes surrounding dirty work that establish status for some, and exclude or degrade others. To do so, in fact, is an imperative that derives from the heart of the New Testament call to discipleship. Scholars of early Christianity have shown that the community Jesus gathered around him both transgressed and radically revised traditional standards for religious and ritual purity. The gospels appear to reject exclusionary practices based on physical purity and dirtiness, as well as related patterns of honor and shame, not selectively, but across the board.[33] As Countryman states, "From the New Testament onward, all genuinely Christian ethics had to explain themselves in terms of purity of the heart, which is itself defined primarily as willingness to respect and unwillingness to harm the neighbor."[34] By this measure, much of what passes for "purity" and "dirt" in contemporary culture, and the behavior that this supports, is wholly counter to the gospels' depiction. Christians demonstrate their religious "purity" precisely through actions that cross the exclusionary boundaries, both visible and invisible, maintained by the concatenation of contemporary physical purity codes, dualistic yearnings, and well-honed habits of pursuing economic security and comfort while disregarding the economic suffering of marginalized others upon whom that pursuit depends. When, for example, affluent Harvard students organize to demand that the lowest-paid workers on campus be accorded a living wage and decent benefits, or when children are taught to undertake their share of bodily-related dirty work and to acknowledge and respect such work and those who perform it, this first Christian task is concretely advanced.

Second, Christian social ethicists ought to ferret out ways in which old dualistic leanings within Christianity continue subtly to reinforce the modern cultural versions of dualism we have identified around issues of bodily dirt and dirty work. And Christianity's considerable, if frequently under-employed, anti-dualist resources, especially its incarnational and sacramental emphases, ought to be enlisted to oppose the denigration of bodies and bodily-related work and workers inscribed in the current culture and economy. An adequate Christian approach will thus eschew both disdainful denial of the physical messiness and dirt that is part of our embodied humanity, and sentimental idealizations of bodily labor that sugar-coat its toil while colluding in its devaluation. Cultivating, instead, a posture of "incarnational realism" will enable Christians to see that the realities of bodily-related dirty work in household and paid workplace call for recognition rather than denial, respect and adequate economic reward rather than disdain.

Third, Christians and social ethicists need to ponder, seriously and explicitly, what just regard, valuation, and distribution of bodily-related dirty work look like. I have already suggested that Christians cultivate an incarnational respect for embodiment, its physical needs and functions, and the dirt and labor that attend it. To do this does not mean that physical cleanliness may no longer be valued, nor does it mean that Christians must regard the economic and social value of bodily-related dirty work as on an exact par with every other kind of work. Instead, it is to affirm with Andolsen, Mary Romero, and others that contending with dirt is not naturally work that results in stigma. There is nothing inherent in such work that makes it despicable or demeaning, far less anything that should besmirch the dignity of the persons who perform it. It is, instead, the structure and context in which such work is carried out, and the way those who perform it are then treated, that makes the work oppressive. On this point, the perceptions of people who do such work are often both more realistic and more incarnational than those of elites who avoid it.[35] A wholesale abandonment of the improved standards for hygiene and cleanliness that most Americans enjoy is not likely, nor is it required. At issue is the human, social, and ecological morality of the ways in which dirt is removed, and cleanliness in reasonable degree attained.

In both households and in the waged sector, how might what is currently a profound under-valuation and stigmatization of socially-reproductive dirty work be transformed? To date, feminist economists and philosophers have done some of the most creative and constructive thinking about this. When asking, in an equitable society, who will do the dirty work, most, like Susan Moller Okin, have affirmed some version of Michael Walzer's suggestion that, "at least in some partial and symbolic sense, we will all have to do it . . . . Otherwise, the men and women who do it not only for themselves but for everyone else too will never be equal members of the political community."[36] If privileged citizens—and, Ehrenreich notes, among the 20% of U.S. households whose members do no domestic work at all, many of our most influential political, cultural, academic, and business leaders may be found—continue to identify their status in terms of (among other things) escaping bodily dirt and related dirty work, what Walzer calls "the link between dirty work and disrespect" will never be broken.[37]

For those of us who *can* afford to insulate ourselves from bodily-related dirty work, one practical Christian-ethical response is to refuse ever to completely do so. But "symbolically" picking up a toilet brush on occasion does not, on its own, begin to address the systemic inequities we have discussed. If Christians' response to the problems with dirty work are not to remain tokenistic, nothing less than a thoroughgoing social re-evaluation, and corresponding economic and cultural re-arrangement, of the work of social reproduction must be moved to the forefront of their social-ethical agendas. This re-evaluation ought not merely commodify socially-reproductive labor by placing a price tag on it. It must, however, redress the unjust consequences that a long history of bodily-related dirty work being provided cheaply or at no cost by less powerful members of society have wrought. A Christian-ethical approach to social reproduction must also confront the interacting effects that racist, sexist, and classist practices have had on dirty work's diminution and invisibility. Renovated ways of valuing and rewarding the work of social reproduction must avoid solving elite women and men's problems with dirt at the expense of less-valued, non-elite others.

As Christian ethicists move to articulate the sort of socio-economic arrangements that a reconciliation with dirt will entail, the work of scholars like social theorist Joan Williams and economist Nancy Folbre offers helpful starting points. Folbre describes two possible future scenarios for the re-organization of socially-reproductive labor, "one in which women have exactly the same rights as men, but class and race inequalities remain unchanged, and one in which men have exactly the same responsibilities as women, across class and race lines." She advocates, as do I, the pursuit of the more challenging second scenario, which refuses to confine flourishing to racial or class elites, and appeals to the intrinsic value of family labor and the social relationships it sustains. In this scenario,

> [M]en would substantially increase their hours of unpaid work, devoting more time to home, children, and community. Their formal labor force participation rate would decline to levels more typical of women today. Forms of work that women once specialized in, such as child care . . . would be re-valued. High skill levels, as well as high wages, would be required. The family would remain an important economic institution, and common commitments to certain kinds of unpaid household labor would reduce class and race inequalities.[38]

Conclusion

I conclude by returning to the earthy insights of Ruether, Maguire, and Andolsen about household chores, diapers, and bedpans. How, in our most intimate living spaces, bodily-related dirty work is regarded, how it gets done, by whom, and at what cost, cannot help but shape the dispositions and horizons by which U.S. Christians confront larger questions of social and economic justice. This awareness, and reflection upon its implications for action, need to be heightened among Christian ethicists, and better incorporated into Christian social teachings. To the extent that Christians continue to acquiesce, however unwittingly, in our culture's systemic degradation and devaluation of dirty work, we undermine the commitment to social and economic justice that is at the heart of our social mission. Perhaps equally seriously, actively ignoring the moral and economic import of private and public treatment of bodily-related dirt fails to address people in the places where we really live. Correcting this omission will enhance the credibility and effectiveness of Christian ethical analysis and the churches' social ministry today.

NOTES

[1] Louise Rafkin, "Houses Too Clean For Comfort," *The New York Times,* February 19, 1999, Op-Ed Section, A 19. The contemporary cultural tendency Rafkin signals, and which figures importantly in this essay, was aptly described by Philip Slater in 1970 as "the Toilet Assumption–the assumption that unwanted matter, unwanted difficulties, unwanted complexities and obstacles will disappear if they are removed from our immediate vision." Philip Slater, *The Pursuit of Loneliness: American Culture at the Breaking Point* (Boston: Beacon Press, 1970), 15, cf. 13-19.

[2] See Rosemary Radford Ruether, "Home and Work: Women's Roles and the Trans-formation of Values," *Theological Studies* 36(4) (December 1975): 647-59.

[3] Daniel Maguire's remarks made at the Presidential Banquet during the annual meeting of the Society of Christian Ethics, National 4-H Center, Washington, D.C., January, 1982.

[4] Barbara Hilkert Andolsen, "Justice, Gender, and the Frail Elderly: Re-examining the Ethic of Care," *Journal of Feminist Studies in Theology* 9/1-2 (Spring/Fall 1993): 127-45, at 135.

[5] Michael Walzer makes a distinction between "hard" work, which corresponds with the first sort of dirty work I describe, and "dirty" work, which is the most despised because the most menial and bodily-linked. Walzer offers as a type of dirty work the labor assigned to India's untouchables: "It is probably true...that a set of activities having to do with dirt, waste, and garbage has been the object of disdain and avoidance in just about every human society. . .[T]he characteristic occupations of the Indian untouchables suggest what we can think of as [the archetype of dirty work]: they are the scavengers and sweepers, the carriers of waste and night soil." Michael Walzer, *Spheres of Justice* (New York: Basic Books, 1983), 176.

[6] Lillian Rubin, *Families on the Fault Line: America's Working Class Speaks About the Family, the Economy, Race, and Ethnicity* (New York: Harper Perennial, 1994), 40.

[7] This more subtle, structural coercion is encountered disproportionately by women, the poor, and subordinated racial-ethnic groups; for poor women of color it is multiply operative.

Evelyn Nakano Glenn, e.g., writes that "subordinate-race women within dual labor systems . . . were drawn into domestic service by a combination of economic need, restricted opportunities, and education and employment tracking mechanisms. Once they were in service, their association with 'degraded' labor affirmed their supposed natural inferiority." "From Servitude to Service Work: Historical Continuities in the Racial Division of Paid Reproductive Labor." *Signs* 18/1 (Autumn 1992): 1-43 at 32.

[8] Rubin, *Families on the Fault Line,* 40.

[9] See ibid; also Katherine S. Newman, *No Shame in My Game: The Working Poor in the Inner City* (New York: Alfred A. Knopf & Russell Sage, 1999), esp. ch. 4; Richard Sennett & Jonathon Cobb, *The Hidden Injuries of Class* (New York: Vintage, 1973).

[10] The latter practice, widespread among domestic workers in the Detroit area during my youth, is still observed among many domestic cleaners today. Both male and female workers who contend with bodily-related dirt are aware that their jobs make them vulnerable to the disdain of others, including peers and family members. See, e.g., "Louis Hayward, Washroom Attendant," "Nick Salerno, Sanitation Truck Driver," "Eric Hoellen, Janitor" in Studs Terkel, *Working: People Talk About What They Do All Day and How They Feel About What They Do* (New York: Pantheon, 1974), Book Three; Rubin, *Families on the Fault Line,* 40, inter alia; Sennett & Cobb, *Hidden Injuries of Class.* On "stigmatized employment" and fast food workers' ambivalence about being seen in their uniforms by peers, see Newman, *No Shame in My Game,* ch. 4, esp. 89-97. Terkel's and Newman's work also makes clear that (as the title of the latter's book suggests) not all "dirty-workers" allow social stigmatization to lead to self-disdain. See, e.g., Ibid., 97-104; Terkel, *Working,* 103, 122, 125.

[11] Glenn, "From Servitude to Service Work," 1. Other theorists identify this general arena of work as "reproductive labor," "family and caring labor," or the work of the "feminine economy."

[12] For an insightful treatment of the features, and distinctions between, exchanges of commodities and of gifts that highlights the latter's connections to the personhood of the giver, see David Klemm, "Economies of Grace," in Charles A. Mathewes & William Schweiker, eds., *Having: Essays on Property, Possessions, and the Theology of Culture* (forthcoming, 2002).

[13] Interviews with such workers abundantly confirm this point. See, e.g., Mary Romero, *Maid in the U.S.A.* (New York: Routledge, 1992), esp. 105-111; Bonnie Thornton Dill, "Making Your Job Good Yourself: Domestic Service and the Construction of Personal Dignity," in Ann Bookman and Sandra Morgen, eds., *Women and the Politics of Empowerment* (Philadelphia: Temple University Press, 1988).

[14] This complex point deserves further development than I am able to provide here. But to affirm non-commodified, personal elements that can make bodily-related caring work a labor of love does not obviate that work's economic and social worth, and the reward due it: to tell one's child care provider or domestic worker that she is worth her weight in gold is no substitute for a living wage and decent benefits. I also wish to resist any romantic or sentimental portrayal of caring labor. Andolsen (drawing on William Jarrett and Sarah Ruddick) captures this insight: " . . . [I]t is helpful to recognize care as a moral duty irrespective of subjective feeling, rather than as work necessarily motivated by loving sentiments. . . [To] recognize human vulnerability as morally salient and to respond to it with practical supportive action are two crucial moral choices involved in all caring labor . . . . [U]seful caretaking work is at least as morally significant as a loving attitude toward the one-cared-for." "Justice, Gender, and the Frail Elderly," 136.

[15] Christianity has also contributed to this tendency to sentimentalize women's labor. Sara Ruddick, e.g., criticizes the way popular Christmas nativity scenes depict the birth scene and newborn: "Birth is clearly not a merely physical event. Yet whatever else it is, birth is physical, a transaction of bodies . . . In the Christian language . . . 'a child is born to us,' the physical realities of birth are at best passed over. The infant, quickly 'wrapped in swaddling clothes,' is quite unlike the crying, shitting, burping, sometimes colicky babies that I have known. . . . Such a conception of birth denies the bodily realities on which the birth relationship depends; this renders natality sentimental." Sarah Ruddick, *Maternal Thinking: Toward A Politics of Peace*

(Boston: Beacon Press), 212. On the need to de-sentimentalize and learn from women's bodily labors, cf. Bonnie Miller McLemore, *Also a Mother: Family and Work as Theological Dilemmas* (Nashville, TN: Abingdon, 1994).

[16] Among those tracing this development are Juliet Schor, *The Overworked American: The Unexpected Decline of Leisure* (New York: Basic Books, 1992), ch. 4; Suellen Hoy, *Chasing Dirt: The American Pursuit of Cleanliness* (New York: Oxford University Press, 1995). Cf. Phyllis Palmer, *Domesticity and Dirt: Housewives and Domestic Servants in the United States, 1920-1945* (Philadelphia: Temple University Press, 1989), ch. 7; Romero, *Maid in the U.S.A.*

[17] See Mary Douglas, *Purity and Danger: An Analysis of Concepts of Pollution and Taboo* (London: Routledge & Kegan Paul, 1966); L. William Countryman, *Dirt, Greed, and Sex: Sexual Ethics in the New Testament and Their Implications for Today* (Minneapolis, MN: Fortress Press, 1988, 1990); Lisa Sowle Cahill, *Sex, Gender, and Christian Ethics* (New York: Cambridge, 1995). To date, theologians have applied Douglas's work to issues in Christian sexual ethics; here I make connections with the arenas of economy and work.

[18] Julia Kristeva's category of the abject, as adapted by Iris Marion Young in *Justice and the Politics of Difference* (Princeton, NJ: Princeton University Press, 1990), ch. 5, provides a useful, more psychoanalytically-oriented description of the phenomenon that Douglas approaches anthropologically, in terms of purity codes. Cf. Julia Kristeva, *Powers of Horror: An Essay in Abjection* (New York: Columbia University Press, 1982).

[19] Countryman, *Dirt, Greed, and Sex*, 13.

[20] Countryman, *Dirt, Greed, and Sex*, 14. The influence of purity-code-related repugnance can often be identified when people, things, or situations evoke what one undergraduate student described as "that eeeewww reaction."

[21] Cahill, *Sex, Gender, and Christian Ethics*, 131.

[22] Labor and birth may also be a prototype for the traditional practice of women taking on bodily-related dirty work as a "labor of love." As shall be noted below, middle-class womanhood from the 19th century forward was also, paradoxically, portrayed as deeply connected to purity and goodness by way of the so-called "cult of true womanhood." The complex relations between images of women's purity, working class and middle class women, and household dirt are analyzed in Palmer, *Domesticity and Dirt*.

[23] Palmer illustrates specific ways in which middle-class women were subject to these twin demands; see esp. ibid., ch. 7.

[24] David Theo Goldberg, *Racist Culture* (New Haven, CT: Yale University Press, 1998), 52, 186-87. He continues: "Impurity, dirt, disease, and pollution are expressed as functions of the transgression of classificatory categories, expressed, that is, in terms of laws, as also are danger and the breakdown of order. Actively undertaking to transgress or pollute the given order necessitates reinventing order by way of confinement and artificially imposed separation." Ibid, 54.

[25] Typical reactions of middle-class urbanites to encounters with homeless "street people" confirm their association. In the cases of foreign immigrants and the poor, actual physical dirtiness and lack of training or opportunity for hygiene prompted large public and philanthropic health campaigns and programs in the early twentieth century, directed at educating and, more importantly, improving the wages and housing available to poor families. While often patronizing or paternalistic, these efforts resulted in a dramatic decrease in disease and infant mortality. See Hoy, *Chasing Dirt*, esp. chs. 3 & 4.

[26] Barbara Ehrenreich, "Maid to Order: The Politics of Other Women's Housework," *Harper's Magazine* 300 (1799) (April 17, 2000), 59-70, at 70..

[27] Cf. note 16 above.

[28] Palmer, *Domesticity and Dirt,* 127-51, cited in Glenn, "From Servitude to Service Work," 7-11.

[29] Glenn, "From Servitude to Service Work," 18-19 (italics supplied), 32. Cf. Phyllis Palmer, "Housewife and Household Worker: Employer-Employee Relationships in the Home, 1928-41," and Elizabeth Clark-Lewis, "'This Work Had An End': African-American Domestic Workers in Washington, D.C., 1910-1940," in Carol Groneman & Mary Beth Norton, eds., *To*

Toil the Livelong Day: America's Women at Work, 1780-1980 (Ithaca, NY: Cornell University Press, 1990), 179-95, 196-212.

[30] Glenn, "From Servitude to Service Work," 3. Palmer notes that through the first half of the 20th century, "Most white middle class women could hire another woman—a recent immigrant, a working class woman, a woman of color, or all three—to perform much of the hard labor of household tasks." Palmer, *Domesticity and Dirt*, 182-83.

[31] The limits of this essay prevent me from adequately elaborating on the moral and practical significance of Western cultural tendencies to treat, in different but related ways, bodies, the earth, and workers assigned to bodily-related tasks "like dirt." Feminists and ethicists have delved into the gender and ecological connections much more thoroughly than I am able to here. See, e.g., Rosemary Radford Ruether, *Gaia and God: A Feminist Eco-Theology of Earth Healing* (San Francisco: HarperSanfrancisco, 1992); James Nash, *Loving Nature: Ecological Integrity and Christian Responsibility* (Nashville: Abingdon, 1991).

[32] See J. R. Balkin, *Cultural Software: A Theory of Ideology* (New Haven, CT: Yale University Press, 1999). By "memetic pattern" Balkin means a a cluster of linked beliefs and assumptions that are transferred and spread through cultures, creating widely shared, often isomorphic (and therefore mutually reinforcing) sets of beliefs and that embody and express cultural identity. The "memetic" patterns inscribed in this individual-and-communal "cultural software" circulate, get rearranged and modified, and are passed down generationally in a manner analogous to genetic transmission and evolution.

[33] This is Countryman's argument in *Dirt, Greed, and Sex*, echoed and developed by Cahill in *Sex, Gender, and Christian Ethics*. An analogous demonstration of the gospel's thorough rejection of extant codes of honor and shame, which also highlights the high price that disciples could expect to pay for abandoning those codes, is Jerome H. Neyrey, *Honor and Shame in the Gospel of Matthew* (Louisville, KY: Westminster John Knox Press, 1998).

[34] Countryman, *Dirt, Greed, and Sex*, 140; cf. 94.

[35] On dirty work as not inherently stigmatizing see esp. Romero, *Maid in the U.S.A.*, 42-45, 178 n. 79; on realism concerning its necessity and reward, see ibid, ch. 7; for the testimony of workers concerning the inherent respectability of their so-called "dirty" work, see citations for Newman and Terkel in endnote 10, above.

[36] Walzer, *Spheres of Justice*, 174-75; cf. Susan Moller Okin, *Justice, Gender and the Family* (New York, Basic Books, 1989), 116.

[37] Walzer, *Spheres of Justice*, 175; Ehrenreich, "Maid to Order," 63.

[38] Nancy Folbre, *Who Pays for the Kids?: Gender and the Structures of Constraint* (New York: Routledge, 1994, 102-103. Cf. Joan Williams's excellent recent contribution on this question: *Unbending Gender: Why Family and Work Conflict and What We Can Do About It* (New York: Oxford University Press, 2000). For discussion of the "social partnership" model of domestic/waged economy this might entail, see Christine Firer Hinze and Mary Stewart Van Leeuwen, "Whose Health? Whose Marriage? A Christian Feminist Ethical Response," in John Wall & Don Browning, eds., *Marriage, Health, and the Professions* (Grand Rapids, MI: Eerdmans, in press).

Inequality, Globalization, and Leadership: "Keeping Up with the Joneses" across National Boundaries[1]

Douglas A. Hicks

Abstract

Economists and sociologists have shown that social norms and relative standing are significant factors in the perception of one's well-being. Globalization increasingly extends the scope of the "neighbors" with whom persons compare themselves. Worldwide income inequality currently stands as high as inequality in Brazil, Guatemala, and South Africa. While Christian ethicists can applaud certain dimensions of globalization, we must also develop critiques of those inequalities that obstruct the full participation of persons in their societies. This paper considers how a social-relational anthropology informed by the preferential option for the poor should understand global inequality and deprivation. It offers a constructive account of how relative factors (local, national, and international) should count alongside absolute concerns in our understanding of well-being, and it suggests ways in which leaders, scholars, and citizens can respond to inequality and globalization.

How are global inequality and perceptions of well-being related? What are the moral implications of high levels of inequality in a world in which people in rich and poor countries are increasingly encouraged to see themselves as "global citizens"—or at least as "global consumers"? How should leaders respond to the paradox of globalization which brings people together but which also makes them discover their vast socioeconomic differences?

Annual of the Society of Christian Ethics, 21 (2001): 63-80

This paper begins with the empirical reality of high levels of global inequality. Sharpened theoretical insights as well as more reliable data have made it increasingly feasible to evaluate inequality at global as well as national levels. As of 1993, over half of total global income went to the world's top 10% of income earners, leaving the other half of global income to 90% of the world population.[2] As of 1998, the world's richest 200 persons held more wealth than the annual income of the poorest 41% of the world's total population, or roughly 2.3 billion people.[3] In terms of consumption, as reported in the *Human Development Report 1998*, the 20% of the world population living in the richest countries consumed 86% of the world's goods and services and used over one-half of the total energy, while the 20% living in the poorest countries accounted for 1.3% of total consumption and used less than 4% of total energy.[4]

A different kind of empirical reality that informs the paper is that the relationship between income and happiness is not as straightforward as traditional economic models would describe it. Richard Easterlin, Fred Hirsch, Tibor Scitovsky, and Robert Frank have helped forge a literature showing that while real income has increased significantly in the postwar period in most industrialized nations, overall or average happiness levels have not increased significantly.[5] These empirical studies have shown that, above certain basic levels, relative income matters more to people than absolute income when they assess their own happiness. This literature considers the "material norms" and the "habit formation" that are perpetuated by persons' interactions with—and comparisons to—their local neighbors, their social class, and society as a whole.

The possibility that a transnational region or the world as a whole could be a significant additional frame of reference for comparison has not been seriously developed. The central question of this paper is as follows: If international or global comparisons become increasingly relevant to persons' social norms, what are the descriptive and moral implications of high levels of inequality for persons' sense of happiness or well-being? We must take care, to be sure, to specify *which* persons we are discussing. I will construct a basic framework for the case that severe levels of inequality—whether in local, national, or transnational contexts—have normatively undesirable effects upon persons at various levels of the distribution—for rich and poor alike as well as for those in between.

The remainder of the paper is divided into five sections. Section I offers a critical review and analysis of global inequality, juxtaposing findings at the global level with more familiar national figures. Section II considers briefly the various economic and humanitarian movements toward the global level, and it argues that such processes increasingly are leading individual persons, for better and for worse, to attend to global social comparisons. Section III explores the role of relative economic status and perceptions of well-being. Section IV critically applies insights from Christian ethics to argue that current inequalities should be factored into the normative evaluation of the various features of globalization.

Section V offers implications for public leadership, suggesting how further research as well as effective action might address the issues raised in the paper.

Global Inequality—Levels and Trends

When considering global inequality, it is first necessary to specify the types of inequality that are relevant. In my recent book, *Inequality and Christian Ethics*, I develop a framework that explains why and how Christian ethics should be interested in multiple forms of inequality, both within and across various demographic groupings.[6] For instance, one must distinguish between inequality among individuals and inequality among groups, between inequality of income and inequality of consumption, and between inequality within nations and inequality across nations.[7]

No single statistic or finding can—or should—capture all aspects of inequality.[8] One way to begin is to examine inequality of income among all the countries for which reliable data are available. A standard measure of inequality is the Gini coefficient, which can have a value between 0 and 1. A value of 0 would represent complete equality; higher values indicate more inequality within a population.[9] As a reference point, the respective Gini coefficients for industrialized countries range from .25 to .40. With a Gini coefficient of .40, the United States experiences the highest level of inequality in the developed world.[10] Among the so-called developing countries, inequality spans from .25 to the .55-.60 range. South Africa, Guatemala, and Brazil are countries which have long held the dubious distinction of having the highest level of inequality.

A United Nations (UN) report in 1993 showed that using three different currency conversion rates, the level of global inequality was indicated by a Gini coefficient between .67 and .73. When the gross domestic product for each country was adjusted to reflect purchasing power parity, the level of inequality lessened but remained in the range of .55 to .58.[11] These calculations do not account for disparities within individual countries. In other words, this approach yields a conservative measure of inequality.[12] Yet by any conversion technique, a Gini coefficient of .55 or higher was obtained for global inequality.

More recently, a number of studies in economics and sociology have further supported the case that international income disparity is at least as wide as reported in the 1993 UN report.[13] In a November 1999 working paper for the World Bank, Branko Milanovic provides the most rigorous recent findings about global inequality. He employs household-level data that include over 85% of the world's population.[14] He finds that when adjusted for purchasing power parity the Gini coefficient of global income inequality was .63 in 1988, and it rose to .66 in 1993. When not adjusted for purchasing power, the Gini coefficient increased to .80 in 1993.[15]

It is important to note that when speaking of the level of global income inequality, virtually all scholars agree that the level is of this magnitude—as large or larger than inequality levels in even the most unequal nations. At the same time, there is significant debate as to whether the global income distribution has widened, narrowed, or stayed the same in the past three decades.[16] A minority of respected scholars argue that global inequality has begun to fall slightly.[17] Whether global inequality is rising, falling, or holding steady is crucial to the globalization debates currently taking place; but no acceptable consensus on inequality trends has been reached. Regardless of *trends*, however, the *level* of inequality demands serious moral attention.

Thus far, the discussion has focused on inequality of income. Even more directly relevant than *income* to the norms, relative standings, and social comparisons that influence perceptions of well-being are inequalities of *consumption*. When Adam Smith spoke of the "relative" need of men in his society to own a linen shirt in order to appear in public without shame,[18] and when Thorstein Veblen issued his sharp criticism against the leisure class,[19] they were focusing not on what individuals or households received economically as income, but on what they could and did consume. What do we know about international or global inequalities of consumption?

Global inequalities of consumption are of the same general magnitude as inequalities of income. Inequalities can be seen in terms of particular goods and services, and it matters morally which goods and services we examine. Not all goods necessarily contribute to healthy and well-lived lives, nor do they necessarily carry positive social benefits. Some do have indirect, positive external effects upon society as a whole. The *Human Development Report 1998*, which focused on the theme of "consumption for human development," received much media attention with its estimates that the global "community" could provide basic education, clean water and sanitary services, reproductive health services for women, and basic health and nutrition for every person in the world for an additional $40 billion per year. This figure was shown to be less than the consumption expenditure each year for cigarettes in Europe or the combination of business entertaining in Japan and cosmetics in the United States.[20] This juxtaposition suggests the importance not only of examining consumption inequalities in general, but also of understanding the *kinds* of goods and services being consumed.

In terms of either income or consumption, the magnitude of global inequality stands at least as great as inequality within South Africa, Guatemala, or Brazil. These are countries in which wealthy persons live in walled compounds made secure by barbed wire and broken glass; parking lots are protected by armed guards; carjackings are common; and street children reportedly "disappear" from urban streets, never to be seen again. Guatemala and South Africa recently undertook high-profile truth and reconciliation commissions that documented not only severe abuses and oppression in political and civil rights, but also deprivation and suffering related to economic division.

Global inequality is arguably enforced by analogous walls, armed guards, and institutional barriers that keep the richer countries well protected from poorer ones. Economist Branko Milanovic makes this comment about global inequality:

> One can conjecture that such a high inequality is sustainable precisely because [the] world is not unified, and rich people do not mingle, meet or even know about the existence of the poor (other than in a most abstract way).[21]

This observation leads to the topic of the next section of the paper: the increasing significance of the global level. What if the processes of globalization, however they are defined, actually do what we are told they can do, that is, increase people's sense of living as global citizens or global consumers? In particular, if globalization moderately increases the awareness by the world's poor that there are rich consumers in the U.S., Europe, Japan, and elsewhere, then this current inequality may not be so benign or sustainable.

Before proceeding to the next section, it is important to consider two possible objections (which can be combined) to the very emphasis on inequality. The first objection asserts that we should only be concerned morally with meeting people's absolute needs, not their relative ones. Poverty, not inequality, is the form of deprivation about which we should be concerned.[22] In this view, Christian ethics demands that individuals and societies work together to meet needs, and not necessarily only the most basic ones. Yet, there should be a limit to the kinds of relative factors involved in determining what people really need. Just because people want to "keep up with the Joneses" does not mean that they *should* "keep up with the Joneses." The second objection is this: Attention to relative concerns such as inequality promotes an emphasis on envy. That is, people should not compare themselves to others next door or around the globe who have more (or less) income or products than they do. According to this objection, such comparisons lead to feelings of resentment and jealousy and the failure to appreciate what one has. Both strands of this objection have some merit. I am not asserting that the absolute aspect of needs (such as minimum nutrition) is unimportant. Rather, I argue that relative factors as well as absolute factors have moral significance. In addition, it is difficult to determine which aspects of need are absolute and which are relative. More substantively, the kinds of goods that presently are distributed very unequally, including health care, education, and the like, are closely related to human "capabilities," which need to be roughly equal in order for persons to view themselves as full participants in their society. Human beings are relational creatures, and their perception—and the reality—that they are full participants within their society are morally desirable. The capability to function in one's society is impacted by absolute and relative factors. My framework is built on a justice-based argument for such human capability and not on the grounds of envy. The normative position detailed in the following sections will seek to develop more fully the relative dimension, while acknowledging that the absolute dimension is also vitally important.

The Increasing Significance of the Global Level

Let us consider why it is relevant and worthwhile to analyze inequalities specifically at the *global* level. Assuming that the prior objection to viewing inequality as morally problematic can be answered adequately, there still may be two possible objections to analyzing *global* inequalities. First, there is a descriptive argument that globalization simply *does not* alter persons' frame of reference. That is, even with international products and marketing campaigns, satellite television, the Internet, and the like, people will continue to think of themselves and to make determinations of their well-being solely in relation to people closer to them geographically. A second objection can be put forth by cultural protectionists who argue that each community has its own particular local values and customs that are not comparable to other communities' values and customs. In this view, even if it were possible to show mathematically that various kinds of global inequalities exist, the inequalities would not have substantive meaning, since people in different parts of the world live truly distinct and separate lives. It would make little more sense, in such a view, to compare the incomes of rural Chinese and urban New Yorkers than to compare the average weight of apples and oranges.

I will address this latter objection first: The assertion that incomes or health expenditures or the proportion of people with access to clean water should not be compared across cultures depends heavily on the view that incomes or health care or clean water are not important in roughly the same ways for all people. There is some validity in this point; it is important to acknowledge that any good carries distinct social meanings in specific local contexts. (In addition, there are significant problems of conversion rates and purchasing power to be worked out, but to recognize such pragmatic difficulties is distinct from denying the comparability across societies for some basic social goods and services.) I have argued elsewhere, building on the capability approach of Amartya Sen, that Christian social ethics should be interested in evaluating a wide range of social goods and services, so as to gain a broad picture of persons' abilities to participate in the life of their society. While goods convey somewhat different social meanings, when seen together, evaluating various basic goods gives a helpful overall picture of social functioning. To the extent that certain basic social goods can be understood as essential to adequate functioning in the life of any society— even if not essential in precisely the same ways—then they should be subject to evaluation, including distributional comparison.

The first objection that people have not altered their determination of well-being also deserves consideration. Indeed, the cross-national studies that have been undertaken thus far are merely suggestive of an "international" effect on their reported happiness. For most people on the globe, their principal frames of reference surely remain some combination of their family, neighborhood, social class, racial/ethnic group, and nationality. Yet it is hard to argue that globalization will not have an increasingly significant impact on the self-understanding of many people in the world. Indeed, it is reasonable to assert that global processes have already made significant impacts on persons' way of life. With the exception of people within committed isolationist states like North Korea, citizens around the world have become part of what Benjamin Barber calls "McWorld."[23] Barber's 1995 book, *Jihad vs. McWorld*, offers an impressively broad set of figures and accounts describing ways in which people in many countries have already dramatically shifted the way they experience culture and commerce. Barber is clear that for people with adequate capital and favorable access to media and markets, the process is an opportunity for expansion of wealth and luxury. But for many citizens of what he calls the "terminal world," the prospects for mere survival have declined.[24]

Statistics of the UNDP bear out, in less vivid but more precise terms, that economic globalization has detrimentally impacted significant numbers of people.[25] Yet to establish causality in any definitive way between globalization and increased inequality is nearly impossible, particularly since it is problematic to specify globalization's economic, technological, political, and cultural impacts and because the actual trends in inequality, as mentioned in the previous section, are disputed.[26] While this paper cannot specify precisely what processes have made global inequality rise to severe levels, the argument does depend upon the claim that people around the world are now, or are becoming, aware of such inequalities in ways that affect their perception of their well-being.

Perceptions of Well-Being and Relative Economic Status

The paper now turns to the question of how relative factors—including inequalities—impact perceptions of one's well-being. With articles entitled "Does Money Buy Happiness?" and "Does Economic Growth Improve the Human Lot?" Richard Easterlin initiated in 1973-74 a debate that has received renewed attention in recent years. Easterlin and other economists have shown that while income is *not* the most important factor in determining an individual's self-reported happiness within a given society, persons with higher incomes do report, on average, greater satisfaction with their lives than do lower-income individuals. The striking feature of this literature, and the most relevant for this paper, is that this phenomenon has been shown to be almost completely attributable to *relative* income status, and not *absolute* income.

In a 1995 article, Easterlin surveys data from the postwar period in many industrialized countries to show that for the United States, Japan, and countries in Europe, although the income of all has risen significantly, there was little or no increase in the self-reported level of happiness. Easterlin concludes that "[t]his is because the material norms on which judgments of well-being are based increase in the same proportion as the actual income of the society."[27] In other words, these studies show that people's conception of what they need to "get along" increases at roughly the same rate as increases in average income. Other economists have responded that while Easterlin's conclusion should be qualified, his overall findings that money "buys," at best, very little happiness do bear out.[28] An important qualification, however, is that up to a certain basic economic standard of living, absolute improvements do, in fact, matter. More research is needed on least-developed countries in order to understand how the relation of absolute and relative factors is different from (or similar to) these findings for industrialized countries.

Thus, in industrialized nations, what matters most at the national and local level is how persons are doing relative to others. In a classic 1949 essay, economist James Duesenberry integrated such a conception into his "theory of consumer behavior." While standard economic models had viewed an individual's satisfaction or utility in terms of an absolute quantity and quality of goods, Duesenberry argued that an individual's utility and, consequently, his or her saving and consuming behavior were impacted by the visible consumption of his or her neighbors. He states:

> What kind of reaction is produced by looking at a friend's new car or looking at houses or apartments better than one's own? The response is likely to be a feeling of dissatisfaction with one's own house or car. If this feeling is produced often enough it will lead to action which eliminates it, that is, to an increase in expenditure.[29]

This effect of comparing oneself with one's neighbors and modifying both one's sense of well-being and one's behaviors has been termed "keeping up with the Joneses." Duesenberry called it, less poetically, the "demonstration effect."[30]

The established model entails the idea that people at different levels or classes of society (that is, at different points in the income distribution) may have different material norms, because they are most often exposed to persons near them in social or economic class.[31] Sheldon Danziger and Robert Haveman add that one's racial or ethnic grouping may be another reference group.[32] Concurrently, there are society-level influences that lead all persons in that society to have common aspirations. This is the reason why richer people, on average and when other factors are controlled, report higher happiness levels than poorer individuals within the same society: to the extent that there are common material aspirations, the rich have, by definition, met them more fully.

If persons perceive themselves as worse off when they have a relative lack of economic goods, does it follow that a wider income or consumption distribution indicates a worse social situation than a narrower distribution? The answer to this question, in the abstract, is "not necessarily." First of all, when speaking of *perceived* well-being, empirical work needs to be undertaken that demonstrates, when distributions are made less unequal, whether people shift their sensitivity to smaller differences in a way that could fully cancel out the improvement towards equality. Further, in a social utilitarian calculus, the increase in perceived happiness of the rich could more than offset the decrease in perceived happiness of the poor (though not if standard assumptions about decreasing marginal utility hold). From the perspective of a preferential option for the poor, however, a strong case can be made that excessively unequal economic distributions are less desirable than more equal ones because of moral priority given both the perceived and actual well-being of the poor. Such an argument will be considered in the next section. Before that, a few issues related to the global level need to be considered.

The study of social comparisons at the cross-national or international level is not as developed as at local and national levels. When comparing happiness among national populations, there is not definitive evidence that the magnitude of income inequality impacts the average level of happiness; it is even postulated that in more egalitarian societies, citizens might become more sensitive to smaller differences among their neighbors.[33] The impact of average income upon national happiness across nations is not nearly as significant as the effect of income upon happiness among individuals within a nation. This finding supports the "relative income" argument that one's primary social norms come from within one's society rather than from international influences. There are also significant cultural factors that lead some countries simply to report higher levels of happiness than are reported in neighboring countries with similar socioeconomic characteristics. (For example, the French, on average, report consistently lower happiness scores than their European neighbors with similar incomes.)[34] A positive relationship has been found, however, between average national income and reported happiness, at least among industrialized nations; higher average GNP predicts a higher average happiness level.[35] The extent to which this effect has to do with difference in achievement of some transnational norm deserves further empirical attention.

The present paper calls for an extension of this framework to transnational levels. Of course, one important aspect of this expansion would be to take into account the cultural factors that affect perceptions of happiness. If this can be done adequately, the framework already developed by economists and sociologists allows for an expansion to include global influences also. The model in its present form views persons as forming their habits and aspirations principally through their local, class-based context, but with a "moderating" effect of the national level that moves all citizens of a society toward common norms and aspirations. Incorporating global influences would then move or "moderate" individuals' norms and aspirations, not toward the national standard, but toward a global one.

Christian Ethics and Global Inequalities

It is not possible to develop here a full normative framework for understanding global influences on well-being. I have sought to construct some elements of a Christian ethical approach to inequality and well-being in *Inequality and Christian Ethics*. The following paragraphs state and then apply relevant features of that approach to global inequalities and perceptions of well-being. Drawing on both Gustavo Gutiérrez and H. Richard Niebuhr, I have developed a strongly relational anthropology that understands persons as socially situated. People are not isolated individuals whose well-being could be determined by some objective, non-contextual, material standard.[36] Within this framework, more important than counting the number of dollars or shoes or dishes that a person has is the wider picture of whether persons understand themselves to be full agents within their societies. It is morally problematic if some persons are excluded from feeling—and actually having—a sense of stake in their societies. Persons' sense of participation is impacted or partially mediated by the social goods that they can own or use.[37] It is not difficult to see that people require access to certain goods and services in order to function within their society. For example, a telephone or refrigerator was not required one hundred years ago in U.S. society, but with some exceptions that is no longer the case. Now, arguably, as the U.S. Internet usage has surpassed 50% of the population, access to the World Wide Web will soon be central to being a full participant in American life.[38]

It is in this context that the preferential option for the poor becomes significant. In *Inequality and Christian Ethics,* I have developed an account of the preferential option of the poor that fits within a Christian ethic of solidarity. That framework has its theological roots in both the *universality* of God's love and the call to *preferential care* for persons who are in need or who are marginalized in one or more dimensions of life. While the liberation theologians give priority to economic deprivations based on a class-based analysis, they also acknowledge the important forms of marginalization or discrimination on the basis of race, gender, age, sexual orientation, and indigenous status. The wider framework of solidarity is inclusive and not partisan—that is, the goal is not to invert the groups or persons who are rich and poor, able-bodied and disabled, and so on. Rather, the goal is to remove the conditions of injustice and deprivation that keep some persons from being full participants.[39]

This account of the preferential option for the poor within a framework of inclusive solidarity allows for a social ethic that gives moral priority to the needs of the poor and marginalized but also recognizes the humanity of the affluent and well-connected. It also enables a view of society as a whole that understands the well-being of all persons as interrelated. When the three dimensions of the framework are developed—solidarity, selfhood, and social goods—a relational anthropology results. Inequalities of important goods impede the sense of full participation in one's society, and for this reason, excessive disparities are seen as morally troubling.

Asserting that persons require some relative (but not complete) equality of important goods in order to be full participants is not to argue against severe inequality on the grounds of envy. Some expressions of "keeping up with the Joneses" may be attributable to envy; those are not normatively acceptable. As Patrick Byrne argues, the preferential option for the poor, when properly under-stood, allows no traces of *ressentiment;* rather it is rooted in agapic love for the poor and non-poor alike.[40] The moral goal is not merely to take consumption from the rich and shift it to the poor, but rather to rethink how and what people consume by critically evaluating the institutional forces that can hamper the well-being of rich and poor alike. In fact, we need to develop a critique of consumption that notes the structural and personal aspects that lead people to pursue their happiness where the Christian tradition and some economists, too, tell us we will not find it.

Not all consumer products or services are actually "goods" in the moral sense. Unlike a basic liberal position that would refuse to make moral judgments about which products and services are actually good for persons, there is space within liberation theology or a Reformed approach like H. Richard Niebuhr's for substantive deliberation about the role of particular goods for living a well-lived life. In distinct ways these Christian ethical approaches pay close attention to the social context; products are goods to the extent that they allow people to participate in the life of their society. More important than any product or service is the instrumental impact that it has on enabling people to pursue their well-being within their society.

If the general contours of such a social-relational anthropology are accepted, Christian social ethicists, I am arguing, should have mixed feelings about movements toward the global—not just "globalization" as an economic process, but also moral and humanitarian efforts towards seeing ourselves as "global citizens" with equal rights and consequent responsibilities.[41] On the positive side, both in practice and in scholarship, national sovereignty has increasingly been "relativized" by concerns about the rights of its citizens. The humanitarian prospects of a global culture of human rights have also contributed to an increasing number of transnational prosecutions based on human rights abuses. These developments are consistent with an account of neighbor-love that sees national boundaries as no limitation on the theological doctrine that all humans are created equal in the image of God.

But as was suggested in one of the objections above, these beneficial aspects of seeing oneself as a global citizen may come at some cost to local identity. Precisely because of the interdependent nature of the human person that is emphasized within a social-relational anthropology, persons flourish when they see themselves as part of local groups, families, and contexts in which they can interrelate on a face-to-face basis with friends and colleagues. It bears emphasizing here that I make no claim that global identity should somehow replace local identity or that it should become the principal form of identity. Rather, I suggest that there are both positive and negative dimensions when persons incorporate global norms, among others, into their acts of social comparison. Progress on the human rights front is perhaps the most promising dimension. I turn now to consider some of the negative dimensions.

As earlier sections of the paper have suggested, a possible negative aspect of global influences concerns economic inequalities. People in poorer countries are increasingly confronted with images of what they do not have but "should" have. Of course, alleviating absolute deprivation is clearly an important end which is . not diminished by attending to additional relative factors. Yet, even if they have a low material standard of living, people can feel a sense of having a stake in their (albeit economically poor) societies. Given current levels of global inequality, global comparisons could undermine that sense (or reality) of being full participants.

There is some empirical evidence that societies in which a broad spectrum of persons have a sense of stake in their society have strong objective results. Richard Wilkinson and colleagues have demonstrated, for instance, that above basic subsistence levels people in more egalitarian societies actually live longer. Wilkinson presents evidence that for countries with a GNP per capita above $5000 per year, life expectancy of the population as a whole is strongly correlated with the level of income distribution but not with the overall level of income. That is, more egalitarian countries, and not necessarily richer ones, have a higher life expectancy.[42] Life itself is arguably the most basic form of human functioning and capability. Poor persons may well be (and not just perceive themselves to be) less able to function in a (highly unequal) global society than in a more locally centered (if it is a more equal) one.

Another kind of problem raised by high economic inequality—and rising consciousness of it—is that the actual well-being of the rich may be detrimentally affected. That is, even if affluent persons perceive themselves to be happier when they see that they are atop the global economic distribution, they may be pursuing happiness in the wrong spheres of life. Indeed, as liberationists emphasize, rich persons' very salvation may be at stake in the response to their own affluence. There are, for instance, financial and psychological costs to protecting oneself and one's possessions from others. On this point, it is significant to remember that the preferential option for the poor concerns itself with the well-being of wealthy as well as poor persons and notes the negative potential consequences of inequality for *all* persons.

One possible reply to these arguments about the impact of global inequality and well-being is to acknowledge that the framework is in general terms correct but then to say that the best response is simply to make international walls higher! That is, the way to address the insight that global inequalities are unsustainable if they are fully recognized is to reinforce, by political and economic means, a global reality of "separate but unequal." In this approach, leaders of affluent nations would make every effort to preserve their privileges and to maintain their disproportionate power over international institutions.

This position should be rejected on three grounds. First, it is unrealistic. It is simply a losing battle to try to preserve local or national isolation. The viable question is not whether to be engaged internationally but *how* to be engaged. Second is an argument couched in terms of enlightened self-interest. All persons could benefit from a movement towards the global if the process were undertaken in a way that attended explicitly to both absolute and relative deprivation. Economists are right that there is a win-win potential that can come from increased trade and information flows across national boundaries. Amartya Sen has emphasized that critics and proponents of the free market alike fail to recognize the important intrinsic value of engaging in market transactions. Free market proponents emphasize the instrumental, efficiency-based benefits of globalized trade, and opponents rightly assert that democratic and social freedoms do not necessarily come with market liberalization. Few people on either side, however, note that engaging in market transactions itself is one form of freedom and participation.[43] Global movements, including liberalization of trade, could have benefits that reach all people. The problem is that with current inequalities persons at the bottom have little ability to participate favorably in these markets. Thus, the focus turns to remedying severe inequalities. Third and finally, the moral argument has the most force here. Why not build bigger walls to maintain separate but unequal? Such a situation denies the fundamental equal dignity of all human beings. If humans derived their perceived and actual well-being solely from relative factors and not also from absolute ones, then this possibility might be morally defensible. In reality, however, it is clear that a large proportion of the world population does not enjoy the basic (absolute) socio-economic conditions that any Christian ethical position would judge to be necessary in order to guarantee human dignity for all persons. Further, it would not be consistent with a commitment to the equality of all persons before God to create barriers to human interaction in order to keep one group's affluence from others.

Implications for Public Leadership

What are the implications of my analysis for effectively addressing issues of inequality, globalization, and well-being? It will be helpful to draw together the strands of the argument and then to suggest how leaders and citizens could respond. I have presented an argument that current levels of global inequality—in various forms of income and consumption—are unacceptable from a theologically informed position. As people increasingly include global influences in the assessment of their condition, global inequality will have more of an impact on both their perceived and their actual well-being. The analysis suggests that the effects of transnational influences will make the global poor perceive themselves as less well-off and the global rich see themselves as better off than if they were not aware of global disparities. The preferential option for the poor criticizes not only decreases in perceived happiness but also the actual decreases in participation and agency that are suffered by people marginalized by a globalizing world. It is true that some global processes—such as increasing human rights protections and even access to the Internet—offer possibilities for improving the actual well-being of poor persons, though the promise of globalization in its current form has not been realized for many people. Even if there were increases in their objective well-being (that is, via human rights protections), the incorporation of a global component could, at the same time, negatively affect their perceived well-being (such as the realization of relative income deprivation).

The detrimental effects of severe economic inequality on the rich deserve fuller attention than could be given in this paper. The "costs" in terms of fear of robbery or violence because of inequality, marked by increases in both local gated communities and international barricades and immigration laws, are of concern in terms of enlightened self-interest and on purely moral grounds.

Empirical studies of transnational effects of social comparisons will help add clarity to how much influence (if any) globalizing economic and technological changes have on persons' perceived well-being. Empirical studies of international disparities will shed more light on the trends, and even causes, of inequality. This paper suggests the importance of understanding these two areas in moral-theological terms. Persons rightly understand their well-being in terms of their capability to be participants in their societies. This paper suggests that we should increasingly ask how global influences impact persons' perceived and actual status as social agents.

These discussions related to inequality and "keeping up" with our neighbors ultimately become value-centered ones that call for creative response by public leaders as well as citizens. If consumers uncritically accept the view that the acquisition of goods and services is a good way to increase their happiness, they will seek more complicated and specialized products to signify their superior position to their neighbors, whether local, national, or foreign. The empirical literature, however, suggests that while there are benefits of consumer climbing for the relatively affluent, there are more promising ways to pursue happiness for almost all individuals. From a wider perspective, as Robert Frank argues, this race for relative position is inefficient for society as a whole; social cooperation leading to public goods could result in lasting and tangible improvements in well-being for all citizens (except perhaps the mega-rich, who may prefer to provide their own infrastructure and even their own security.)[44] Benjamin Barber's framework suggests that the kinds of global comparisons that individuals currently undertake (and will probably do increasingly) similarly focus on conspicuous consumption. That is, Barber's analysis of McWorld as the dominant dimension of globalization leads to global comparisons of the sort that Robert Frank laments at the national level. Shifting priorities from private consumption to public provision at the national level or beyond requires serious moral reflection about public goods and effective leadership to implement the vision. Leaders can also articulate the difference between spending for basic needs and spending for luxury consumption.

The normative perspective of this paper suggests that the effectiveness of public leadership can be evaluated in terms of the impact on the capability of citizens to be participants in their societies. Such capability is seen to be affected by both absolute and relative factors. It is reasonable that for poorer societies, leaders should focus on overcoming "absolute" deprivations—such as basic nutrition, clean water, basic shelter, and the like—while also taking into account the impact on poor persons' perceived well-being of affluent persons within and beyond their societies. For wealthier societies, leaders should increasingly focus on the relative dimensions of need that can result in people, even those with relatively high incomes, who are marginalized from the public life of their society.

Leaders at various levels—local, national, and beyond, and in political, business, nonprofit and religious spheres—must be sure that they are accounting for how global influences affect their constituencies. They should encourage a public debate about society-wide goals while also acknowledging the reality that social norms matter for citizens who are pursuing their individual well-being. Because people are social-relational beings, addressing the needs of marginalized persons through provision of more goods and services can amount to chasing a moving goal post. (Whether the goal post is moving almost as fast as people progress towards it is a matter for further empirical work.) On this point, leaders and scholars alike can distinguish goods and services that are necessary for functioning and participating in one's context from luxury goods that are not essential. Other key issues for ethical reflection and for the practice of leadership, then, include these: Leaders should use their positional authority and visibility to emphasize the moral and self-interested reasons for attending to the needs of the most vulnerable citizens, both domestically and internationally. Addressing the basic needs of those at the bottom of the distribution is a way to lessen both poverty and inequality. Further, an effective leadership process will address the potential inefficiencies of "keeping up with the Joneses" by incentivizing and coordinating individual efforts to produce socially desirable outcomes, such as public infrastructure whose benefits reach all citizens. Although these leadership challenges become more complicated beyond the national level, responses to globalization in its various forms will require such thoughtful, committed, and creative leadership in the coming decades.

NOTES

[1] I would like to thank Terry L. Price, Elizabeth H. Rickert, and three anonymous referees from *The Annual* for their helpful comments on this paper.

[2] Branko Milanovic, "True World Income Distribution, 1998 and 1993: First Calculation Based on Household Surveys Alone," World Bank, Development Research Group working paper, November 1999, 29.

[3] United Nations Development Programme (UNDP), *Human Development Report 1999* (New York: Oxford University Press, 1999), 38.

[4] UNDP, *Human Development Report 1998* (New York: Oxford University Press, 1998), 2.

[5] Easterlin summarized the literature in 1995: "Will raising the incomes of all increase the happiness of all? The answer to this question can now be given with somewhat greater assurance than twenty years ago (Easterlin, 1973; Easterlin, 1974). It is 'no'." Richard J. Easterlin, "Will Raising the Incomes of All Increase the Happiness of All?" *Journal of Economic Behavior and Organization* 27 (1995): 35-47. The references are to Easterlin, "Does Money Buy Happiness?" *The Public Interest* 30 (Winter 1973): 3-10; and Easterlin, "Does Economic Growth Improve the Human Lot?" In Paul A. David and Melvin W. Reder, eds., *Nations and Households in Economic Growth: Essays in Honour of Moses Abramowitz* (New York: Academic Press, 1974). See also Fred Hirsch, *Social Limits to Growth* (Cambridge, MA: Harvard University Press, 1976); Tibor Scitovsky, *The Joyless Economy: An Inquiry into Human Satisfaction and Consumer Dissatisfaction* (New York: Oxford University Press, 1976); Robert Frank, "The Frame of Reference as an Economic Good" *Economic Journal* 107 (November 1997): 1832-1847; Frank, *Luxury Fever: Why Money Fails to Satisfy in an Era of Excess* (New York: Free Press, 1999).

[6] Douglas A. Hicks, *Inequality and Christian Ethics* (Cambridge: Cambridge University Press, 2000).

[7] See especially Hicks, 203-214.

[8] For inequality in any sphere, it is possible to calculate that inequality in many ways. Three of the most standard are these: 1) the ratio of the amount of a given good held by the top 20% of the population to the amount held by the bottom 20% (or the top 10% to the bottom 10%); 2) Theil's measure of entropy; or 3) the Gini coefficient of inequality. For reasons both theoretical and pragmatic, I focus here on the third measure.

[9] For a fuller discussion of the Gini coefficient, with its virtues and limitations, see Hicks, 247-251 (Appendix A).

[10] World Bank, *World Development Report 2000/2001* (New York: Oxford University Press, 2000), 282-283 (Table 5).

[11] United Nations Department for Economic and Social Information and Policy Analysis—Statistical Division, *Trends in International Distribution of Gross World Product*, National Accounts Statistics Special Issue Series X, No.18 (New York: United Nations, 1993), 7-26.

[12] A fuller discussion is included in Hicks, 46-48.

[13] T. Paul Schultz, "Inequality in the Distribution of Personal Income in the World: How It Is Changing and Why," *Journal of Population Economics* 11(1998): 307-344; Glenn Firebaugh, "Empirics of World Income Inequality," *American Journal of Sociology* 6 (May 1999): 1597-1630; Milanovic, "True World Income Distribution"; see also Lundberg and Milanovic, "Globalization and Inequality."

[14] Milanovic, 10.

[15] Milanovic, 51.

[16] For various perspectives, see Schultz, "Inequality in the Distribution of Personal Income in the World"; Firebaugh, "Empirics of World Income Inequality"; Andrea Boltho and Gianni Toniolo, "The Assessment: The Twentieth Century—Achievements, Failure, Lessons," *Oxford Review of Economic Policy* 15 (Winter 1999): 1-17; Milanovic, "True World Income Distribution."

[17] Boltho and Toniolo do not find that the level of international inequality is much different from figures cited above; they state that the international Gini stood at .54 in 1980 and at .50 in 1998 (Boltho and Toniolo, "The Assessment," as quoted in Lundberg and Milanovic, 1-2). This argument is worthy of careful attention, though as Lundberg and Milanovic assert, there are serious limitations to the methodology employed by Boltho and Toniolo, most notably that they only include 49 countries in their analysis (Lundberg and Milanovic, "Globalización and Inequality," 2).

[18] Adam Smith, *An Inquiry into the Nature and Causes of the Wealth of Nations* (London: Everyman Edition, Home University Library, 1776), 351-352; see also Hicks, 192.

[19] Thorstein Veblen, *The Theory of the Leisure Class* (New York: Macmillan, 1967 [1899]).

[20] *Human Development Report 1998*, 37.

[21] Milanovic, 51.

[22] Note that for the purposes of this paper, poverty is associated with absolute deprivation, while inequality entails relative deprivation. It is possible, of course, to define poverty to include a relative component. In that case, some of the concerns described here as inequality-related ones are incorporated within the analysis of poverty. Inequality, however, is a phenomenon of the entire distribution, not just of persons at the bottom, an important point that informs my Christian ethical account with a social-relational anthropology.

[23] Benjamin Barber, *Jihad Vs. McWorld: How Globalism and Tribalism Are Reshaping the World* (New York: Ballantine Books, 1995).

[24] Barber, *passim*.

[25] The most explicit treatment of globalization and inequality is the UNDP's *Human Development Report 1999*, which bears the theme, "Globalization with a Human Face."

[26] See, for instance, the special issue on "The Global Economy" in *Current History: A Journal of Contemporary World Affairs* 96/613 (November 1997), especially these articles: Blanca Heredia, "Prosper or Perish?: Development in the Age of Global Capital"; Douglas Watson, "Indigenous Peoples and the Global Economy"; and Thomas M. Callaghy, "Globalization and Marginalization: Debt and the International Underclass."

[27] Easterlin, "Will Raising the Incomes. . . ?" 44.

[28] See Andrew J. Oswald, "Happiness and Economic Performance," *Economic Journal* 107 (November 1997): 1815-1831; and Robert H. Frank, "The Frame of Reference as an Economic Good."

[29] James Duesenberry, *Income, Saving, and the Theory of Consumer Behavior* (Cambridge, MA: Harvard University Press, 1962 [1949]), 27.

[30] Ibid.

[31] Easterlin, "Will Raising the Incomes . . . ?" 36-37.

[32] Sheldon Danziger and Robert Haveman, "An Economic Concept of Solidarity: Its Application to Poverty and Income Distribution Policy in the United States." Research Series No. 37, International Institute for Labour Studies (Geneva: IILS, 1978).

[33] See Easterlin, "Does Economic Growth Improve the Human Lot?" 119.

[34] See Easterlin, "Will Raising the Incomes?" 39 (Figure 2). See also Alex Inkeles, "Industrialization, Modernization, and the Quality of Life," *International Journal of Comparative Sociology* XXXIV (1993): 1-23.

[35] Easterlin, "Will Raising the Incomes?" 42-44. Easterlin focuses on data and analysis from Ronald Inglehart, "The Renaissance of Political Culture," *American Political Science Review* 82:4 (December 1988): 1203-1230.

[36] Hicks, 179-187.

[37] Hicks, 187-194.

[38] Nua Internet Surveys provide estimates that show that just over half of U.S. Americans now have online access. See http://www.nua.ie/survey/how_many_online/index.html.

[39] Hicks, 168-176. The emphasis on both universality and preferential attention of God's love runs throughout Gustavo Gutiérrez's work. See, for example, *Evangelización y Opción por los Pobres* (Buenos Aires: Ediciones Paulinas, 1987), 53. See also Stephen J. Pope, "Proper and

Improper Partiality and the Preferential Option for the Poor," *Theological Studies* 54/2 (1993): 242-271, esp. 256-262.

[40] Patrick Byrne, "Ressentiment and the Preferential Option for the Poor," *Theological Studies* 54 (1993): 213-241.

[41] See Martha Nussbaum et al., *For Love of Country: Debating the Limits of Patriotism* (Boston: Beacon Press, 1996).

[42] Richard Wilkinson, "The Epidemiological Transition: From Material Scarcity to Social Disadvantage?" *Daedalus* 123/4 (Fall 1994): 61-77.

[43] Amartya Sen, *Development as Freedom* (New York: Alfred A. Knopf, 1999), 111-116.

[44] Frank, "The Frame of Reference as an Economic Good" and *Luxury Fever: Why Money Fails to Satisfy in an Era of Excess*; See also Hirsch, *Social Limits to Growth*.

RELIGION AND LIBERALISM REVISITED

Panel

Theology Beyond the Liberal Paradigm: Civil Society and its Discontents

Nature, Grace, and Toleration:
Civil Society and the Twinned Church

John R. Bowlin

Abstract

Various theological benefits accrue as similarities are noted between Christian churches and other intermediate associations in societies like ours. Above all, we come to regard the church in ancient ways, as a twinned body, as a *gemina persona*, one thing by nature, another by grace. This in turn helps us see the morally ambiguous character of graced nature, even ecclesiastical nature, exemplified most plainly in the mixture of virtue and vice that natural societies yield, but also in the church's ambivalence about natural virtue and its supernatural transformation in time.

I have two stories about civil society to tell and I want to try to give each their due. They are, I think, competing stories, but not entirely so, and when told together they shed light on each other. Above all, they disclose something of the twinned character of the Church *in via* and something of the morally ambiguous character of nature, even nature transformed by virtue and sanctified by grace.

Churches and Gamecock Clubs

The first story regards the Christian churches in America and goes something like this. Constantinian Protestantism has passed. The Catholic moment never arrived. The churches have retreated to the social space between the household and the state that we have come to call civil society. In the company of other intermediate powers, they play their part, they do their job. Within their walls, "the taste and habit of self-rule" are cultivated.[1] Shared interests are pursued and collective efforts made, and along the way, social capital accumulates. Informal networks form, trust grows, and toleration emerges, all in a context of cooperation for the sake of mutual protection and common welfare.

The consequences are political and altogether positive, or so the story goes. A people schooled in these tastes and habits will most likely become active, robust citizens. "Engaged men and women tend to be multiply engaged."[2] Already disposed to care for the welfare of one kind of society, they will understand the importance of caring for the common good of political society. Already skilled in cooperative ventures at the parochial level, they will not be threatened by the conflicts and compromises of public life. With little effort they will come to understand that give and take among equals is the soul of democratic politics, and they will realize that this soul flourishes only as certain moral virtues—good will, respect, toleration, and trust—are cultivated and exercised. And, perhaps most importantly, they will be disposed to resist the most common unintended harms and hidden tyrannies of societies like ours, societies that place a premium upon individuals and their choices. Accustomed to self-rule and to the pursuit of their own ends, they will most likely oppose both the soft despotism of the market and the corporatist tendencies of the modern state.[3] Accustomed to living their lives in the company of others, they will be less likely to think that their rights are possessions, their obligations are burdens, and their choices are constrained by nothing but their preferences.[4]

Sociologists, political theorists, and pundits are, more often than not, the tellers of this tale, and although it includes repeated reference to the churches, it is not about them.[5] It is, rather, a story about the prospects and discontents of liberal democracy, and the churches figure in the tale only as they benefit political societies like ours. The tone is secular and instrumental throughout. America flourishes when the churches do, not because of their unique ability to transform political life, but rather because healthy liberal democracies require vibrant civil societies. The churches are important, not because they mediate God's grace to the temporal order, but rather because they mediate, and thus perpetuate, the virtues and practices that sustain liberal democracies and the interests that sustain particular political establishments. At the same time, they help generate resistance to those political establishments and institutional arrangements that threaten democratic virtues and liberal freedoms. When intermediate powers, the churches among others, fulfill these functions, America prospers.[6]

So goes the first story. Its moral should be obvious: intermediate associations are good, when threatened they ought to be protected, and the churches are significant precisely because they help reproduce our political order and chasten its pretensions without first acquiring the establishment privileges that now elude them. Nonetheless, one can imagine a different collection of responses from our theological critics, the most interesting being the least favorable. Some will object to the fact that the churches have only subsidiary significance in this story. Locate them among the intermediate powers of civil society, praise them for the important services they render there to democracy and you will tempt them to forgo their critical purchase upon every temporal politics, even the best imaginable. Indeed, if the churches accept this supporting role in the political drama, they will have difficulty imaging themselves (let alone asserting themselves) as an eschatological witness to an altogether different arrangement of political affairs, to the rule of God revealed in Christ.[7] Still others will wonder whether anything useful can be learned about the church from a secular story about its sociological location and political function. The Church is, after all, a sacramental reality, a consequence and vehicle of God's grace, and thus one might suspect that only theology could speak truthfully about its place and significance in the temporal order.[8] In a similar vein, one might suspect that the Church ought to forsake the virtues it happens to generate in its secular, civic capacities. No doubt, it ought to lay claim to those virtues that follow from its sacramental reality, those that grace cultivates for the sake of supernatural ends. But why bother with those that follows from its location in civil society, toleration in particular? The tolerant quiet their outrage and make agreements with the vicious, all in the hope of securing some measure of civil peace. But why call this habit a virtue, when the peace that it promises is no more that a suspension of warfare, a mockery of the peace of Christ?[9]

These worries demand a response, which I hope to offer, but before I do, consider another story about civil society, a story about the Collinsville Gamecock Club. In Oklahoma, the state where I live, cockfighting is legal and popular. Cockfight clubs dot the countryside, gamecock weekends attract thousands to the county seat towns of the southeast, and legislators have been known to float bills that would enshrine in the state constitution the right of roosters to fight and of Oklahomans to bet and cheer.[10] During the heyday of the cold war, a state senator from Sallisaw was reported to have said that cockfighting would be the first thing to go when America caved in and the communists took over. Freedom is just another word for cockfighting, or so it seems. Yet, these days, the threat to freedom lies closer to home, in the petition drives of the animal rights activists. Mostly from Tulsa and Oklahoma City, their aim has been to put before the voters a proposed amendment to the state constitution that would ban cockfighting. As the signature count mounted late last spring, the divide between rural and urban became sharp and nasty. The animal rights activists were described by their opponents in predictable terms—as liberal elites, as outsiders from the coasts, people who have never had red dirt stuck on their boots, people who do not understand our rural traditions—or, they were, that is, until it appeared that the petition drive would succeed. Then the tone became conciliatory and the Oklahoma Gamecock Breeders Association invited all registered voters to attend a weekend fight at any one of their member clubs. A flyer spelled out the motive: "Let all come to see that cocks were made by God to fight, that nature compels them to battle, and that we ought not oppose what the hand of God has fashioned."[11]

Peace-loving by conviction, and by habit a sucker for anti-cosmopolitan sentiments of any sort, I was of divided mind about the matter. I needed to know more. So, mustering my courage—I said to my wife, if Clifford Geertz can stomach this, so can I!—and with three colleagues in tow, I drove thirty miles north of Tulsa one Saturday morning to Collinsville. What I found there, among other things, was a sturdy intermediate association, doing the kinds of things political scientists tell us intermediate associations are supposed to do in societies like ours. Here was a seedbed of citizenship if ever there was one, and the means of cultivation were surprisingly familiar. Weekend rituals and mid-week gatherings, youth groups, potlucks, educational opportunities (in gamecock lore, of course), a women's fellowship, a boy scout troop, a softball team, a board of trustees, benevolent activities (they tithe 10% of their receipts to the local John 3:16 mission), a newsletter, a website, membership that crossed generations, and collective memory that went back to before statehood. Here was a thriving social world situated between *oikos* and *polis*. Here was an independent community, accustomed to self-rule, and primed for the rigors of democratic life. Indeed, evidence of political participation was everywhere, and not only in the efforts to resist the campaign against cockfighting. Counted among their dues paying members were a state representative, a county commissioner, two school board members, and various judges. Perhaps Robert Putnam is right about the decline of civil society and the rise of rootless individualism, but at least in Collinsville, neither trend was apparent. No one was cockfighting alone.[12]

The fights themselves are pretty horrible. Rising bleachers surround a small ring on a dirt floor. The cocks, angry and eager, are made lethal by their handlers, who fit each leg with two inch, razor-sharp spurs. When placed center ring, the birds explode at each other, leaping and slashing. The excitement is brief. Gamecocks tire easily, and if neither receives a lethal blow in the first few minutes, the fight quickly degenerates into pecking and rolling. After about ten minutes, both birds are bloodied, blinded, and breathless. Their handlers remove them to a smaller ring behind the far bleachers where a small crowd gathers— friends of the handlers, gamblers following a bet, gawkers following death. The fight ends only as one bird dies.

After the first fight, I could not watch any more, so I concentrated on the audience. There were many children in the crowd, children of all ages, scampering over and under the bleachers, some watching the proceedings, some ignoring them, some shouting encouragement to their favorite cock, some gazing passively on the contest before them. My eyes followed a small boy of about seven or eight who was being chased by three or four other children of about the same age. He slipped between the seats and dropped beneath the bleachers, trying to escape, but his pursuers were faster and cornered him just below us. "Get him! Get his eyes!" one of them shouted, and they began to peck and pinch his head and face with thumbs and fingers. The boy fought back with kicks and jabs, broke out of the circle, and then, crying, fled the building into the yard with the others close at his heals.

We had seen enough and followed the children out the door. We too were pursued. "Whad'ya think? Pretty exciting, eh?" We turned, and there was a man in his seventies, flanked by three others, fifty-ish and scowling. Apparently the seed caps I had distributed in the car did nothing to conceal our geeky, out-of-place identities. The older man was eager to talk, and so we did. We gave our impressions, our mixed feelings about what we had seen, and he gave us what was plainly the party line, that same old Stoic theology. Gamecocks love to fight. It is in their blood. By pitting them together, we allow nature to take its course, nothing more. Yes, the consequences are violent and bloody, but nature is like that. Indeed, death by this noble *agon* is a fate far better than the one met by most of their kind, far better than the pathetic pluck and chop at the local Tyson plant. He then encouraged us to vote against the proposed constitutional amendment.

The other men said nothing, but we could tell that they did not like us. In their eyes, we were the enemy. Active hostilities had ceased, but for tactical reasons, and it was plain that they neither welcomed nor accepted our company. We were tolerated, if only just barely. As we thanked them for their hospitality and turned to go, we noticed the children repeating their imitation of the cock fight ritual with a new victim among the cars in the parking lot. The boy we had watched was now an aggressor, pecking and kicking with a ferocity unmatched by the others. We got into our car and drove back to Tulsa.

When told together, these two stories accent the similarities between actual Christian churches and the Collinsville Gamecock Club. Both are intermediate associations. Both are seminaries of citizenship and habit. Both are natural human societies, not because they share proximate causes in nature's necessities, not because intermediate associations are natural to our kind as such,[13] but rather because the social world between family and state is now common, and because both now occupy that world. It is by noting these similarities that we can, I think, develop a different kind of theological response to the familiar, first story. In particular, these similarities can help us recognize something of the natural character of the churches in societies like ours and something of the gracious character of those same churches in Christian confession. This in turn, should help us think about the church in rather ancient ways, as a twinned body, as a *gemina persona*, one thing by nature, another by grace.[14] It should also help us better understand the church's traditional theological self-description as *civitas*, not *pourvoir interméditaire*. And finally, it should help us see the morally ambiguous character of nature *sub gratia*, even ecclesiastical nature, exemplified most plainly in the mixture of virtue and vice that natural societies yield, but also in the Church's ambivalence about both natural virtue and its supernatural transformation in time.[15]

To put these benefits of comparison in plain sight, a detour is needed through a different discussion of nature and the church—the one found in Aquinas's treatment of religion.

Religion, Justice, and Nature

Religion, according to Aquinas, is annexed to justice (*ST* II-II.80.1), the virtue that sets right our relations with others by disposing us to render each their due (*ST* II-II.57.1; 58.1; I-II.60.3).[16] Religion sets right our relation to God, insofar as it disposes us to pay due honor to God with a perpetual will (*ST* II-II.81.2). It cannot, of course, establish the equality between human beings and God that is characteristic of perfect justice, if only because whatever honors we render to God fall short of what is owed. It is for this reason that Aquinas calls religion a potential part of justice, not an essential part (*ST* II-II.80.1).

Justice is, as everyone knows, a moral virtue, a habit that specifies and perfects an inclination to act; in this instance, our inclination to act for the sake of objects we have judged good (*ST* I-II.58.1). Aquinas also calls it a *virtus humana* (*ST* II-II.58.3), a habit that specifies and perfects those inclinations characteristic of our kind—our natural, rational, human inclinations. Here Aquinas has in mind those inclinations that God creates in the human will as He promulgates the natural law. We are a creature of one sort and not another, we act in this way and not that, precisely because God directs us to a small collection of ends specified by the first precepts of the natural law. We consider these ends good, and we do so immediately, without reflection or inference (*per se nota*). Our wills are inclined to these ends simply and absolutely, and all that we do in particular is designed to achieve at least one specific instance of them. Thus, when Aquinas says that the first precepts of the natural law are the seminaries of virtue and that the moral virtues are natural to us, he means that the virtues perfect the inclinations to act that the first precepts set in order. God creates rational human agency as He commands us with this law, and it is our agency—rational and human—that the virtues perfect.[17]

Justice perfects those actions that regard external doings and external things (*exteriones actiones et res*), precisely because our relations with others that justice makes right are mediated through the external doings and things that we use as we act.[18] Justice sets right those relations by attending to the way we communicate with each other as we act in the world and move about its things (*ST* II-II.58.8).

Gather together these observations about justice as a virtue and notice what follows. Justice is natural to us; not the virtue, not the perfection itself, but the concept and the concern. God has set us forth in the world doing human kinds of things, making use of this and that. Our various doings and makings have consequences for others and for ourselves in our relations with others. Since we are inclined by nature to want some sort of human society, some sort of peaceful fellowship with other human beings, we are also inclined by nature to care about right relations with those human beings who are members of our society.[19] Peaceful fellowship requires this kind of care. It also requires judgments about those external actions and things that mediate right relations between human beings in society. It requires judgments about justice and care for the just, and it is our created nature that compels us to each.

Of course, our nature does not compel us to judge well or to care as we should. It does not grant us virtue. More often than not, our judgments miss the mark and our care falls short. The relations that we call right are not, and the actions we call just are mere semblances. Nonetheless, nature does dispose us to think about justice and to think that it matters. Look around, Aquinas seems to say, and we find human beings in all times and places concerned with conduct that creates right relations among those with whom they share some sort of society. No doubt, we will also find judgments we consider mistaken and relations we consider misplaced, but disagreements and misperceptions about justice cannot go all the way down without forsaking the humanity that unites us with the rest of our kind. That possibility, Aquinas seems to say, would be unnatural, not as vice is, but as madness is, and few face that prospect. Our natural inclinations dispose most of us to care about justice, to acquire basic mastery of the concept, and Aquinas doubts that conceptual mastery can be had without accepting certain conclusions about justice, certain judgments about its most basic instantiations (*ST* I-II.95.2). Nature presses the concept upon us only as it conspires with reflection (just a bit, *cum modica*) to derive the truth of certain *conclusiones* (*ST* I-II.100.1). Aquinas admits that not all human beings will accept all of the items on *his* list of *conclusiones*. He notes that the Germans in Julius Cæsar's account of the Gallic wars did not conclude that taking another's property was unjust (*ST* I-II.94.5). But these concessions serve only to sharpen the point. All of us must accept some basic *conclusiones* about justice in order to make use of the concept, and we can recognize that others make use of the concept only as we notice that they share a number of our *conclusiones*. Thus, Cæsar can recognize that the Germans speak of things just and unjust in their remarks about property precisely because they use these concepts pretty much as he does and because their shared use follow from substantial agreement in *conclusiones*. By the same token, Aquinas can report their disagreement as a matter that regards justice, and we can makes sense of his report, precisely because our *conclusiones* about things just and unjust are not all that different from his, and his are not all that different from theirs.

In philosophical abridgment, meaning and truth are assigned together or not at all.[20] Look around, says Aquinas, and you will find human beings speaking of justice as we do, not exactly so, but with enough conceptual overlap for us to recognize their talk for what it is. And we can recognize that they use something like our concept of justice precisely because they share with us a collection of judgments about proper human relations. Observations like these convince

Aquinas that attention to justice and its semblances is natural to us. We would be hard pressed, he believes, to find a human being unable to speak meaningfully of justice, precisely because we could scarcely find anyone who doubted all that we consider true about justice and who acted in accord with her doubts (*ST* II-II. 58.1.3).

Religion is, Aquinas contends, a feature of this natural moral reality. Consider, for example, what he says about sacrifice, one of the principle external acts of religion. He writes, "at all times and among all nations, there has always been the offering of sacrifices. Now that which is observed by all is seemingly natural. Therefore offering of sacrifices is of the natural law."[21] Acts of religious worship are, by these lights, one of the things we do according to our kind. Look around, religion is everywhere, or at least something very much like it. The caveat is important, because religion is a moral virtue, a perfection of our nature, and thus it is no more likely that true religion abounds than perfect justice does. Better then to note among our kind the ubiquity of religion and its semblances, what Aquinas calls *superstitione*. True religion is the fruit of charity and the truly religious give due honor to the triune God of Christian confession (*ST* II-II.81.6). *Superstitione*, by contrast, "offers divine worship, but either to whom it ought not, or in a manner it ought not" (*ST* II-II.92.1). The difference between them is as real as the difference between virtue and vice, nature and grace, and yet Thomas is determined to treat them together and gather them under a single heading precisely because of their common origin in our shared nature.[22] "Natural reason," according to Aquinas, "tells man that he is subject to a higher being, on account of the defects which he perceives in himself, and in which he needs help and direction from someone above him: and whatever this superior being may be, it is known to all under the name of God" (*ST* II-II.85.1; cf. 81.2.3; 86.4). Religion has its origin in this knowledge. Of course, notoriously, Aquinas insists that by nature we know neither who nor what this superior being is. Our natural knowledge of God is empty and impersonal. We recognize no more than that some thing—we know not what—is the cause of all things (*ST* I-II.3.8). Nevertheless, Aquinas believes this scant natural knowledge of God suffices to explain the abundant natural reality of religion, both true and apparent. Everywhere and always this knowledge has compelled human beings pay due honor to the power (or powers) that they consider in some way responsible for their life and welfare in this world.[23]

As a natural phenomenon, as a human virtue, religion has natural aims. Neither its external acts, such as sacrifice, nor its internal acts, such as prayer, reach out to God or unite us with God. Of course, acts of religion caused by grace do indeed intend this end, they do achieve this supernatural union, but in that event their religious character is largely overcome (*ST* II-II.81.5.1). An action takes its moral species from the end it seeks. Just as "he who steals in order to commit adultery is, strictly speaking, more adulterer than thief," so too, he who worships God at the command of the theological virtues for the sake of a supernatural end acts more in accord with faith, hope, and charity than with religion (*ST* I-II.18.6; II-II.81.5.1). Acts of religion *in se* have far more banal aims. We give honor and reverence to God for our own sake. God has no need for what we can provide, but we need the benefits of justice. When we worship God we set right our relations with God, we subject ourselves to God, and in so doing, we secure the good that this just state of affairs provides in itself. Similarly, when we revere God by habit, we secure the good that simply *is* this perfection of the will (*ST* II-II.81.7). And note, these individual benefits accrue only as the acts of religion that generate them are directed to the common good of some society. Religion is a part of justice, and justice always directs us to common goods, civic harmony above all (*ST* II-II.58.5). We care about right relations with others, at least in part, because we desire the peaceful society that those right relations yield. By the same token, we care about the right relations with God that are the fruit of divine worship, at least in part, because we desire the benefits that come to a society whose members stand in right relation with the divine powers that sustain it. In any community, justice in the parts must ultimately be directed to the good of the whole. As such, it is right and good for individuals to show reverence to God for their own sake only as they direct these acts of religion to the common weal of their society.

Notice what follows. Because religion is annexed to justice, it has an irreducibly public character. Religious worship is always established within social arrangements of some sort and even its private acts are ultimately directed to the goods that sustain those arrangements. The reverse is also true. Every society has an established religion of some sort. Whether by legal statute, indirect coercion, or gentle persuasion, every society encourages acts of worship that bestow honor on the powers, real or imagined, that are thought to sustain it. This public character of religion is, Aquinas contends, an unavoidable feature of the natural moral world. He encourages us to look around, and as we do he thinks we will find, more often than not, private acts of religion mediating care for the common good. We will find individuals moved to revere the power or powers they consider divine, in part for their own sake, but also for the sake of their community, which will benefit from the right relations with the divine that their worship helps secure. We will also find that most societies organize acts of public worship in order to accrue those benefits immediately.[24] These are priestly functions. Priests, Aquinas remarks, administer "divine worship, not only for themselves, but also for others" and "for the welfare of the whole people" (*ST* II-II.85.4.3; 87.1). This too is a feature of natural religion.[25]

Civil Society as Nature

Aquinas's remarks about religion, nature, and society provide us with what I consider a useful vocabulary for thinking about the churches and civil society. To say that the American churches are located between family and state, but not assimilated to either, is to deny that they play a priestly role in our political society. They do not act as the established religion of our political order. They do not fulfill this natural function.[26] Of course, it may well be that the prayers and devotions of the churches fulfill a religious function for some other society, for the welfare of some other temporal community.[27] But to admit that the churches abide in civil society is to deny that their religious practices are designed to secure the welfare of the state before the powers that sustain it. This task, it appears, has passed to some other religious community, some other order of priests and priestesses.[28]

No doubt, these are matters of degree. Many churches pray for the well being of our political communities and for the wisdom of our leaders. These are prayers of citizens and they are designed to uphold the political order. Nonetheless, when we note that the churches are located in civil society and that their effects upon the political are now principally indirect (encouraging civic participation, building up social capital, agitating for reform, and so on) we assert what is, no doubt, true—that the churches have largely lost their religious function with respect to the political order.

To say that the churches *are* intermediate associations, to say that this is the best way to regard them now, is to say something slightly different. It is to deny that the prayers and devotions of the churches fulfill a religious function for some other society. It is to say that their religious practices are designed to look after their own welfare, their own temporal community. One might object that this is nothing new, that the churches have always been intermediate associations. They have, from the beginning, staked out a place between family and state. They have always been a *tertia* on the social map, neither nation nor clan, but drawing on each for its members. They have always offered prayers for themselves.

Perhaps, but this particular natural reality of the church, and of its religious devotions, has not always been obvious, and was not in the modern period until quite recently. Recall that in the late classical world there was no independent *tertia* between *oikos* and *polis*, either in thought or practice. The voluntary associations that did emerge tended to be incorporated into some larger political society, either nation or empire.[29] The early church may well have tried to stake out this ground and secure some measure of independence, but there was no obvious place for it to occupy. It had to slip in between the categories and was, as a result, an odd duck—out of place, drawing fire, and easy to shoot. Indeed, Christians were persecuted for their atheism, not simply because they failed to bring benefit to the empire by refusing to worship Rome's gods, but also because of the ambiguous social location of their religious practices. It was never clear what society their prayers and devotions were designed to serve. Jews, by contrast, were often tolerated, in part because their religious practices fit nicely within the available categories. They offered worship to a God who promised to look after their national, political community. This made sense. Christian worship did not, precisely because the independent community that the Church seemed to constitute—neither nation, nor class, nor family, nor city—was itself unimaginable.[30] Indeed, it may well have been difficult for the first Christians themselves to say just what sort of natural body the Church had. If it was difficult to speak of the church as an independent intermediate power, it was no less difficult to fit it into one of the available options. Of course, the kingship theology inherited from the Hebrew bible made it easy for Christians to speak of the reign of Christ and of his rule over creation through the Church, but as a claim about the natural reality of the ecclesiastical body it was never easy to make out. *Civitas* was not the most obvious reply to those who wondered what kind of human society the Church might be.

With Constantine and Theodosius, conditions emerged that put these antinomies to rest, but in a fashion that made it even more difficult to conceive of the Church as an independent social reality with a natural body of its own. With the temporal order ruled by Christians, the ecclesiastical was quickly incorporated into the political. The Church was, quite literally, brought into the political body so that it might serve a religious function for Christendom's political society. No doubt, different spheres of influence were occupied, different swords were swung, and conflict between them was constant. Still, it was conflict over a single natural body, a single human society. Each side tried to extend its influence over what was shared and beheld in a common vision. This is best seen in the Christological account of temporal and ecclesiastical rule found in the twelfth century, *Norman Anonymous*.[31] The prince is vicar of Christ the King. The bishop is vicar of Christ the Priest. Both participate in Christ's rule of the *corpus mysticum* by grace, and yet, as creatures in time, both rule through the medium of the natural, social body that they share. Thus the prince participates in Christ's rule *pedes in terra*, while the priest rules *caput in caelo*.[32]

The advantages of this corporatist model follow in turn. Our natural inclinations for society and for right relation with the divine are held together in a single Christological vision. Both are consummated in the grandest temporal society. But there are dangers as well, which became plain as religious and political authorities proliferated in the early modern period. It was now possible for this or that church to note the heretical piety of this or that prince and refuse incorporation into his political body. Wanting religious worship offered to the divine on behalf of his political community and fearing an ecclesiastical authority with an independent natural body rousting about his realm, casting doubt upon his dominion over all terrestrial affairs, the early modern prince endeavored to unite his church into the political body that he ruled head and feet. *Cuis regio, euis religio*, whoever rules, his religion. Hobbes, as in so many matters, is the best guide here. Part iv of the *Leviathan*, "Of the Kingdome of Darknesse," is devoted to the prospect of an unincorporated, independent church that is, by his lights, an instrument of Satan's rule in temporal affairs. The devil is cast out, he contends, only as we deny that the Church constitutes a new Israel, a "Peculiar People," a visible society ruled by God through temporal intermediaries—popes, prophets, or presbyters—other than "our Civill Soveraigns."[33] That God has put one rule on earth, the *Deus mortalis*, and that all communities are to be brought into the political body, is, Hobbes contends, a prescription of nature. In response to the objection that bishops derive their authority from the See of St. Peter, he writes, "But by the law of nature, which is a better principle of right and wrong than the word of any doctor that is but a man, the civil sovereign in every Commonwealth is the head, the source, the root, and the sun, from which all jurisdiction is derived. And therefore the jurisdiction of bishops is derived from the Civil Sovereign."[34]

The settlement Hobbes defended was, most historians agree, the established norm in Europe and the unofficial rule in the United States until quite recently. Aquinas would not have been surprised. Political societies almost always elicit religious practices designed to find favor with the powers that are thought to sustain them. Since most citizens thought that the Christian God sustained the temporal order, Christian worship was well positioned to play this religious role. By the end of the nineteenth century, forces unleashed by the French Revolution made it imperative for the Catholic church to demand its independence from the civil sovereigns of Europe.[35] Protestant churches were beginning to decouple from the political body at about the same time, but largely by default. On both sides of the Atlantic, political societies were emerging that Protestant worship could no longer sustain. Some other sort of religious piety was needed, and in most instances, a substitute was already beginning to emerge.[36]

Thus to say that the churches are now best regarded as intermediate associations within civil society is to say something about the their natural reality. It is to say that they are, more or less, independent societies precisely because their religious practices are more or less designed to secure their own welfare. What Hobbes feared has in fact happened. The great advantage of this state of affairs, it seems to me, is that we can now see the natural reality of the church. Disentangled from political society, it emerges as a temporal society in its own right. This, in turn, helps us make better sense of its eschatological reality caught in time: it is twinned, one thing by nature, another by grace. Two traditional claims about the Church—that it is the body of Christ and an eternal city in exile—should help make the point.

What Robert Jenson says about the church seems just right: "the church is founded in the triune life of God because the church anticipates being taken into that life, and because, as the gospel interprets reality, it is precisely what creatures may anticipate from God that is their deepest being."[37] Because of its triune reality, Christians cannot say one thing about the church, any more than they can say one thing about God. Nevertheless, one of the things they do say is that the church is the mystical body of Christ, which in turn is to say, among other things, that it is a sacramental reality, a real means of grace in time. But this means that church must have, as Christ did, and as the bread and wine do, an independent natural body, one that exists in time. The incorporation of the ecclesiastical into the political during Christendom obscured the reality of that body, which in turn tended to mask its sacramental character. Or, more demonically, Christendom's corporatism tempted Christians to sacralize the political body. By contrast, if the church is in fact an intermediate association, then Christians have a good chance of resisting this temptation and a far better chance of making sense of the claim that the church is a natural reality, a temporal society that can be transformed by grace into a real means of grace.[38]

Christians have also said that the church is a city. The claim is an eschatological one. The church is a political society, as Jenson would have it, only by anticipation. Like other societies, a city is a union of wills, but unlike others, its union regards goods that can be had together and held in common by the greatest number. In this instance, it is a union forged out of love for God and for that fellowship with the blessed that Christians hope to enjoy. During the heyday of incorporation, the church's supernatural expectation and its natural reality merged. It was a city in anticipation and in actuality, and this tended to obscure the fact that the church becomes the political reality of Christian confession only as grace sanctifies and redeems its natural body. Put another way, when the church was incorporated into the political body, Christians were tempted to think that its political reality in time confirmed its eschatological hopes. If subtle minds like Augustine avoided this temptation, others like Eusebius did not. Here again we see a theological advantage that comes from finding the church among the intermediate associations of civil society. If its natural body is not assimilated to the political body through its religious functions, then Christians can more easily regard its political hopes as founded in God's promises and fulfilled by God's grace. Indeed, its natural reality in civil society makes its supernatural destiny unimaginable without divine assistance.

Of course, there are temptations to resist here as well. A church decoupled from the political body will have to imagine its terrestrial authority in new ways, lest it mystify itself in time. It cannot influence those who rule through its priestly functions, for it can no longer act as the principal religion of its political community. It can, however, pursue other channels that nature provides. It can, for example, note that intermediate associations have always been hotbeds of energies, activities, and ideas that transform the political realm. In our own country, they have not only provided the social capital needed to sustain citizenship in a political culture often hostile to it, they have also been the place where criticism of political arrangements most often emerge. Indeed, as Charles Taylor points out, when one invokes civil society in our time, one draws a two edged sword.[39] With it, one might slay the beasts that threaten American democracy or one might challenge democracy itself. Both edges are available to the church as it looks to the political from the vantage point of civil society.

That an intermediate association might have this ambiguous relation to the goods of this or that political society, that it might help or harm, that it might generate virtue or vice, will come as a surprise to those who read only what our political scientists and sociologists write about civil society. Most (not all, see note 31) give the impression that the social world between family and state is always good, and always unambiguously so. But if I am right to interpret what they say through the lens provided by Aquinas's remarks about nature and religion, then the morally ambiguous character of that world comes as no surprise at all. Intermediate associations are natural, not because they are necessary but because they are common among us now, and the natural in time, at least by Aquinas's lights, is always morally ambiguous, always *permixte*, even when transformed by virtue and sanctified by grace.

Ambiguous Nature

Of course, to say that Aquinas considers nature itself morally ambiguous is somewhat misleading. Everything is what it is and not some other thing because it is inclined to some good, and thus, in a sense there is nothing morally ambiguous at all about anything that is. Aquinas could only agree. But human beings and human conduct are slightly different. We are inclined by God's eternal law to know and desire a small collection of general goods—life, friendship, knowledge, and a few others—and with nature's necessity we are disposed to will them simply and absolutely. We are not, however, disposed to intend any particular instantiation of any one of these goods, to arrange our preferences for them in any particular way, or to employ any particular means to achieve them. In these matters, judgment and choice hold sway, and each can go astray. From this combination of necessity and freedom, Aquinas concludes that "every act of reason and will in us is based on that which is according to nature" (*ST* I-II.91.2.2). Ultimately, *every* human action is done for the sake of one of the goods we know and will by nature. But whether we intend this or that particular end by this or that means, nature remains silent. From our participation in God's eternal law, from the human nature that follows, either virtue or vice may ensue. [40]

In this sense, our nature *is* morally ambiguous, and so too are the conclusions that follow from it after very little consideration. [41] As Cæsar's Germans make plain, some will track the truth, some will not. We have already seen that Aquinas thinks we are disposed by nature to know that our lives are gifts from another and that as a result of this natural knowledge, and after a little reflection, we are inclined to acts of religion. We have also noted that when we regard religion in this way, as a deliverance of nature and not as one of its perfections, Aquinas encourages us to see its morally ambiguous character. Divine worship can be offered virtuously or viciously, and in either case, nature is discharged.

My suggestion is that we regard intermediate associations in precisely this way. We are disposed by nature's necessity to live in human society, and in societies like ours we have come to occupy the social world between family and state. Our nature did not compel us there, but it did put us in a position to conclude that given our history and circumstance we belong there now. Like nature and its other proximate conclusions, these intermediate associations are morally ambiguous. They can be seminaries of virtue or vice. They can create the social capital we need "to make American democratic pluralism work," [42] or they can generate sentiments and energies hostile to those arrangements. Given the uneven and contradictory character of the forces that form our natural inclinations into concrete intentions and particular habits, it is likely that both virtue and vice, help and harm, will come forth from most intermediate associations. Moral ambiguity of precisely this kind abounds in the churches, as everyone knows, in the Collinsville Gamecock Club, or so it appeared to me, and elsewhere in civil society, and it does so in each precisely because these are natural locations and because, to borrow a turn of phrase from one of my informants in Collinsville, nature is like that.

Of course, temporal nature perfected as well as it can be by natural virtue, and then again by grace, lacks a full measure of this moral ambiguity, but for Christians, traces remain. Those of us who take our moral bearings from our supernatural hope, from that communion with God and the blessed that we hope to share, find moral ambiguity everywhere in time.[43] Toleration provides a good example. It is a virtue that salutary intermediate associations are said to cultivate, and most do, the Collinsville Gamecock Club among them. Every thriving temporal society seems to cultivate some version of it and to find reason to praise what they cultivate. The goods that move us to act are many and thus disagreement about them abounds. Some disagreements threaten the union of wills upon which the community rests. These require rough magics—coercion, constraint, expulsion, or withdrawal. Other disagreements are less threatening to that union, and it is to these that the tolerant respond well, not with indifference, but with disregard for the union that can be had in spite of these disagreements. This much is plain. But perhaps the first thing to say about toleration is that few of us want to tolerate or to be tolerated. This, it seems, is at the root of every criticism of it. The tolerant do not want to restrain their outrage and the tolerated would prefer to be accepted. The first acts with regret and the second accepts what is given with little gratitude. Both would prefer to live in a world where toleration was unnecessary.

Given these preferences, one might be tempted to say that moral ambiguity is built into the very nature of toleration, but I think this is a temptation to avoid. The mixed mind that most of us have in response to toleration is, it seems to me, more evidence of our lack of virtue than of our moral or theological acuity. This is not a claim that I can defend in the space that follows, but it seems to me that the truly tolerant are, in this respect, similar to those great in courage. Neither lament the conditions of this world that make their virtue necessary, if only because neither believes that the combination of those conditions and their virtue prevents them from securing happiness in this world, at least for the most part.[44] If lament remains in the company of *true* virtue, then it must follow from their eschatological yearning for conditions that will make it unnecessary for them to predicate community upon natural virtue, upon toleration, courage, and the rest.

If an argument to this effect could be made, and made compelling, then it seems that we could find moral ambiguity in toleration only as virtue falls short of perfection or as grace sanctifies our moral vision. This may seem like an odd conclusion, lumping together perfection and imperfection across the nature-grace distinction, but perhaps it can be made sensible by noting that toleration transformed by grace deserves a similar assessment. As intermediate associations, the churches are natural societies that, with luck, generate natural virtues, toleration among the rest. As a twinned reality, something by nature, something else by grace, the church and its sacraments generate twinned virtues. In this instance, the toleration that follows from the church's natural reality is transformed into forbearance, its gracious twin, which is an act of charity. Difference and disagreement confound the church in time, just as it confounds gamecock clubs. But here, the burdens of our brothers and sisters are born, not only for the sake of temporal goals, but also for that eternal fellowship for which we yearn and that we trust is now breaking in upon us.[45] Given that hope and goal, an act of forbearance will always come packaged with moral ambivalence about itself, if only because those who forbear act for the sake of a state of affairs that when achieved will make forbearance unnecessary.

Transformed by grace in time, natural virtue is like that. It elicits that kind of response from those whom grace has blessed with supernatural hope, and it is only as we take of note of the twinned reality of the church that we see why this response must attend that hope. The church and its virtues appear as a twinned realities only as we recognize its natural body in time, and in political societies like ours, we find its natural body among the intermediate powers of civil society. That it is found there is a lesson of natural reason, which can, it appears, yield benefits of this kind.[46]

NOTES

[1] Charles Taylor, "Invoking Civil Society," in *Philosophical Arguments* (Cambridge: Harvard University Press, 1995), 222.

[2] Michael Walzer, *What it Means to be an American* (New York: Marsilio, 1992), 11.

[3] In Augustine's words, the members of an intermediate association will "dissent and become onerous" when the political community they inhabit pursues ends and activities they cannot (*De civ. Dei.* 19.17).

[4] Here I follow Charles Taylor's example ("Invoking Civil Society," 215-224). Since intermediate associations fulfill both legitimating and critical functions, appeal must be made to quite different treatments of them in order to make sense of civil society. On the one hand, we must appeal to the tradition that Taylor traces back to Montesquieu, the tradition that denies the independence of intermediate associations. Most are assimilated to a political society that they perpetuate by reproducing its virtues and norms. But appeal must also be made to the tradition Taylor traces back to Locke. Here intermediate associations are regarded as societies with aims, actions, and origins all their own. So set apart from political society, they tend to be its critic, at

times its revolutionary opponent. Borrowing and adapting Michael Mosher's image, intermediate associations are the transmission belts of political tradition. They can also be a monkey wrench in its gears, at times for better, at times for worse. See, Michael Mosher, "Are Civil Societies Transmission Belts of Ethical Tradition?" in *The Ethical Traditions and Civil Society*, eds. Simone Chambers and William Kymlicka (Princeton: Princeton University Press, forthcoming, fall 2001).

[5] A representative list includes: Benjamin Barber, *A Place For Us: How to Make Civil Society and Democracy Strong* (New York: Hill and Wang, 1998); Jean Bethke Elshtain, *Democracy on Trial* (New York: Basic Books, 1995); Thomas Janoski, *Citizenship and Civil Society: A Framework of Rights and Obligations in Liberal, Traditional, and Social Democratic Regimes* (Cambridge: Cambridge University Press, 1998).

[6] For a useful discussion of the contemporary American churches and civil society see Robert Wuthnow, *Christianity and Civil Society: The Contemporary Debate* (Valley Forge, PA: Trinity Press International, 1996).

[7] Stanley Hauerwas has advanced the objection in a number places over a number of years. For representative examples see *The Peaceable Community* (Notre Dame: University of Notre Dame Press, 1983), 96-115; and, *After Christendom?* (Nashville: Abingdon Press, 1991), 23-44.

[8] This is, I take it, the conclusion of John Milbank's essay, "A Critique of the Theology of Right," in *The Word Made Strange: Theology, Language, and Culture* (Oxford: Blackwell, 1997), 32.

[9] John Milbank, *Theology and Social Theory: Beyond Secular Reason* (Oxford: Blackwell, 1990), 331.

[10] As I write, the Oklahoma State Senate has legislation pending that would call for a vote of the people on a proposal that would give constitutional protection to hunting, trapping, rodeo, raising livestock, and cockfighting, activities that Speaker of the House Larry Adair calls "the traditions and long-standing customs of people in certain areas of our state," *Tulsa World*, Sunday April 22, 2001.

[11] From the flyer distributed by the OGCA in late May 2000, inviting all registered voters in the state to visit one of their member clubs.

[12] Robert D. Putnam, "Bowling Alone: America's Declining Social Capital," *Journal of Democracy* 6 (1995): 65-78. Since the publication of this famous essay, Putnam's view has become more nuanced. See his *Bowling Alone: The Collapse and Revival of American Community* (New York: Simon & Schuster, 2000).

[13] Indeed, there is abundant historical evidence that they are not. See, for example, Ernest Gellner, *Conditions of Liberty: Civil Society and its Rivals* (New York: Penguin, 1994).

[14] The discussion that follows is informed by Ernst Kantorowicz' s magisterial work, *The King's Two Bodies: A Study in Medieval Political Theology* (Princeton: Princeton University Press, 1957). Kantorowicz reports that his epiphany occurred when he realized that American Benedictines were legally incorporated: "The Order of Saint Benedict, Inc." (vii). For me, the heavens opened when I realized that American churches and Oklahoma cockfight clubs have largely identical natural bodies. Suppose I had visited a different intermediate association: e.g., the Junior League, the Cherry Street Merchants Association, the Akdar Shrine Temple. Might the heavens have opened above these venues as well? Surely they could have, for like cockfight clubs, these societies bear nature's marks, at least in some measure. But still, I wonder. They are gentler societies, and more subtle. They mask and ignore what cockfight clubs make explicit— the violence of nature unredeemed, the moral ambiguity of nature perfected in time. This means that sharper eyes and keener judgment are indeed required to see the heavens open above the PTA or the Rotary Club.

[15] The distinction between nature and grace drawn here does not compel me to include pure nature in my ontology, any more than Aristotle's distinction between form and matter compels him to include prime matter in his. Neither are empirical realities. Both are best regarded as conceptual placeholders. Thus when Aristotle refers to a piece of bronze as the matter that receives form from a sculptor, he does not assume that bronze is unformed matter (*Ph.* II.iii). This he explicitly denies (*Metaph.* Z.viii). Rather, he assumes that the bronze is

formed matter, but not entirely so. It has potencies that can take on new forms. By the same token, when I speak of natural societies and bodies, I do not assume they exist apart from grace. Rather, like Aquinas (who parses the natural law in terms of God's free and gracious command) and Barth (who regards creation as unmerited grace from the One who loves in freedom), I assume that creation is gift, that grace preserves nature in being. And just as Aristotle distinguishes matter and form in order to speak of the different ways that matter's potency can be informed, so too Christians have distinguished nature and grace in order to speak of the different ways that nature—God's creation, graciously given—can be transformed by grace. Indeed, the distinction is indispensable for preserving the bodily significance of Israel and the church in the biblical drama of salvation. After Sinai and Calvary, grace intermingles with nature in new ways, redeeming and sanctifying. But created nature is, for the most part, temporal and bodily, and thus so too is redemption and sanctification. It is the people Israel—a particular body in time—that grace redeems and sanctifies, not Moab, not Edom. Similarly, it is through the sacraments of the church—and not through some other natural society in time—that the Gentiles are redeemed and sanctified.

[16] Reference to the *Summa* will appear in the text. I have used the translation of the Fathers of the English Dominican Province: *The Summa Theologica of Thomas Aquinas*, 3 vols. (New York: Benzinger, 1947-48). I have adapted some translations through consultation with the most recent complete edition of the Leonine text: *Thomae Aquinatis Opera omnia: cum hypertextibus in CD-ROM*, 2nd ed., *auctore*, Roberto Busa (Milano: Editoria Elettronica Editel, 1996).

[17] This discussion assumes another, my much longer treatment of Aquinas's account of the natural law in *Contingency and Fortune in Aquinas's Ethics* (Cambridge University Press, 1999), 93-137.

[18] For an excellent discussion of the "externality" of Aquinas's account of human action and of the importance of *usus* in that account see Stephen T. Brock, *Action and Conduct: Thomas Aquinas and the Theory of Action* (Edinburgh: T&T Clark, 1998), 49-93, 137-196.

[19] *ST* I-II.10.1; 94.2. Aquinas speaks in the most general possible terms. We are inclined by nature to live in the company of others, but we are not inclined by nature to live in a society of this or that sort. Thomas knows there are varieties—friendships, families, political communities, and possibilities he has not imagined—and he sees evidence of our natural inclination in each.

[20] In this respect at least, Aquinas's view tracks contemporary accounts of conceptual mastery. Ludwig Wittgenstein, *Philosophical Investigations*, trans. G.E.M. Anscombe (New York: Macmillan, 1953), 242: "If language is to be a means of communication there must be agreement not only in definitions but also (queer as this may sound) in judgments. This seems to abolish logic, but does not so.—It is one thing to describe methods of measurement, and another to obtain and state results of measurement. But what we call "measuring" is partly determined by a certain constancy in results of measurement." Donald Davidson, "On the Very Idea of a Conceptual Scheme, in *Inquiries Into Truth and Interpretation* (Oxford: Clarendon Press, 1985), 196: "What matters is this: if all we know is what sentences a speaker holds true, and we cannot assume that his language is our own, then we cannot take even a first step towards interpretation without knowing or assuming a great deal about the speaker's beliefs."

[21] "*In qualibet aetate, et apud quaslibet hominum nationes, semper fuit aliqua sacrificiorm oblatio. Quod autem est apud omnes, videtur naturale esse. Ergo et oblatio sacrificii est de iure naturali*" (*ST* II-II.85.1.*sed contra*).

[22] Thus, Aquinas contends that "religion" is like "prudence." Both terms may be taken in two senses precisely because both regard a natural capacity and its perfection. On the one hand, both terms can apply univocally to both a virtue and its semblance. It is this sense of "religion" that Aquinas highlights when he insists that religion is natural to us. On the other hand, both can apply equivocally to a virtue in contradistinction to its semblance. It is this latter sense that Aquinas highlights when he insists that true religion acts at the command of charity (*ST* II-II.92.1.1; 94.1.2; cf. II-II. 55.1-2).

[23] Counter-examples immediately come to mind, but no real challenges. Most modern secular societies are religious by these natural lights, offering sacrifices to the nation, the

market, the working class, the mysteries of sex and death, or to some other great power. Even those philosophers who encourage us to show reverence to no such power either do so unwittingly (Nietzsche) or recant and encourage reverence for some powers but not all (Rorty).

[24] The distinction between public acts of religion that are directed to the common good immediately and private acts of religion that are directed to common goods through the mediation of private benefit tracks the distinction between legal and particular justice (*ST* II-II.58.5, 7).

[25] Those who consider contemporary America an exception to this rule should read my colleague Eldon Eisenach's most recent book, *The Next Religious Establishment: National Identity and Political Theology in Post-Protestant America* (Lanham, ND: Rowman & Littlefield, 2000). Eisenach's argument confirms Aquinas's suspicion that established, priestly religion is a natural feature of most human societies, even contemporary American society.

[26] This way of putting the matter avoids the pitfalls of saying that the American churches are now distinguished by their independence from *oikos* and *polis*. Plainly, they are not and never will be. Better then to speak of the specific functions that may or may not connect churches to the families and states they are said to stand between. My point is that the contemporary American churches fulfill few, if any, *religious* functions in our political society. As a result, they are not bound to the political in this direct way.

[27] Thus, for example, we might say that from the last decade of the nineteenth century through the first half of the twentieth, the United Lutheran Norwegian Church in America served a religious function for the society of Norwegian immigrants that lived in the Cedar-Riverside neighborhood of South Minneapolis. See James S. Hamre, *From Immigrant Parish to Inner City Ministry: Trinity Lutheran Congregation, 1868-1998* (Minneapolis: Trinity Church, 1998).

[28] For speculation about where we might find that religious community and who its priest might be, see Eisenach, *The Next Religious Establishment*, 121-141.

[29] Albert Baumgarten, "Graeco-Roman Voluntary Associations and Ancient Jewish Sects," in *Jews in a Graeco-Roman World*, ed. Martin Goodman (New York: Oxford University Press, 1998).

[30] E. Mary Smallwood, *The Jews Under Roman Rule From Pompey to Diocletian* (Leiden: Brill, 1981).

[31] Heinrich Böhmer, *Monumenta Germaniae Historica, Libelli de Lite*, vol. III, 642-678. For selected ET see, O. O'Donovan and J.L. O'Donovan, *From Irenaeus to Grotius: A Sourcebook in Christian Political Thought* (Grand Rapids, MI: Eerdmans, 1999), 250-259.

[32] For a useful discussion of the *Norman Anonymous* see, Kantorowicz, *The King's Two Bodies*, 42-61.

[33] Thomas Hobbes, *Leviathan*, edited by C. B. Macpherson (Harmondsworth: Penguin, 1981), IV.xliv.629-630.

[34] Ibid., II.xlii. 596. I am grateful to Russell Hittinger for bringing these passages to my attention.

[35] In a soon to be published book on nineteenth and twentieth century papal social thought, my colleague Russell Hittinger argues that concern for the church's freedom from political authority dominate the encyclicals of this period.

[36] Recent events in Sweden exemplify this decoupling. Formal disestablishment occurred precisely because the Lutheran church no longer served a religious function in Swedish political society. It could not, given the character of that society. Indeed, if we assume the ubiquity of natural religion, it is likely that some other religious practices had already replaced it. For and excellent account of the rise and fall of Protestant establishment in American see, Eisenach, *The Next Religious Establishment*, 29-98.

[37] Robert W. Jenson, "The Church as *Communio*," in *The Catholicity of the Reformation*, eds. Carl E. Braaten and Robert W. Jenson (Grand Rapids, MI: Eerdmans, 1996), 2.

[38] Of course, whether we can, in good faith, call the church's natural reality a *body* is another matter altogether. In fact, one might argue that as the church emerges within civil society, as it decouples from the political body, its own embodied character becomes harder to

imagine. With luck and effort, we can still regard families and nations in this way, as organic wholes with different parts grafted on to a common body. But we tend to describe intermediate powers in terms of agreements and contracts, individuals and their rights. They are *voluntary* associations, or so we say. Whether this description captures their full reality is, I suspect, doubtful. But that said, there is some truth in this talk and American Christians will have to resist it in order to speak of the natural body of the church, as of course they must, if they wish to remain faithful to the biblical witness.

[39] See Charles Taylor's discussion of the competing Lockean and Montesquieuian versions of civil society in "Invoking Civil Society." See also Michael Walzer's discussion of the threats to political union that parochial associations frequently generate in *What it Means to be an American*, 23-49.

[40] I discuss these matters in more detail in Bowlin, *Contingency and Fortune*, 93-137.

[41] Aquinas contends that a principle can be derived from the natural law's first precepts "as a conclusion of premises." Or, alternatively, a principle can be derived from the first precepts "by way of determination" (*ST* I-II.95.2). *Conclusiones* are principles derived from the first precepts "after very little consideration (*cum modica*). Determinations, by contrast, require "much consideration of the various circumstances" of human action, and as such, can be derived from the first precepts of the natural law only by those who are wise (*ST* I-II.100.1).

[42] Stanley M. Hauerwas and William H. Willimon, *The Truth about God: The Ten Commandments in Christian Life* (Nashville: Abingdon Press, 1999), 14.

[43] Without the supernatural perspective that grace provides, no such traces could be seen, or so I argue in Bowlin, *Contingency and Fortune*, 138-221.

[44] I make this argument with respect to courage in ibid., 138-212.

[45] Throughout, I follow Aquinas's discussion of forbearance, which he nestles within his treatment of fraternal correction (*ST* II-II. 33.1-6).

[46] William Cavanaugh, Jean Elshtain, Stanley Hauerwas, Jennifer Herdt, Russell Hittinger, Charles Mathewes, Charles Pinches, and three readers from *The Annual* offered comments and criticism on an earlier draft of this paper. Thanks to them all. The usual disclaimers apply.

Is Public Theology Really Public?
Some Problems with Civil Society

William T. Cavanaugh

Abstract

This paper sketches two ways in which the concept of civil society is currently being used to carve out a space for Christians to be "public," and makes some suggestions of problems that arise from these models. The first way involves the theoretical appropriation of John Courtney Murray's work by authors who advocate a "public theology." The second is a practical application of Harry Boyte's work on civil society which is being appropriated in Catholic schools to advance the public mission of Christian education. Despite differences, this essay argues that, though both seek to create a space for the church which is both "public" and "free," neither succeed. At the end of the paper, suggestions are made of a more adequate ecclesiology of the public.

In trying to make sense of the recent explosion of literature in political theory and social ethics on "civil society,"[1] it is not hard to feel like the Native Americans must have felt when the Europeans began talking excitedly about the "discovery" of America. Civil society would appear to have been here all along, and yet the term is invoked, especially since the fall of the Berlin Wall, as representing some important new possibilities in democratic revitalization. The term has its origins in the Scottish Enlightenment and Hegel, but reappeared with renewed vigor in the 1970s. It names a space that, above all, is public without being political in the usual sense of direct involvement with the state. This distinction between state and society is seen by some Christian social ethicists as a breakthrough concept because it seems to allow the church to avoid mere privatization on the one hand, and the Constantinian specter of implication in state coercion on the other. Chastened by its experience with rule, yet aware of the absence of a privatized Christianity from the biblical and traditional witness, the church seeks to speak clearly in the public arena without carrying a big stick.

In this paper I will sketch two ways (of many, I hasten to add) in which the concept of civil society is currently being used to carve out a space for Christians to be "public," and then suggest certain problems that arise from these models. The first way involves the theoretical appropriation of John Courtney Murray's work by authors who advocate a "public theology." The second is a practical application of Harry Boyte's work on civil society which is being appropriated in Catholic schools to advance the public mission of Christian education. The first way is more oriented toward public policy, the second toward grassroots activism. Despite differences, however, I will argue that, though both seek to create a space for the church which is both "public" and "free," neither succeed. At the end of the paper, then, I will suggest ways toward a more adequate ecclesiology of the public.

Murray and Friends

In Catholic circles the father of public theology is John Courtney Murray, who put tremendous emphasis on a sharp distinction between state and society. According to Murray, this distinction originates in the medieval distinction between, on the one hand, the *imperium*, and on the other the *ecclesia*, by which he indicates the entire Christendom, or *christianitas*. This distinction mirrors the distinction between temporal and spiritual. Just as the *imperium* served a limited role in medieval Christendom, so the American constitutional order establishes limits on the state.[2] The state in Murray's thought is but one limited part of society, that part responsible for the maintenance of public law and political administration. The importance of this distinction is to carve out free space beyond the direct grasp of the state, a space which contemporary theorists call "civil society." Murray puts it this way: "In general, 'society' signifies an area of freedom, personal and corporate, whereas 'state' signifies the area in which public powers may legitimately apply their coercive powers. To deny the distinction is to espouse the notion of government as totalitarian."[3]

For the sake of civil peace, religion is excluded from the state but allowed to flourish in the remaining public space defined by civil society. Here the various religious "conspiracies," as he called them, could meet on common ground and debate public life in the language—not of theology, which tends to divide one from the other conspiracies—but of natural law, the language of cool, dry reason. Natural law, Murray thought, has no theological presuppositions; rather it provides for the possibility of reasoned discourse among religions and even with that "conspiracy" which does not acknowledge God at all.[4] Underlying this reasoned discourse, and in part proceeding from it, is a public philosophy or public consensus.[5] This consensus is not the sum of public opinion or self-interest, but is based on certain truths that structure the political system of the United States; "we hold these truths" because they are true.[6] This consensus does not eliminate conflict, but rather serves as an agreed basis upon which conflicts are in theory resolvable.

For my present purpose it is important to see that for Murray this consensus manages to maintain the fences which make his distinction of state and society work. In the first place, society is free of coercion precisely because there are commonly agreed rules for discourse which are built into the American proposition and are part of American experience. Reasoned discourse guarantees that public conversation will take place on the basis of persuasion, and not coercion. In the second place—and this is seldom noticed in Murray's thought—this consensus also maintains a proper distinction between civil society and economic activity. Murray acknowledges the power and omnipresence of economic forces from which neither state nor church, family nor individual is immune. However, it is precisely the idea of the "public consensus" that saves us from the overweening power of corporations and economic forces. Murray adopts his exposition of the "public consensus" from Adolf Berle, who attributes the relative freedom America enjoys from abuses of economic power to this consensus: "[T]he ultimate protection of individuals lies not in the play of economic forces in free markets, but in a set of value judgments so widely accepted and deeply held in the United States that public opinion can energize political action when needed to prevent power from violating these values."[7] Through the public consensus, the state is mobilized in its coercive function to keep economic power in check, without the state thereby overstepping the boundaries of its own power. State, civil society, and work are all separable into semi-autonomous, though interrelated, spheres.

Contemporary interpreters of Murray's project have adopted his distinction of state and society as central. In Richard John Neuhaus' conception of democracy, for example, it is crucial that there be many different actors in the "public square."

> The state is one actor among others. Indispensable to this arrangement are the institutional actors, such as the institutions of religion, that make claims of ultimate or transcendent meaning. The several actors in the public square—government, corporations, education, communications, religion—are there to challenge, check, and compete with one another.[8]

The churches, then, take their rightful place as public institutions without direct implication in wielding coercive state power, entanglements which have had disastrous consequences in Western history.[9] As another Murrayite, George Weigel says:

> Those who enter the civil public square have a right to speak from religious conviction. But those who claim a right to speak assume a responsibility to speak in such a way that they can be heard... In concrete practice, this will mean "translating" religiously-based moral claims and arguments into concepts and language that can be heard and contested by fellow-citizens of different faiths.[10]

This follows from Weigel's definition of "public" as "understandable to all."[11]

Not all interpreters of Murray are content with Murray's banishment of theological language from the public square. Michael and Kenneth Himes, for example, in their book *The Fullness of Faith*, have pleaded for the public significance of theology, though under certain limited conditions. According to the Himeses, clarity about the distinction between state and society ought not to obscure the fact that there is some interpenetration between the two. This recognition likewise demands a recognition that people who act in the realm of the state do so having been formed by religion.[12] This formation takes place primarily in the hearts and minds of believers who, though acting publicly, have been shaped in their "basic orienting attitudes" by explicitly religious symbols. More than this, however, the Himeses wish to allow the use of theological language in the public forum, even though the listeners may not share the faith of the speaker. Although public debate in civil society must be based on a consensus among all people, religious or not, on what can be considered reasonable, religious people should not shy away from using religious symbols, such as the Trinity, in the hope that they may communicate something universal even to those who reject the theological origins of such symbols. Here the Himeses turn to David Tracy's concept of the "classic," defined as "a phenomenon whose excess and permanence of meaning resists definitive interpretation."[13] In the presence of such a classic in art or religion, for example, even the uninitiated is subject to the transmission of some truth which is therefore a public truth. The Himeses also adopt Tracy's suggestion that one should concentrate on the "effects" of such truth, and not its non-public "origins" in the doctrine of one particular religion.[14]

Theology has, therefore, an important contribution to make to the public life of a society. Nevertheless, when moving from civil society to state, the "basic orienting attitudes" that theological symbols elicit must be translated into public policy by means of a social ethic, that is, theories of justice, the state, and so on, which cannot be derived directly from theology; "public theology is several steps removed from public policy."[15] The Trinity, for example, must first be translated into a concept of "relationality" which belongs to social ethics, and then into an affirmation of a certain kind of rights-language.[16] The result in theory is a theology which is free to function in a fully public manner, yet not in a way that seeks to impose its alien beliefs on the other. The church stands in a position to form hearts and minds, to equip them for public life, but it remains outside access to the coercive power of the state, and theology remains subject to the bar of what the society can consider "reasonable."

Public Achievement

The Murrayite models sketched so briefly here depend on the maintenance of a space in society beyond the reach of the state, yet Murray and his successors share a tendency to see that space as oriented toward the state. Free discussion takes place outside of the state in civil society, yet such debate is oriented ultimately toward the making of public policy. Although theoretically limited, the state is still the primary means for the establishment of justice. This is the case whether what is primarily in mind are either lobbying efforts by the social justice arms of the church bureaucracy aimed at producing legislation, or efforts aimed at affecting "culture" as a whole. There is talk of "the" (singular) public square. The "common" to which the "common good" refers is the nation-state. "The health-care debate," for example, has to do with legislation before Congress on government-sponsored health care insurance, prescription drug price controls, Medicare, and so on.

There is another model of civil society, however, which is beginning to have an increasing impact in Christian circles. It shares with the Murrayite models an emphasis on the creation and maintenance of free spaces in society beyond the direct purview of the state. Unlike the Murrayite models, however, its accent is not on public policy but on the democratic potential of civil society itself. One important exemplification of this model is based on the work of Harry Boyte, one of the principal interlocutors in the debates over civil society. From the Humphrey Institute at the University of Minnesota, Boyte has been advocating for the renewal of American democracy through the empowerment of grassroots citizens' groups. In addition to extensive publishing in the field, Boyte is also something of an activist. One of his more prominent endeavors is called "Public Achievement," an attempt to instill the virtues of citizenship into school-age children. Public Achievement has been very active in Catholic schools in my area, and the social justice office of the archdiocese has just begun a major collaboration with Boyte to use Public Achievement as a means of training Catholic school students in the public use of Catholic social teaching. At St. Bernard's Catholic school, Public Achievement has taken root and changed the culture of the school. Every Thursday morning is given over to Public Achievement, facilitating involvement for every student in every grade. St.

Bernard's has been made a national model for the creation of a Catholic School of Democracy and Social Justice.[17]

For Boyte the term "civil society" conveys three important themes in democratic theory, all derived from recent democratic movements in the U.S., the Third World, and especially Eastern Europe during the fall of communism.[18] The first is a renewed appreciation for the quotidian and mundane types of power wielded by ordinary citizens. There is a small movement to break the preponderant concentration of political science on electoral politics and parties to the exclusion of the actual decision-making taking place in concrete communities. Boyte has been structuring his work around case studies of community organizations.[19] The second is the importance of alternative sources of power as bulwarks against the state. It has long been a bias of left-wing politics especially to think big, to "see like a state," as the title of James Scott's recent book has it.[20] "Civil society" became an energizing concept for the movements of 1989 that brought down totalitarian regimes from the inside. The third is an appreciation for the free and uncoerced nature of discourse in voluntary community settings. Boyte and Sara Evans have pioneered the study of what they call "free spaces," defined as "settings between private lives and large-scale institutions where people can act with dignity, independence and vision. These are, in the main, voluntary forms of association with a relatively open and participatory character" which include many religious organizations, clubs, self-help groups, and so on.[21] The black church is singled out as an autonomous institution which has, at various points in American history, allowed the very possibility of free speech that opposed the dominant culture. For Boyte, such institutions are not merely important for their own sake, but as seedbeds of democratic movements with much broader impact. The civil rights movement, begun in the black church, is, for Boyte, a particularly important paradigm of "democratic renewal."[22]

Rather than fix on "the" public debate as supervised by the state, therefore, Boyte wants to encourage democratic renewal as it springs from local community action. That said, however, Boyte is critical of those he calls "voluntarists," who would locate active citizenship in voluntary organizations and leave it there. Can we seriously expect, Boyte sharply asks, to confront power with "volunteers?"[23] Here Boyte is critical of theorists such as Benjamin Barber who define "civil society" (like Murray) over against both government and economic activity. For Barber, civil society is a kind of refuge from the coercion of the state and the consumerism of the market, a position which Boyte regards as fatalistic.[24] According to Boyte, democratic renewal must not remain confined to "free spaces," but must challenge institutions such as the state and the corporation. Crucial to this challenge is the idea of "public work," which Boyte and Nancy Kari define as "patterns of work that have public dimensions (that is, work with public purposes, work by a public, work in public settings) as well as the 'works' or products themselves."[25] In blurring the lines between "public" and "work," Boyte and Kari hope to renew a sense that America is not built in volunteers' spare time, but is the product of people's day to day labors. The workplace is reclaimed as a potentially public space, and what is usually considered public is recast as the work of ordinary citizens, not merely the operations of the distant state bureaucracy.

Boyte is also critical of those he calls "moralists," who blame the deterioration in democratic practice not on government or the economy but on declining morality and a lack of personal responsibility. While Boyte advocates a renewal of citizens' sense of personal ownership for what is public, he believes it is wrong to blame the citizens for what has gone wrong in American democracy. Absent from the moralists' considerations, says Boyte, is a serious analysis of why Americans feel so powerless, and the overwhelming forces of government and market which produce passivity in people.[26] To practice civil society is unavoidably to speak in terms of power. Boyte would perhaps be critical at this point of the Murrayite emphasis on reason over power. Boyte himself accents consensus-building, such emerges in the rough-and-tumble of competing power, not in some arid forum of public reasonableness.

One place where theory meets practice in Boyte's work is in Public Achievement. The stated goal is to educate young people "to think and act as citizens";[27] St. Bernard's School has adopted the theme "Educating Catholic Citizens for the 21st Century."[28] The method is to engage students in "public work," here defined as "the hard, ongoing effort of working with a diverse group of people to solve public problems and to make things of lasting contribution in shaping and creating our communities and the wider world."[29] Guided by a coach, a team of young people decides on a problem to address, then takes action. Examples of issues range from the need for a skateboarding park to racism in the community to U.S. policy on endangered animals or undocumented workers.[30] Actions include appeals to responsible authorities, letter-writing, fundraising, community awareness projects, and other activities.

A theory of civil society is embedded in this practice, and Public Achievement is centered on inculcating this theory and developing "public identities" in young people. Weekly debriefing sessions offer reflection on core Public Achievement concepts, such as "cocreation of learning, public work, self-interest, and power."[31] Democracy is defined as the "work of the people,"[32] not merely the work of political professionals. Furthermore, democracy means "more than a people's right to participate in governance, it means all people hold power and can exercise it to create our common world."[33] Freedom is defined as the ability of individuals to "choose their life and their ends unobstructed by others," though it is acknowledged as possible that the collective self-determination of the society could override an individual's self-determination.[34]

This last point is significant. No particular ends are given, other than the renewal of American democracy. Much emphasis is put on dealing with a diversity of people who will have a diversity of ends. How issues are chosen therefore depends on the self-interest of participants:

> Traditional forms of civic education focus on institutional politics . . . or community service (e.g., helping those in need). Public Achievement departs from these approaches by giving explicit attention to the self-interest of participants, and to concepts of public contribution in a world of diverse values and cultures.[35]

As this passage indicates, self-interest is not defined narrowly. One of Public Achievement's primary themes is moving away from a view of politics as based on what I/we can get from the government.[36] The Public Achievement participant is made aware that a range of interests exists from self-interest to a broader conception of the public interest. Nevertheless, the participant is alerted to the importance of interests, and informed that "a basic premise of public work is that people are more likely to become active on an issue that they feel strongly about."[37] With no ends given, Public Achievement must recognize that the self-interest of individuals and groups will play a key role in determining what problems are approached and how they are approached. Public interest, therefore, emerges from a process of consensus building by which it is hoped that agreement on ends can be reached among diverse people with diverse interests.[38] Consensus is by no means undergirded by a strong conception of truth, as it is for Murray.

Problems

I am entirely in agreement with the attempt to envision a space for the church that is neither Constantinian nor privatized. There is much to applaud in the Himeses' attempt to move theology out of the ghetto of private discourse. Boyte's scheme goes further in breaking out of a narrow focus on the making of public policy. I am in deep sympathy with Boyte's populism, in particular his appreciation for the churches as potential "free spaces" which escape the hegemony of the state. Christian educators' attempts to use Boyte's ideas in the form of Public Achievement have the potential to aid in moving the churches' political discourse and activism beyond limp recommendations on how to vote. Nevertheless, I want to point to some problems that undercut these attempts to give the church a significant public presence.

To begin with, both the Murrayites and Boyte are far too reticent about the interpenetration of state and society. In both models civil society appears as an essentially free space beyond the coercive reach of the state. The flows of power tend to move from civil society to the state, such that the ultimate goal of democratic organization and social movement—even for Boyte—is to generalize the impact of such movements through influencing the state. The potential of every person to limit, control, and use the state is highlighted in a fashion not too distinct from the "civics" approach that Boyte criticizes. Although Boyte's approach emphasizes power more than the Murrayite stress on reasoned consensus, power nevertheless tends to be envisioned as flowing in one direction, from civil society to state.

Insofar as its proponents are speaking descriptively, however, I find this view of civil society far from convincing. Indeed, other political theorists beginning with Hegel have drawn the flows of power in the opposite direction, from state to civil society. For Hegel, the associations of civil society take on an educative function between the state and the individual. Work is not excluded from Hegel's definition of civil society. Rather, civil society is where concrete labor is converted to abstract labor, that is, where the raw, untamed forces of labor are taken up by the institutions of civil society—such as trade unions, schools, and corporations—and domesticated for the sake of the universal interest of society. Labor, and all the interests and ends of individuals, must pass through the educative project of civil society before they can be fully realized, gathered, and universalized in the state, which is the "actuality of the ethical Idea."[39] Though based on production and family, the state is not the result of them, but rather comes first and is the true ground of them according to Hegel.[40] Work, family, and the person herself only become "real," take on objectivity, by participation in the state.

Michel Foucault has shown in great detail how what Hegel considered the ideal has become a baleful reality. The institutions of civil society—the party, the union, the school, the church, the prison—have an educative or disciplinary function which realizes the state project.[41] Surveillance has become a general feature of Western society, a feature that is one with state hegemony but does not depend on a totalitarian center to enforce its rule. The power of Foucault's Panopticon image is precisely that *self*-discipline becomes the norm, reinforced by the pedagogical function of the apparently free institutions of civil society. As Michael Hardt argues in an essay entitled "The Withering of Civil Society," it is perhaps most descriptively accurate to say that there is no longer any significant distinction to be made between civil society and state, the two having been fused to such a great extent.[42] For example, government regulation—much of it for good ends—reaches into every facet of society and every type of activity. Furthermore, fully a third of the U.S. economy is implicated directly or indirectly with the state, and government is increasingly seen as a bureaucratic provider of goods and services whose primary job is to serve its "customers," a fact which Boyte himself laments. In arguing against the voluntarists, Boyte acknowledges the extent to which spaces in state, business, and civil society have come to resemble each other because they have been colonized by the rationalization of the market. He singles out the managerial culture of the mega-church, with its emphasis on attracting new congregants by providing them specialized service, as a particularly bleak example.[43] Today's gods do not respect the neat divisions between state, civil society, and economy, a point made sharply by Michel de Certeau:

> Seized from the moment of awakening by the radio (the voice is the law), the listener walks all day through a forest of narrativities, journalistic, advertising and televised, which, at night, slip a few final messages under the door of sleep. More than the God recounted to us by the theologians of the past, these tales have a function of providence and predestination: they organize our work, our celebrations—even our dreams—in advance. Social life multiplies the gestures and modes of behaviour *imprinted* by the narrative models: it continually reproduces and stores up the "copies" of narratives.[44]

If this interpenetration of state, society, and economy is indeed the case, then appeals to the idea of free space outside the state may not be sufficient for the creation of true alternative spaces. Indeed, a project like Public Achievement can be seen as fulfilling the kind of educative or disciplinary role that Hegel and Foucault envision for the institutions of civil society. Embedded in Public Achievement's definition of freedom, for instance, is an anthropology that allows assimilation to a democratic capitalist order but is not so easily assimilable to a Christian anthropology in which a person's ends are not chosen but given by God. If Christian children's "public identities" are being formed to be citizens of the nation-state, those same students can perhaps be forgiven for forgetting that by baptism their "citizenship is in heaven," as Paul tells the Philippians (3:20), and that their fellow citizens are the saints, as the Ephesians are reminded (2:19). In other words, it is difficult to conceive of the church as a "free space" when we have been self-disciplined to avoid public Christian language even within our own schools.

In both the Murrayite and the Boyte models, the price to the church of admission to the "public" is a submission of its particular truth claims to the bar of public reason, a self-discipline of Christian speech. In the case of Public Achievement, particular Christian ends—such as an especial care for the poor before considerations of self-interest—are subjugated to a purely procedural search for consensus among a diversity of ends, none of which can ultimately claim a larger warrant than what issues from self-interested choice. Political theorist Romand Coles criticizes Boyte's pragmatism for its propensity—contrary to Boyte's intentions—to silence minority positions and unpopular claims to some measure of truth. An emphasis on drawing together many diverse voices can foster a need to converge *prematurely* around common goals. Coles argues that proposals to change the terms of political discourse that seem "absurd" or "divisive" to the mainstream are in danger of being silenced. "Pragmatic politics can foster poor listening and a restless intolerance toward those who speak from angles and in idioms that are foreign to many in the organization or those in the middle to whom an organization would appeal."[45] Thus although Boyte holds up the black church as a model of a "free space," it is not clear how he could accommodate as public the outrageous truth claims some black churches might want to make, claims such as "Jesus is Lord, and not just for us." An even deeper problem, however, is the fact that Public Achievement, despite its claims, does present as given one ultimate end: the renewal of American democracy. On this point there is no talk of a diversity of ends; the achievement of American democracy is simply presented as the *telos* of one's actions and the proper object of one's faith.

Murray is at least clear that the public consensus is built not upon self-interest but upon God-given truth. Nevertheless, the Murrayite project represents the self-disciplining of the church's ability to make theological claims in public. Theology must submit to what "the public" can consider reasonable, where "the public" is understood in terms of the nation-state. Christian symbols must be run through the sausage-grinder of social ethics before coming out on the other end as publicly digestible policy. As Talal Asad has shown, however, religion as a symbol system theoretically detachable from communities of discipleship is a modern invention which facilitated the absorption of the church into the modern secular state. For the Himeses, ritual and symbol are generically distinct from instrumental or pragmatic actions. Christian symbols function (as Clifford Geertz maintains) to elicit motivations which are then translatable into publicly available actions. Christian symbols can elicit transformations apart from participation in a community of discipleship. However, as Asad points out in his study of medieval—especially Benedictine—practices, ritual was never imagined as a distinct activity separate from a complete program of Christian discipline and discipleship. Indeed, religious symbols are never separable from bodily practices of discipline and power; it is simply that in the modern West the primary locus of discipline has become the state-society complex, and the church has been essentially transformed into a semi-private voluntary association.[46]

The great irony, then, is that in trying to arrange for the church to influence "the public," rather than simply *be* public, the public has reduced the church to its own terms. Citizenship has displaced discipleship as the church's public key. In banishing theology from the public sphere, the church has found it difficult to speak with theological integrity even within the church. The flows of power from church to public are reversed, threatening to flood the church itself.

It is little wonder that many people find liturgy, sacrament, and doctrine to be irrelevant to the "real world" of social problems. Christian symbol floats free from the church, which theologically is a social reality in its own right. Christian symbol must be translated and replaced in order to escape ghettoization. In the Christian tradition, by contrast, the liturgy is more than a generator of symbols for individual consumption. It is, as the original Greek *leitourgia* suggests—and despite Public Achievement—the true "work of the people," the *ergon* of the *laos*. The church gathered around the altar does not simply disperse and be absorbed into civil society when God's blessing sends it forth. The liturgy does more than generate interior motivations to be better citizens. The liturgy generates a body, the Body of Christ—the Eucharist makes the church, in Henri de Lubac's words—which is itself a *sui generis* social body, a public presence irreducible to a voluntary association of civil society.

As this critique suggests, I think the deepest problem with the two models of civil society we have been examining is their anemic ecclesiology. Their search for a public Christian presence which is neither private nor in the thrall of the state simply bypasses the possibility of the church as a significant social space. Missing is even a basic Augustinian sense that the church is itself an alternative "space" or set of practices whose citizenship is in some sort of tension with citizenship in the *civitas terrena*. For Augustine not the *imperium* but the church is the true *res publica*, the "public thing"; the *imperium* has forfeited any such claim to be truly public by its refusal to do justice, by refusing to give God his due.[47] For the Murrayite and Boyte models, on the other hand, what is public is that space bounded by the nation-state. To enter the public is to leave behind the church as a body. Individual Christians, fortified by "basic orienting attitudes," can enter public space, but the church itself drops out of the picture. The church is an essentially asocial entity which provides only "motivations" and "values" for public action. Christians must therefore find their politics and their public role elsewhere, borrowing from the available options presented by the secular nation-state. If we wish to go public, we must take on the language of citizenship. When Catholic schoolchildren embrace the plight of undocumented workers they are told they are being "citizens," unaware that the very fact that these workers are denied citizenship is the cause of their plight.

The Church as Public Space

What would it mean to construe the church as a public space in its own right? First we must be more precise about what "public" means. In one sense I have been using the term negatively to mean "not private," that is, not confined to the individual or the home. It would be a mistake, however, simply to accept the dichotomy of public and private as it is currently construed. In the Christian tradition, the home is not simply private space, simply *oikos*, in part because the home is always open to the community through the practice of hospitality (Luke 10:3-11), but also because the church itself is a new "family" that breaks down the isolation of the old family unit (Mark 3:20-35). As John Paul II says in his "Letter to Families," the family through the church opens up to a wider "public" space, the widest imaginable; the family is the "fundamental 'cell' of society" whose task is to extend its own "communion of persons" to the creation of a "civilization of love." John Paul reminds us that etymologically the word "civilization" is derived from *civis*, or citizen, but this meaning should not be confined to what is ordinarily construed as the civic or political; "the most profound meaning of the term 'civilization' is not merely political, but rather pertains to human culture."[48]

The church appears then as a term which is neither *polis* nor *oikos*. Ephesians 2:19 uses both "public" and "private" language simultaneously: "you are citizens (*sympolitai*) with the saints and also members of the household (*oikeioi*) of God."[49] The early Christians borrowed the term *ekklesia* or "assembly" from the Greek city-state, where *ekklesia* meant the assembly of all those with citizen rights in a given city. The early Christians thus refused the available language of guild or association (such as *koinon*, *collegium*) and asserted that the church was not gathered around particular interests, but was interested in all things; it was an assembly of the whole. And yet the whole was not the city-state or empire, but the people of God. As Gerhard Lohfink points out, the ultimate source for the language of *ekklesia* is not the Greek city-state but the assembly of Israel at Sinai. In Deuteronomy the foundational assembly of Israel at Mt. Sinai takes place according to the formulaic phrase "the day of the assembly."[50] In using the term *ekklesia* the church understood itself as the eschatological gathering of Israel. In this gathering those who are by definition excluded from being citizens of the *polis* and consigned to the *oikos*—women, children, slaves— are given full membership through baptism.

The gathering of Israel is made possible by certain detailed practices, structured by the Torah, and oriented toward the exclusive worship of God. What makes these practices "public" is that no aspect of life is excluded from them. The Law makes clear that what one does with one's money, one's body, one's neighbor, even one's feces are all within the ambit of the people's worship of God, and all these practices combined form a distinctive body of people. In the church, the practices of the liturgy, the creeds, the scriptural canon, hospitality, binding and loosing, the exercise of episcopal authority, all constitute the church as a distinctive public body.[51] Augustine goes beyond saying that the church is public like the Roman Empire is public, however, arguing that the Empire is not public at all because its practices are not oriented toward the worship of God. A true *res publica* is based on justice, which must include giving God his due in sacrifice, for only when God is loved can there be love of others and a mutual acknowledgment of right. According to Augustine, the true public thing is thus constituted by the Eucharist, which offers true sacrifice to God and makes the church into Christ's body.[52]

Having discussed what it means to call the church "public," we need also to be more precise about what it means to call the church a "space." One option here is to produce a two-dimensional mapping of the nation-state, then configure the borders of the church on this grid. Those borders could be drawn as coterminous with the borders of the nation-state (theocracy), or as an isolated island geographically within the nation-state but not participating in it (Amish), or as a space within "civil society," that is, within the national borders but outside the state apparatus (Murray). What these models have in common is the map, a formal figure of abstract places from which the dimension of time has been eliminated.[53] Placing the church on such a grid is a peculiarly modern phenomenon. In medieval theology, the temporal indicated a time between the first and second comings of Christ, during which the coercive sword of civil authority, under the tutelage of the church, was "temporarily" necessary. One need not endorse the Constantinian arrangements of medieval Christendom to lament the fact that in modern times the temporal has become not a time but a space, a realm or sphere, one which is usually located *outside* the spiritual realm occupied by the church.

There is a much richer concept of space to be found in the work of Jesuit social theorist Michel de Certeau. Certeau contrasts the "place" (*lieu*) of the map with "space" (*espace*). Place is a static order in which all the elements are arranged in their proper location, *beside* one another, no two things occupying the same location. The map produces a place by means of an abstract, two-dimensional grid produced by observation, allowing surveillance and control of a particular territory. After the fifteenth century, maps gradually replaced itineraries, which had described journeys or pilgrimages in terms of the actions prescribed at different points (e.g., spend the night here, pray at this shrine). Such itineraries describe not place but space. A space takes into account the vector of time, such that different spaces are created by the ensemble of movements and actions on them. Space is produced by people performing operations on places, using things in different ways for different ends. According to Certeau it is stories that "organize the play of changing relationships between spaces and places."[54] For example, the stories told in history books (Manifest Destiny) and on the evening news induce belief in a national territory, which mobilizes certain actions such as participation in war. The stories told by Native Americans might, on the other hand, refract space in entirely different ways, and mobilize other types of actions. In theological terms we can think of Certeau's work here as a gloss on Augustine's conception of the two cities. They do not exist beside each other on a territorial grid, but are formed by telling different stories about ends, and by thus using matter and motion in different ways.

The Eucharistic liturgy can be understood as what Certeau calls a "spatial story," an operation performed on matter and place—in this case by God, with human cooperation—which produces a different kind of space. The liturgy is not a symbol to be "read," its "meaning" formally detached from its signs, internalized by the individual, and smuggled as "attitudes" or "values" into another space outside of the church. Just as eating and drinking together do not merely symbolize a family, but help to constitute a family, so eating and drinking the body and blood of Christ transform the partakers into a body with a social dimension. For this reason the discipline of the Christian community has since the very beginning taken the form of excommunication; who is and who is not partaking of the table defines the spatial limit of the community gathered around the table.

David Schindler uses the home-cooked meal to illustrate how the family is a different practice of space. The home-cooked meal, Schindler says, is itself a different economy, one which *transforms* material objects and reconfigures space and time. Lest this be seen as a quaint and strictly private practice, Schindler describes how the Christian is called to extend this space into ever wider circles; the task of the church is to "domesticate" the world, to heal the homelessness and anomie of the modern condition by extending the "community of persons" that exists in the family—and that mirrors the Trinitarian life—to the whole world. The church does this by performing actions on matter and motion, space and time.[55]

To speak of the church as a public space means, then, that Christians perform stories which transform the way space is configured. The preeminent "spatial story" is that of the formation of the Body of Christ in the Eucharist. Imagine if Christian students, such as those involved in Public Achievement, were trained to see others not through the lens of self-interest but as fellow members of the mystical body of Christ? Why not tell them that in taking action on the plight of undocumented workers they are not reinforcing the borders of the national territory defined by "citizenship," but rather building up the body of Christ, which transcends those borders, and in which all—Christian or not—have a share? This approach shares with Boyte a concern to move beyond the image of the unitary "public square" to the fostering of a multiplicity of free spaces that are nonetheless fully public. Far from a withdrawal, this approach asserts the full public currency of the most basic Christian convictions. Furthermore, the international nature of the church challenges the sectarian narrowness of the nation-state for which citizenship stops at the border.

To take the church seriously as a "free space" would mean more than encouraging Christians to look for the public elsewhere. Boyte's work helpfully suggests that our imaginations have been limited by a narrow focus on one public forum supervised by the state. When Christians approach the creation and use of material goods, for example, we have been trained to think in terms of "economic policy," by which is meant the conversation in civil society and state among banks, the Federal Reserve, corporations, labor unions, Congress and other concerned parties over how the state ought to manage or not manage the flow of money, taxes, tariffs, etc. When framed in these terms, the only responsible reaction seems to be lobbying. Under certain circumstances lobbying—or, better, "witnessing"—may be helpful. The most fruitful way to dialogue with those outside of the church, however, is through concrete practices that do not need translation into some putatively "neutral" language to be understood. A significant response would be creating spaces in which alternative stories about material goods are told, and alternative forms of economics are made possible. For example, churches in my area have already begun to establish relationships with CSA (community supported agriculture) farms. In CSAs, a community is formed by buying shares of a farm's produce at the beginning of the growing season, thus sharing the risks involved in farming. The community is invited to help with the work of the farm and receives the benefits of its produce. In a significant and material way, the imagination of globalization is short-circuited and replaced by an alternative economic space which gives priority to personal relationships, community responsibility, a livable income for farmers, and a direct stewardship of the land from which our food comes.

The irony implicit in the models of civil society I have examined is that in our attempts to do social justice and to make theology public, we in fact consign the church to public irrelevance. Public theology is simply not public enough. What is lost is an important possibility of challenging in a fundamental way the dreary calculus of state and individual by creating truly free alternative spaces, cities of God in time.

NOTES

[1] Among many examples, see Andrew Arato, *Civil Society, Constitution, and Legitimacy* (Lanham, MD: Rowman and Littlefield, 2000); Benjamin R. Barber, "The Search for Civil Society," *The New Democrat*, no. 7 (March/April): 1995; Benjamin R. Barber, *Strong Democracy: Participatory Politics for a New Age* (Berkeley: University of California Press, 1984); Harry Boyte, *CommonWealth: A Return to Citizen Politics* (New York: Free Press, 1989); Sara Evans and Harry Boyte, *Free Spaces: The Sources of Democratic Change in America* (New York: Harper & Row, 1986); Jurgen Habermas, *Between Facts and Norms: Contributions to a Discourse Theory of Law and Democracy*, trans. William Rehg (Cambridge: MIT Press, 1996). For a history of the concept, see John Ehrenberg, *Civil Society: The Critical History of an Idea* (New York: New York University Press, 1999).

[2] John Courtney Murray, SJ, "The Problem of Religious Freedom," in *Religious Liberty: Catholic Struggles with Pluralism*, ed. J. Leon Hooper, SJ (Louisville: Westminster/John Knox Press, 1993), 144. Murray does not appear to deal with the problem of transposing the homogeneous wholeness of the term "society" from the complex of overlapping personal loyalties which constituted medieval Christendom.

[3] Ibid., 144-5.

[4] John Courtney Murray, SJ, "The Origins and Authority of the Public Consensus" in *We Hold These Truths* (New York: Sheed and Ward, 1960), 109-23.

[5] Murray uses the terms synonymously, saying that "public philosophy" emphasizes objectivity of content, whereas "consensus" emphasizes a subjectivity of persuasion; Murray, "Two Cases for the Public Consensus: Fact or Need" in *We Hold These Truths*, 79.

[6] Murray, "The Origins and Authority of the Public Consensus," in *We Hold These Truths*, 98-106.

[7] Adolf Berle, quoted in Murray, "The Origins and Authority of the Public Consensus," 101.

[8] Richard John Neuhaus, *The Naked Public Square: Religion and Democracy in America* (Grand Rapids, MI: Wm. B. Eerdmans, 1984), 84.

[9] Ibid., 116-17.

[10] George Weigel, *Catholicism and the Renewal of American Democracy* (New York: Paulist Press, 1989), 116.

[11] Ibid., 115.

[12] Michael J. Himes and Kenneth R. Himes, OFM, *The Fullness of Faith: The Public Significance of Theology* (New York: Paulist Press, 1993), 14-15.

[13] David Tracy, quoted in ibid., 16.

[14] Ibid.

[15] Ibid., 22-3.

[16] Ibid., 55-73.

[17] Harry Boyte, Nancy Kari, Jim Lewis, Nan Skelton, and Jennifer O'Donoghue, *Creating the Commonwealth: Public Politics and the Philosophy of Public Work* (Dayton, OH: Kettering Foundation, n.d.), 18.

[18] Harry C. Boyte, "Off the Playground of Civil Society," *The Good Society* 9, no. 2 (1999): 1, 4.

[19] Boyte's book *Citizen Action and the New American Populism*, co-authored with Heather Booth and Steve Max (Philadelphia: Temple University Press, 1986) consists almost entirely of such case studies. Boyte's *CommonWealth: A Return to Citizen Politics* interweaves such case studies with a more general democratic theory.

[20] See James Scott, *Seeing Like a State* (New Haven, CT: Yale University Press, 1998). Scott's earlier work includes a fascinating book called *Weapons of the Weak*, a study of poor people's ordinary ways of resistance to power, which typically involve foot-dragging, false compliance, sabotage, and the like, and not more dramatic revolutionary uprisings.

[21] Sara M. Evans and Harry C. Boyte, *Free Spaces: Sources of Democratic Change in America* (New York: Harper & Row, 1986), 17-18.

[22] Ibid., 26-68.

[23] Boyte, "Off the Playground of Civil Society," 4-5.

[24] Ibid., 4-5. For Barber's position, see his *A Place for Us: How to Make Society Civil and Democracy Strong* (New York: Hill and Wang, 1998). Habermas likewise writes of the "self-limitation of civil society" to those spheres outside of the economy and the state, since both state bureaucracies and markets are now too complex to be directed by democratic processes; see Habermas, *Between Facts and Norms*, 366-73.

[25] Harry C. Boyte and Nancy N. Kari, *Building America: The Democratic Promise of Public Work* (Philadelphia: Temple University Press, 1996), 202.

[26] Boyte, "Off the Playground of Civil Society," 5-6. Boyte has in mind especially *A Call to Civil Society: Why Democracy Needs Moral Truths*, a statement put out in the summer of 1998 by the Council on Civil Society, chaired by Jean Bethke Elshtain. The statement had a wide range of signatories, from Cornel West to Republican Senator Dan Coats of Indiana. For a summary of *A Call*, see www.americanvalues.org.

[27] *Building Worlds, Transforming Lives, Making History: A Guide to Public Achievement*, 2nd ed. (Minneapolis: Center for Democracy and Citizenship, 1998), 1. This is the training manual for coaches and participants in Public Achievement.

[28] Boyte, et al., *Creating the Commonwealth*, 23.

[29] *Building Worlds, Transforming Lives, Making History*, 1.

[30] The students and teachers of St. Bernard's were cited by Governor Jesse Ventura in his 1999 State of the State address for their successful attempt to build a new playground.

[31] Boyte, et al., *Creating the Commonwealth*, 18.

[32] *Building Worlds, Transforming Lives, Making History*, 40.

[33] Ibid., 23.

[34] Ibid.

[35] Boyte, et al., *Creating the Commonwealth*, 14.

[36] *Building Worlds, Transforming Lives, Making History*, 39. Public Achievement is differentiated from the "civics approach," which stresses receiving goods and services from the government, and the "communitarian approach," which can become too narrowly focused on the interests and experience of one relatively homogeneous group. For Boyte's own criticism of interest-organizing, see his *CommonWealth*, 12-13.

[37] Ibid., 23. Self-interest appears to be a legitimate starting point provided it result in public action. Thus Public Achievement at St. Bernard's is described as "a vehicle for students to act on their self-interest in public ways around work to make change"; Boyte, et al., *Creating the CommonWealth*, 15.

[38] Ibid., 16.

[39] G.W.F. Hegel, *The Philosophy of Right*, trans. T.M. Knox (Oxford: Clarendon Press, 1952), §257.

[40] Ibid., §256.

[41] See, for example, Michel Foucault, *Discipline and Punish: The Birth of the Prison*, trans. Alan Sheridan (New York: Vintage Books, 1977), 293-308.

[42] Michael Hardt, "The Withering of Civil Society," *Social Text* 45, vol. 14, no. 4 (Winter 1995): 27-44.

[43] Boyte, "Off the Playground of Civil Society," 5. Examples of the interpenetration of state and society can be multiplied. One that comes immediately to mind is the official encouragement given to corporate mergers by government "regulators." What debate there is over such mergers is conducted around the question, "Will this particular merger be good or bad for consumers?" People are defined as consumers, not citizens, by state management of the debate.

[44] Michel de Certeau, "Believing and Making People Believe" in Graham Ward, ed., *The Certeau Reader* (Oxford: Blackwell Publishers, 2000), 125.

[45] Romand Coles, "Toward an Uncommon Commonwealth: Reflections on Boyte's Critique of Civil Society," *The Good Society* 9, no. 2 (1999): 26. As examples of prematurely silenced forms of discourse, Coles cites "supporting non-anthropocentric ecological ethics, animal rights, radical bending of gender roles, challenges to mainstream political, economic, and cultural practices from the vantage point of small minority positions."

[46] Talal Asad, *Genealogies of Religion: Discipline and Reasons of Power in Christianity and Islam* (Baltimore: Johns Hopkins University Press, 1993), 27-54.

[47] St. Augustine of Hippo, *The City of God*, trans. Marcus Dods (New York: The Modern Library, 1950), XIX, 21-2.

[48] Pope John Paul II, "Letter to Families," 13.

[49] See Reinhard Hütter, "The Church as 'Public': Dogma, Practice, and the Holy Spirit," *Pro Ecclesia* 3, no. 3 (Summer 1994): 334-61.

[50] Gerhard Lohfink, *Does God Need the Church?: Toward a Theology of the People of God*, trans. Linda M. Maloney (Collegeville, MN: Liturgical Press, 1999), 218-20.

[51] Hütter, "The Church as 'Public.'"

[52] Augustine, XIX.21-3, X.6.

[53] Michel de Certeau explains what happens when the "trajectory" (we might substitute the word "pilgrimage") is replaced by a mapping. The category of "trajectory":

"was intended to suggest a temporal movement through space, that is the unity of a diachronic *succession* of points through which it passes, and not the *figure* that these points form on a space that is supposed to be synchronic or achronic. Indeed, this "representation" is insufficient, precisely because a trajectory is drawn, and time and movement are thus reduced to a line that can be seized as a whole by the eye and read in a single moment, as one projects onto a map the path taken by someone walking through a city. However useful this "flattening out" may be, it transforms the *temporal* articulation of places into a *spatial* sequence of points . . . ." (Michel de Certeau, *The Practice of Everyday Life*, trans. Steven Rendall [Berkeley: University of California Press, 1984], 35).

[54] Ibid., 118. See 34-42, 115-30.

[55] David L. Schindler, "Homelessness and the Modern Condition: The Family, Evangelization, and the Global Economy," *Logos* 3, no. 4 (Fall 2000): 34-56.

Faith, Hope, and Agony:
Christian Political Participation Beyond Liberalism[1]

Charles T. Mathewes

Abstract

The recent emergence and maturation of "agonistic" political thought, in explicit opposition to liberal political theory, offers opportunities for Christian thinkers in two ways. First, it releases Christians from the unnecessarily narrow political etiquette of received liberal political theory, and makes possible a more comprehensive public debate in which thick Christian commitments can plausibly play a role. Second, it sets Christian thinkers the task of determining how they can legitimately participate in this movement for a more "agonistic" democratic theory (and, by extension, a more agonistic democracy.) Some agonists argue that Christianity is the sort of worldview which is blind to the ineliminable pervasiveness of violence, and so is potentially a dangerous participant in the development of agonistic theory. Others challenge the idea that Christians can comfortably participate in a pluralistic conversation at all, given that their aim inevitably is (or should be) the conversion of other participants. The former group claims others ought not allow Christians to participate; the latter claims Christians ought not want to participate.

This paper explores and responds to these challenges in order to uncover a new and properly Christian approach to understanding political life, by contesting both sorts of challenges about Christian participation in agonistic democracy. It argues that, in contrast to agonists who see conflict as necessarily violent because essentially governed by a zero-sum logic of winners and losers, Christians can imagine and approach moments of conflict in the conviction that no one need lose or win, but that the struggle can be a struggle for conversion of one's loves and the

Annual of the Society of Christian Ethics, 21 (2001): 125-150

loves of one's interlocutor. By so interpreting conflict, Christians can re-imagine politics as a conflict about loves, and the movement for "agonistic democracy" can be seen as clarifying the possibility of re-interpreting politics as a struggle over peoples' loves.

Introduction

Contemporary political thought is currently undergoing a sea-change, away from a dominant "liberal" paradigm to a more complex and heterogeneous array of alternatives. Whereas even ten years ago most work in political thought was organized around exploring or critiquing the proper contours of a "liberal" political theory—typically thought to be exemplified by the work of John Rawls or Jürgen Habermas—today thinkers are pursuing a variety of inquiries which, whether they derive from the defenders of a "liberal" political theory (for example, exponents of "liberal virtue" and "deliberative democracy" theories) or from the critics of it (for example, exponents of "civic republicanism"), are no longer confined to the agenda of high liberal political theory. These alternative positions represent the growing sense that something important, perhaps even essential, goes unthought in the typical liberal fixation on articulating a consensual adjudicative framework for resolving sociopolitical issues in a pluralistic society—specifically, the idea that political life cannot be wholly supplanted by an algorithm or decision procedure, and that exclusive attention to such a framework for adjudication may blind theorists to other significant needs. The changes in political theory promise to transform political theory in exciting ways, and Christian ethicists should take note—and advantage—of them.

This paper attempts to do this by engaging so-called "agonistic" political thought in order to uncover a new and properly Christian approach to understanding political life. "Agonistic" political theorists argue that liberal political theory is concerned with constructing a social order which is invulnerable to destabilizing dissent, and that preoccupation with this concern will (1) undercut the very energies that most would-be participants in politics bring to the political process, in part because it (2) covertly and (by liberal lights) unjustifiably marginalize or silence many significant potential participants. In contrast, "agonists" see the appropriate political task as the fostering of disagreement, debate, and conflict among groups (and within them) with the aim of encouraging the full participation of all members of society. Because of this, agonists are often more interested in religious positions than the mainstream "liberal" theorists they critique, and more willing to take seriously religiously-informed positions as interlocutors, and not just curiosities.[2] The emergence of these agonistic theories thus opens a new and more fruitful avenue for Christian political thought, and I want here to offer an initial "scouting report" on what lies open beyond that frontier.

Part I briefly maps the general contours of the "liberal paradigm," in order to describe how agonistic political theorists understand themselves to have escaped from it. Part II argues that this "agonistic" alternative is not a panacea for Christians wishing to free themselves from the liberal paradigm, both because agonism faces serious challenges, and because agonism itself presents some very significant and interesting challenges to Christians as to the political implications of Christian commitment. Finally, Part III attempts to show how Christian political thought, in responding to the challenges agonism sets before it, may discover resources within itself to offer a more thoroughly agonistic, and more post-liberal (though not anti-liberal) political vision. By re-imagining conflict as a conflict about our loves, Christians can see the movement of "agonistic democracy" as opening up the possibility for re-interpreting politics as a struggle over peoples' loves. I conclude with some comments about the root cause of this different vision, which I see as entailed by some rather odd—and, to my mind, attractive—fundamental elements of Christianity's cosmological vision.

Agonism Beyond Liberalism

The need for some new vision of political life is urgent. Both in terms of our larger civic culture and the state of Christian religious institutions in America today, we are experiencing a crisis that many think is unprecedented. In terms of civic life, Americans seem gripped by deep disaffections regarding politics, and public life more generally. Part of the problem seems to lie in the impoverished character of our contemporary political imagination. In our setting many thinkers have criticized what most see as the dominant "liberal" vision of political life, and the quest for a new approach to politics, what Michael Sandel calls a new "public philosophy," to rejuvenate our understanding of and attitudes toward public life.[3] Generally these proposals begin by diagnosing the problems attendant upon "liberal political theory," which they see as the dominant, indeed almost hegemonic, approach to thinking about political matters in a normative register in academic political theorizing. I turn, then, to a brief sketch of why so many are disenchanted with this position.

Liberal Political Theory and its Discontents

Take "liberal political theory" to refer to a collection of assumptions and projects about politics. These assumptions are complex and perhaps even self-contradictory, and have never totally filled the space of our political imagination, or even held unquestioned dominance on any political scene. (Indeed some of the most interesting recent work done on liberalism's conceptual shape today suggests that there are multiple and incompatible projects beneath liberalism's carapace, which we would do well not to conflate with the single term "liberal."[4]) Nonetheless, in the last half-century this position has generally set the terms of debate for academic political theory, determining and positioning its opponents as much as its advocates.[5] The general problem with liberal theory is that its strictures are too narrow and confining for the political challenges we face today. In the liberal political paradigm our questions are restricted largely to two: First, how are we to manage the problem of pluralism? Second, what structures of governance will most justly meet the needs of the populace? These are good questions; the debates from which they spring are valuable, perhaps even essential, and at one point they were historically quite urgent. But today they set a too-comfortable task for thinkers, because they ask a too-narrow range of questions, and hence play a problematically restrictive role in public deliberation.[6] While liberal political theory as an approach is by no means finished—and there is some reason to believe we inhabit a society with "liberal" political institutions—the hegemony that liberalism has had over our political vision has begun to loosen, and a variety of alternative positions are becoming imaginable.[7]

Most basically, the project of the liberal paradigm can be identified as the project of establishing a set of political structures which cannot (ultimately) legitimately be the subjects of seriously contentious, and hence socially straining, public dispute. But many today find the tasks this project sets to be an inadequate guide to understanding and guiding political life today. There is an historiographical challenge to liberalism's "myth of beginnings," a philosophical challenge to its ideal of consent and its conceptual underpinnings, and a profound socio-political challenge to its faith in structures—from both the rise of toxic ethnic nationalisms and identity politics, and the large-scale anomie of the populaces of democracies worldwide. I want briefly to unpack these dimensions, and the challenges to them.

First of all, the liberal paradigm sees the task of political thought as structural or institutional—a matter of establishing just structures of deliberation, decision-making, and complaint—to the neglect of concern for the development of personal characteristics on the part of the citizenry. Liberalism is a deeply technological model of political thinking, one impatient with problems that are not yet clearly defined, much less ones that have no clear route to a solution.[8] Yet the socio-cultural developments of the last several decades have not been kind to this liberal. First of all, the massive re-ethnization of peoples around the world— the explosive self-identification through restrictive or exclusionary identities—has challenged the liberal assumption that such identities could be effectively filtered out of the political process by liberal political procedures and institutions. The "veil of ignorance" turned out to be too flimsy a boundary, and all sorts of (for liberals) problematic "non-public" identities started appearing in the public square, claiming it as their own. The liberal paradigm provides us no theoretical resources to address the presence of such "thick" identities, and so liberals can only scold those who hold to them, or bomb them into submission—and if it is the latter, they have no good legitimation of that bombing as a policy. Furthermore, there appears another deeper problem, namely the massive malaise, anomie, and deep suspicion that many citizens increasingly feel towards their governments.[9] But received liberal theory finds it difficult even to see the problem, let alone suggest fruitful ways to respond to it.

Secondly, this received theory sees its task not only primarily as the articulation of political structures but also their articulation in ways which can be ideally affirmed by all—or if not affirmed, at least not legitimately contested. There have been a number of philosophical challenges to the conceptual framework elaborated as the underpinning of the liberal fixation on consent, highlighting the dubiousness of the philosophical anthropology this framework entails. Briefly put, the argument goes: One imagines that consent is the basic problem only if one imagines that somehow individuals are ontologically prior to the communities in which they exist. But human beings are not so prior; we are essentially (though not exclusively) socially constructed beings.[10] Hence the question of consent is a question secondary to that of shaping humans to be real agents; the right is not prior to the good. Furthermore, the aim of maximal consent slides too easily into the goal of delegitimating dissent—the project of finding ways of ruling out of bounds principled dissents to the liberal picture of the political order, typically by assuming, with entirely good will, disputable anthropological and metaphysical principles in ways which liberal theorists could not defend by their own set canons of public reason. (I read this problem as the heart of the failure both of Rawls, early and late, and also of Habermas.) The received liberal fixation on the ideal of consent as the holy grail of political theory implies a "dangerous utopia of reconciliation" and renders liberal theory blind to the ineliminable presence of conflict and disagreement, which in turn means that such political thought must essentially seek to eliminate, not foster, dissent—which in turn leads to the annihilation of politics itself. Liberal theorists claim to aim at consent, but they consistently hit the target of silence. *Solitudinem faciunt, et pacem appelant*; they make a desolation and call it peace.[11]

Thirdly, the liberal paradigm worries about legitimation because it sees the great danger of political life as the polarization of opponents, normally due to irreconcilable (usually religious) differences which lead ultimately to warfare. All political imaginations have their nightmares, and the nightmare of the liberal imagination is the horrific religious wars of the sixteenth and seventeenth centuries.[12] Such liberal theorists fear that, given a situation of real value-pluralism, we must find ways of ensuring that value pluralism does not fracture the political order.[13] But historians are busy challenging this "usable past," both in its interpretation of its self-proclaimed originary moment—the religious wars of the seventeenth century—and also in its claim to be motivated by such a distant genesis at all. Most historians working on the seventeenth century today argue that what happened in that era was not the creation of political tolerance as a reaction to inter-religious violence, but rather the rise of the centralized and absolutist state as the locus of all legitimate violence and political sovereignty. The ruthless simplification of the bestiary of politics in this era, what we might call "the era of the birth of the Westphalian state," was the real story behind the violence of the religious wars, which were used significantly (though not exclusively) as convenient excuses for the further entrenchment of power on the part of various political actors; as Richard Dunn put it, the Holy Roman Emperor "Charles V's soldiers sacked Rome, not Wittenberg, in 1527."[14] The liberal paradigm has picked up the epiphenomena of the era of its (putative) origins and missed the real story of what was happening. (Indeed, the liberal paradigm's real roots can be found in its anxious recoil from the threat of totalitarianism in the 1940s and 50s.)[15] After all, the famous doctrine of *cuius regio eius religio*, purportedly one of the building blocks of toleration, is as much a doctrine of intolerance—of the legitimation of a ruler's right to compel his subjects to believe as he did, no matter what others outside the realm may wish—as of tolerance. The belief that "the liberal state" is the response to the challenge of pluralism gets things the wrong way round; pluralism is a problem only when you have a monotheism of the state, when the state claims to be the only game in town as regards power and authority. Without such an essentially aggrandizing political structure, diversity in belief and heterogeneity on the ground are much less difficult. Pluralism is a central problem for modern states not because of pluralism, but because of modern states.

None of these challenges, nor all of them together, euthanize particular liberal proposals. The death of liberal hegemony in no way means the end of liberalism as a viable political position; a chastened "political liberalism" or "civic liberalism" or "liberal republicanism" can still exist.[16] But the liberal paradigm's conceptual dominance is overcome. What comes after liberalism? Is it an altered, but still self-described "liberal" theory, or something else, eschewing the name? That question will, I think, increasingly occupy political thinking in the years to come.

Most people working on these issues have tried to address them by appeal to a more capacious sense of what politics might be, one that acknowledges genuine political activity to be more than mere lobbying. Politics, on this view, is a human good in a way that the liberal hegemony makes it difficult for us to acknowledge. This recognition of the value of politics is tied up with the resurgence of the concept of "civil society," which designates the realm of human sociability outside of the state and the market, beyond sheer governance and bare commerce. "Civil society" expresses the growing sense that something important, perhaps even essential, goes unthought in liberalism's fixation on articulating a consensual adjudicative framework for resolving sociopolitical issues in a pluralistic society such as our own; and what goes unthought, civil society's advocates suggest, is the idea of political life itself, the idea that understanding and guiding the cultivation and sustenance of political life is a crucial task for political thinkers.[17]

Political life cannot be wholly supplanted by an algorithm or decision procedure, and exclusive attention to such a decision procedure may blind theorists to other significant needs, most especially the cultivation of civic virtues for the sustenance of a responsible citizenry. Many people still think that this concept represents what it is that we need to recover—a kind of model Tocquevillean polis of debating clubs, volunteer organizations, town meetings, and knitting circles which double as political discussion groups. It promises to reinvigorate civic discourse and public culture in crucial ways, and thereby replenish the dangerously alkaloid soil of contemporary American political culture; by engaging others in civil society, thinkers hope, we can help to revitalize public life and achieve, in Michael Sandel's words, "a good in common that we cannot know alone."[18]

But the concept of civil society is no panacea; it cannot point the way to its own reinstitution, and we cannot rest content with the incantation of the words. The idea has functioned best in settings significantly different from ours. Historically, civil society is an oppositional concept, first in opposition to ecclesiastical society, as in eighteenth-century Scotland, then later in opposition to totalitarian society as in Eastern Europe. While it can thrive when it has an opponent, civil society seems equally to rely on other conditions which it is equally difficult to imagine pertaining to contemporary America, such as a reduction in work time and a large-scale shift away from the fundamentally isolating pleasures (such as television) which capture most citizens' leisure time. The need to re-institute civil society is precisely our problem, as we can sense its lack; but we cannot simply re-institute an earlier model of civic activity. We do need what civil society gives us; but saying that we need it is not the way to get it.[19] What can help us here?

Agonism

One of the most promising routes towards recovering something of the political energies symbolized by civil society, and passed over by received liberal political thought, is found in the work of recent political theorists, who offer what they call an "agonistic" alternative opposed to liberal political theory. "Agonists" think that genuine human flourishing entails real engagement with public matters, and that such engagement will inevitably take the form of a struggle. For them, democratic participation is a primary end in itself, not just a means to other ends. As they see it, the point of politics is not simply to settle on policies, but at least equally significantly to un-settle participants, as far as that is possible; hence the central task of political theory is not avoiding conflict, but maximizing peoples' access to and participation in it.

Agonistic theorists argue that received liberal theory is so concerned about the possibility of conflict that it dismisses concerns with the public good in order to secure the peace and prosperity of the private. They insist that, while liberal theorists acknowledge the inescapability of pluralism, they often do so out of regret. As Chantal Mouffe says, John Rawls's political liberalism "tends to erase the very place of the adversary, thereby expelling any legitimate opposition from the democratic public sphere"; for Rawls, "a well-ordered society is a society from which politics has been eliminated."[20] Against this, agonists see pluralism as a happy part of our condition, one worth fostering. The central question for agonists is not really how to design structures for resolving political conflict, but rather how to induce enough people to start disagreeing with one another to enable thick and contentious dispute to flourish.

Agonists begin with the axiom that society is non-natural, a human artifact whose reality is significantly a product of human decisions, not of inevitable natural structures. There is no "natural" or even necessarily eternally best way to organize society; the organization of society is always ultimately up to the people who inhabit it.[21] No political structure is transcendentally the best; what matters is what the constitutive agents of political life decide. Secondly, agonists argue that complete consensus is both impossible and undesirable. It is impossible empirically, because modern states' actions are so complex and comprehensive and the citizenry is so diverse; it is impossible theoretically, because no decision can avoid exclusion, and the dynamic of inclusion and exclusion is essential to political life. Conflict and struggle are ineliminable; as Stanley Fish (who is as much an agonist as he is anything else) says, "Hobbes was right."[22] For agonists, political life should be carried on in full recognition of the essentially fabricated and inevitably conflictual nature of political order: "every discourse, even one filled with words like 'fair' and 'impartial,' is an engine of exclusion and therefore a means of coercion . . . . The real question is: 'Is this the coercion we want, or the coercion favored by our opponents?'"[23] We must resist "the sacralization of consensus" and "the closing of the gap between justice and law that is a constitutive space of modern democracy;" we must "constantly challeng[e] the relations of inclusion-exclusion," in order both to resist the rigor mortis of some particular political configuration, and to ensure that political life remains vigorous.[24]

Nevertheless, the recognition of the inevitability of conflict and exclusion does not entail the celebration of violence. On the contrary, agonists argue, this very recognition will help resist conflict's tendencies to turn bloody. It is precisely those political theories for which ultimate challenge to some political framework is unthinkable (sometimes, as in the case of Habermas, quite literally) which are prone to a much greater danger of violence. Agonists believe we can begin to imagine a non-violent political struggle by thinking not in terms of enemies, but in terms of adversaries; in imagining the "us" versus "them" dynamics inherent in political life, we should "construct the 'them' in such a way that it is no longer perceived as an enemy to be destroyed, but as an 'adversary,' that is, somebody whose ideas we combat but whose right to defend those ideas we do not put into question."[25] By so imagining our opponents as engaged with us not in an ethical dispute about what is morally good, but rather as engaged with us in a political dispute about what is politically the best thing to do, we resist the temptation to subsume politics into the ethical project of "the recognition of the Other," and instead imagine the political as a realm of debate and dissent relatively free of the anxieties and aggressions we invariably bring to our moral projects.[26]

While this may sound disturbing, the project of the agonists is exciting and fruitful. It offers opportunities for Christian thinkers, because it releases Christians from the unnecessarily narrow political etiquette of liberalism and thereby renders possible a more comprehensive public debate in which thick Christian commitments can plausibly play a role. Furthermore, such involvement could help revivify Christian belief and participation, as it would engage Christians in the project of explaining themselves to their fellow citizens (and each other—for, after all, there is no guarantee that all "Christians" will align on the same side of any position).

Nonetheless, agonism is not a wholly satisfactory solution. It has its own internal problems, and even if it did not, it would present serious challenges to Christians attempting to appropriate it. Indeed it is more interesting and useful as a provocation to Christian political thought than as a model to imitate.

Beyond Agonism

Agonism's root problem is that, in the end, it is doubtful whether it really fulfills its claim to escape the logic of received liberal political theory; it seems merely to represent the recognition of intractable difficulties with the received liberalism, the bankruptcy of its fundamental conceptual constituents—and, as such, it is simply another form of the same "hermeneutics of suspicion" which has seduced political thought repeatedly since 1968.[27] Furthermore, Christians cannot directly and simply appropriate agonism because it challenges some basic Christian commitments in profound ways. Some agonists argue that Christianity is the sort of worldview which is blind to the ineliminable pervasiveness of violence, and so is a dangerous potential participant for such agonism. Others challenge the idea that Christians can comfortably participate in a pluralistic conversation at all, given that their aim inevitably is (or should be) the conversion of other participants. The former group claims others ought not to allow Christians to participate; the latter claims Christians ought not to want to participate. I will address these difficulties in turn.

Problems with Agonism

The concerns about agonism ultimately resolve into the worry that it does not so much transcend the dominant liberal political approach as manifest its intractable difficulties. For all its trumpeting of the inescapability of conflict, agonism finally aims via such acknowledgments to contain conflict, to be as magisterially (and managerially) non-partisan as the liberal model promised to be. As Stanley Fish says, agonists fall into "the theorist's most rarefied temptation, the temptation of thinking that recognizing the unavoidability of politics is a way of avoiding it."[28] Ultimately the ambitions of agonists are incoherent: like liberal theorists such as Rawls, they still want to be referees, offering a theory of politics capable of accommodating and organizing the conflicts among the very divergent political positions present in any society. But—as we will see manifest when we turn to agonism's relation to Christianity—this very focus on accommodating conflict, and including all possible viewpoints, is premised on a prior exclusion of any positions which would imagine politics in radically different terms. Agonism is what happens when liberal elites recognize the contestability of their positions but still hold on to the hope that there can be an essentially neutral and descriptive political philosophy within which such contestations can occur—which is to say, agonism is just another attempt to avoid politics after all.

We can see this by returning to Mouffe's distinction between adversaries and enemies. This distinction is an attempt to contain conflict, and this is our first clue that agonists have commitments to peace which can override their privileging of conflict. Mouffe may want to distance agonism from liberalism, but he eventually falls into the same problem of attempting to manage conflict. Again, Fish puts this well: While agonists believe in "openness to revision" and argue "that some forms of organization are more open to revision than others," they fail to recognize

> that openness to revision as a principle is itself a form of closure, not at all open to ways of thinking or acting that would bring revision to an end. "Openness to revision" is an internal, not an absolute, measure; it is relative to whatever understood exclusions—and there will always be some—give the politically organized space its shape.[29]

Where agonists claim to offer "a political philosophy that makes room for contingency," Fish argues, "contingency is precisely what you can't make room for; contingency is what befalls the best laid plans of mice and men—and that includes plans to take it into account or guard against its eruption."[30] Agonism remains crippled, like the liberal theories its advocates want to supplant, by being essentially a strategy based around a root fixation on the problem of conflict, and how best to accommodate it: "The [agonist's] assertion that forms of order and stability are always provisional is equivalent to the ["liberal"] assertion that values are plural and nonadjudicable. Both are offered as reasons for withdrawing from conflict."[31]

This failure is connected to another: agonists assume a moral psychology which is interestingly self-contradictory, as is revealed in their treatment of the relevance of individuals' commitments, their concerns and interests, to politics. Agonists cannot take these commitments seriously enough; on their picture, the "grip" of commitments has a certain phenomenological "lightness," as if they could be easily jettisoned, as if our aim must be not to be stuck to any of them: "if the clash of values is irremediable and if the forms of order (and thus the configurations of 'us' against 'them') are continually shifting, it is best not to insist too strongly on the values you happen to favor or the forms of order you prefer. If everything is up for grabs, why grab anything with the intent of hanging on to it?"[32] Yet this is a lightness that many commitments do not in fact have. Paradoxically and ironically, agonists are "backed into" affirming this vision of our relation to our "commitments" by their vision of our commitments' very intransigence, their intractability; for agonists, it is madness to expect that our commitments can be changed or commensurated, and so we must be resigned to that. (There is, in this way, a deep Stoical resignation or despair at the center of the agonists' political ontology.) They depict our commitments as permanent interests, "objectively" given in our constitution and fundamentally unquestionable (*de gustibus non est disputandem*). Hence agonists also take our commitments too seriously, accepting them as absolute and inflexible, fixed forever in ways we must accommodate, and cannot hope to change.[33]

In sum, like the liberal theorists they disparage, the agonists never actually theorize conflict, never actually go behind the fact of conflict to discern its constituent parts. They simply assume conflict as the bedrock fact from which all political thought must begin, and, like the liberal theorists, they offer what is essentially a protectionist response to conflict, one aimed at ensuring that it does not become too dangerous. But agonism can only ensure this containment of conflict—or, rather, convince itself that it can ensure it—if, like the liberal theory it attempts to supplant, it makes us not too tied to our aims, willing to renounce them for the sake of the agony. And that position is simply manifestly false to human psychology. By fixating on conflict, agonists back into asking humans to be the kind of creatures we cannot be, and so attempt (again) to "solve" politics before anyone actually begins to engage in it.

Challenge to Christianity

Agonism's internal difficulties are not the only reason we cannot simply swallow the theory whole; it also sets us the task of determining how, and how far, Christians can legitimately participate in public life imagined as ongoing agonistic engagement. For, given this agonistic picture of political life, some argue that Christians ought not be allowed to participate; others argue that Christians ought not want to participate. Let me lay out these challenges in more detail.

Some agonists argue that Christians are dangerous political participants who fantasize an ideal world without violence, and so necessarily disdain this world, and the actions necessary for its sustenance, in ways which corrode our attachment to it. Despite Christians' recognition of the inescapability of violence in this-worldly politics, especially through the doctrine of sin, they typically retain a theoretical idealism, believing that there is some sort of "pure community" whose existence (now or eschatologically) bears, in some ambiguous way, on the sordid and sloppy realities of life in this world. (Just-war theory, on both "presumption of peace" and "presumption of justice" interpretations, exhibits this idealism.) Furthermore, the idealism presses Christians toward demonizing their opponents in dangerous ways; for to disagree with their plan is to place oneself firmly in the camp of evil. Agonists argue that this Christian idealism invariably arises from and in turn reinforces an otherworldly, nay-saying *ressentiment* which poisons Christian participation in the political bargaining necessary for the sustenance of the world.

Other thinkers, Christian and non-Christian alike, challenge the idea that Christians can or should comfortably participate in a pluralistic conversation at all, given that their aim inevitably is (or should be) the conversion of other participants; under the guise of politics, such critics claim, Christians are secretly playing another game. On this view, Christians cannot be serious about political engagement, because their participation always governed by rules that counsel a final indifference concerning politics; Christians would rather be nice than win. Religious participants are implicitly seeking converts, not conversation-partners. Furthermore, Christianity seems essentially just the sort of "final" discourse that agonists cannot countenance; its dogmas are incontestable, and thus would only resist the deliberations agonists would cultivate. Is there a way for religious voices to participate as religious voices without simply evangelizing? And can distinctly religious speech operate as other than a political conversation-stopper? Can religiously committed individuals take politics seriously as politics, and not use politics merely as a convenient camouflage for evangelization? Can Christians be citizens of an earthly city, while undertaking the pilgrimage towards the City of God?

Agonism's challenges, both to our vision of political life and the place of Christian participation in that life, are profound. And I think they deserve and reward serious reflection by Christian ethicists, among others. In the final part of this essay, I want to make a start at such reflection—with no pretense of achieving any sort of conclusive answer to the agonists. I begin from the suspicion that we typically too totally oppose "love" and "conflict." Perhaps, as the title of this paper implies, charity and agony have something interesting in common. Perhaps love itself is the ultimate form of struggle, and struggle is unintelligible apart from love.

A Christian Response to Agonism

The agonists' concerns should worry Christians. But precisely because they can worry Christians—because they already have a place within Christian political thought—we can use these concerns to re-think the appropriate form of

Christian political engagement, and to uncover a new and properly Christian approach to understanding political life. The worries misconstrue what "winning" is for Christians, as well as the sort of "struggle" Christians understand themselves to undertake. For Christians, conflict is not the most basic fact about human society; conflict is merely the symbol (and the symptom) of the reality of our disordered loves. The struggle of politics can be a struggle for conversion, conversion of one's loves and the loves of one's interlocutor. By so interpreting political conflict, Christians re-imagine it as a conflict about our loves, and the movement of "agonistic democracy" can be seen as one opening up the possibility for re-interpreting politics as a struggle over peoples' loves. Ironically enough, in doing so Christians can in fact be more "agonistic," more playful, and more valuing of politics than non-Christian agonists can be. Let me explain.

Proper Otherworldiness: Eschatology versus Apocalypticism

I want to begin by addressing the concern that Christians cannot properly theorize the essential presence of conflict in political life. Certainly Christians oppose agonists' naturalization of conflict, which seems problematic to them in two ways. First of all, Christians think that this too thoroughly absolutizes conflict, refusing all imaginative possibilities for some sort of ideal absolute harmony. This stands in manifest tension with the agonists' own insistence that patterns of human interaction are radically contingent, always open to contestation and re-imagination. It also, I would argue, reinforces our temptation towards an enervating pessimism and despair by too thoroughly renouncing all hope for some sort of final reconciliation of all with all. This imaginative ideal has considerable power to shape political attitudes in the present; as a positive desire it is a political motivation distinct in kind from the motivation of fear for what we might lose—a motivation dear to the received liberal theorists and agonists alike—and it should not be collapsed into it.[34] Secondly, the agonists' naturalization of conflict is also problematic because, as we saw earlier, this naturalization can easily become a domestication. By trying to normalize conflict, they implicitly and unintentionally ignore its extremities. They do not allow conflict to be absolute enough. Sometimes politics does lead to war, and some of those wars—again, not many, but some—are just. The construction of the category of adversary is all very nice, but sometimes we face enemies, and we must not allow the concept of adversary wholly to eclipse that of enemy. Occasionally good and evil do appear in the political sphere. Some forms of political argument are simply right or simply wrong; it is just a fact that some political programs may not be the objects of legitimate contestation, or understandable support, and it is unrealistic to imagine that people should not operate with ethical motivations in the political realm.[35] Politics and ethics exist on a continuum just as much as do other putative conceptual dichotomies, such as public and private; and while we may want to keep alive to the distinction between the two ends of the continuum, we cannot imagine that they are radically separate spheres of reality. The agonists' particular vision of politics as a sphere of "conflict" wholly distinct from the realm of the ethical may be a salutary warning for most of our political engagements; but it cannot be allowed the privileged place of metaphysical dogma that agonists seem to want to grant it, for it forecloses the possibility that politics may be more important, both positively and negatively, than we normally experience it as being.

In contrast to agonists, Christian political theory gives "conflict" a quite complicated role, organized around the symbolics of sin. For Christians, because the necessary "violence" has already occurred, once and for all, in sin and in God's "overcoming" of our sin (which is actually not a second act of God, but simply God's refusal to allow us to complete our attempted violence of original sin), violence is simply not essential to politics. On all levels but the most primordial, Christians recognize the inextirpable reality of conflict and tension— after all, we live East of Eden, and it may be politically necessary for properly authorized agents to use violence as a defense against further acts of violence, in the realm of the political.[36] But that should not obscure the essentially non-violent character of the cosmological vision Christianity expresses.

Indeed Christians recognize conflict not only between human beings but within them, through the concept of sin. The idea that conflict is more primordially psychological than socio-political informs Christian belief in the ineliminability of conflict in this life and Christian belief that the meaning of this conflict is not what agonists purport it to be, but something both more profound and more hopeful. It is more hopeful, because conflict in the political realm is not understood to reflect humans' ultimate estrangement from one another. But it is equally more profound, because political conflict is not only itself; it also symbolizes our own brokenness. Still, just as it symbolizes that brokenness, our converse hope in our ultimate unity can bear a political significance as well.

Most basically, then, the agonists misconstrue the nature of Christian hope, by characterizing it in immanent terms as hope for the this-worldly realization of the Kingdom of God. But true Christian hope's eschatological orientation precludes such desires for any such ending in time. Christians do not want to "win," because Christ has already won. Because of Christ's victory, Christians should not conceive of either history in general or politics in particular as essentially agonistic, essentially a struggle or a war, but as a pilgrimage. Thus, against those who see conflict as necessarily and essentially violent, governed by a zero-sum logic in which some must lose for others to win, Christians can imagine and approach moments of conflict in the eschatological conviction that "losing" and "winning" need not be objects of ultimate concern.

Still, the simple idea of eschatology is no panacea; like all other human artifacts, "eschatology" can be turned to terrible misuse. To protect against such misuses, I contrast (too simply, I admit) what I call the "eschatological" imagination with what I call the "apocalyptic" imagination. The apocalyptic imagination, which has as its most famous representative Eusebius of Caesarea, claims that the "signs of the times" can be read in such a way as to provide an accurate reading of the course of history, which typically means reading history as coming to an end (the connections between Eusebian apocalypticism and Hegelian readings of contemporary history, by thinkers such as Francis Fukuyama, should be apparent.)[37] History is interpreted as narratively intelligible from inside, as having enough coherence to be rendered intelligible, given the right key (typically Scripture). But to be so intelligible, to connect up with our extra-textual apprehension of how things are going, we must be relatively near the end of history; the patterns must be "finally" coming into resolution (in several senses). Thus the project of understanding history in this way is essentially apocalyptic: history can only be understood as completed, as over; our desire to understand history is actually a desire to be able to say what it meant "in the end," a desire to have it finished, which is another way of saying that we want to escape history. In contrast, the eschatological imagination, as I understand it here (again too simplistically, not to mention entirely stipulatively), is exemplified in Augustine's refusal, in *City of God*, to read the signs of the end times literally, and his suggestion that they be read symbolically, to keep us "awake" and unpresumptuous of our lives in this world.[38] It reads the course of Providence through history not as developing a pattern, but rather as vexing all attempts to discern pattern in history; the lesson of providence is not that history can be finally solved, like a cryptogram, but that it must be endured, inhabited as a mystery which we cannot fully understand from the inside, but which we cannot escape of our own powers. All we can know is that a living God is in charge of history; the movement of history to the end which God has appointed for it is beyond our ability to discern. "Providence" here is not a tool to predict the future; instead, appreciation of Providence teaches one to remain humble and open to God's new thing, not to get too comfortable in any worldly dispensation, because we remain aware of the distance separating it from our ultimate home.

This attention to cultivating some level of alienation or estrangement helps us understand our lives here as a "training in longing," a process of learning fully to feel (and bewail) what Augustine called our condition of *distensio*—our experience of being "stretched," scattered, disordered, torn, confused.[39] We should learn to live in suspense and resistance to closure. This is how this mode of inhabiting time partakes of what I termed earlier the eschatological imagination, one which opposes all apocalypticisms, all desires to be able to anticipate the end of time. This eschatological imagination accepts that the world will end; but it further acknowledges that we would not be the ones to end it.[40]

In being so suspicious of utopianisms and perfectionist energies, this proposal may seem deeply conservative. But I do not think it needs to be so. It merely does not claim that any change will be a change of divine significance. The same basic problems will remain, because *we* will remain. We ought not hope that any future change will bring heaven on earth, in large part because when that change is enacted we will be tempted to imagine that we have instituted heaven—or really, returned to Eden. But Eden is lost to us forever. And good riddance: *felix culpa*. What lies ahead of us is greater than that Paradise ever was.

Hence, because the political horizon is ruptured by the eschatological assurance that God is sovereign over history, Christians' attitude to history should not be one of anxious grasping after control, but of a relaxed playfulness.[41] Because Christians can treat conflict as not ultimate, they can harbor hopes for politics which extend well beyond the grim zero-sum vision of agonists. Instead of treating politics (as agonism does) as the ultimate realm of human achievement (i.e., salvation), Christians think it is better seen as a site for conversion, for further transformation for all participants in the long waiting for the realization of our longings. By so interpreting conflict, Christians re-imagine it as a conflict about our loves, and the movement of "agonistic democracy" can be seen as one opening up the possibility for re-interpreting politics as a struggle over peoples' loves. They are not only less necessarily violent than agonists, they also have a richer notion of "politics" as well, one which makes our engagement in it all the more urgent. Indeed the two advantages are connected, because agonists, who think that history and politics is all there is, will invariably invest it with a desperate seriousness licensing almost anything—which will in turn mean that, for them, violence is an inevitable, inescapable, part of politics. (Hence their assumption that conflict is inevitable becomes an inescapably self-fulfilling prophecy.) And their only response to Christian descriptions of an alternative is a weak, unverifiable appeal to "bad faith" and *ressentiment* on the part of Christian participants. Nonetheless, those appeals must be confronted; and so I turn to them next.

"Relaxed Playfulness": Politics as Conversation and Conversion

The language of "relaxed playfulness" will immediately provoke the agonists' second concern. For if Christians do have such a more capacious vision of politics, perhaps this vision occludes politics' central realities, the nature of political give and take; perhaps Christians cannot take politics seriously enough. How are we to respond to this concern? Do Christians really care enough about politics to be truly political, or are they always going to be interested in politics for purely instrumental reasons? For Christians, is politics—understood as the murky and painful "boring of hard boards" as Max Weber put it—only a distraction, a necessary evil? Is this vision of politics so valuing of it as to actually end up rendering real politics disappointing and finally unfulfilling in a way which undermines Christians' desire to engage in it?

I do not think so. Christians allow politics its full significance; they simply refuse to grant it more importance than it merits. They can combine a "relaxing" realization that "all will be well" with genuine though proximate commitment to political ends. This is not a devaluing of politics but a re-valuing of it, based on a radical rethinking of its point. This attitude enables Christians to see political action as not just immanent activity, not only about itself, but as also a space of openness to other things. In a way not entirely unlike close emotional relations (like family or communal life), the struggle of politics exposes our loves to one another, exposes our commitments; and so politics, properly undertaken, can be a struggle for conversion, conversion of one's loves and the loves of one's interlocutor, without ceasing to be genuinely political—without, that is, luring our interest and attention away from the proximately ("this worldly") and immanent concerns of the matter directly at hand.[42] Furthermore, this attitude also releases Christians from the terrible presumption of acting as if they were the ultimate guardians of goodness in the world, as if they were God. Indeed it is precisely Christians' capacity to see beyond the this-worldly horizon of the agonists' self-proclaimed "political" vision that allows them to value rightly the political conflicts as political, and not of ultimate significance. As Rowan Williams says,

> the only reliable political leader, the only ruler who can be guaranteed to safeguard authentically political values (order, equity, and the nurture of souls in these things) is the man [sic] who is, at the end of the day, indifferent to their survival in the relative shape of the existing order, because he knows them to be safeguarded at the level of God's eternal and immutable providence, vindicated in the eternal *civitas Dei*.[43]

That this idea sounds so wrong to us bespeaks not our greater disillusioned "realism" or post-Marxist savvy about the consolatory comforts of theoretical or metaphysical dogmas. (Such savvy was not invented by Marx or other moderns, they only invented the conceit that we have invented it.) Instead its oddity is due precisely to our *un*-realism, to our enthrallment to—indeed, our stubborn refusal to surrender—a bad theoretical dogma: namely, the dogma that any such attitude of ultimate "indifference" or "relaxation" inevitably dissipates our political energies. And it is well past that dogma's expiration date.

When one thinks of the great political struggles of the twentieth century, those in which one would most expect struggle to characterize the events, one thinks of episodes such as the U.S. civil rights campaigns of the 1950s and '60s, or struggles against oppressive regimes such as Gandhi's struggles in South Africa and India, the struggle against apartheid in South Africa, resistance to Pinochet in Chile, or to the communist regimes of Eastern Europe. In all of these, the presence of religious bodies expressly committed to presumably "otherworldly" values was essential to the movements' present-day success and the relative non-violence. Of course, the agonists (or other thoroughgoing "materialists") may cry foul, claiming that I have stacked the deck against their position; in which case I invite them to undertake their own historical inventory, for they will discover that it is not I, but history, which has stacked the deck against them. Despite the slanders often launched at "otherworldly" motives, the agonists, I would argue, can point to no comparative set of successful movements informed or led by those with thoroughgoing "immanent" orientations.[44]

Granting that Christians will undertake politics with this relaxed attitude, and that this attitude is potentially quite fruitful, how precisely will Christians actively reach out and engage others? Most central here is the idea that Christians must genuinely put their beliefs at risk in this engagement. And this I think is right: Christians can legitimately (and ought to, theologically) engage others in ways that put their own convictions at risk. Such risk is central to, and nourishing of, Christian faith, which possess an inner dynamic that drives its adherents towards just the sort of risky openness our society needs in order to flourish. This openness is central to the Christian kerygma, which communicates (to speak in dangerously abstract terms) the reconciliations of othernesses: within God's own being in the Trinity, with God and the world, and especially a fallen humanity, and finally, among humans themselves. Christian faith is not parochially "local" or fundamentally narcissistic, but is always already cracked open to, and involved with, alternative modes of being. Thus we can argue, in a distinctly Christian dialect, for the necessity of understanding and engaging non-Christian positions.[45]

How "risky" can this agonistic engagement be? No less risky than the agonists' more typical Nietzschean approach would be. Central to both is a conviction that one's beliefs cannot but be radically challenged, transformed and deepened by what (or who) one encounters in one's engagement, and that such challenging is central to keeping one's beliefs (even oneself) alive. To engage one another in good faith—faith that such engagement is the route to (and of) true communion; to undertake such engagements with the ever-renewed hope that the other will respond in such good faith; and finally, to behave in such engagements with a genuine love for the other, manifest certainly in respect of them, but also in a refusal to let them be less than worthy of that respect (to love them agonistically, as it were)—to do all these things in public life is to participate in the truly dynamic life of Christ, acting with faith, hope, and even charity, where, in public life, charity appears as not so totally different from the agonists' engagement.

All of this may sound sheerly individualistic. But it need not be. It is certainly a program that starts with individuals' attitudes, and works on their dispositions, to mold them in a Christoform way; but it does so only in order to encourage people to participate in a particular sort of community, the community of the Christian churches.[46] The idea that we can undertake these practices largely in independence from one another is merely a symptom of the atomic individualism so pervasive today. But, put too weakly, in fact we cannot be the sorts of individuals we want to be outside of some community such as the church—and, to put it more strongly and perhaps more accurately, even on a sociological level, churches remain among the few social formations in our culture that even theoretically put us in a condition of being able to become the sorts of people we should be. I am not simply saying this as a nice pious cliché; I mean that contemporary socio-economic conditions and patterns work against the development of some of those characteristics fundamental to who we should be, for we have collectively organized our social lives in ways which allow us often to evade one another.[47] This point is made nicely by an exchange between Robin Lovin and Stanley Hauerwas. Lovin, in critiquing Hauerwas's focus on "the church" having a "common story," described the church in which he worshipped:

> At church I stand in the circle with a group of people that includes a couple of welfare mothers, a commodities broker, two or three Filipino nurses, and a Filipino schizophrenic who carries a three-foot-high doll. I look around that circle and I say to myself, "Whatever it is that I share with these people, surely it's not a common story—or at least that's not all that's involved here."

To this thought Hauerwas replied: "I don't think that that group of people is possible anywhere else outside the Christian community. I think it's wonderful that Robin stands there worshiping with a schizophrenic holding a doll. I don't see American society desiring that. That's exactly the kind of critical edge that we need."[48] And I suspect that Hauerwas is right (though note he does not really respond to Lovin's concern about the ineffectiveness of "common story"-talk to understand the church). Ours is a time in which, according to Joseph Turow, advertisers have begun to carve up our society into "image tribes," interest groups clustered around focal self-identifications with various "lifestyles," anything that works against that atomization is potentially a powerful device for the right sort of existence.[49] Those communities where people gather in groups—groups that attempt expressly and harmoniously to connect multiple, complex, and diverse personal histories, rather than treat them as monolithic fetishes or inflexible distinguishing marks—are just the sorts of communities that can enable a rebirth of a real politics.[50] And it seems to me that the churches, whatever their failures and frailties today, remain one of the very few institutional spaces in America where we may occasionally run into people who are not clones of ourselves. And I think that this is a crucial thing to realize. Churches are spaces, and potentially genuine public spaces, in a world where such public spaces are increasingly disappearing.

But I would be wrong to end by instrumentalizing the church into one more support strut for our civic life; it would also be misleading, for that is not my main aim. My main point is not that Christianity is good for civic life; it is that civic life is good for Christianity. As Ellen Charry has argued, Christian life is a life of inquiry into God, and the practices we engage in are meant to aid us in that inquiry.[51] *Askesis* is theology, properly understood. By engaging in this encounter in public with others, and enduring the risk—the risks of time—that such engagement entails, we come better to see God's face for us, we come to participate in God *pro nobis*. If, speaking civically, it is only by appealing to the local languages of our faiths that we will find the resources to meet our problems, it is equally the case that, speaking theologically, it is only by returning upon the deep sources of the religious traditions that we can find the energies to revitalize our religious commitments. If Christianity is in important part about the reconciliation of apparent opposites, it should not be surprising that a vibrant Christian faith presses us outward towards one another, not centrally as social workers, doing nice things for those less fortunate than us, but as fellow citizens, and not just of any worldly kingdom, but citizens of the kingdom of heaven.

Conclusion

This vision of Christian political philosophy not only offers the rudiments of an adequate answer to the agonists' challenges; it also shows how a Christian political philosophy, unlike agonism, can offer a real alternative to the "liberalism of indifference" to which so many thinkers—Christian and non-Christian alike—today remain bewitched. For it imagines that the basic challenge of political life is not simply conflict between people, but the ordering of our loves.

This sort of "politics with a theological face," and "theology with a political face," is not uncontroversial. And it cannot be irrefutably proved to be truth. It may seem wildly optimistic on sociological grounds, both to those Christians more dubious about political life, and to those (Christian and non-Christian) more suspicious about Christian involvement in it. But I think that both sorts of doubts cannot finally be serious; we have to engage in politics in this life, and Christians will be involved in that engagement, in America. The question then becomes, how that engagement will go forward; and my project here has been merely to offer one answer to that question.

There are other serious worries about this position that cannot—in this dispensation, at least—be answered. It may seem perilously optimistic, assuming that our lives are genuinely what we think they are: that we are most deeply constituted by our loves; that those loves are fundamentally excessive, marked by a "giftedness" that no object in the world can ever earn; that we can bring our loves into some sort of integral ordering; and that we actually benefit from this sort of integration, that we are made whole by being so integrated. And I think we can all feel the doubtability of this view. Our suspicion, and our fear, that our gratitudes are not in fact such—that we are in fact marked more by exchanges than gifts, that we are concerned with others only in the register of merit—partly (but only partly) explains why the encroachment of politics on our lives is a source of so much anxiety for us. This essay's counter-claims can hence be easily misread as being overly optimistic, even naive. But it should help to quiet concerns about naiveté that it is an Augustinian, that most dour of mythic beasts, who suggests it. Politics will never, in this dispensation at least, be simply a means of joy (and not only will politics never be wholly joyful, not only are there good parts and bad parts, but the whole of any part will never be simple joy.) Good and bad overlay each other, so that the results of politics, and the practice of it, will be forever mixed. The point of this essay has simply been to insist on its mixedness, not its complete corruption, and on the possibility that good can come out of our being political in this way.

It is worth noting, finally, the radicality of the alternative offered here, and the historical background that enables us to offer it. This Christian vision is rooted in a fundamentally different ontology and cosmology than that of the agonists and liberals. It has taken Christians a long time to come to this vision; it is rooted in the cosmological revolution undertaken by Christianity on its inherited Ancient Near Eastern cosmology. This revolution rejected the received view of the cosmos as formed in an agonic struggle between two (or more) divine entities, replacing it with a cosmology of a single monarchic Deity from whom creation has tragically and inexplicably swerved.[52] It is worth noting the nearly-unique character of this Christian cosmology, and the way in which it makes all appropriations of alternative resources for understanding our lives quite complex. Many of the root myths of the universe, the worldviews from which Christianity borrows many of its concepts—such as the concept of virtue—are agonistic, fundamentally conflictual; Christianity's claim to transform them is quite radical, and we should appreciate, and reflect upon, that radicality more thoroughly than we have yet done.

Further exploration of this cosmology is out of place here. I have simply tried to show that Christian faith, far from being innately opposed to activity we would recognize as political, instead builds out of a disposition to charity a motive for politics that is quite powerful, rooted as it is in basic human desires for integrity. And even if I have not accomplished that task completely—or even partially—I hope to have convinced you that the challenge of the agonists to our usual ways of thinking about politics are worth considering, if only for the fruitful thoughts that challenge provokes by way of resisting it.

NOTES

[1] Thanks are due to Leora Batnitsky, Colin Bird, John Bowlin, Talbot Brewer, William Cavanaugh, Patrick Deneen, Jean Bethke Elshtain, Jennifer L. Geddes, Eric Gregory, R. Marie Griffith, Krishan Kumar, Richard Miller, John Owen, Gerald Schlabach, Lisa Sideris, Jeffrey Stout, Darlene Weaver, Robert Wuthnow, and Joshua Yates for conversations regarding issues in this essay. Discussions in 1999 with Ashley Woodiwiss, and a reading of one of his essays, led me to think about agonistic political theory, and its attractions for Christian political thought; I thank him for it. Two anonymous readers for *The Annual*, and *Annual* co-editor John Kelsay, provided very helpful criticisms as well. The essay grew out of discussions at the Institute for Advanced Studies in Culture at the University of Virginia, and it was composed during my stay as a visiting fellow at the Center for the Study of Religion at Princeton University; I am grateful for both institutions' support. For all the flaws remaining, I have only myself to thank.

[2]For examples of such sustained engagement, see William E. Connolly, *Why I Am Not a Secularist* (Minneapolis: University of Minnesota Press, 1999), Stephen K. White, *Sustaining Affirmation: The Strengths of Weak Ontology in Political Theory* (Princeton: Princeton

University Press, 2000), and Romand Coles, *Rethinking Generosity: Critical Theory and the Politics of Caritas* (Ithaca: Cornell University Press, 1997).

[3]Michael Sandel, *Democracy's Discontent: America In Search of A Public Philosophy* (Cambridge, MA: Belknap Press of Harvard University Press, 1996). This is a truly remarkable book, which has not yet received the attention it deserves. See also Benjamin Barber, *The Conquest of Politics: Liberal Philosophy in Democratic Times* (Princeton: Princeton University Press, 1988).

[4]See, e.g., Colin Bird, *The Myth of Liberal Individualism* (Cambridge: Cambridge University Press, 1999).

[5]An idiosyncratic series of works have informed my understanding of this discontent; see Alan Brinkley, *Liberalism and Its Discontents* (Cambridge, MA: Harvard University Press, 1998), Daniel T. Rogers, "Republicanism: The Career of a Concept," in *Journal of American History* (June 1992): 11-38; W. B. Gallie, "Essentially Contested Concepts," in *Proceedings of the Aristotelian Society (New Series)* 56 (1955-56): 167-98; and David Johnston, *The Idea of a Liberal Theory* (Princeton: Princeton University Press, 1994).

[6]Furthermore, they are not only minimalist, they are *too* minimalist, incomplete even as a putatively minimal range of issues; even to secure the goals that the liberal paradigm sees as paramount—say, the stable governance of a complex modern society—we must ask questions that that paradigm at best ignores, and at worst dismisses as irrelevant—such as the question of how to sustain civic virtue. See Jean Bethke Elshtain, *Democracy on Trial* (New York: Basic Books, 1995), and Peter Berkowitz, *Virtue and the Making of Modern Liberalism* (Princeton: Princeton University Press, 1999).

[7]Much could be said here regarding the associations of this decline with the supposed ongoing decline of the Westphalian state system, but I do not do so here, because the nature of this other purported decline is hard for me to characterize. For an account that does something of this, see Allen Buchanan, "Rawls's Law of Peoples: Rules for a Vanished Westphalian World" in *Ethics* 110:4 (July 2000): 697-721. For an ambitious and thought-provoking discussion of this presumed decline and its consequences, see Michael Hardt and Antonio Negri, *Empire* (Cambridge MA: Harvard University Press, 2000).

[8]The technological model is partly the expression of the rise of an elite managerial class of experts in the Twentieth century. For background on "expert culture," see Steven Brint, *In an Age of Experts: The Changing Role of Professionals in Politics and Public Life* (Princeton: Princeton University Press, 1994), and Peter Dobkin Hall, *The Organization of American Culture, 1700-1900: Private Institutions, Elites, and the Origins of American Nationality* (New York: New York University Press, 1984). For more on the "therapeutic state," see James L. Nolan Jr., *The Therapeutic State: Justifying Government at Century's End* (New York: New York University Press, 1998), and Andrew J. Polsky, *The Rise of the Therapeutic State* (Princeton: Princeton University Press, 1991).

[9]See Danilo Zolo, *Democracy and Complexity: A Realist Approach* (State College, PA: Pennsylvania State University Press, 1992).

[10]An exemplary critic of this sort is Michael Sandel, whose *Liberalism and the Limits of Justice* (New York: Cambridge University Press, 1982) brilliantly anatomized and perspicaciously critiqued the "punctual self" of Rawlsian liberalism.

[11]Tacitus, *Agricola*, § 30. See Chantal Mouffe, *The Democratic Paradox* (New York: Verso, 2000), 29, and *The Return of the Political* (New York: Verso, 1993). See also the earlier mentioned works by William E. Connolly, Stephen K. White, and Romand Coles. The roots of this concern go back at least to Hannah Arendt; see her *The Human Condition* (Chicago: The University of Chicago Press, 1958). On dissent, see Stephen L. Carter, *The Dissent of the Governed: A Meditation on Law, Religion, and Loyalty* (Cambridge, MA: Harvard University Press, 1998), esp. 26-7, on the puzzle of how the "dissent of the governed" can fit into a "liberal constitutional regime". See also Don Herzog, *Happy Slaves: A Critique of Consent Theory* (Chicago: University of Chicago Press, 1989), Nicholas Rescher, *Pluralism: Against the Demand for Consensus* (Oxford: Clarendon Press, 1993), and Steven H. Shiffrin, *Dissent, Injustice, and the Meanings of America* (Princeton: Princeton University Press, 1999). For a

fascinating discussion of "unknowing," on which I am modeling this picture of how the liberal hegemony constructs its vision of the problems facing it, see Eve Kosofsky Sedgwick, *Epistemology Of the Closet* (Berkeley: University of California Press, 1990).

[12]Thus Jeffrey Stout, *The Flight from Authority: Religion, Morality, and the Quest for Autonomy* (Notre Dame, 1981). One example of the fear of religion may be found in John Rawls's recent *The Law of Peoples* (Cambridge, MA: Harvard University Press, 1999), under the index heading "Christianity." The entire entry is as follows: "Christianity: and heresy, 21, 166n; persecuting zeal of, its curse, 21, 166n" (the heading is found on p. 182). See also Judith Shklar, *Ordinary Vices* (Cambridge, MA: Belknap Press of Harvard University Press, 1984), and Mark Juergensmeyer, *Terror in the Mind of God: The Global Rise of Religious Violence* (Berkeley: University of California Press, 2000) and *The New Cold War? Religious Nationalism Confronts the Secular State* (Berkeley: University of California Press, 1993).

[13]It is worth noting that this focus centers political attention upon those problems that best fit this model of difficulty, such as abortion. Other worries—about, for example, the *anomie* or selfishness which some thinkers claim increasingly marks our political life—are typically read as sub-categories of the "religious war" model. By making the question "how can we avoid bloody conflict?" as their basic problem, liberal theory reads all other challenges in a descending scale of seriousness therefrom (on this see Ronald Beiner, *What's the Matter with Liberalism?* (Chicago: University of Chicago Press, 1992)).

[14]Richard Dunn, *The Age of Religious Wars 1559-1689* (New York: W.W. Norton & Company, 1970), 6. I first read this passage in William T. Cavanaugh, "'A Fire Strong Enough to Consume the House:' The Wars of Religion and the Rise of the State" in *Modern Theology* 11:4 (October 1995): 397-420; this article began my reading on this issue. The nationalizing of religious life which the Reformation enabled was also harnessed by the political actors of the day as well. See Charles Tilly, *Coercion, Capital, and the European States AD 990-1990* (Cambridge MA: Basil Blackwell, 1989), and *European Revolutions, 1492-1992* (New York: Blackwell, 1993). Before the Reformation, and contrary to popular images of constant Gestapo-like oppression by sadistic Inquisitors, there was not the constant presence of theological thought-police; as R. I. Moore points out: "In the West, far from being 'normal' in medieval society, it [religious persecution] faded away with the Roman Empire, and did not reappear until the eleventh century; even then…it became regular and established only gradually during the next hundred years or so," and then in deep connection to large-scale social and political changes (*The Formation of a Persecuting Society* (Oxford: Blackwell, 1987), 4, 99, 102-3, 110). There are no recorded executions for heresy between 383 (and the accusers in that case were later excommunicated by Ambrose and Pope Siricus), and 1022 (Moore, 12-13). On "Constantinianism," see Hal Drake, *Constantine and the Bishops: The Politics of Intolerance* (Baltimore: Johns Hopkins University Press, 2000).

[15]Jeffrey Isaac, *Democracy in Dark Times* (Ithaca: Cornell University Press, 1997), pp. 26-8; Alan Brinkley, *Liberalism and Its Discontents*, 296-7.

[16]See, e.g., Steven Macedo, *Liberal Virtues* (Oxford: Clarendon Press, 1993), William Galston, *Liberal Purposes* (New York: Cambridge University Press, 1991), John Rawls, *Political Liberalism* (New York: Columbia University Press, 1993).

[17]Note that this means that what counts as genuinely "political" activity, or a "political" life, may very well be activity only obliquely concerned with the direct governance of a state— at times, such as in Eastern Europe in the 1970s and 1980s, it can be the case that real political activity could only occur where the state was *absent*. See George Konrad, *Antipolitics: An essay* (San Diego: Harcourt, Brace, Jovanovich, 1984).

[18]Sandel, *Liberalism and the Limits of Justice*, 183. The literature on civil society is immense: for starters, see E. J. Dionne, ed., *Community Works: The Revival of Civil Society in America* (Washington: Brookings Institution Press, 1998) for a more discursive (though highly intelligent) series of brief essays; John A. Hall, ed., *Civil Society: Theory, History, Comparison* (Cambridge, UK: Polity Press, 1995) for a slightly defensive one; Chris Hann and Elizabeth Dunn, eds., *Civil Society: Challenging Western Models* (New York: Routledge, 1996) for an interesting "global" perspective; John Ehrenberg, *Civil Society: The Critical History of an Idea*

(New York: New York University Press, 1999) for a relatively decent history; Andrew Arato and Jean Cohen, *Civil Society and Political Theory* (Cambridge, MA: MIT Press, 1992) for a far more intimidating one; and Adam Seligman, *The Idea of Civil Society* (New York: Free Press, 1992), for a very nice, brief, occasionally obscure, but probably the best, account of the concept and its problems.

[19]Thanks to Krishan Kumar and Colin Bird for discussions on the concept of civil society. Seligman, *The Idea of Civil Society*, notes the concept's essential localness and ironic belatedness (168-9, 179, 184-88). Michael Walzer argues that "civil society" talk is a liberal corrective to communitarian-republican, socialist, libertarian capitalist, and nationalist accounts of political life (in "The Idea of Civil Society: A Path to Social Reconstruction," 123-43 in Dionne, *Community Works*).

[20]Mouffe, *The Democratic Paradox*, 14, 29, see 31; she launches the same complaint against so-called "deliberative democrats," who (she thinks) destroy real pluralism—Mouffe, 46-9, 55, 81-2, 91-2

[21]As Chantal Mouffe puts it: "Breaking with the symbolic representation of society as an organic body...a democratic society acknowledges the pluralism of values, the 'disenchantment of the world' diagnosed by Max Weber and the unavoidable conflicts that it entails" (in her *The Democratic Paradox* (New York: Verso, 2000), 103).

[22]Stanley Fish, *The Trouble with Principle* (Harvard University Press, 1999), 12. See Mouffe, *The Democratic Paradox*, e.g., 107 n. 31, against those who would "leave open the possibility that the political could under certain conditions be made absolutely congruent with the ethical, optimism which I do not share."

[23]Fish, *The Trouble with Principle*, 223.

[24]Mouffe, *The Democratic Paradox*, 10, 32, 113. Mouffe also thinks that modern "liberal democracies" contain conceptual tensions between "liberalism" and "democracy," especially in their conceptions of equality, which retain an "irreducible alterity" (p. 32); we need to resist "any attempts at closure" (33), because, when articulated together, they usefully challenge pretensions of either singularity. For theoretical support, she also appeals to the thought of Jacques Derrida (12, 21, 33-4, 135) and René Girard on violence (131). On the "social imaginary," see Cornelius Castoriadis, *The Imaginary Institution of Society* (Cambridge, MA: MIT Press, 1987), esp.131. For a similar analytic approach, see Fred D'Agostino, *Free Public Reason: Making It Up As We Go* (New York: Oxford University Press, 1996).

[25]Mouffe, *The Democratic Paradox*, 101-2.

[26]Mouffe, *The Democratic Paradox*, 129-40.

[27]Mark Edmundson, in his *Nightmare on Main Street: Angels, Sadomasochism, and the Culture of Gothic* (Cambridge MA: Harvard University Press, 1997), argues that contemporary "critical theory" operates within an essentially "gothic" understanding of power (see pp. 40ff.). For supporting views see Tobin Siebers, *Cold War Criticism and the Politics of Skepticism* (New York: Oxford University Press, 1993), esp. 68-70, and Jeffrey Isaac, *Democracy in Dark Times* (Ithaca: Cornell University Press, 1997), esp. 41-58.

[28]Fish, *The Trouble with Principle*, 233.

[29]Fish, *The Trouble with Principle*, 235.

[30]Fish, *The Trouble with Principle*, 237.

[31]Fish, *The Trouble with Principle*, 239.

[32]Fish, *The Trouble with Principle*, 239. Note the similarities with Michael Sandel's critique of John Rawls's anthropology in *Liberalism and the Limits of Justice*, 154-65.

[33]See Marcel Lieberman, *Commitment, Value, and Moral Realism* (New York: Cambridge University Press, 1998), Harry Frankfurt, *The importance of what we care about: Philosophical Essays* (New York: Cambridge University Press, 1988). See also Albert O. Hirschman, *The Passions and the Interests: Political Arguments for Capitalism Before its Triumph* (Princeton: Princeton University Press, 1977); this is where the Enlightenment's turn to cool "interests" as opposed to more volatile "passions" may have deleterious consequences. One of the advantages of my proposed Augustinian-Christian account is that its psychology is built around the concept of love, and the language of love seems more amenable to development over time; while one

can change one's interests (presumably by rejecting them for some others), it sounds strained to say that the "interests" themselves can change.

³⁴Tyler Cowen, in *What Price Fame?* (Cambridge, MA: Harvard University Press, 2000) suggests an interesting critique of the "liberalism of fear" from an economic standpoint. He argues that an excessive attention to the role of fear in establishing civic order makes it difficult for us to appreciate the equally primordial desire for fame, honor, and glory. His example is Hobbes (*What Price Fame?*, 169-70), but it seems to me that the concern is more general. In contrast, Augustine's work readily accommodates our desire for fame, and all the other symptoms of our ever-expansionist self-love.

³⁵Note that the agonists separate what Mouffe calls "the political" and "the ethical" in a way that echoes the received liberalism's disjunction between "the right" and "the good".

³⁶The complexities of this approach to violence are often overlooked, but can be glimpsed by looking at Augustine's understanding and justification of coercion. It is now recognized that Augustine was unique in offering a justification of violence and coercion in his time (see John Bowlin, "Augustine on Justifying Coercion" in *Annual of the Society of Christian Ethics* 17 (1997): 49-70). What is less well known is that the character of his justification was not at all theological or, more specifically, evangelical; he never thought souls could be won for Christ by the edge of the sword. On his understanding, coercion was, rather, an essentially *political* act, one expressly concerned with the stability of the civic order. It took the form of religious coercion (and forced conversion) only because it responded to the danger presented by people who understood their religious identities to be necessarily and violently opposed to that order. In Augustine's world, it was the Donatists who offered an explicitly *religious* warrant for violence (or engaged in religiously motivated violence without condemnation by their leaders). Augustine's justification of the necessity of force was made wholly on non-ecclesial civic grounds; he wanted them "converted"—which meant forced to publicly repent their views, as they disparaged the "Catholics" for having done in the past—in the hope that such experiences would undercut the righteous zeal fueling their violence. (See Neal Wood, *"Populares* and *circumcelliones*: The vocabulary of "Fallen Man" in Cicero and St. Augustine" in *History of Political Thought* VII (1986): 33-51, esp. 46-48.)

³⁷See, e.g., Eusebius's *Life of Constantine*, introduction, translation, and commentary by Averil Cameron and Stuart G. Hall. (Oxford: Clarendon Press, 1999), and his *In praise of Constantine: a historical study and new translation of Eusebius' Tricennial orations*, by H. A. Drake. (Berkeley: University of California Press, 1976).

³⁸See, e.g., *City of God* XX.2. For a modern take on this, Lincoln's "Second Inaugural Address" is perhaps the best. See also Reinhold Niebuhr, *The Irony of American History* (New York: Charles Scribner's Sons, 1962).

³⁹See Harrison, *Augustine: Christian Truth and Fractured Humanity* (New York: Oxford University Press, 2000), 97. This theme of course predates Augustine; see Hans Dieter Betz, "The Human Being in the Antagonisms of Life according to the Apostle Paul," in *The Journal of Religion* 80:4 (October 2000): 557-576.

⁴⁰ I think this eschatological imagination can identify the essential continuity of apocalyptic longings and utopian fantasies, as equally impatient desires to bring the kingdom of heaven to earth on our own terms. Hence there is an interesting debate to be had with various liberationist theology perspectives, including European liberationists such as Metz and Moltmann; but I cannot engage in that debate here. For two earlier and still potent Niebuhrian critiques of such liberationists, see Langdon Gilkey, "Reinhold Niebuhr's Theology of History," in Nathan A. Scott, Jr., ed., *The Legacy of Reinhold Niebuhr*. (Chicago: The University of Chicago Press, 1975), 36-62 and Dennis McCann, *Christian Realism and Liberation Theology: Practical Theologies in Creative Conflict* (Maryknoll: Orbis Books, 1981).

⁴¹For more on play, see Johan Huizinga, *Homo Ludens: A Study of the Play-Element in Culture* (Boston: Beacon Press, 1955), and Hugo Rahner, *Man At Play* (New York: Herder and Herder, 1972). The exploration of a disposition of play is a task for another essay. My sense is that it would combine both the responsibility ethics of H. Richard Niebuhr and William Schweiker, and the hermeneutical theory of Hans-Georg Gadamer (a task already begun in

Schweiker, *Responsibility and Christian Ethics* (New York: Cambridge University Press, 1995)).

[42]It is important to recognize that the agonists' primary strategy in response to this claim—the insistence that such a position annihilates the real "political" character of politics—is, by their own lights, a contestable political argument; it cannot be a dogmatic claim, for they have ruled any dogmatic claims out, and such a statement would be simply the implicit re-imposition of illegitimate discourse rules, of exactly the sort that agonists excoriate liberals for imposing.

[43]"Politics and the Soul: A Reading of *The City of God*," *Milltown Studies* 19/20 (1987): 55-92; at 67. See also Oliver O'Donovan, "Augustine's *City of God* XIX and Western Political Thought," in *Dionysius* XI (December 1987): 89-110. Note that this does not mean taking on Augustine whole-heartedly; as Williams himself says, "the most disturbing and uncongenial feature of this analysis for most modern students is probably the absence of any idea that the actual *structures* of government and society are answerable to some critical principle." (67).

[44]For an early attempt by a traditional intellectual to work out the implications of this, see Adam Michnik, *The Church and the Left*, trans. David Ost (Chicago: The University of Chicago Press, 1993). It remains a relevant book in part because, sadly enough, there are few other works similar to it.

[45]As I have argued elsewhere; see my "Pluralism, Otherness, and the Augustinian Tradition," in *Modern Theology* 14:1 (January 1998): 83-112.

[46]Any ecclesiology I would deploy would be done in thick conversation with William Cavanaugh's *Torture and Eucharist* (Cambridge MA: Blackwell, 1998), and Kenneth P. Serbin, *Secret Dialogues: Church-state relations, torture, and social justice in authoritarian Brazil* (Pittsburgh: University of Pittsburgh Press, 2000).

[47]As is argued by the forthcoming book *Quietly Influential: The Public Role of Mainline Protestantism*, ed. Robert Wuthnow and John H. Evans (Berkeley: University of California Press, 2002).

[48]*Reinhold Niebuhr Today*, ed. and with a foreword by Richard John Neuhaus (Grand Rapids, MI: William B. Eerdmans, 1989). Lovin's comments are on page 127, Hauerwas's on page 129.

[49]Joseph Turow, *Breaking Up America: Advertisers and the New Media World* (Chicago: The University of Chicago Press, 1997). See also Cass Sunstein, *republic.com* (Princeton: Princeton University Press, 2001), on the very real dangers of a loss of exposure to others in contemporary American society, and the damage that would do to civil society.

[50]This entails a certain populism, a subdued resistance to the typical intellectual bemoaning of the loss of "public intellectuals" as a specific class of people. The problem with most political thought is not with the lack of "intellectuals," but with the absence of a "public," or any sense of obligation to be open to public engagement. This is a common charge leveled against "deliberative democrats," but is a more general problem. For a good investigation of the paradoxes attendant upon the fact that putatively "democratic" theory is conducted by academics working at an essentially elitist level, see Christopher Bertram, "Political Justification, Theoretical Complexity, and Democratic Community," in *Ethics* 107:4 (July 1997): 563-583.

[51]Ellen Charry, *By the Renewing of Your Minds: The Pastoral Roots of Christian Doctrine* (New York: Oxford University Press, 1997).

[52]The crucial intellectual figure in this revolution is Augustine; see Neil Forsyth, *The Old Enemy: Satan and the Combat Myth* (Princeton: Princeton University Press, 1987), and my own *Evil and the Augustinian Tradition* (Cambridge: Cambridge University Press, 2001).

Response to Panel Papers

Jean Bethke Elshtain

Each of these essays is provocative and powerful in its own right; together, they give one a keen sense of hopefulness about the future of theologically grounded Christian ethics. Each paper responds to powerful, contemporary challenges and does so in a way that takes no easy route to enlightenment: no cheap theoretical grace here. As one whose primary formation was in Western political theory, I especially appreciate the engagement with current political and theoretical battles in the field of political and social theory. My one regret is that, given the interdisciplinary boundaries we all labor under, fewer of my colleagues in the world of political and social theory will read these papers than ideally ought to read them as each adds much to debates that have grown a bit stale within the confines of political science. The strategy I have pursued for this response consists in elaborating on a few questions—and they *are* questions and not simply rhetorical devices of the sort used by panel chairs to get the conversational ball rolling.

First, to John Bowlin's witty essay. Bowlin is no doubt correct that in a rush to baptize all local efforts that generate what social and political analysts indebted to economic theory call "social capital," insufficient attention has been paid to what I would call the normative dimensions of such efforts. One can certainly observe in action, as Bowlin did with his Geertzian trip to the gamecock clubs, an intermediate association in full flower with its self-ruling norms, its keen sense of perpetuating itself over time, its generation of friendship and solidarity. But does that suffice to make it a "seedbed of citizenship if ever there was one?" Not in my book. And not according to many social and political theorists who find somewhat wanting, or "thin," the accounts of the building of social capital indebted primarily to Harvard political scientist Robert Putnam and his famous

Bowling Alone. The problem, for many of us, begins right at the beginning with the locution "social capital" itself for that is held to be a neutral category, one that "secretes" (as Charles Taylor might put it) no normative dimensions. But to think in terms of "social capital" rather than, say, civic commitment or a civic conscience or a commitment to a common good that takes us outside the boundaries of our particular and immediate commitments to family, friends, and yes, gamecock clubs, is to narrow the horizon of civic life before one even starts. The moral ambiguity of which Bowlin writes seems to me a fact of life. But not all associations are morally ambiguous in the same way. One needs a way of sorting out and evaluating associations using criteria that include but go beyond the "social capital" dimension. Bowlin resists the notion that a real fleshing out of his argument means necessarily to bring in some consideration of explicit anthropological presuppositions. To coin a phrase: *who are we?* This is a question that partakes of certainly fundamental facts about human beings as creatures and, at the same time, gestures toward aspirations. It isn't clear to me how Bowlin can evoke Aquinas as clearly and deftly as he does, and yet try to avoid the anthropological question at the same time. There is one other important matter in Bowlin's fine paper that I cannot here touch on given space constraints but that requires more acute, critical attention, namely, whether churches have largely "lost their religious function with respect to the political order." It is not clear to me why seeing churches as abiding in that realm we call "civil society," not being creatures of the state, means that one is perforce required to "deny that the prayers and devotions of the churches fulfill a religious function for a society other than themselves." Why must this latter follow from the former?

William Cavanaugh's paper is challenging as a reminder of the ambiguity of the very concept of civil society depending, in part, on whether one is approaching matters from a Hegelian or Tocquevillian direction. That is for starters. (I should note that Cavanaugh does not reference Tocqueville, but it is the Tocquevillian understanding of association life that prevailed in America, not the more elaborated Hegelian schema that culminates, as we all know, in an overarching *Kriegstaat* that serves a potent synthetic political and ethical function.) Instead, he contrasts the activist-populism he associates with community organizers and thinkers along the lines of Harry Boyte and the precise attunement to the rhetoric of public life he ties to John Courtney Murray. Cavanaugh rather likes the Boyte "empowerment" route but finds problems in this attempt to "give the church a significant public presence." This problem links both the "Murrayites and Boyte," insofar as both are too naïve in seeing civil society as an "essentially free space outside the coercive reach of the state." Not so, argues Cavanaugh: power oozes and courses through the system and flows not only from civil society to state but from state down, so to speak.

It is hard to take exception to this observation. I am less clear about the upshot or meaning of the observation, however. I don't think the Foucault turn is particularly helpful: Foucault's dark utopia of immanent power lost its shock value and power to persuade some time ago as more nuanced histories and works in social theory emerged. *Pace* Foucault, self discipline has always been a norm of one sort or another, whether one is speaking of early Christian martyrs, or even earlier Roman gladiators, or any other category of person at any time. Cavanaugh is rightly worried about the "price of admission" to contemporary civil society grounded citizenship. Self-discipline does not provide that entree. But—and he hits this theme in the last fourth of his essay—the anthropological presuppositions do. What sort of self is being disciplined to or toward what ends? Indeed it is the case that Christian anthropology does not comport very well with the sorts of selves we are bidden to be in order to be "productive" members of a consumerist society. Here playing even a complex "identity" card isn't going to help very much as the issue is not just about capacious listening to all sorts of voices but strict if sympathetic (at least most of the time) evaluation of what these diverse voices represent by way of an anthropology: what sorts of people and to what ends?

Finally, to Charles Mathewes and his energetically thrown gauntlet that endorses simultaneously agonism and a politics based on love or loves. There is so much that is interesting going on in Mathewes' paper that I will only hit a few highlights, each of which warrants a more substantive discussion. I am sympathetic overall to his critique of philosophical liberalism and to his claim that the rules of engagement afforded within that framework, insofar as these are applied to religious communities and commitments, has the clear intent of "privatizing" such communities and commitments: hence Locke's strict division between statescraft as public and civic; soulcraft as private and quite uncivic. (Not uncivil but just as having no civic role of importance, at least not one that is legitimate.) In practice, of course, no liberal society looks like liberal political philosophy—whether Lockean or Rawlsian—but that is another story. The theory certainly pushes the direction Mathewes suggests, although the fact that liberalism is an "essentially contested concept" (W. B. Gallie's term) is not itself a problem at all as all great political terms are thus contested. A good bit of politics derives from ironing out such contested meanings and their implications. (As a kind of footnote: It is not at all the case that most historians working on the seventeenth century are now committed to the view that the rise of the centralized state, not inter-religious violence, is the source of political intolerance: no such operating consensus has emerged. But the challenge has been mounted quite vigorously. Moreover, to criticize liberals for bombing those with "thick identities" even as one speaks of the "balkanization of tribalism," is to take away what one has just given. It is precisely the language of "balkanization" and "tribalism" that evokes the intolerant response Mathewes credits to liberalism.)

How much help is the agonistic alternative to philosophical liberalism? Not very when you get down to brass tacks and Mathewes credits the agonists more than I would. A problem is that many write as if they have suddenly awakened to discover . . . *conflict*—and this is shocking news. It is not shocking at all to those of us who study history and who are aware of human sin and evil. This is a wakeup call only for those who were first lulled to sleep by consensus theory or some such. The unbridgeable gulf between agonists and Christian thinkers lies in the ontology of violence and coercion such agonists presume: Hobbes and Jesus of Nazareth cannot both be right. The kind of conflict Hobbes presupposes is conflict-unto-death or unto-submission-to-the-leviathan. The kind of conflict Christians presuppose derives from an awareness of human brokenness and weakness, the wrenchings and cruelties of sin, without abandoning the ground of hope and the prayerful recognition of grace. Many agonists also play tricks with the category "the natural." To say that human society is in some sense an artifact is to belabor the obvious. To go on to claim, boldly, that this artifact does not derive from "inevitable natural structures" is to belabor the even more obvious. But it does not follow from either of these claims that there is no such thing as "nature" or "the natural": that there is, in fact, no *there there*. No one working with a doctrine of Creation can credit that. I dare say, no one who has observed closely a newborn infant can credit that. The question is how this nature is to be understood and whether or not nature or the natural can serve as guides or assessments of any kind. But Mathewes, in any case, would take us "beyond agonism" and to what? To a politics of loves. He cites Stanley Fish's appraisal of certain thinkers with favor, namely, that they are "moved more by what they fear than by what they desire." But surely any *responsible* political thinker and actor is going to have to be moved in part by fear, aware as he or she surely is of the darkness attendant upon the human heart and human society. To desire peace is at the same time to fear war: how can one separate these? The challenge that confronts Mathewes, surely, is to offer up a robust defense of what a politics that involves a struggle over loves would look like in practice if it is not to become a struggle unto death. What institutional forms and structures would help to form such a politics? What rules of engagement would perforce enable and contain such a politics at one and the same time? Add to this the obligation to evaluate contrasting and competing loves, as one cannot simply endorse uncritically whatever it is a person or group claims to love given how easy it is for loves to be false and distorted, and Mathewes has his work cut out for him.

Once again, it was a pleasure to read and to respond to these challenging papers.

Augustine and Arendt on Love:
New Dimensions in the Religion and Liberalism Debates

Eric Gregory

Abstract

This paper illustrates the need for a more integrated theoretical account of two large but typically isolated subjects in twentieth century Augustine studies: love and the ambiguous relation of Augustinianism to liberalism. The paper is divided into three parts. First, by aligning Augustinian *caritas* with a feminist "ethic of care," it presents a morally robust ethics of liberalism that differs from both liberal-realist and antiliberal extrapolations of the Augustinian tradition. Second, and most extensively, it presents Hannah Arendt's provocative reading of Augustine that issues both "Kantian" and "Nietzschean" challenges to a political ethic that moves beyond liberal reciprocity and relates love for neighbor to love for God. Finally, and more tentatively, it argues that Augustine's much maligned categories of "use" and "enjoyment" should be redeemed by those who defend a version of Augustinian liberalism that does not sentimentalize or privatize love.

Introduction

The recent publication of the first English annotated edition of Hannah Arendt's 1929 dissertation, *Der Liebesbegriff bei Augustin*, signals emerging interest in what her translators call "the Augustinian root of Arendt's critique of modernity."[1] While Arendt scholars debate the influence of Augustine in Arendt's writings, this neglected text in both Augustine and Arendt studies does raise a promising but troubled site for political Augustinianism: the difficult conceptual relation between love for God and love for neighbor. My interest in Arendt stems both from her dissertation, which interestingly predates Anders Nygren's more influential *Agape and Eros*, and her representatively liberal analysis of the relation of love to politics in later works.[2]

The central claim of the paper is that two large but typically isolated subjects in twentieth century Augustine studies—love and the ambiguous relation of Augustinianism to liberalism—require a more integrated theoretical account. The segregation of these two fields of inquiry both misinterprets Augustine and limits the capacity of extending the Augustinian tradition in light of the need to promote a richer understanding of citizenship in a liberal democracy. Arendt's dissertation issues a provocative challenge to the tradition's capacity to offer this integrated account. While I do sketch what such an account might look like in the context of a "morally robust" Augustinian liberalism, the paper primarily exposes the need for the account. In addition to responding to Arendt, the inadequacies of traditional liberal interpretations of Augustinianism and the dramatic under-theorizing of love in liberalism also motivate my interest in this account. The paper argues for an alliance between Augustinianism and feminist moral and political thought that resists the subordination of love in the ethics of liberal citizenship.[3]

On its own terms, such an account is justified by the significance of love as both the form of goodness in Augustine's ethics and as constitutive of what it means to be human in his anthropology. One could relate this account of love to the extended debates about the right and the good in political theory and the contested status of politics as "natural" in political theology. But this paper aims primarily to promote love as a political virtue that is rejected or only weakly valued in both the ethics of liberalism and political Augustinianism.

The success of Augustinian realism has eclipsed analytic attention to the phenomenology of loving others in relation to the love of God as basic to Augustine's motivational structure of agency and action. Approaches to Augustinian political ethics rarely display more than the requisite gesture to love itself before turning to the sinful persistence of self-love, the complex relation of neighbor-love to "politically relevant" themes of justice and freedom, or the prominent two cities formulation that itself trades on the opposition of the love of self and the love of God. This neglect of love parallels or, more cynically, imitates the conceptual fate of love in modern political theory. It also perpetuates premature interpretations of Augustinianism that align a desacralization of politics with the developed arts of suspicion about the aspirations of virtue that currently dominate liberal thinking about morality and politics.

Dissents from liberal readings of Augustinianism combine with increasingly diverse kinds of liberalisms in ways that also warrant this revisionist account of

Augustinian liberalism. Since ideas about love reveal a host of broader theological and philosophical commitments that tend to be sublimated in Christian social ethics, bringing together these two aspects of Augustinian interpretation yields a more coherent extension of this formative tradition. Conventional readings of political Augustinianism tend to rely on scattered proof texts related to Augustine's two cities imagery or his polemical treatment of virtue in classical philosophy. Focusing on Augustine on love elevates a core aspect of his theology and broadens the terms on which Augustinianism might engage contemporary political theory and its renewed interest in virtue and the ethics of citizenship.[4] Moreover, since love is both a metaphysical and psychological category for Augustine, attending to love helps broaden the narrowness of liberal pre-occupations with the appropriate sorts of epistemic restraint placed upon the moral citizen subscribing to "public reason."[5]

In rethinking love as a *public* virtue in need of *political* affirmation, Augustinians have good reasons to support developments in feminist political theory that draw from Carol Gilligan's seminal work on an "ethic of care."[6] For many feminists, the subordination of love as an aspect of moral motivation (especially among neo-Kantian and pragmatic liberals) is part of an unwarranted larger pattern of domesticating and marginalizing various practices and relations that rely on an ethic of care. These critics show that works of love, like many other goods in liberal theory, are presupposed but not affirmed in the ethics of liberalism. Increasingly, this aversion to thinking about love is linked to a general philosophical neglect of the extent to which human beings are both vulnerable and dependent.[7] Liberal theorizing, following this argument, starts off on the wrong foot by positing the desiring individual as the erotic problem of politics. This anthropological starting point leads to a conception of love as a politically irrelevant, even dangerous, virtue.

Many feminists, however, are rightly skeptical of communitarian alternatives and have tried to accommodate an ethic of care within liberalism.[8] In religious ethics, Timothy P. Jackson in his various writings on love and liberalism helpfully highlights the significance of love for Christian social theory and its putative relation to liberalism.[9] His chastened account of civic virtue demonstrates that incorporating love into a liberal framework does not commit one to sentimentalism or political romanticism. By connecting Augustinianism with these projects, my aim is not to bring Augustine into an emancipatory feminist model, but to appeal to these developments as constructive efforts in the ethics of liberal citizenship that do not privatize love.

The aversion to theorizing love in relation to the political is limiting for both Augustinians and liberals in their ethical proposals for the self-images of citizens in a liberal society. Apart from Jackson's strong thesis about the "morally brutalizing and practically self-defeating" hostility of Rawlsian liberalism toward the value of love, the monolithic treatments of love in modern political philosophy perpetuate a narrow preoccupation with the conative and altruistic dimensions of love.[10] They enforce stereotypical notions that love is a blindly possessive desire not analyzable within the terms of either morality or politics. This tendency to reduce love either to moralistic notions of benevolence or to irrational feeling is equally a danger for advocates of the ethic of care. Pursuing connections between love and political Augustinianism illuminates, then, not only the tradition itself but raises new dimensions for any alignment of Augustinianism with modern political traditions like liberalism.

The paper is divided into three parts. First, I situate the paper in terms of a morally robust version of Augustinian liberalism which differs from dominant liberal-realist or antiliberal extrapolations of the tradition. I focus the specific interests of the paper in terms of an ethics of citizenship which seeks something other than mere liberal reciprocity as a motivational ideal. Second, and most extensively, I identify two distinctive challenges to an Augustinian ethics of liberal citizenship that highlights the perspective of love. These challenges issue from 1) Arendt's "Kantian" rejection of love and espousal of "respect" as the more relevant political virtue of a liberal society and 2) her "Nietzschean" rejection of eudaimonism that challenges Augustine's particular account of loving others in relation to the love for God. Finally, and more tentatively, I argue that Augustine's much maligned categories of "use" and "enjoyment" should be redeemed by those who defend a version of Augustinian liberalism that does not sentimentalize, privatize or marginalize love.

Love, Liberalism, and Political Augustinianism

Augustinian dispositions toward politics often make common cause with repudiations of "thick" accounts of civic virtue and "perfectionist" efforts to justify a broad range of goods in the domain of the political. It was Augustine who famously polemicized against the prideful vanities of Roman civic culture, poking fun at its impotent yet violent efforts to secure a false virtue.[11] This unmasking of Rome and pagan moral culture often is taken to anticipate modern (and now postmodern) suspicions about politics and virtue. Augustine, so to speak, was an early voice in exposing the illusions of consoling metanarratives and their techniques of domination.[12] It was also Augustine who canonized a doctrine of the "two cities" whose imagery of exile and pilgrimage proved to be a decisive break from the variants of Eusebian imperial theology that arose in the wake of the Constantinian settlement. This "two cities" formulation was not only formative throughout the period of Christendom but continues to hold sway in many Christian defenses of liberalism.[13] Augustine's separation of earthly politics from the economy of salvation—coupled with a radically ambiguous vision of history and the hiddenness of divine providence—often are taken to anticipate both later formulas of a separation of "church" and "state" and a realist approach to the possibilities of politics. These much remarked upon aspects of Augustine's thought figure prominently in political extensions of both academic and folk Augustinianism.

Despite his many critics, R. A. Markus' interpretation of these well-known characterizations is representative of their liberal (and, typically, liberal-realist) appropriation.[14] For Markus, the great achievement of Augustine's image of the *civitas peregrina* is the restriction of political concern to the mundane yet precarious task of securing, as Augustine famously puts it, "things relevant to this mortal life."[15] Two passages from Markus capture the allure of this point of view for a pluralist society:

> In Augustine's mature thought there is no trace of a theory of the state as concerned with man's self-fulfilment, perfection, the good life, felicity, or with "educating" man towards such purposes. Its function is more restricted: it is to cancel out at least some of the effects of sin...All the institutions of political and judicial authority, with their coercive machinery, serve this purpose . . . to secure the space for the free exercise of virtue in a society racked by the insecurity which is woven into the very texture of human existence.[16]

> Augustine's attack on the "sacral" conception of the Empire liberated the Roman state, and by implication, all politics, from the direct hegemony of the sacred. Society became intrinsically "secular" in the sense that it is not committed to any particular ultimate loyalty. It is the sphere in which different individuals with different beliefs and loyalties pursue their common objectives in so far as they coincide. His "secularisation" of the realm of politics implies a pluralistic, religiously neutral civil community . . . Augustinian theology should at least undermine Christian opposition to an open, pluralist, secular society.[17]

These passages reflect an influential view from a prominent Augustine scholar that is echoed throughout the textbooks of political theory. Alongside Reinhold Niebuhr's more popular writings, they have generally secured the classification of Augustine as a proto-liberal—wary of virtue and progressive utopianism in a political society. I begin with Markus, however, for what he does *not* say about Augustinianism and the ethics of liberal citizenship.

Augustinianism, while not offering a political theory as such, is rightly seen as supporting liberalism in deflating the pretensions of politics, diminishing expectations of political authority in relation to civil society, and promoting important distinctions between the economy of salvation and the legitimate boundaries of state concern. Augustinian dispositions, to be sure, issue from a very different narrative about the world than many contemporary liberal accounts. Indeed, Augustine often is vilified as the source of many philosophical and cultural maladies that we struggle to overcome. But Augustinian dispositions do share a tendency to highlight the limits of politics, the need to restrain evil through the rule of law, and suggest a more palliative approach to the various ills and pathologies that beset political society. This tendency contrasts with an emphasis on the creative possibilities of politics, the active cultivation of goodness, and a more transformative political assault on social injustice. Liberals and Augustinians rightly emphasize the tragic persistence of conflict, the frustrations that haunt even our best moral efforts, the value of stability (or "earthly peace"), and the perennial danger of totalitarianism (or "idolatry"). These background characterizations play an important role in Augustinian liberalism—particularly in terms of the appropriate differentiation of political and social identity, and the emphasis on ways in which disordered passions perpetually obstruct justice and the stability of the regime.

While sympathetic with these emphases and the descriptive power of observations about politics that claim Augustinian influence, such as those mediated by Markus and Niebuhr, I believe they have overwhelmed the theoretical significance of love for retrievals of Augustinianism for politics. Augustinianism appears most strained when it is translated into contemporary liberalism on its own terms—whether as warrant for a general philosophical justification of neutrality, a theological validation of the exclusion of religious motivation from political ethics, or a commitment to public/private distinctions that condemn love to the cloisters of domesticity. It was Augustine (after all) who, in addition to his subversive reading of Roman virtue and powerful articulation of the "two cities," was responsible for placing the twofold love commands at the heart of Christian moral and social reflection. Christ commanded the love of God and the love of neighbor as the sum of the law, but Augustine was the first to theorize the implications of this centrality of the doubleness of love for rational and affective creatures capable of community. This aspect of Augustine's theology is obscured by exclusive political attention to his doctrine of sin or relatively anachronistic notions of a theory of the state in Augustine.

The theocentric understanding of love that governs the Augustinian tradition, however, complicates the affinity with contemporary proposals for a liberal "ethics of care." It has been the source of deep criticism in both philosophical and theological ethics. These criticisms center on the supposed failure of Augustinian piety to correlate non-competitively the "horizontal" and "vertical" dimensions of love in a common life with others.[18] In particular, Augustine's early and undeveloped effort at relating the two love commands in terms of a distinction between "using" one's neighbors and "enjoying" God has come under sustained assault. As Oliver O'Donovan puts it, "this is one of those rare opinions in the history of thought which have had a more conspicuous influence through being rejected than through being held."[19] Apart from this particular construal of religious devotion, Augustine's whole formulation of "ordered love" has more recently been identified as the root of the authoritarian antiliberalism that puts the lie to any notion of "Augustinian liberalism."[20] Ironically, these criticisms suggest that Augustinian ethics is either too preoccupied with goodness or too preoccupied with evil to be of use for liberal politics. Caught between good and evil, Augustinianism yields a schizophrenic political morality that seems to apply to any theocentric social ethics that would relate love for others with love for God. For these critics, Augustine's ambiguous attitude toward any temporal project at best renders political action radically indeterminate and sponsors indifference and ascetic inwardness (in the deceptive guise of love for God as the *summum bonum*). At worst, it promotes the violent legitimation of coercion and undermines the central value of autonomy in liberalism (in the manipulative guise of love for neighbor). The "pastoral" endorsement of religious persecution is seen as the inexorable development of the Augustinian logic of love.[21]

Much of contemporary theology, whether explicitly or implicitly, seeks to interrupt this ostensible tournament of loves by imagining alternate ways of coordinating or even identifying the love of God and the love of neighbor. For instance, one thinks of Karl Rahner's non-univocal identification of love of God and love of neighbor, liberationist readings of Matthew 25 that equate love of the oppressed with love of God, and more recently appeals to Emmanuel Levinas that link the two love commands in a post-metaphysical vision of drawing near to God through the face of the other.[22] In Augustine studies, this more sacramental direction toward an *una caritas* can be found in the exegetical work of Raymond Canning and Tarcisius von Bavel.[23] Indeed, for Canning's Augustine, "turning to the neighbor forms such an integral part of human turning to God that the latter may be defined by it."[24] At the end of this paper, I return to this re-reading of Augustine, but at this point set it against one of his more curious political readers.

Arendt's "Kantian" Challenge

At the heart of Hannah Arendt's thought is a defense of the freedom of political action from both ancient and modern depoliticizing subordinations of the world. In a kind of inverted Augustinianism, the structure of Arendt's thought is governed by the theme of "love for the world."[25] Yet, the "love" for the world relevant to Arendt's vision of citizenship is a particular notion of love—one drained of piety, personality, and affectivity so as to be suitable for the political world of action and appearance. For Arendt, unlike the worldly *eros* of the Greeks and the Renaissance humanists or the Kantian notion of respect, true Christian love—like the European revolutionary spirit or the strict conscience of a Thoreau or Socrates—is worldless. It can not withstand liberal politics because it is wedded to what she calls the "activity of goodness."[26] Christian love, in particular, is too concerned with the integrity of the self and responsibility for the neighbor.[27] It is too demanding, too intimate, and ultimately too dangerous for liberal politics.

Arendt's rejection of love runs throughout her writings. In a revealing passage from *The Human Condition*, she writes:

> love, for reasons of its passion, destroys the in-between which relates us to and separates us from others...love by its very nature is unworldly, and it is for this reason rather than its rarity that it is not only apolitical but antipolitical, perhaps the most powerful of all antipolitical forces.[28]

Love, like pity, is an emotion that overwhelms and corrupts politics—which for Arendt, by its very freedom from the self-absorbed need for moral authenticity, is the only redemptive sphere of human striving.[29] Love may be a moral virtue for the sentimental soul or the romantic embrace, but it is a political vice. In fact, love as the spring of political virtue is the source of cruelty itself. Jesus, according to Arendt, recognized the dangers of the publicity of love when he counseled his followers to "let not thy left hand know what thy right hand doeth" (Matthew 6:3).[30] Public love too often becomes the intense, violent destroyer of freedom, as Arendt sees in figures like Robespierre, Saint-Just, and Melville's Billy Budd. "Because of its inherent worldlessness," Arendt warns, "love can only become false and perverted when it is used for political purposes."[31] For Arendt, love needs to be kept in check, while "respect" is to govern the sphere of politics. She writes:

> Yet what love is in its own, narrowly circumscribed sphere, respect is in the larger domain of human affairs. Respect, not unlike the Aristotelian *philia politike*, is a kind of "friendship" without intimacy and without closeness; it is a regard for the person from the distance which the space of the world puts between us.[32]

Rather than imagining respect as an appropriate form of love in politics, Arendt consistently follows the liberal tradition in characterizing love as a passionate sentiment of intimacy and altruism.

This characterization of love reflects the Kantian account of "pathological" love as being at odds with respect.[33] As Kant strikingly puts it, "According to the principle of *mutual love* [persons] are directed constantly to approach one another; by the principle of *respect* which they owe one another they are directed to keep themselves at a distance."[34] Respect, universalized in the moral law and motivated by reverence for the ideal of the rational will, places constraints on intimacy. It privileges justice and autonomy against love and intimacy as the appropriate public goods of the "enlarged mentality" of political judgment. Love, on the other hand, is vulnerable and particular. It exposes us and draws us to others. As one author puts it, "love motivates a risky attunement to embodied particulars, whereas a Kantian respect maintains a safe distance."[35] As such, for those with liberal sensitivities, it threatens to make other's ends my own rather than simply treating them as ends and not using them as mere means.

Even John Rawls, who initially linked his difference principle with the virtue of fraternity and Christian neighbor-love, becomes uncharacteristically lyrical when he sounds this Kantian note.[36] Arendt would affirm Rawls when he writes:

> those who love one another or acquire strong attachments to persons and to forms of life, at the same time become liable to ruin: their love makes them hostages to misfortune and injustice of others...once we love we are vulnerable: there is no such thing as loving while being ready to consider whether to love, just like that. And the loves that hurt the least are not the best loves.[37]

Love, for modern liberals, is then a sensitivity that destabilizes politics. To say too much about love in a political context raises the pathological spectre of relentless altruism, dangerous sentimentalism, and paternalistic moralism. This caricature of love is why many liberals are willing to accept Hume's famous characterization of justice as a cautious, jealous virtue.[38] One wonders how love, if it is so dangerous and irrational on this account, ought not be banished from marriage and other social institutions as well—but for liberals even deeper problems attach themselves to Augustine's particular theocentric vision of love.

Arendt's "Nietzschean" Challenge

In 1929, at the age of twenty-three and after her studies with Heidegger, Hannah Arendt published her Heidelberg dissertation under the direction of Karl Jaspers. Throughout her dissertation, with echoes of Feuerbach and Luther, Arendt exploits what Kierkegaard called the "frightful collision" between the love of God and the love of neighbor.[39] The possibility of such a collision arises from the priority that the biblical tradition assigns to the love of God. The concrete encounter with the neighbor as neighbor is always mediated through the vertical relation to God. The essential argument of the dissertation relies on the familiar reading of the neo-Platonic structure of Augustine's thought in such a way that worldly loves are stripped of value.[40] Augustine's contrasting of *cupiditas* and *caritas* and *uti* and *frui* makes, as she strikingly puts it, "a desert out of this world" (18). Yet Arendt is fascinated by Augustine's struggle to find a place for neighbor-love in the context of the overwhelming desire for God in the tensed living between time and eternity. The question that guides her—"how the person in God's presence, isolated from all things mundane, can be at all interested in his neighbor"—expands throughout the dissertation into a discussion of the grounds for collective political action itself (7).

In the first part of the dissertation, Arendt puts forward her reading of the metaphysics of Augustine's eudaimonism. To love, Augustine learned from the Greeks, is a craving (*appetitus*), a motion of desire. Desire as craving, however, gives rise to a menacing fear of losing the good against our will. Love seeks the good, indeed the *summum bonum*, that casts out anxiety and fear; as Augustine puts it, "what you cannot lose against your will."[41] As such, it is the good that cannot be lost (even in death) that is most to be desired. What Augustine yearns for is that life where "our existence will have no death, our knowledge no error, our love no obstacle."[42]

The tragedy of the world quickly becomes apparent. Lovers sacrifice the true good and become lovers of the world, enslaved by the multitude of its false promises. Love that turns to the world, the wrong object, is *cupiditas*. In the end, slavery. Love that turns to eternity and "the absolute future," the right object, is *caritas*. In the end, freedom. Here, Arendt claims, is the force of Augustine's warning, "Love, but be careful what you love."[43]

All love remains a craving desire, a movement of the will from isolation to possession in happiness, from dispersion to recollection. Unlike the Stoics, Augustine cannot advocate the suppression of desire itself (even if right desire is not fixed upon things of this world). The problem for Augustine at this point, claims Arendt, is the very notion of love as desire and the demand to reconcile the "internal" motion of desire and the "external" object of the divine. How can this gap between lover and beloved be overcome? How can the highest good be both eternal and internal?

Arendt hints that Augustine tries to resolve the problem by imagining God's love as "circulating within us."[44] Perhaps, she rightly imagines, eternity functions differently for Augustine than Plotinus. In the *Confessions*, Augustine makes it clear that God is his helper, the guide of right self-love. It is this God that Augustine calls out "to gather [him] in from dispersion where [he] was torn asunder."[45] But the self that is to be loved, Arendt argues, remains the true self projected into the future that stands in relation to God in eternity. It is this self, the inner invisible self of the future, that belongs to the invisible God.

Love as desire, Arendt continues, lies at the root of Augustine's distinction between that which is to be enjoyed (*frui*) and loved for its own sake (*propter se ipsum*) and that which is to be used (*uti*) and loved for the sake of something else (*propter aliud*). Following a standard reading of Augustine, Arendt reasons, "if the object of desire is God, the world is related to God by using it. Since it is used, the world loses its independent meaningfulness and thus ceases to tempt man" (33). *Amor mundi*, so to speak, competes with *amor Dei* for attention and loses. The world, Arendt writes with telling pathos, "loses its awesome character" (34). Returning from the absolute future, everything in the world, including the self, is now a thing among things. Things are to be loved proportionately, in right order and proper measure, and under a mode of living marked only by hope and anticipation. This ordering, however, comes from the absolute future and is not given by an internal relation between God and the world. The command to "love thy neighbor" in this framework, Arendt argues, "appears like a *deus ex machina*" (39).

This dead-end is manifest in Augustine's tortured explanation of the command to "love thy enemies." He writes, "hence it comes to pass that we even love our enemies: for we do not fear them since they cannot snatch from us what we love."[46] On this account, love of enemies is not really love at all, but a fearless and abstract calm inspired by the objectivity of the highest good. The neighbor is relevant not in concrete reality but only as a possible companion or, more likely, a mutual help in the enjoyment of God.

In the second part of the essay, Arendt explores a different possibility for Augustine. In remembering the absolute past, the self can be guided not so much by a love of God of the future (*amor Dei*), but by a love of the love that God bestows in the past (*amor amoris Dei*). To remember this love, this past, is to "confess" it. This confession changes the mode of desire from craving to a different mode of creaturely dependence in recollection. To love rightly is, then, to return. Love as desire for the future, which was determined by the fear of death, is now reconfigured by remembrance and a "gratitude for life" (52). This divine memory allows Augustine to escape the dead-end of love as desire for the highest good, but it preserves the problem of loving in a world that is not representative of one's "true being" (57). Augustine remains a "question to himself" in such a way that he continues to "ask himself out of the world in his quest for 'true being'" (58). Just as the desire for the future yielded insecurity and love of the world, remembrance can become forgetfulness and yield the same insecurity and love of the world *as worldly*. In short, "the lover reaches beyond the beloved to God in whom alone both his existence and his love have meaning" (96). Love of neighbor remains merely an occasion to love God in the neighbor.

Can Augustine escape these two trains of thought that have left the neighbor irrelevant? Arendt turns briefly in the third part of her essay toward such a possibility. Perhaps it is in Adam, she muses, that Augustine locates the "foundation of a definite and obligatory equality among all people" (100). Equality in Adam creates a kinship among humanity, not in terms of traits or talents but "of situation" (100). All people stand before God as equally sinful, and this sinfulness "necessarily attaches to everyone" (102). Arendt paradoxically writes, "the human race as such originates in Adam and not in the Creator." (103).

An account of neighbor-love in this theological context is different than the lonely philosophical meditations of the individual concerned with Being. In Adam, the world becomes "familiar" (104). Love of neighbor can now be understood as an authentic feature of mutuality and shared nature. And, yet, this love is grounded not in shared dependence on the Creator but in common sinfulness and rebellion against the Creator. The equality of humanity is both concealed and revealed by sin.

This strange worldliness is overcome in Christ, the second Adam. But the possibility of grace in Christ means that the neighbor "appears either as one in whom God has already worked his grace . . . or . . . as one who is still entangled in sin" (106). The neighbor remains inscribed in their God-relatedness, which for

Arendt threatens to obscure their particularity. Indeed, for Arendt, to love the neighbor according to Augustine is finally "to bring one's neighbor to this explicitness of his own being, to 'carry him off to God' (*rapere ad Deum*)" (108).

Rather than securing the relevance of the neighbor *qua* neighbor, even the coming of God in Christ finally transfers attention away from the neighbor to God. Arendt writes, "When Augustine frequently quotes Paul's words that love never fails, he means solely the love of God, or Christ, for which all human neighborly love can only provide the impetus" (111). In a passage that resonates with Nygren, Arendt writes that for Augustine:

> I never love my neighbor for his own sake, only for the sake of divine grace. This indirectness, which is unique to love of neighbor, puts an even more radical stop to the self-evident living together in the earthly city. This indirectness turns my relation to my neighbor into a mere passage for the direct relation of God himself (111).[47]

The fellowship of saints, then, is a wandering collection of individuals—truly resident aliens—knit together by the indirect love of God as a defense against the world. One's true being is found only in relation to God, not in relation to other human beings.

Thomas Breidenthal helpfully summarizes this aspect of Arendt's reading of Augustine:

> For Arendt, Christianity's anti-politicality is one with its belief in the incarnation of God in Jesus. To state Arendt's view plainly: if God has become my neighbor, then love of God has outsmarted love of neighbor on its home turf. The claim of Jesus is greater than all other human claims...so to love him as neighbor is to be drawn away from all other human loves, except as they serve and repeat the love of Jesus.[48]

For Breidenthal, this reading turns the Incarnation on its head and misses the persistent Augustinian claim that the God who comes in the form of the servant Jesus seeks to interrupt this very tension between love for neighbor and love for God. Jesus is "the neighbor who directs us to other neighbors" and "the neighbor who is able to give us the means to address other neighbors out of abundance rather than out of lack."[49] Rather than either being morally paralyzed by the infinite claims of the neighbor or spiritually distracted by the jealous claims of God, the self is liberated by Jesus to genuinely love the neighbor. This resolution again recalls Rahnerian moves that imply the coincidence of love for God and love for neighbor in loving God by loving the neighbor.[50]

Love, "Use/Enjoyment," and the Ethics of Liberalism

There is much to criticize in Arendt's account. Like many other strong readings of a means/end subordinationist teleology in Augustine's ethics, she pays a costly analytic price for abstracting his account of love from his biblical exegesis and his more explicitly trinitarian moments. She pushes Augustine into false dichotomies that he and others who share his theological commitments might otherwise avoid. To be sure, Augustine's rhetoric, especially in polemical or homiletic settings, invites both the "Kantian" and "Nietzschean" criticisms. Given the pilgrimage imagery of the journey to our true homeland, the sense that the neighbor is merely a temporal vehicle for the individual's journey to eternal beatitude is particularly acute. This picture of love threatens the equal dignity of human beings that motivates liberal fears of paternalism because it assumes a love that loses sight of the neighbor in the vision of God or primarily aims to promote the neighbor's well-being—not only in terms of their moral virtue but their eternal well-being in God.

Recent studies suggest several strategies that defenders of Augustine might employ in order to avoid the most objectionable features of Augustine's supposed monism in his account of the relation of the love commands. Some argue that the "use" and "enjoyment" distinction is a tentative and exploratory formula that Augustine later abandons.[51] Others expand the semantic range of *usus*, pointing both to its non-Kantian meaning in standard Latin locution and Augustine's creative appeal to *usus* as a term for the engagement of the will in discussing the intersubjective relations of the persons of the Trinity.[52] The most sustained reading of Augustine's understanding of the two love commands is Raymond Canning's massive and meticulous study, *The Unity of Love for God and Neighbor in St. Augustine*.[53] Placing Augustine in both immediate theological controversies and distinctively Christian breaks from classical culture, Canning makes a compelling case that Augustine's mature conception of love is thoroughly social and avoids both the egocentric and instrumentalist readings of his critics.

Technical interpretations of Augustine on love do relieve some of the pressures of popular misreadings and help the case for promoting love as a political virtue. For Arendt and other modern political theorists, however, the real problematic for Augustinianism is not simply the debated influence of neo-Platonism that is thought to engender the "use" and "enjoyment" distinction. Rather, it seems to be the very framework of theocentric reference itself. This framework is what Romand Coles identifies as the "malignancy at the heart" of Christian interpretations of love—the refusal to relinquish the claim that all human life finds its meaning and destiny in reference to the story of God in Christ.[54] The self that confesses Augustine's God and cares for others in God produces the ungenerous ethic of hostility and imperialism that many theorists identify with Christianity and Platonism alike.

Although I cannot make this argument here, Augustinianism is well suited to address these concerns. Its theistic orientation preserves the sort of politics that Arendt and other agonistic liberals most value: one that activates citizenship but releases politics from pressures it cannot bear. Augustinianism is morally serious but alert to the disjunctures of morality and politics. The spirit of Augustine's "use" and "enjoyment" distinction captures this disposition even as it secures love as an appropriate political virtue that does not violate central elements of liberal politics. However one judges the Rahnerian turn in Augustinian interpretation, Augustine provides a model for thinking about the perils of affective self-enclosure and the perennial recapitulations of choosing partial goods and false ultimate loves. What does this model have to do with new dimensions for religion and liberalism debates?

As mentioned at the beginning of the paper, the most influential political readings of Augustine in the twentieth century are liberal. Augustinian liberals highlight Augustine's anthropology and eschatology in ways that encourage an association with core features of liberal traditions of secular and pluralist politics. While liberal-communitarian typologies continue to define central tropes in contemporary theory, dissatisfaction with these debates as well as a changing political world suggests that the revival of interest in Augustine needs to move beyond the familiar realm of emphasizing the limits of politics. There have been a number of important dissents from standard liberal readings of Augustinianism.[55] But these works operate at the grand level, and fail to capitalize on a more piecemeal dispositional engagement with liberal political ethics. How might Augustinians do this? I want to close by suggesting how attention to love might shift the focus of political Augustinianism.

Despite the self-congratulatory mood of some interpreters of the globalization of democratic liberalism, there are a number of signs that liberal political societies and the intellectual environments that sustain them are (to borrow from Arendt) in "dark times."[56] It is not only the brutal violence of Bosnia and Rwanda or the fragile situation in post-1989 democracies that cast doubt on liberal enthusiasm.[57] Rather, as Toqueville predicted, even the most consolidated democracies suffer from dramatic political alienation and a growing sense of impotence about the possibilities of collective action. Even in this situation, the sin of pride and the limits of politics are essential features of political Augustinianism. Counsels against utopianism abide. But for a cynical liberal culture that also suffers from the sin of sloth and a false humility that impoverishes political and moral discourse, narrow debates about epistemology neglect questions of motivation and moral psychology in a liberal society.[58] My aim in this paper is not to invoke "love" in the abstract as a panacea or moralistic consolation for the discontents of liberalism. No retrieval of Augustinianism for contemporary liberalism could bear such idealism or sentimentalism. But challenging the terms of liberal debates that marginalize love is a way for Augustinians to imagine a better liberalism less open to the charges of radical individualism, bourgeois commercialism, and narrow rationalism. Theorizing the virtue of neighbor love and its relation to the thematization of God may not create a healthier politics, but for Augustinians— liberal or otherwise—it remains an unfinished theological task. Responding to the Kantian and Nietzschean anxieties might also require sociological arguments about what ails liberalism—is it really too much responsibility and love for others? But for Christians, for whom their encounter with the neighbor often passes through the relation of citizen, restoring the virtue of love to the ethics of citizenship is an obligation.[59] Good citizenship, like a good anything for Augustine, is good loving. Incorporating the sophisticated treatment of love in the literature of theological ethics, however, remains a difficult but rich challenge for advocates of a "morally robust" Augustinian liberalism.

NOTES

[1]Hannah Arendt, *Love and Saint Augustine*, eds. Joanna Scott and Judith Stark, (Chicago: University of Chicago Press, 1996), 115. References in the text refer to this translation. A strong case can be made that Arendt's reading of Augustine, and the conceptual categories that govern this reading, remain with her throughout her career. In addition to the lengthy interpretive essay by Scott and Stark that defends these connections, see Ronald Beiner, "Love and Worldliness: Hannah Arendt's Reading of Saint Augustine," in eds., Larry May and Jerome Kohn, *Hannah Arendt: Twenty Years Later*, (Cambridge: MIT Press, 1996), 269-284; and *Amor Mundi: Explorations in the Faith and Thought of Hannah Arendt*, ed. James W. Bernauer, S.J., (Dordrecht: Martinus Nijhoff Publishers, 1987). Some reviews of the new translation, however, push these connections too far and mistake the influence of Augustinianism for an endorsement. See, for example, Peter Bathory, "Augustine Through a Modern Prism," *Society* 34:4 (May/June 1997): 72-76, and Leah Bradshaw, "Communion with Others, Communion with Truth," *Review of Politics*, 59:2 (Spring 1997): 368-372.

[2]Anders Nygren, *Agape and Eros*, trans. Philip Watson, (Philadelphia: Westminster Press, 1953). The conceptual analysis of love in modern religious ethics tends to be dated from Nygren's work, originally published in the 1930's.

[3]The connection between feminist "ethics of care" and Augustinian *caritas* has not been noted in the literature of moral and political philosophy. My thoughts on these connections were provoked by Jean Bethke Elshtain's claim that Augustine's "metaphors are fascinating and fascinatingly feminine, if I may dare say so, having to do with collecting, emptying, receiving, rather than mastering, attacking, gaining." Jean Bethke Elshtain, *Augustine and the Limits of Politics*, (Notre Dame: University of Notre Dame Press, 1995), 56. Elshtain explores the relationship between Augustine and Arendt, but not in terms of the philosophical or theological analysis of love.

[4]See *Theorizing Citizenship*, ed. Ronald Beiner, (Albany: State University of New York Press, 1995); and, Peter Berkowitz, *Virtue and the Making of Modern Liberalism* (Princeton: Princeton University Press, 1999).

[5]For love as both metaphysical and psychological category, see Oliver O'Donovan, *The Problem of Self-Love in St. Augustine* (New Haven: Yale University Press, 1980), 10-36 and 137-159.

[6]The "ethic of care" debates, once dominated by discussion of the Gilligan's research on women's moral reasoning in relation to issues of gender, have proved illuminating for broader questions in moral and political theory. See Joan Tronto, *Moral Boundaries: A Political*

Argument for an Ethic of Care (New York: Routledge, 1994), and Grace Clement, *Care, Autonomy, and Justice*, (Boulder: Westview Press, 1998). For specifically theological interests, see, Kathryn Tanner, "The Care That Does Justice: Recent Writings on Feminist Ethics and Theology," *Journal of Religious Ethics* 24:1 (Spring 1996): 171-191.

[7]See, for example, Eva Feder Kittay, *Love's Labor: Essays on Women, Equality, and Dependency*, (New York: Routledge Press, 1999).

[8]In addition to Tronto, see Susan Miller Okin's influential article, "Reason and Feeling in Thinking about Justice," *Ethics* (January 1989): 229-249.

[9]See, for example, Timothy P. Jackson, "To Bedlam and Part Way Back: John Rawls and Christian Justice," *Faith and Philosophy* 8.4 (October 1991): 423-447; idem, "The Disconsolation of Theology: Irony, Cruelty, and Putting Charity First," *Journal of Religious Ethics* 20.1 (Spring 1992): 1-35, "Liberalism and Agape: The Priority of Charity to Democracy and Philosophy," *The Annual of the Society of Christian Ethics* 13 (1993): 47-72, and "Love in a Liberal Society," *Journal of Religious Ethics* 22.1 (Spring 1994): 28-38.

[10]Timothy P. Jackson, "Love in a Liberal Society," 35.

[11]On the complexities of Augustine's relation to classical virtue, see James Wetzel, *Augustine and the Limits of Virtue* (Cambridge: Cambridge University Press, 1992), and Carol Harrison, *Augustine: Christian Truth and Fractured Humanity*, (Oxford: Oxford University Press, 2001), 79-114.

[12]Postmodern appropriations of Augustine for political ethics are growing. In addition to the influential work of John Milbank, see Robert Dodaro, "Eloquent Lies, Just Wars and the Politics of Persuasion: Reading Augustine's *City of God* in a 'Postmodern' World," *Augustinian Studies* 25 (1994): 77-138, and J. Joyce Schuld, "Augustine, Foucault, and the Politics of Imperfection," *Journal of Religion* (2000): 1-22.

[13]The standard treatment of this theme remains R.A. Markus, *Saeculum: History and Society in The Theology of St. Augustine* (Cambridge: Cambridge University Press, 1970). For two sophisticated defenses that follow this kind of Augustinian liberalism, see Edmund Santurri, "Rawlsian Liberalism, Moral Truth, and Augustinian Politics," *Journal for Peace & Justice Studies* 8:2 (1997): 1-36, and Paul Weithman, "Toward an Augustinian Liberalism," in *The Augustinian Tradition*, ed. Gareth B. Matthews (Berkeley: University of California Press, 1999), 304-322.

[14]For criticisms of Markus, see Michael J. White, "Pluralism and Secularism in the Political Order: St. Augustine and Theoretical Liberalism," *The University of Dayton Review* 22:3 (Summer 1994): 137-154, and John R. Bowlin, "Augustine on Justifying Coercion," *The Annual of the Society of Christian Ethics* 17 (1997): 49-70.

[15]*City of God*, 19.17.

[16]Markus, 94-95.

[17]Ibid., 173.

[18]For a similar use of "horizontal" and "vertical" metaphors that links the two love commands to the two tables of the Decalogue, see Timothy P. Jackson, *Love Disconsoled: Meditations on Christian Charity* (Cambridge: Cambridge University Press, 1999), 1-31.

[19]Oliver O'Donovan, *Resurrection and Moral Order* (Leicester: InterVarsity Press, 1986), 234. For a concise re-statement of this criticism in light of recent ethical theory, see Robert M. Adams, *Finite and Infinite Goods* (Oxford: Oxford Univeristy Press, 1999), 186-187.

[20]See Romand Coles, *Self/Power/Other: Political Theory and Dialogical Ethics*, (Ithaca: Cornell University Press, 1992) and William Connolly, *The Augustinian Imperative: A Reflection on the Politics of Morality* (Newbury Park, CA: Sage Publications, Inc., 1993).

[21]For a compelling discussion of the problem of coercion in Augustine, see John R. Bowlin, "Augustine on Justifying Coercion," *The Annual of the Society of Christian Ethics* 17 (1997): 49-70.

[22] Karl Rahner, *The Love of Jesus and the Love of Neighbor* (New York: Crossroad, 1983); Gustavo Gutierrez, *A Theology of Liberation*, second edition (Maryknoll, NY: Orbis, 1988); and Emmanuel Levinas, *Totality and Infinity* (Pittsburgh: Duquesne University Press, 1969).

[23]Raymond Canning, *The Unity of the Love for God and Neighbor in St. Augustine,* (Heverlee, Belgium: Augustinian Historical Institute, 1993), and Tarcisius J. van Bavel, "The Double Face of Love in Augustine," *Augustininan Studies* 17 (1986): 169-181.

[24]Canning, 420.

[25]See Elisabeth Young-Bruehl, *Hannah Arendt: For Love of the World,* (New Haven: Yale University Press, 1982), and Shin Chiba, "Hannah Arendt on Love and the Political: Love, Friendship, and Citizenship," *Review of Politics* 57:3 (Summer 1995): 505-535.

[26]See Hannah Arendt, *On Revolution* (New York: Penguin, 1962), 76, and *The Human Condition,* (Chicago: University of Chicago Press, 1958): 76.

[27]For a rare theological review of Arendt that develops this theme, see Thomas Breidenthal, "Arendt, Augustine, and the Politics of Incarnation," *Modern Theology,* 14:4 (October 1998): 489-503.

[28]Hannah Arendt, *The Human Condition,* 242.

[29]For a fuller discussion of this aspect of Arendt's thought, see George Kateb, *Hannah Arendt: Politics, Conscience, Evil* (Totowa, NJ: Rowman & Littlefield, 1983), 25-29 and 89-96.

[30]*The Human Condition,* 73-78.

[31]Ibid., 52.

[32]Ibid., 243.

[33]Kant's own account of love and emotion, as opposed to the later Kantian tradition, is an important feature of contemporary scholarship. For a compelling attempt to "juxtapose love and Kantian respect in a way that is illuminating to both," see J. David Velleman, "Love as a Moral Emotion," *Ethics* 109 (January 1999): 338-374 (esp. 344).

[34]Immanuel Kant, *Metaphysical Principles of Virtue,* trans. James W. Ellington, (Indianapolis: Hackett, 1983), 449.

[35]Henry S. Richardson, "Nussbaum: Love and Respect," *Metaphilosophy* (1998): 254-261 (esp. 257).

[36]The case of Rawls is instructive given his influence on contemporary liberalism. The early Rawls provides a notable exception in recent liberal theory because he pursues an extended discussion of love (understood, however, primarily as benevolence). See Susan Mendus, "The Importance of Love in Rawls' Theory of Justice," *British Journal of Political Science* 29 (1999): 57-75.

[37]Rawls, *Theory of Justice* (Cambridge: Harvard University Press, 1971), 573.

[38]See Rawls, *Theory of Justice,* 8.

[39]Soren Kierkegaard, *Either/Or* II, trans. Walter Lowrie (Garden City: Doubleday, 1959), 205.

[40]See Gregory Vlastos, "The Individual as Object of Love in Plato," *Platonic Studies,* second edition (Princeton: Princeton University Press, 1981), 3-42.

[41]*The Free Choice of the Will,* I.16.34 (Cited by Arendt, 12).

[42]*City of God,* 11.28. The original German text of the dissertation contains a reference to this passage (Arendt, 10n6).

[43]*Commentaries on the Psalms,* 31,5 (Cited by Arendt, 17). Annette Baier numbers Augustine among the theological pessimists for whom "love of God will be a sort of live vaccine that will block any riskier loving" in "Unsafe Loves," *Moral Prejudices* (Cambridge: Harvard University Press, 1994), 36.

[44]*Sermon* 163, I, 1. (Cited by Arendt, 21).

[45]*Confessions* II, I, I. (Cited by Arendt, 23).

[46]*On Christian Doctrine,* I, 29, 30. (Cited by Arendt, 43).

[47]Compare, for example, Nygren, 550 and 735.

[48]Thomas Breidenthal, "Arendt, Augustine, and the Politics of Incarnation," 491.

[49]Ibid., 499.

[50]See Mark Lloyd Taylor, *God is Love: A Study in the Theology of Karl Rahner,* American Academy of Religion Series 50 (Atlanta: Scholars Press, 1986): 84-87.

[51]See Oliver O'Donovan, "*Usus* and *Fruitio* in Augustine, *De Doctrina Christiana* I," *Journal of Theological Studies,* 33:2 (October 1982): 361-397.

[52]See Helmut David Baer, "The Fruit of Charity: Using the Neighbor in *De doctrina christiana*," *Journal of Religious Ethics*, 24.1 (1996); and, William Riordan O'Connor, "The *Uti/Frui* Distinction in Augustine's Ethics," *Augustinian Studies* 14 (1983): 45-62.

[53]Raymond Canning, *The Unity of Love for God and Neighbor in St. Augustine* (Heverlee, Belgium: Augustinian Historical Institute, 1993).

[54]Romand Coles, *Rethinking Generosity: Critical Theory and the Politics of Caritas*, (Ithaca: Cornell University Press, 1997), 3.

[55]John Milbank, *Theology and Social Theory*, (Oxford: Basil Blackwell, 1990), and Oliver O'Donovan, *The Desire of the Nations*, (Cambridge: Cambridge University Press, 1996).

[56]See also Jeffrey Isaac, *Democracy in Dark Times* (Ithaca: Cornell University Press, 1998).

[57]For a discussion of resurgent interest in Augustinianism after the Cold War, see Joshua Mitchell, "The Use of Augustine, After 1989," *Political Theory* 27.5 (October 1999): 694-705.

[58]In his impressive study of Reinhold Niebuhr and contemporary ethics, Robin Lovin hints at a salutary shift in the focus of Christian realism by "reintroducing the motive power of moral and religious ideals to those who learned too well the earlier lesson against sentimentality." In this context, "the role of Christian realism is not to talk about realistic limits, but to expand political imagination." See Robin Lovin, *Reinhold Niebuhr and Christian Realism*, (Cambridge: Cambridge University Press, 1995): 232 and 246.

[59]See Paul Ricouer, "The *Socius* and the Neighbor," *History and Truth*, trans. Charles A. Kelbley, (Evanston: Northwestern University Press, 1965), 98-109.

CRITIQUES AND NEW DIRECTIONS IN CATHOLIC MORAL THEOLOGY

The Catholic Church's Public Confession: Theological and Ethical Implications

Aline H. Kalbian

Abstract

The Catholic Church, as part of the year 2000 Jubilee celebrations, issued a prayer of confession for sins committed in the past. Most notable was the confession for "actions that may have caused suffering to the people of Israel." In this paper I identify two prominent metaphors in the magisterial literature associated with this act of contrition—the metaphor of Church as mother, and the metaphor of repentance as purification of memory. I analyze these metaphors and place them in the context of important conversations about the Catholic Church and the Holocaust, and about collective responsibility and repentance.

Introduction

On March 12, 2000, Pope John Paul II led the Catholic Church in a Universal Prayer for Pardon, asking God "to accept the repentance of his people who humbly confess their sins . . . ." Perhaps the most controversial of these sins were the ones described as "any actions that may have caused suffering to the people of Israel."[1] In a trip to Palestine and Israel a week later, the Pope offered similar expressions of contrition, especially during his visit to the *Yad Vashem* Holocaust Museum in Jerusalem and his prayer at the Western Wall. The prayer and the statements made during his Holy Land trip were the culmination of a series of more detailed documents that address the nature and significance of this act of repentance by the Church.

Annual of the Society of Christian Ethics, 21 (2001): 175-189

These documents feature two prominent metaphors. One is the metaphor of the Church as the "sinless" mother of the "sinful" laity; the other is the metaphor of repentance as "purification of memory." Both metaphors can be read as diluting the potentially positive impact of this Catholic response to the Holocaust. The first, by drawing a sharp distinction between the Church and the laity, appears to deflect blame from the institutional Church. The second, by pairing the term purification with memory, conjures an image of erasure and forgetfulness—a negation of memory. In this paper I explore these metaphors and suggest that they deserve a more nuanced and careful interpretation. To that end, I situate them as part of several larger conversations—one about the Catholic Church's response to the Holocaust and the other about issues of collective responsibility and repentance.[2]

Most of the immediate responses to this confession, from both within and outside of the Church, were filled with emotion. Some questioned whether the Church had gone far enough in accepting responsibility for its actions.[3] Others wondered whether it was appropriate for the Church to speak so publicly and negatively about its past.[4] The questions raised about the confessions by these critics focused on matters of *sincerity*, *effectiveness*, and *sufficiency*.[5] It is the power of these responses that animates my analysis of the metaphors in this paper.

The Context of the Metaphors

The metaphors discussed in this essay are found in two documents: John Paul II's Apostolic Letter *Tertio Millennio Adveniente* (TMA), issued in late 1994 to prepare the Church for the Jubilee year 2000, and the International Theological Commission's document *Memory and Reconciliation: The Church and the Faults of the Past* (M&R), issued in 1998 to clarify and elaborate points from the Pope's earlier letter.[6] Read together, these documents answer many of the questions that have been raised about the Church's confession.

The Pope begins *Tertio Millenio Advenniente* by emphasizing what he calls the *cosmic value* of the birth of Christ 2000 years ago—the "fulfillment of the yearning present in all the religions of mankind" (TMA 6). He notes that: "In Christianity time has a fundamental importance. Within the dimension of time the world was created; within it the history of salvation unfolds, finding its culmination in the 'fullness of time' of the Incarnation, and its goal in the glorious return of the Son of God at the end of time" (TMA 10). The theological significance of time for Christians combined with their relationship to God leads to a duty "to sanctify time." This duty captures the essence of the Jubilee rooted in the Old Testament—a symbolic action that sets aside a certain period of time for God.

According to the 1994 apostolic letter, it is this tradition, derived from ancient Israel and fulfilled by the coming of the Messiah, that sets the stage for the "extraordinarily great Jubilee" that is to take place in 2000. This celebration of the 2000 years since the birth of Christ is to focus on the preceding century, marked in particular by the providential event of Vatican II, the "disturbing experiences" of two world wars, and the massacres at the Nazi concentration camps. The juxtaposition by the Pope of such radically different expressions of Jewish-Catholic relations as illustrative of the twentieth century is noteworthy, particularly in light of the papal apologies to the Jewish people. At one extreme, Vatican II affirmed Catholic-Jewish relations in the document *Aeterni Patris*, a document that David Novak has dubbed "undoubtedly the most significant statement of the Church regarding the Jews in modern times, perhaps ever."[7] The events of the Holocaust stand in sharp contrast. Thus, for the Pope, these two contradictory expressions of Catholic-Jewish relations frame the century that has passed and give particular meaning to his statements of confession.

This tension—between the joyfulness of the celebration (Vatican II) and the sadness of memorial (the Holocaust)—preoccupy the Pope in the latter part of this document. Thus, he calls for a "joy based upon forgiveness of sins" and the consequent need to emphasize penance and reconciliation (TMA 32). The penance and reconciliation by the Church is to consist of four parts. The metaphors Church as Mother and repentance as purification are introduced in the context of this four-part penance and reconciliation.

The first part is described as an increased *consciousness* of "the sinfulness of her [the Church's] children." This is followed by an *acknowledgment* of that sinfulness. Note that the Pope is careful to distinguish the sinfulness of the Church's sons and daughters from the Church itself which, in the words of *Lumen Gentium*, is "at the same time holy and always in need of being purified" (TMA 33). The third step addresses the Church's *response* to these children—"embracing them to her bosom." The fourth part, enacted by the Pope in this letter, is to encourage the laity to *purify themselves* of these past sinful actions. The Pope writes, "she [the Church] cannot cross the threshold of the new millennium without encouraging her children to purify themselves, through repentance, of past errors and instances of infidelity, inconsistency, and slowness to act. Acknowledging the weaknesses of the past is an act of honesty and courage which helps us to strengthen our faith . . . ." (TMA 33).

It is important to note that these Jubilee year expressions are the culmination of many years of reflection and commentary by the Pope on the Holocaust, Judaism, and the Catholic Church. Karol Wojtyla's childhood in Poland and his first-hand experiences of World War II and the Nazi regime are central chapters in his biography. He is diligent in bringing this fact to attention whenever possible. In fact, autobiographical references are commonplace in his many statements about Judaism and the Holocaust. Perhaps the most poignant was his speech during the historic visit to the *Yad Vashem* Museum in Jerusalem in March of 2000. The Pope begins the speech,

> In this place of memories, the mind and heart and soul feel an extreme need for silence. Silence in which to remember. Silence in which to try to make sense of the memories which come flooding back. Silence because there are no words strong enough to deplore the terrible tragedy of *Shoah*. My own personal memories are of all that happened when the Nazis occupied Poland during the War. I remember my Jewish friends and neighbors, some of whom perished, while others survived.[8]

The appeal to personal experience adds an important element of credibility to the Pope's reflections on the Holocaust. In addition to the personal dimension, several important themes mark his papacy in regard to Catholic-Jewish relations. Eugene Fisher has identified and organized them into thematic categories.[9] The first four relate to theological issues concerning the relationship between Christians and Jews. All address serious flaws in the history of Christian polemics regarding Judaism and point to the advances made by the present Pope. Fisher notes, for example, that John Paul II carefully prefaces the term heritage with the term living, thus replacing earlier negative images of Judaism as a heritage of the past. On another theological point, Fisher quotes the Pope's 1980 speech to representatives of the Jewish community in Mainz, West Germany. There, John Paul referred to the Jewish community as "the people of God of the Old Covenant, which has never been revoked by God," as a way to emphasize the permanent validity of God's covenant with the Jewish people.[10]

Fisher identifies three other categories that, while less theological, address contemporary Catholic-Jewish relations more directly. They are: 1) recognition of the State of Israel; 2) controversies; and 3) condemnation of anti-Semitism and the remembrance of Shoah. The 1993 agreement between Israel and the Holy See ushered in an era of full diplomatic relations between the two, and it certainly has gone a long way in strengthening Catholic-Jewish relations. The category, "controversies," includes three events: the beatification of Edith Stein, the location of the Carmelite convent at Auschwitz, and the Pope's meetings with Yasser Arafat and Kurt Waldheim. To these, one can add the more recent controversies surrounding the canonization of Pope Pius XII.[11] Such controversies are a sharp contrast to what Fisher sees as John Paul II's record in the area of Catholic-Jewish relations—a record that he describes as "the most solid and extensive advances . . . perhaps in the history of the Church."[12]

The third and most important category identified by Fisher is condemnation of anti-Semitism and the remembrance of the Shoah. These are constant themes in all the Pope's many addresses to Jewish communities worldwide. In one of his most famous addresses, given during his historic visit to the Synagogue in Rome in 1986, the Pope touched on both of these themes: "the acts of discrimination, unjustified limitation of religious freedom, oppression also on the level of civil freedom in regard to the Jews were, from an objective point of view, gravely deplorable manifestations." The Pope then quotes the passage from *Nostra Aetate*, the Vatican II "Declaration on the Relationship of the Church to non-Christian Religions," that the Church "deplores the hatred, persecutions, and displays of anti-Semitism directed against the Jews at any time by anyone."[13] In that same address, John Paul II invokes the Holocaust: "I would like once more to express a word of abhorrence for the genocide decreed against the Jewish people during the last war, which led to the Holocaust of millions of innocent victims."[14] There are countless other examples of attention both to anti-Semitism and the Holocaust in the Pope's addresses.

These expressions denouncing the Holocaust and expressing Catholic solidarity with victims and survivors culminated in the 1998 Vatican document *We Remember: A Reflection on the Shoah*.[15] The statement received widespread attention. Most significant is the fact that much of the reaction from Jewish leaders was negative.[16] While the statement clearly condemns the Holocaust and all forms of anti-Semitism, it falls short, in the eyes of many, of apologizing for the "Church as such." The language of the statement urges that the Church cannot remain indifferent to what happened to the Jewish people. "Recalling the past," it is deemed, is not sufficient—there is a demand to remember and "a moral imperative to insure that never again will selfishness and hatred grow to the point of sowing such suffering and death" (WR, I).

The crucial phrase, in terms of apology, appears towards the end of the document: "At the end of this Millennium the Catholic Church desires to express her deep sorrow for the failures of her sons and daughters in every age. This is an act of repentance (*teshuva*), since as members of the Church, we are linked to the sins as well as the merits of all her children" (WR, V). The prayers of confession offered as part of the Jubilee also echo this sentiment, but the two metaphors that I discuss in this paper set a significantly different tone. Both memory and the maternal aspect of the Church are mentioned in the *We Remember* document, but in both cases the emphasis is different. For instance, the maternal image is balanced with language that is suggestive of the Church as people of God; and memory and repentance are promoted without the troublesome language of purification.

I turn now to a more detailed discussion of these metaphors and of the problems they raise about collective responsibility and collective repentance.

Analysis of the Metaphors

Church as Mother

The maternal image of the Church bearing the sins of her children is meant to illustrate the sense of responsibility that the Church feels for its actions, but as we shall see, this metaphor is open to various interpretations. Describing the Church as mother is certainly not a new metaphor—it can be traced back to the early

Church fathers. More recently in Vatican II's *Lumen Gentium*, the Church is described as "becoming herself a mother" as a result of contemplation on Mary's mysterious sanctity. Also like Mary, the Church is described as virgin—whole and pure in fidelity (LG 64).

The authors of *Memory and Reconciliation* note the important theological contribution made by Vatican II on the precise point this metaphor is meant to convey—the distinction between "the indefectible fidelity of the Church and the weakness of her members, clergy or laity" (M&R 1.2). The Vatican II documents describe the Church as bride of Christ and the laity as her children. The bride (also mother) thus remains pure and unblemished, while her children are sinners to be pardoned. To many, particularly those outside the Church, reliance on this imagery in the context of repentance for actions toward the Jewish people seems to obscure the repentance itself. Thus, on one reading of the metaphor, it reveals the failure of the Church to take adequate responsibility for its actions.

Nevertheless, one needs to note that the imagery of family is prominent in the Pope's apostolic letter *Tertio Millenio*. The first paragraph is replete with familial language—God sending forth his Son, born of woman, who comes into the world so that all "might receive adoption as sons and daughters" (TMA 1). Certainly, in the context of the millennial celebration of Christ's birth, the imagery makes sense. In fact, the Jubilee year is placed in the context of the Marian 1986/87 year and the Year of the Family, both of which are labeled by the Pope as anticipatory of the Jubilee.

This context supports a more sympathetic reading of the metaphor of Church as mother. In this light, the maternal image evokes a sense of closeness between a mother and her children as she comforts them and bears their burdens. Furthermore, one could argue that assigning blame to children does not automatically absolve the parents. It is commonly held that parents are responsible, at least to some extent, for their children's actions. For example, when a child commits a crime, we ask why the parents did not foresee the act, or we wonder whether a lack of parental guidance brought it about.

Even in the context of a sympathetic reading, we must note that the metaphor is maternal, rather than more generally parental. This is particularly troubling in light of the Magisterium's attitudes towards women's roles in the institutional Church. Thus the connection of Church, a male-dominated hierarchy, with motherhood, a role associated with women, is problematic—a point that is overlooked in these documents. Furthermore, the maternal role of the Church has also traditionally been distinguished from its teaching role. The title of John XXIII's social encyclical *Mater et Magistra* is one example of this distinction. More recently John Paul II's *Vertiatis Splendor* also relies on this trope. He suggests that the Church in her maternal role exhibits "genuine understanding and compassion" about the often difficult demands of the moral life, while the Church as teacher "never tires of proclaiming the moral norm."[17]

A more critical interpretation of this metaphor suggests that its central purpose is to explain how the Church can ask forgiveness for actions while maintaining holiness. On this reading, the metaphor establishes a distance between the Church and the laity (her sinful children)—a distance that keeps the Church, as Church, secure in holiness while placing the burden of the sins on the laity. As Francis Sullivan notes, while the distinction between Church as mother and her sinful children solves the problem of how to reconcile the Church's holiness with the request for forgiveness, it does leave two negative consequences. First, it overlooks the fact that some of the children were in fact members of the hierarchy of the Church. Second, it hides the fact that some of the policies and practices of the Church "have been objectively in contradiction to the Gospel and have caused harm to many people." Thus for Sullivan, this metaphor muddies the issue of responsibility. He proposes instead the use of the metaphor "pilgrim people of God."[18]

The image of Church as pilgrim people of God is most often associated with Vatican II documents like *Lumen Gentium*. It suggests a teleological image of the Church as on a journey, and de-emphasizes the hierarchical and static nature of the Church. Charles Curran notes a correlation between the image of pilgrim church and dynamic change in the Church. He writes, "The Church lives in the tension between the now and the future of the fullness of grace. The church is a pilgrim church. In the light of its eschatological fullness the church is never perfect and always in need of change and reform."[19] In the more recent 1994 edition of the Catechism of the Catholic Church, *Lumen Gentium's* discussion of the "symbols of the Church" is referenced as central for understanding the nature of the Church. This discussion, while not using the explicit language of "pilgrim people of God," does suggest some alternative metaphors that are sanctioned by the magisterium, all of which resonate with the people of God language that Sullivan favors.[20]

Regardless of whether one interprets this metaphor as distancing the Church from the laity, or as drawing the two closer together, it does raise two interrelated questions: what is the relationship of individual responsibility to the collective, and what does it means for an institution to be guilty?

These questions are addressed in one way by the ITC's claims that sin is always personal and that the expression "social sin" is merely an analogy for the "accumulation and concentration of many personal sins" (M&R 1.3).[21] The commission develops this point further, noting an ethical distinction common to Catholic moral theology, between objective and subjective responsibility. Objective responsibility concerns the action itself understood apart from the perception of good or evil by the moral agent. Subjective responsibility refers to the perception of the individual's conscience. In other words, if I commit a harm against another, I am objectively responsible, regardless of whether I take responsibility for the action. The subjective element of the responsibility has to do with my perception of the goodness or evil of my act—it resides in my conscience. Thus, it is only relevant when the guilty party and the persons harmed by an action are contemporaneous. "Subjective responsibility ceases with the death of the one who performed the act" (M&R, 5.1). The descendants of the responsible parties continue to experience the objective responsibility, which develops as a solidarity based on the continuing burden on the conscience of those descendants between their contemporary experience and the wrongdoing or evil of the past. "An objective common responsibility" is the result. It is through this trans-historical responsibility that the memory exists today—the memory that is to be the subject of purification.

What does it mean morally to speak of common or collective responsibility? To what extent can we impute responsibility to corporate entities? Larry May and David Novak offer two helpful ways to think about these questions.[22] They both argue, albeit in different ways, that we can hold the collective responsible for the actions of its individual members. They both want to narrow the gap between the individual and the collective. In fact, their reflections on this issue provide a way to move beyond the negative implications of the metaphor discussed above.

May offer a three-part scheme for understanding collective responsibility.[23] He claims first that it is appropriate to attribute responsibility to people for some of their attitudes, even if those attitudes are not the direct cause of harm. As long as persons share attitudes, such as racist ones, they are responsible for any harms that result from the actions of those holding similar attitudes. May bases his view on an existentialist conception of consciousness combined with a virtue-based ethical theory. In essence, he rejects the idea that agents are only responsible for those attitudes that are *fully* under their control. He writes, "I advocate a weaker requirement, namely, that a person is responsible for those attitudes that he or she could partially change (or could have partially changed) and that it is reasonable to say the person should change (or should have changed)."[24]

This discussion illuminates concerns about whether the Church's confession was sufficient. Ultimately, it serves to put aside the thorny historical questions about the precise extent of the Church's guilt since responsibility can be assigned for attitudes as well as for actions. May's suggestion that we can hold agents responsible for attitudes provides those who are dissatisfied with the Church's confession another angle of criticism on the point of the Church's attempt to distance itself from responsibility.

The second part of May's scheme is the claim that individuals who are part of a larger collective are blameworthy for their omissions and inactions. Here, May wants to counter the notion that membership in a collective diffuses individual responsibility. An individual's values become deeply connected with the values of the group. This theory of collectivism enables May to develop a view of how individuals function within larger institutions. May concludes his argument by focusing on the greater responsibilities that attach to persons in various roles and positions within a group.

May's emphasis on narrowing the gap between the individual and the collective is echoed by Novak's theological treatment of the issue of collective responsibility. For Novak, Catholicism shares with Judaism a theological framework for making sense of communal responsibility, namely the covenant. The nature of covenant of both religious traditions affirms the idea that "the relationship with God is primarily a communal affair."[25] Within the context of such a covenant, collective responsibility takes on a different meaning. Novak writes, "Thus in a covenanted community, even though one is not morally responsible for the sins of fellow members of the community, there still is an *existential* sense of collective sorrow and shame when another member of the community—even those as estranged from the community as the Nazis were—commits a sin, especially a sin having great public consequences."[26]

This sense of existential connection with members of one's community raises the question of what, precisely, the Pope takes responsibility for in these confessions. In the earlier *We Remember* (WR) document, the notion that "the spiritual resistance and concrete action of other Christians was not that which might have been expected from Christ's followers" is attributed to the Pope (WR, IV). This appears in contrast to those Christians who did risk their lives to save their Jewish neighbors. Thus the implication is that the worst one can say about Christians is that they failed to resist and act appropriately in the face of evil. Also in *We Remember*, the Vatican distinguishes anti-Judaism from anti-Semitism. Anti-Semitism is the Nazi's National Socialist ideology that totally rejects all teachings of the Church. It is thus identified as anti-Christian and as developing on a parallel, yet different trajectory than anti-Judaism, which is described as "the long-standing sentiments of mistrust and hostility" that have developed over time within the Christian community. Christians, therefore, should be held responsible for anti-Judaism, but not for anti-Semitism (WR, III).

Both May and Novak provide arguments for collective responsibility that counter the sense of distance evoked by the image of the motherhood of the Church. There is nevertheless one element of Catholic teaching that does resonate with elements of both their views, and it can be found in the John Paul II's discussion of the relation of personal to social sin (or structures of sin).[27] Like May, the Pope argues that social sin or responsibility is really made up of many personal sins. In other words, the individual is ultimately responsible. There is, however, one interesting difference of emphasis in their arguments. May wants to insure that individuals cannot hide behind the collective, whereas the Pope's critics claim that his confession is an instance of the collective (Church) hiding behind individuals.

Novak's discussion of the individual and the collective draws our attention to a different issue, namely, do people today have responsibility for what members of their community did in the past? Novak provides a theological argument claiming that they do. In the context of the action of purification being encouraged by the Pope, we might ask what connection these Jubilee acts of repentance have to the past. The Church as pilgrim people of God metaphor provides one way to address this issue. Its teleological thrust would enable today's Church to connect existentially with the actions of Catholics in the past. The issue of repentance, discussed in the next section, addresses this point more directly.

Purification of Memory

The metaphor "purification of memory," used by the Pope in *Tertio Millenio*, is interpreted more fully in the ITC document. There, one finds a description of the exact nature and significance of this purification. The commission's attempt to clarify it is important, because many of the responses to these apologies, particularly the more negative ones, have focused on this metaphor. For example, Leon Weiseltier writes in the *New Republic*, "I must confess that I do not quite understand the concept. The purification of memory seems less urgent than the purification by memory. Memory has not been the problem. The neglect of memory has been the problem."[28] On hearing this phrase in the context of the Holocaust, one is struck by the immediate dissonance of the terms purification and memory. The concept of memory has been central to Jewish understandings and responses to the Holocaust. Anxiety about erasing or losing memory is a central experience for most victims of trauma, and forms the basis of many Jewish responses to the events of the Holocaust. Unfortunately, the connotation of a term like purification offers little comfort to those desperate to keep the memory alive.

Purification of memory is both a sign and an action according to the ITC's description. As a sign, it is one among others "which may help people to live the exceptional grace of the Jubilee with greater fervor." Furthermore, it can be a sign of exemplary behavior that "draws attention to something good and stimulates the imitation of it" (M&R 5.1). These utilitarian benefits of the purification as a sign are important elements of the Jubilee message. Put simply, Catholics can benefit from actions that embody the sign; others will benefit by witnessing this commitment and will hopefully be motivated by this exceptional display of remorse.

As an action, the purification of memory is described as both an act of courage and humility. It is difficult to pinpoint a practical description of this act; we are told more about what it will achieve than about how it is to be done. The individual Catholic is urged to begin with a thorough and careful theological and historical evaluation of the relevant events. More precisely, purification of memory entails an act of *substitution*—the negative elements of the memory of the past history are to be eliminated from personal and collective conscience. The negative elements are described as "all forms of resentment or violence left by the inheritance of the past"—specifically the past which has been deemed through rigorous theological and historical judgments to be worthy of remorse. The purification is thus the elimination of the negative feelings which are then substituted by "a reconciled memory" (M&R 5.1).

Purification of memory liberates the conscience, both personal and communal. The document refers to it as an "historical examination of conscience before God" (M&R 5). There is talk of a recognition of guilt and of setting out on a "path of reconciliation," but the theological end is paramount—glorification of God. The attendant moral result, according to the ITC, is a renewed moral way of acting, but few specifics are offered. The earlier Vatican document, *We Remember*, draws a distinction between historical and religious memory. Historical memory is the attempt to learn about the "reality" of the Shoah and its causes. Moral/religious memory is described as "a very serious reflection of what gave rise to it" (WR, II). This distinction is not developed in the document, but the implication is that ordinary historical research is incapable of revealing what was really in the hearts of those involved in the Nazi persecutions.

There are several significant observations to be made about the purification of memory and the imagery that it evokes. On the one hand, it describes concrete acts—recognition of guilt, attempts at reconciliation, and ultimately a renewed mode of moral behavior—all acts to be admired, and all acts that mirror the description of the sacrament of reconciliation as described in the Catechism.[29] On the other hand, less concrete elements having to do with what exactly happens to the memory pose more serious questions. What appears troubling is that the image of purification is reminiscent of the phrase "whitewashing," which is used to describe the act of covering up something unpleasant. The process described by the ITC, of recognizing guilt and "owning up" to the historical acts requires the opposite of whitewashing. In other words, claiming responsibility is a way of accepting the stain associated with the action.

While the acceptance of a stain is hinted at throughout these documents, the most explicit description of what the purification of memory will achieve can be seen in the following quote. The ITC claims, "If the cause of possible resentment for evils suffered and the negative influences stemming from what was done in the past can be removed as a result of dialogue and the patient search for mutual understanding with those who feel injured by the words and deeds of the past, such a removal may help the community of the Church grow in holiness through reconciliation and peace in obedience to the Truth" (M&R 6.1).

In the earlier *We Remember* document, the language of purification of memory is not evident. Instead, the notion of the "duty of remembrance" is stressed. Interestingly, in *We Remember* the Vatican suggests that that duty arises not only because of the "close bonds of spiritual kinship" between Christians and Jews, but also because the future demands it. Thus, while memory is a reflection on the past, it serves a purpose for the future. Remembering this Shoah, then, will lead to full consciousness of the "salutary warning it entails: the spoiled seeds of anti-Judaism and anti-Semitism must never again be allowed to take root in any human heart" (WR, V). The language of "purified memory" develops further what this memory for the sake of the future is to look like.

While there is a clear theological appeal to the language of purification because of its connection to expiation and atonement, one wonders whether the use of such language ignores and possibly insults the sensibilities of many Holocaust victims and their survivors. Read in a thoroughly Catholic context, the language of purification is not intended to be insulting. And the description offered of what that purification entails is quite different than what one might expect from the metaphor of purification. Regardless of that fact, we are left with serious questions about the way this powerful metaphor has affected the reception of the Jubilee year apologies.

Like the earlier metaphor discussed, this one can also be interpreted both positively and negatively. The detailed account given by the ITC reveals that the purification is intended not as a way to delete memory, but rather as a way to remove all vestiges of the negative feelings that led to the horror of the Shoah. By substituting these memories with a reconciled memory, the foundation of "a renewed way of acting" (M&R, 5.1), the memory is purified without being destroyed. It is clear throughout many of the Church documents that the activities of remembering and meditating on the events of the past are encouraged. Note the title of the Vatican document *We Remember: Reflections on the Shoah*.

Nevertheless, the metaphor does reveal the vexing question: What is the appropriate way for the Church to respond? If not purification of memory, then what? In the same way that the language of the Church as mother suggests that the difficult question of collective guilt is left unanswered in these documents, this metaphor leaves unanswered what the appropriate Catholic response ought to be. What ought to be done with memory? And what if anything does that have to do with reconciliation and progress in Catholic-Jewish relations?

Whatever the extent of Catholic guilt and responsibility, either through action, inaction or complicity, the Pope and the magisterium are attempting to address the events of the Holocaust and to reach some resolution—in essence trying to remove any guilt. Part of the confusion raised by these apologies relates to a proper understanding of what such removal entails. Richard Swinburne suggests that the process of removing guilt has two parts. He writes, "In so far as guilt is analogous to debt, it can be removed either by the action of the wrongdoer in (some way) paying it off; or by the action of the victim in (some way) taking compensation . . . . For perfect removal of guilt, then, the wrongdoer must make atonement for his [sic] wrong act, and the victim must forgive him [sic]."[30]

Reducing the process to these two component parts focuses our attention on the central questions. First, what exactly is the Church doing in these statements to atone for its actions? The language of purification of memory for the reasons just stated simply obscures the essence of the Church's actions. Second, in the context of the Holocaust, receiving forgiveness from the victims who perished would be impossible, but what of the survivors, or relatives of the victim. To what extent would their forgiveness suffice? The Catholic documents relating to the apologies fail to address this very important question.

Swinburne goes on to describe four components of atonement: *repentance*, *apology* to the victim, *reparation*, and *penance*. This distinction between repentance and apology is helpful because by distinguishing repentance as the more private act of conscience from apology to the victim as the more public expression, Swinburne draws our attention to what might be the source of confusion here. The purification of memory, as described in the magisterial documents, blends components of both actions. It is at once both a private act and a public expression. The controversial aspect, however, is its role as a public expression.

Thus, while the public prayer of pardon offered by the Pope is a clear example of public confession, the traditional Catholic view of response to personal sin, described in the language of penance and conversion, encourages both public and private activity. Penance, as an interior act, according to the Catechism, can be expressed in various ways. Most prominent are fasting, prayer, and almsgiving. These activities express a conversion in relation to oneself, to God, and to others.[31] In *Sollicitudo Rei Socialis*, John Paul II describes the conversion as entailing "a relationship to God, to the sin committed, to the consequences, and hence to one's neighbor, either an individual or a community" (SRS, 38). It seems clear that theologically, the activity of penance must occur on both interior and exterior levels.

I think the Vatican texts about the confession of sins against the Jewish people are quite clear that in its essence, the purification of memory, is primarily an act of personal transformation. By contrast, the descriptions of penance and conversion in the Catechism and *Sollicitudo* capture the way in which the activity blends private and public acts. These descriptions would be more appropriate than the metaphor "purification of memory" in the context of the Holocaust where memory has been moved from the merely private realm into the public, and where for survivors, victims, and their families the act of remembering is both a collective ritual and an intensely personal act.

Swinburne makes another interesting point that is quite similar to the message the Vatican documents are trying to convey about purification. He claims that while a person cannot change the fact that she committed a certain act, what he or she can do is make sure that the present self is as different in attitude and action from the past self as possible. The activity of transformation by the agent who committed the act is the closest one can come to undoing that act, according to Swinburne.[32] This notion of transformation is quite similar to the purification of memory, which requires that the memory be formed anew.

The Catholic Church will continue the difficult process of formulating appropriate and adequate responses to the Holocaust. These jubilee year confessions are certainly not the final word. The analysis of the metaphorical language presented in this paper helps to pinpoint the troublesome issues that underlie such confessions. In the midst of these difficulties, however, the *Catechism* offers a useful reminder about the ultimate goal of these actions: "The confession (or disclosure) of sins, even from a simply human point of view, frees us and facilitates our reconciliation with others."[33]

NOTES

[1] The Pope's universal prayer for pardon covered a wide array of sins, including Christian intolerance, lack of faithfulness to the love commandment, intra-Christian fighting and condemnation, violation of the rights of entire groups and peoples, actions depriving women of their dignity and their rights, actions against the poor, the alienated and the unborn, and any actions that may have caused suffering to the people of Israel. This prayer can be viewed online at www.vatican.va/news_services/liturg..../ns_lit_doc_2000312_prayer-day-pardon_en.htm.

[2] For the purposes of this analysis of metaphorical language, I bracket an in-depth discussion of some of the fundamental questions about ecclesiology and the theology of repentance that these confessions provoke. For example, is this confession of sins and plea for forgiveness meant to be an apology? If so, to whom is the Pope apologizing? On whose behalf is he apologizing? Who has ultimate responsibility for the actions of the Church? What exactly does it mean for the Church to sin? These are clearly important questions that must be addressed by theologians.

[3] See for example, Katha Pollitt, "Regrets Only," *The Nation* v. 27, n. 13 (April 3, 2000), 10.

[4] See for example, Mary Ann Glendon, "Public Acts of Contrition in the Age of Spin Control," www.vatican.va/jubilee_2000/magazine/documents/ju_mag_01071997_p-26_en.html.

[5] The issue of sufficiency is complicated by the fact that, at present, a complete account of the precise nature and scope of the responsibility and guilt of Catholics and of the Catholic Church for the events of the Holocaust is lacking. Whether (and how much) blame rests on individual Catholics or on the Church as institution is certainly an important element of the context of these apologies and the reactions to them. For the purposes of this essay, however, I acknowledge that the Church and its members share *some* responsibility, both by omission and commission, and that therefore, an apology by the head of the Church was necessary and appropriate. As the full extent of that responsibility continues to be explored by scholars, the question of whether these apologies are sufficient will need to be revisited.

[6] Both documents can be viewed on line at www.vatican.va/.

[7] David Novak, "Jewish-Christian Relations in a Secular Age," The 1998 Swig Lecture, May 4, 1998, University of San Francisco, 2.

[8] John Paul II, Yad Vashem Speech, (March 23, 2000), Paragraph 1. Available online at www.vatican.va/holy_father/john_paul_ii/travels/documents/hf_jp-ii_spe_20000323_yad-vashem-mausoleum_en.html

[9] Eugene J. Fisher and Leon Klenicki, eds., *Spiritual Pilgrimage: Texts on Jews and Judaism 1979-1995, Pope John Paul II*, (New York: Crossroad, 1995), xxii-xxxvii.

[10] John Paul II, "Address to the Jewish Community, West Germany, (November 17, 1980)," in Fisher and Klenicki, eds., *Spiritual Pilgrimage*, 13-16.

[11] A recent brief summary of the controversy about Pius XII and the Holocaust appears in Judity Shulevitz, "The Close Reader: The Case of Pius XII," *The New York Times Book Review*, (April 8, 2001).

[12] Eugene J. Fisher, "A Commentary on the Texts..." in Fisher and Klenicki, eds. *Spiritual Pilgrimage*, xxxv.

[13] John Paul II, "Address given at the Synagogue of Rome, (April 13, 1986)," in Fisher and Klenicki, eds., *Spiritual Pilgrimage*, 62.

[14] Ibid.

[15] Directed by Edward Idris Cardinal Cassidy, President of the Church's Commission for Religious Relations with the Jews.

[16] See David Novak, "Jews and Catholics: Beyond Apologies," *First Things*, n. 89, 20-25 for a discussion of these responses.

[17] He does emphasize however that the "the Church's motherhood can never in fact be separated from her teaching mission . . . . " John Paul II, *Veritatis Splendor* (Boston: St. Paul's Books and Media, 1993), 117.

[18] Francis Sullivan, "The Papal Apology," *America* v. 18, n. 12 (April 8 2000), 17-22.

[19] Charles E. Curran, "What Catholic Ecclesiology Can Learn from Official Catholic Social Teaching," in *A Democratic Catholic Church: The Reconstruction of Catholicism*, Eugene C. Bianchi and Rosemary Radford Ruether, eds. (New York: Crossroad, 1992), 98.

[20] *Catechism of the Catholic Church (Libreria Editrice Vaticana)* (Mahwah: Paulist Press, 1994), part I, article 9, paragraph 753.

[21] The relation of personal sin to social sin is described in detail in two documents authored by John Paul II: the encyclical letter *Sollicitudo Rei Socialis* (1987) and the apostolic exhortation *Reconciliatio et Paenitentia* (1984). The claim that "social sin" is an analogy for many personal sins is based on the notion that even when sinful behavior can be attributed to a collective, "the real responsibility lies with individuals" (RP 16). Structures of sin are "rooted in personal sin, and thus always linked to the *concrete acts* of individuals who introduce these structures, consolidate them and make them difficult to remove. And thus they grow stronger, spread, and become the source of other sins, and so influence people's behavior" (SRS 36). See John Paul II, *Sollicitudo Rei Socialis* in *Catholic Social Thought, The Documentary Heritage*, David J. O'Brien and Thomas A. Shannon, eds. (Maryknoll: Orbis, 1992). *Reconciliatio et Paenitentia* is available online at www.vatican.va/

[22] For a different treatment of this issue see, Marion Smiley, *Moral Responsibility and the Boundaries of Community* (Chicago: University of Chicago Press, 1992).

[23] Larry May, *Sharing Responsibility* (Chicago: The University of Chicago Press, 1992).

[24] Ibid., p. 7.

[25] Novak, "Jewish-Christian Relations, " 9.

[26] Ibid.

[27] See footnote 21 for more detail.

[28] Leon Weiselteir, "Sorry," *The New Republic*, v. 22, n. 13 (March 27, 2000), 6.

[29] *Catechism*, part II, section 2, article 4.

[30] Richard Swinburne, *Responsibility and Atonement* (Oxford: Clarendon Press, 1989), 81.

[31] *Catechism,* part II, section 2, article 4, paragraphs 1434, 1435.

[32] Swinburne, *Responsibility and Atonement*, 83.

[33] *Catechism*, paragraph 1455. I am grateful to the three anonymous referees for the *Annual*, whose insightful comments helped me revise this paper. I thank John Kelsay and Carlos Lopez for their specific suggestions, and David Kangas for encouraging me to pursue this topic.

Alasdair MacIntyre as Help for Rethinking Catholic Natural Law Estimates of Same-Sex Life Partnerships

William McDonough

Abstract

Christian ethics struggles to articulate a method for thinking about homosexuality and the sexual acts of same-sex oriented persons. In 1988, Hanigan suggested a promising "social import" approach and then judged homosexual acts deficient. MacIntyre's *Dependent Rational Animals* (1999) articulates a fuller social import approach to morality. Although he does not address homosexuality, MacIntyre rejects narrow understandings of family and of "disinterested friendship": we need "communal relations that engage our affections" to grow in "the virtues of acknowledged dependence." How do gay people grow in these virtues? What if Hanigan got the method right, but the evaluation wrong?

Introduction

Do homosexuality and homosexual sex prove that what Stephen Pope recently referred to as a "wall between natural law theory and narrative ethics" is permanent and impassable?[1] Catholicism's natural law proscriptions and the narratives of homosexual persons, it would seem, have no possibility of meeting. Against such a thesis this paper argues that in his latest book Alasdair MacIntyre provides a rationale for why the Catholic Church, precisely because it is committed to natural law thinking, must re-think homosexuality.

Annual of the Society of Christian Ethics, 21 (2001): 191-213

Before I introduce my main argument that MacIntyre's recent work should lead to deepened Catholic natural law thinking about homosexuality, I briefly lay out a commonly accepted, and I think wrong, view that has set natural law and narrative approaches to ethical thinking in opposition. Here, in its baldest form, is the opposition that is often set up between narrative and natural law moralities: natural law is "an impersonal system of law applied abstractly to the individual [while narrative ethics prizes] a consideration of the person and his or her acts as the moral standard."[2]

According to this view, natural law theories "typically propose some set of basic principles as definitive of the moral law. Then they propose a method for applying those principles to cases."[3] What both proponents and opponents of Catholicism's evaluation of homosexuality seem to agree on is that natural law thinking leads almost inexorably to the rejection of homosexuality. The 1994 English edition of *The Catechism of the Catholic Church* summarizes such a natural law approach to homosexuality:

> (T)radition has always declared that "homosexual acts are intrinsically disordered." They are contrary to the natural law . . . . The number of men and women who have deep-seated homosexual tendencies is not negligible. They do not choose their homosexual condition; for most of them it is a trial . . . . Homosexual persons are called to chastity. By the virtues of self-mastery that teach them inner freedom, at times by the support of disinterested friendship, by prayer and sacramental grace, they can and should gradually and resolutely approach Christian perfection.[4]

Natural law moralities, it would seem, exhibit compassion for homosexual persons but can never accept homosexual sex.

On the other side of the wall there are narrative approaches to ethics. In his own earlier writing, MacIntyre proposed narrative as the best alternative to what he called, first, the "social conservatism" and, then later, the "metaphysical biology" of natural law thinking influenced by Aristotle.[5] In his 1981 work *After Virtue,* MacIntyre proposed that ". . . all attempts to elucidate the notion of personal identity independently of and in isolation from the notions of narrative, intelligibility and accountability are bound to fail . . . . What is better or worse for X depends upon the character of that intelligible narrative which provides X's life with its unity."[6]

MacIntyre's emphasis on "narrative unity" was then taken up by gay writers. Gay Catholic Andrew Sullivan is a case in point. He wrote that, for homosexual persons, Catholic natural law thinking is ". . . an unethic, a statement that some people are effectively beneath even the project of an ethical teaching."[7] Sullivan even over-optimistically extended his argument by saying that the narratives of gay lives had to affect Catholic natural law thinking:

What finally convinced me of the wrongness of the Church's teachings was not that they were intellectually so confused, but that in the circumstances of my own life—and of the lives I discovered around me—they seemed so destructive of human love and self-realization . . . . This truth is not an argument; it is merely an observation. But observations are at the heart . . . of the Church's traditional Thomist philosophy . . . . (S)uch lives as those of countless gay men and lesbians must ultimately affect the Church not because our lives are perfect, or without contradiction, or without sin, but because our lives are in some sense also the life of the Church. [8]

But appeals by gay people to the "narrative unity" of their lives have not (yet) affected official Catholic thinking in the way Sullivan hoped. They have had the opposite effect. Against appeals to gay experience, Catholic teaching has invoked natural law thinking to reiterate, even to strengthen, its rejection of homosexual sex. So, when the *Catechism* was given final form in 1997, Rome added the following italicized phrase into the text of its earlier rejection of homosexual sex: "This inclination, *which is objectively disordered*, constitutes for most of them a trial." [9]

Now Catholic natural law thinking has always made room for the distortion of human experience by original sin. Garry Wills recently summarized the tradition: ". . . there is something kinky or askew in ordinary human nature." [10] Metaphorically, then, Catholic natural law thinking has always known that there are stumbling stones on the path all human beings must travel to understand their own experience. "Narrative" does not translate easily to "nature" for any human being. But, in the last decade, official Catholicism has claimed more than this for homosexual persons: not only stumbling stones, but an impassable wall separates homosexual persons from their own experience.

In shoring up its teaching against homosexual sex in this way, official Catholicism is in danger of undermining its own natural law tradition. To construct a wall between narrative and nature is to leave natural law thinking behind. Gregory Baum, in an article on "Homosexuality and the Natural Law," put it this way:

The natural law tradition (holds)…that human beings are by their God-created nature oriented toward the *bonum*—toward their personal good as well as humanity's common good . . . . Some theologians have insisted that this natural law is discoverable by unaided human reason….while others, more conscious of the confusion sin has produced in the human mind, have proposed that reason needs God's gracious help to discover the inner structure that guides people toward the *bonum* . . . . (But) rejection of natural law is rooted in the conviction that the original sin that weighs upon us has damaged the human nature in us and weakened our intelligence so that we inevitably go astray if we presume to follow our own wisdom or our own inclination."[11]

In short, my introductory argument is that natural law thinking knows there is a stumbling stone between narrative and nature, but it cannot tolerate a wall. I have two aims in this paper. First, I want to contribute to a more general re-thinking of natural law methodologies in morality through the test case of homosexuality. My general point is that Catholic natural law thinking never was intended to be "an impersonal system of law" or "some basic set of principles . . . applied to cases."[12] A better theological understanding of natural law was given by Walter Kasper:

> What is already given and laid upon human freedom as the condition which makes it possible is what we call nature. Nature is God's creation. It is not made by human beings and cannot be made by them. It therefore has its own dignity. It has to be cultivated by human beings, but it must not be manipulated arbitrarily and at will. This suggests that the idea of natural law ought to be creatively renewed.[13]

My more particular aim here is to contribute to the dismantling of the wall separating natural law and narrative methods of thinking about homosexuality. This essay argues that a "creative renewal of natural law," and not just narrative ethics, requires the Catholic tradition to re-think its position on homosexuality. Specifically, I want to demonstrate that the *Catechism's* labeling of the homosexual inclination as "disordered" coupled to its invitation to homosexual persons to accept the support of "disinterested friendship" and so move "toward Christian perfection" is incoherent.[14] I will show that the *Catechism's* idea of "disinterested friendship" rests on a mistaken idea of the Stoics; it does not rest on the best of the Catholic tradition of natural law thinking.

In making my particular argument I rely on Alasdair MacIntyre, both substantively and methodologically. Substantively, this paper argues that natural law morality can and should recognize the sanctity of the life partnerships of homosexual persons. I am claiming here that MacIntyre's new book *Dependent Rational Animals* provides exactly what Stephen Pope claims is necessary for an adequate moral assessment of homosexuality, namely "a more precise and comprehensive account of genuine human flourishing."[15]

Methodologically, I am beginning to do here what MacIntyre said a decade ago one must do if one wishes to argue with a tradition. I am suggesting how we might move beyond the impasse—what MacIntyre called an "epistemological crisis" —in Catholic thinking about homosexuality. MacIntyre says three things must be done to move through such a crisis:

(First, one's proposal) must furnish a solution to the problems which had previously proved intractable in a systematic and coherent way. Second, it must also provide an explanation of just what it was which rendered the tradition, before it had acquired these new resources, sterile or incoherent or both. And third, these first two tasks must be carried out in a way which exhibits some fundamental continuity of the new conceptual and theoretical structures with the shared beliefs in terms of which the tradition of enquiry had been defined up to this point.[16]

My paper proceeds in three steps, corresponding to the three tasks MacIntyre lays out above. First, I outline the contribution of MacIntyre's new book, seeing in it a breakthrough toward an adequate notion of human flourishing. Second, I suggest that the failures of the natural law tradition on homosexuality flow from its too close association with Stoicism, particularly the mistaken Stoic understanding of disinterested friendship. Third, I point to twentieth century Catholicism's revised understanding of marriage as a *totius vitae communio* as already a demonstration of continuity-within-change in its thinking about sexuality. My conclusion comes back to the logic for recognizing the sanctity of same-sex life partnerships.

Dependent Rational Animals' Account of Human Flourishing: Breaking Down the Wall between Narrative and Natural Law Moralities

In another place I have argued that Alasdair MacIntyre's new book *Dependent Rational Animals* is his best and most coherent.[17] There I emphasize that MacIntyre's admission of error at the beginning of the new book constitutes a significant, though under-noticed, revision in his own thinking. On this book's second page, MacIntyre writes: "In *After Virtue* I had attempted to give an account of the place of the virtues...within social practices, the lives of individuals and the lives of communities . . . . I now judge that I was in error in supposing an ethics independent of biology to be possible."[18]

In another paper, I argued that MacIntyre's shift signals a move from a "sociologically grounded" morality of communal practices to a "biologically grounded" morality of human nature. Though not precise enough, those categories describe a real and helpful shift in MacIntyre's thought: in recognizing his own need to connect "social practices" and "biology," MacIntyre is naming moral theory's need to re-connect personal narrative and natural law.

MacIntyre's new book offers the more precise account of human flourishing contemporary morality needs, a "culturally neutral" and "pre-conventional" account of human goodness.[19] Here is one more piece of evidence for the important shift taking place in the new book. One of the oddest assertions of

MacIntyre's "sociological" period of moral theorizing came in his 1988 work *Whose Justice? Which Rationality?* There, he wrote that "facts, like telescopes and wigs for gentlemen, were a seventeenth-century invention . . . . There are in fact no nontrivial statements which have appeared evidently true to *all* human beings of moderate intelligence."[20] But MacIntyre has abandoned this view, for his new book is full of references to facts. His first chapter opens with such a reference: "(T)wo related sets of facts . . . are so evidently of singular importance that it might seem that no account of the human condition whose authors hoped to achieve credibility could avoid giving them a central place."[21]

What, to go now to the substance of MacIntyre's view, are these facts that ground human flourishing? There are two of them, "those concerning our vulnerabilities and afflictions and those concerning the extent of our dependence on particular others."[22] The most basic truth about every human being is that "from the outset she or he is in debt," for the "facts of affliction and dependence" are given in all our lives.[23]

MacIntyre's singling out of vulnerability and dependence as determinative for morality certainly is an interpretation of given facts, but as Jean Porter says this is what natural law thinking has always done: it involves an "interpretation of universal principles of moral action, which therefore apply to all persons."[24] MacIntyre proposes his two facts as the central, morally relevant ones because they reveal our "initial directedness to certain goods . . . . Having been cared for, (we) care for others."[25]

MacIntyre's facts add up to a twofold view of human flourishing, encompassing both an account of goodness and of the virtues that support that goodness. A good human being has "learned to act without thought of any justification beyond the need of those given into (her) care."[26] MacIntyre says three times in the book that the facts of vulnerability and dependence require that a good person must come to be able to give to another human being, after herself having first received, unconditional love.[27] Over a lifetime of being cared for and caring, I will have become good when one can see in the way I live that "the good of the individual . . . (is neither) subordinate to the good of the community nor vice versa."[28]

The facts about us and the moral goodness that stems from them give MacIntyre what he calls his "central thesis . . . that the virtues we need . . . (are) the distinctive virtues of dependent rational animals, whose dependence, rationality, and animality have to be understood in relationship to each other."[29] These are "the virtues of acknowledged dependence," and MacIntyre emphasizes two of them: "just generosity" and "elementary truthfulness."[30] Just generosity summarizes three patterns of giving and receiving that I must learn in my life: affective relationship, hospitality, and openness to urgent need. Truthfulness demands that I allow the other to learn what he needs to learn, that I do not conceal my own need to learn, and that I do not withdraw from the circle of learning in what MacIntyre calls "ironic detachment."

In sum, we have in MacIntyre's new book a fuller account of human flourishing than he has ever given. This is a natural law ethic of care in which "flourishing . . . is in itself a question of fact": a good human being is one who has learned to give and receive a love that is disinterested in the sense of unconditional.[31]

My argument here is that this account should lead us to recognize the sanctity of same-sex life partnerships. But before I come to that, I need to show both what has blocked the Catholic tradition from reaching this deeper vision of the good and that the tradition has the resources to move toward it. First, the blocks.

Either MacIntyre and Plutarch or the *Catechism* and the Stoics: What is "Disinterested Friendship" and How Does One Come to It?

Many have shown the Stoic influences on Catholic Church thinking about sex. John Noonan says that early on Western Christianity accepted "the Stoic ideal" about sex, adding:

> The Stoics sought to control bodily desire by reason, to the end of being rationally self-sufficient, dependent on no external force . . . . In fact, the Stoic view of marital intercourse, the stress on procreative purpose, the failure to connect intercourse and love, were profound influences on the Christian approach; the doctrine of contraception, as it was fashioned, largely depended upon [Stoicism].[32]

Jean Porter says Christian natural law thinking transcended the impersonal, fatalistic Stoic understanding of natural law in most areas, except sex: "(The) Stoic view (is) that the wise person will engage in sexual acts only for the sake of procreation . . . . (T)he actual negative evaluation of sexual desire (in Christianity) seems to owe more to the Stoics than to Scripture."[33] In the next section of this paper, I will show signs of the waning influence of Stoicism in Catholic sexual morality. In this section, I show that Stoic thinking is very much alive in Catholic thinking about homosexuality.

I am interested in one Stoic mistake about sex, more precisely in a mistake about human friendship, because it has carried over into the *Catechism*'s treatment of homosexuality. My claim here is that the *Catechism*'s offer of disinterested friendship to homosexual persons is an offer of Stoic friendship, disembodied and lacking in affective content. It is not an offer of the kind of friendship MacIntyre knows all of us to need, an "unconditional care for the human being as such."[34]

MacIntyre shows us this Stoic mistake about friendship by citing a text from Plutarch (c. 47-120 CE), "the most valuable of the opponents of Stoicism."[35]

Plutarch is cited within MacIntyre's own argument that human beings must not neglect our animal identities:

> To become an effective independent practical reasoner is an achievement, but it is always one to which others have made essential contributions. The earliest of these relate directly to our animal existence, to what we share in our development with members of other intelligent species. We owe to parents . . . that care from conception through birth and infancy to childhood that dolphins also owe to elders who provide maternal and other care. And in human as in dolphin life there are patterns of receiving and giving, enduring through and beyond the life-span of particular individuals. Dolphins, having been cared for, care for others, sometimes extending such care beyond their own species to human beings. So Plutarch, in a dialogue comparing the excellences of sea creatures to those of land animals, ascribed to dolphins . . . "that virtue so much sought after by the best philosophers: the capacity for disinterested friendship."[36]

Plutarch's text is from his dialogue "Whether Land or Sea Animals are Cleverer," and is spoken by an advocate for the superiority of sea animals.[37] The dialogue, however, is not intended to decide this question and ends with neither position winning the day. Rather, it ends with the narrator making an anti-Stoic point: "For by combining what you have said about each other, you will together put up a good fight against those (Stoics) who would deprive animals of reason and understanding." [38]

Plutarch's anti-Stoic point is not lost on MacIntyre, who uses the text to argue for the essential animal identities of human beings: "Both dolphins and humans have animal identities and animal histories. (But) human beings are able on occasion to ignore or conceal from themselves this fact."[39] Human animality and the necessary grounding of morality in that animality is the central point of MacIntyre's book, and just here a brief look into Plutarch's anti-Stoic writings helps with why this point is so important. For Plutarch already argued against the very error I see in the Catholic *Catechism*'s approach to homosexuality.

Plutarch's anti-Stoic polemic perhaps reached its height in "Beasts are Rational," a short dialogue whose protagonist is a pig speaking to Odysseus on how mistaken the Stoics are "to consider all creatures except man irrational and senseless." [40] So Plutarch chides the Stoics for forgetting the animal identities of human beings. This chiding does not appear in the three dialogues Plutarch specifically entitled as attacks on the Stoics.[41] I make a brief foray into one of these dialogues, though, because what does appear in Plutarch's dialogue "Against the Stoics on Common Conceptions" is a fuller argument against the Stoics' "stale" notion of the good.[42]

What is stale for Plutarch is the Stoic philosopher Chrysippus' (280-206 BCE) paradoxical use of the most "common conceptions," including the concept of nature. For Plutarch, the Stoics' understanding of nature became unhinged from human beings' "common experiences" in the world. Plutarch quotes Chrysippus as writing: " . . . the standard by which life must be measured is not goods and evils but the things in conformity with nature and contrary to it." To defend the wise person as alone living *kata physein* and as essentially self-sufficient, Chrysippus and the Stoics had to say that all other goods a person seeks, except that of living *kata physein,* are indifferent (*adiaphora*). Plutarch comments wryly, "This is the way they save common experience for men and philosophize with a view to the common conceptions."[43] In fact, Plutarch thinks the Stoics have not saved common experience at all. They have obfuscated and undermined any connection between the philosophically "natural" and the good of persons in the real world. Plutarch continues:

> Consider straight away, then (whether the doctrine of the Stoics itself is in accord with the common conceptions . . . [and is] in agreement with nature). Is it in accord with the common conceptions to say that they are in agreement with nature who believe indifferent (*adiaphora*) the things that are in conformity with nature and who hold health and vigour and beauty and strength not to be objects of choice or beneficial or advantageous or constitutive of natural perfections and their opposites— mutilations, pains, deformities, diseases—not to be injurious and objects of avoidance? . . . While making life in conformity with nature a goal, they believe the things that are in conformity to nature to be indifferent.[44]

By the time the Stoic finishes defending this "nature" there is no content left to it other than conforming to duty. In concluding this attack on Stoic natural law, Plutarch summarizes and provides a metaphor. The summary: ". . . the Stoics in their works and acts cling to the things that are in conformity with nature as good things and objects of choice, but in word and speech they reject and spurn them as indifferent and useless and insignificant for happiness."[45] And the metaphor: to try to live this morality is to be like "those who are leaping from the ground and tumbling down on it again."[46] Stoic natural law turns out to be separated by more than a wall from the narratives of persons in the world; it is separated from narrative by a magic trick. All one has to do to live the Stoic natural law is defy gravity.

I read MacIntyre's insistence on the moral significance of human animality as a gloss on Plutarch's critique of the Stoics. As Plutarch critiqued the Stoic natural law for its ungroundedness, so MacIntyre critiques the "blandly generalized benevolence" of too much contemporary thinking about moral goodness:

> What such benevolence presents us with is a generalized Other—one whose only relationship to us is to provide an occasion for the exercise of *our* benevolence, so that we can reassure ourselves about our own good will—in place of those particular others with whom we must learn to share common goods, and participate in ongoing relationships.[47]

Blandly generalized benevolence is a perfect summary of the Stoic notion of "disinterested friendship." What the Stoic achieves is not a friendship that has calmed self-seeking by ongoing and shared life. If Stoic friendship is disinterested, it has become so by considering all human relationships indifferent. It has not become so by finding in them the movement toward unconditional love. It is an ersatz friendship without affective content and commitment.[48]

It is this ersatz Stoic account of friendship that has rendered the Catholic tradition incoherent on homosexuality. The account of human flourishing offered by MacIntyre offers an alternative to Stoicism's friendship: having been cared for, we will then care for others; we will learn to act toward them without any other reason than that they are given in our care. In this paper's next section, I show that Catholicism is already moving toward this MacIntyrean, non-Stoic understanding of marriage as a committed partnership moving outward in love; this opens the way for our reconsideration of same-sex life partnerships.

Vatican II and the Development of Catholic Thinking about Sexuality: Evidence for the Continuity-in-Change of Acknowledging the Sanctity of Same-Sex Life Partnerships

British theologian Kevin Kelly said a while ago that although at Vatican II the Catholic Church articulated a profound theology of marriage, this was not yet a profound theology of sexuality.[49] But there is another perspective. Without pretending that it summarizes all Catholic thinking about marriage and sexuality, the following generalization is accurate: the twentieth century saw a Catholic flight from Stoicism in its sexual morality. That this flight has not yet affected Catholic thinking about homosexuality is an indication that the flight has not been far and fast enough.

Giuseppe Baldanza's recent historical-critical study of the development of official Catholic thinking on marriage claims that twentieth century Catholic thinking here comprises a "progress in continuity" leading to an understanding of marriage "as a state of sanctification."[50] I briefly summarize Baldanza on the profoundly non-Stoic development in Catholicism's understanding of marriage and summarize this development by connecting it to one systematic theological view of love.

Baldanza says Catholics are so used to reading their tradition on marriage and sexuality for its "juridical-moral focus" that they are in danger of missing the more essential development of the church's theology of marriage in the just completed century.[51] Though Baldanza sees "a serene and positive vision of marriage and sexuality" in the documents of the sixteenth century Council of Trent, he says Trent's assertion that in marriage *gratia perficit amorem naturalem* risked an "extrinsicist conception" of God's workings in the lives of married couples.[52]

He highlights two twentieth century changes in Catholic teaching that transcend this extrinsicism. First, the 1930 encyclical *Casti connubii* (usually read only for its condemnation of birth control) should be read for its definition of marriage as "the blending of life as a whole," a *totius vitae communio*.[53] The encyclical introduced into the tradition an anthropology of marriage which "encompasses the affective and sexual life of the spouses." *Casti connubii* is the first teaching of the Catholic Church to include sexual love in marriage's sacramental symbolism.[54] Baldanza summarizes the change:

> *Casti connubii* signals progress with respect to scholastic theology and that of the manuals. In a general way, there is in those earlier theologies a distinction between matrimony as a state and conjugal acts as an exercise of matrimony. This distinction was made to account for marriage's concrete structure being conditioned by original sin . . . . Even St. Thomas, who accepted the three *bona* of St. Augustine, added the distinction that these goods were excusing because they brought an equilibrium to the conjugal act, there being a *iactura* (a losing of oneself) in that act ever since the first sin . . . . Even though sexual acts were considered as meritorious if performed in the state of grace and according to the divine law, nevertheless, those acts were not encompassed into marriage's signification.[55]

A second essential development in twentieth century Catholic thinking about marriage was necessary to overcome the juridical-moral perspective that had prevailed for centuries. It came when *Gaudium et spes* claimed that "conjugal love is assumed into divine love" in marriage.[56] Baldanza thinks a revolution is in the making in the change of a Latin verb from Trent's *perficit* to Vatican II's *assumit*:

> The difference between the traditional perspective and that of *Gaudium et spes* can be summarized in this way: in the first, divine action is directed at healing, empowering, elevating the love of the spouses, and giving them the spiritual helps for the various duties of marriage. In the second perspective, without excluding all that, the emphasis is that Christ goes out to the spouses to encounter them, *to assume their own love into his spousal love for the church*. And this in force of the

incarnation and the paschal mystery that constitutes the new and eternal covenant, an alliance of communion and salvation for all.[57]

In sum, two changes occurred in Catholic thinking about marriage in the twentieth century: first, sexual love is seen to be of the essence of marriage; second, that sexual love itself is assumed into God and becomes sacramental of God's love. Certainly this is not the whole story of official Catholic teaching about marriage and sexuality.[58] But I am not trying to tell that whole story here. Instead I am showing an unmistakable move by Catholicism away from Stoicism in the last century. Something very different from Stoicism's rescuing of sexual acts by their procreative purpose is underway when *Gaudium et spes* repeated *Casti connubii*'s new definition of marriage, and added: "Even in cases where despite the intense desire of the spouses there are no children, marriage still retains its character of being a whole manner and communion of life (*totius vitae communio*) and preserves its value and indissolubility." [59]

Where is this history leading? In his magisterial article "Love," in the *New Dictionary of Theology,* Enda McDonagh systematizes the point made in Baldanza's history. McDonagh rejects as "specious" the strict separation Anders Nygren and others see "between the spontaneous unmerited creative love of *agape* and the responsive, desiring love of *eros* . . . . In Nygren's version such love of desire turns the beloved into a means of satisfaction for the lover."[60] McDonagh instead says all human love is imperfect and has its beginnings in an ambiguity that can open itself out or close itself down. Says McDonagh:

> The movements of desire for the good, essential to a material historical being, can be distinguished in their ambiguity as they open the way to concern for the good in itself or simply to the good for the self. Grace and power of agape may develop and transform the movement to the good in itself. *Eros* in that positive sense provides the substrate for human agapeic regard with its responsive recognizing of value in its creative letting-be of the other. Of course, no human movement entirely sheds its ambiguity, so that elements of self-centered *eros* persist. It was perhaps the distinction within the ambiguity and the inevitable persistence of selfish elements which misled Nygren and others.[61]

From within the ambiguity of all human loving (and not from outside of it), McDonagh tells us to find the signs of a love that is being assumed into God. He offers two criteria:

> The first is the concrete and inviolable value of the divine other and of the human other. It is this which provokes desire, recognition and response whether for its own sake or to satisfy the desire of the

recognizer. And it is this 'independent,' inviolable value of the other which exposes the movement of simple desire as finally inadequate . . . .

> (The second is that) only in the reciprocity of communion is the other-regarding, self-giving of authentic loving able to provide the . . . shared flourishing which is the thrust of the divine love for and in human beings . . . . The communal thrust of Christian loving is already apparent in its demand for communion, once it is clear that such a communion cannot be confined to some *égoisme à deux* but must incorporate each in all her or his ramifying relationships . . . . One imagines a God-given love as a field of forces within which human beings seek to orient themselves.[62]

McDonagh gives systematic definition to Baldanza's history: a love being assumed into God is one that both does no harm to the beloved (that lets the beloved be) and is joined with the beloved in a "shared flourishing" that widens more and more to include others in the circle. What both Baldanza's history and McDonagh's systematics highlight is that the Catholic tradition is moving further and further away from its (Stoic derived) schematized division of marriage's "two ends" of procreation and interpersonal love.[63] Instead of speaking of those "two ends," an adequate theology of sexuality will talk of the two mutually dependent and mutually enhancing characteristics of authentic love: love lets be, and it enables the partners (and others) to be. Let McDonagh again give voice to these two characteristics of authentic love:

> Letting be and enabling to be between God and human beings, as well as between human beings themselves require reciprocity for continuance and fulfillment. To continue to give oneself in true regard for the other requires the development of the self also, so that there is more to give. It is part of the rich paradox of divine creation and giving that human beings develop through giving, in the end through unconditional giving.[64]

Again, here, love's "disinterest" is in its move toward unconditionality, not in its indifference. We have, almost, come full circle. McDonagh's two characteristics of love (letting be and enabling to be) correlate nicely to MacIntyre's two virtues of acknowledged dependence (elementary truthfulness and just generosity). McDonagh and MacIntyre meet to provide an account of human flourishing adequate for a natural law recognition of the sanctity of same-sex life partnerships.

Conclusion:
Toward a MacIntyrean Ethic of Same-Sex Life Partnerships

I end this paper by returning to MacIntyre's twin virtues of acknowledged dependence to sketch a case for acknowledging the sanctity of same-sex life partnerships. I take elementary truthfulness first because its three qualities (allowing the other to learn, allowing myself to learn, and not withdrawing in irony) correlate so well with the "letting be" that McDonagh labels the first characteristic of love. Both MacIntyre and McDonagh give homosexual persons room to rest long enough in their desire to see what it might mean, room for what the tradition has called desire's needed complacency: the acknowledgment of some "presence already of the good and hence (allowing) a state of rest." [65] The biggest problem with the Catholic *Catechism*'s labeling of homosexual desire as *intrinsice inordinata* is that it gives a homosexual person no room to rest, to let desire be. It achieves "disinterested friendship" only by a Stoic leap away from desire. This cannot be the way to truthfulness.

But can same-sex life partnerships embody elementary truthfulness? The common objection to (male) homosexual sexuality's ability to instantiate truthfulness is that such sexuality almost inevitably becomes eroticism. Jean Porter, for example, writes that "there do appear to be some characteristically gay lifestyles . . . . (that) are typically characterized by a celebration of the erotic, as expressed through a cult of personal beauty and the practice of widespread sexual activity." [66] Such eroticism would not meet the test of MacIntyre's virtue of truthfulness: it lacks an acknowledgment of human vulnerability.[67]

Porter herself envisions the possibility of "an argument for the naturalness of homosexuality precisely in terms of its intelligible purpose," though she does not develop one.[68] J. Michael Clark does develop such an argument, "oppos(ing) the commoditization of our gay male sexuality and any eroticization of peoples which might encourage their exploitation" and "celebrat(ing) relationships, especially our human coupled commitments."[69] On what (non-Stoic) grounds could we judge such relationships to lack elementary truthfulness?

Vatican II acknowledged that marriage partnerships are where some human beings learn to live an ever-deepening truthfulness. Their *totius vitae* commitments are the place where their imperfect love and their imperfect lives are gradually "assumed" into God. Why would not physically embodied commitment also be the place where homosexual persons grow in love?

What of MacIntyre's second virtue, just generosity, and its three patterns of affective relationship, hospitality, and openness to urgent need? Can the "enabling to be" that just generosity allows be lived in same-sex partnerships? Just to phrase the questions in this way is helpful. Twelve years ago, James Hanigan tried to rearticulate the tradition's procreative concern as one about the "social import" of same-sex life partnerships:

> We must ask whether homosexual unions can and sometimes should be understood to be graced callings oriented to the service of God's people . . . . When married couples engage in sexual intercourse they are exercising and realizing both the personal and social meaning of their calling, to be for one another and thereby to establish and secure that center of life and love around which family develops and grows and serves society. While homosexual couples can certainly mirror some of these characteristics in their life together, why is sexual activity essential to their efforts? Their sexual activity undoubtedly has personal and private significance to them, but what is its social import? In what way does it edify the community, or sustain its unity, or add to its numbers?[70]

Hanigan's "social import" criterion melts right back into the procreative principle. But this is exactly the move that *Gaudium et spes* refused to make when it claimed infertile heterosexual couples can live the same *totius vitae communio* that couples with children live.[71]

What MacIntyre's three qualities of affective relationship, hospitality and openness to urgent need offer the tradition is a non-Stoic understanding of the outward movement of love. Thirty-five years ago Rosemary Haughton responded sharply to a bit of Stoicism she saw in Bernhard Häring's assertion that "The stronger and purer the sense of family is, the more is the directly sexual love of the spouses subdued, but also the freer are their charitable impulses." Haughton shot back:

> But this "subduing" of sexual love means that the relationship is developing naturally, growing and opening outwards as it should do. It is not "subdued," but empowered, and the "charitable impulses" are the natural and proper result of sexual love that forms and expresses and increases a true community of the Spirit, which is of course *diffusivum sui* . . . . There is no should about it. If this human love is real then it *does* come from God and lead back to him.[72]

I am asking that we look harder than Hanigan does for the "opening outwards" of same-sex life partnerships. A first place to see the evidence of such opening is in adoption of children by same-sex partners. In her latest book Haughton is busy "reimagining the meaning of family in terms of hospitality," and writes that this makes it "easier to accept the existence of 'unconventional' households...of homosexual partners . . . . In (such) households we can envisage children growing up."[73] My home county (Hennepin County, Minnesota—including Minneapolis) is one of a limited number of counties nation-wide openly encouraging homosexual persons to adopt children. Firm data are not yet available, but anecdotal evidence suggests that single and partnered homosexual persons make up a significant and increasing number of the adoptive parents in my county.[74] Yet, just generosity's three patterns of affective relationship, hospitality, and openness to urgent need do not only manifest themselves in raising children. In claiming that partnerships are where gay persons can move toward "human love and self-realization" and away from "solitary eccentricity, frustrated bitterness, and incapacitating anxiety," Andrew Sullivan is making a natural law argument for the just generosity of same-sex life partnerships.[75]

To be sure, whether same-sex life partnerships can embody and encourage the virtues of acknowledged dependence is not MacIntyre's concern. He is concerned rather to challenge a "social environment" that does not support the care of its most vulnerable and dependent members and in which "we ourselves will continue to lead distorted lives."[76] I link MacIntyre's concern to my own because the distortion he points out is the Stoic flight from animality, the same flight I claim is distorting Christian understanding of homosexuality.

MacIntyre does write this: "All happy families are not alike and only a very great novelist could have gotten away with telling us otherwise."[77] It is time for my religious tradition, which now sees that God comes down into the lives of married persons and assumes them into God's own life, to see that families established by same-sex life partners can also be happy families. Not to do so is to continue asking homosexual persons to live the Stoic mistake about friendship in their lives; it is to ask them to find unconditional love by becoming indifferent to their deepest desires. But indifference does not bring unconditional love; it brings distortion. Simone Weil names both the distortion and the way out of it: "We cannot take a single step toward heaven. It is not in our power to travel in a vertical direction. If, however, we look heavenward for a long time, God comes and takes us up."[78] The Catholic natural law tradition should celebrate the *totius vitae communio* of same-sex partners, just as it celebrates it for heterosexual partners, as a place into which God can come and "take us up" into God's own life.

NOTES

[1]Stephen Pope, "Scientific and Natural Law Analyses of Homosexuality: A Methodological Study," *Journal of Religious Ethics* 25 (1997): 117.

[2] Thomas Shannon, "*Gaudium et spes*: Its Prologue and Legacy," *The Eighth Annual Lecture in Catholic Studies Sponsored by the Edmundite Trust Fund for Catholic Studies and Ministry at St. Michael's College* (Colchester, VT: St. Michael's College, 1996), 11.

See my critique of this understanding of Catholic morality: McDonough, "The Church in the Modern World: Rereading *Gaudium et Spes* after Thirty Years," in Anthony Cernera, ed. *Vatican II: The Continuing Agenda* (Fairfield, CT: Sacred Heart University Press, 1997), at 116-117.

[3] Jeffrey Stout, "Truth, Natural Law and Ethical Theory," in Robert P. George, ed. *Natural Law Theory: Contemporary Essays* (New York: Oxford University Press, 1992), 84.

[4] *Catechism of the Catholic Church* (Città del Vaticano: Libreria Editrice Vaticano,1994), paragraphs 2358-2359.

[5] MacIntyre's rejection of Aristotle's "social conservatism" is found at Alasdair MacIntyre, *A Short History of Ethics*, reprinted (Notre Dame, IN: University of Notre Dame Press, 1998) 80; his rejection of Aristotle's "metaphysical biology" is in MacIntyre, *After Virtue*, revised ed. (Notre Dame, IN: University of Notre Dame Press, 1984)196-197.

[6] MacIntyre, *After Virtue*, 218, 225.

[7] Andrew Sullivan, *Love Undetectable: Notes onFriendship, Sex, and Survival* (New York: Alfred A. Knopf, 1998), 45. Gerald Schner says "The appeal to experience is a negative moment which alerts us . . . to the unexpressed, that is, to the fact that the speaker is absent, is not represented by the conversation partner." Schner, "The appeal to experience," *Theological Studies* 53 (1992): 45.

[8] Sullivan, "Alone again, Naturally: The Catholic Church and the Homosexual," *The New Republic* 28 (November 28, 1994): 55.

[9] *Catechism of the Catholic* Church, revised in accordance with the official Latin text promulgated by Pope John Paul II (Città del Vaticano: Libreria Editrice Vaticano, 1997), paragraph 2358. Two studies summarize the addition of the *obiective inordinata* text to the catechism: Jack Bosnor, "Homosexual Orientation and Anthropology: Reflections on the Category 'Objective Disorder,'" *Theological Studies* 59 (1998): 60-83; and Peter Black, "Revisions of Homosexuality: The Catechism and 'Always our Children," *Louvain Studies* 25 (2000): 72-81.
    The addition of *obiective inordinata* is curious, given the principles expressed by Cardinal Josef Ratzinger for what was to be included in the text: "The methodology of the catechism was a tricky problem. Should we follow a more 'inductive' method...or should we start from the faith itself and argue from within its own logic, that is, testifying rather than reasoning? . . . .In the end, we agreed that analyses of our time always involve an element of arbitrariness and depend too much on the point of view adopted in advance . . . . (T)he *Catechism* avoids tying itself too much to the circumstances of the moment, since it aims to offer the service of unity not merely synchronically . . . but also diachronically." Cardinal Josef Ratzinger, *"The Catechism of the Catholic Church* and the optimism of the redeemed." *Communio* 20 (1993): 475-476.

[10] Garry Wills, *Saint Augustine* (New York: Penguin Books, 1999), 131.

[11] Gregory Baum, "Homosexuality and the Natural Law," *The Ecumenist* 1/2 (January-February, 1994): 33.

[12] Shannon, *"Gaudium et spes*: Its Prologue and Legacy," 11; Stout, "Truth, Natural Law and Ethical Theory," 84.

[13] Walter Kasper, *Theology and Church*, trans. by Margaret Kohl (New York: Crossroad Publishing Company, 1989), 52-53, 92. MacIntyre defines natural law in a similar way: "The precepts of the natural law are those precepts promulgated by God through reason without conformity to which human beings cannot achieve their common good." MacIntyre, *Dependent Rational Animals*, 111.
    This understanding of nature is misunderstood in Bosnor's article. Bosnor thinks Aquinas's "metaphysical anthropology" consists in "the notion of a stable human nature (which) might itself contradict objectivity. . . . If one accepts Aquinas's anthropology, the data about sexual orientation from other disciplines are irrelevant . . . . [In this view judgments about homosexuality are] *a priori* declarations [in which] new evidence is irrelevant." Bosnor, 64-65, 80.
    Stephen Pope better summarizes what the Catholic tradition on nature indicates: ". . . scientific findings and theories about the naturalness of homosexuality will be held to be relevant to but not definitive of the kind of moral assessment of sexual activity among homosexual that is appropriate to natural law ethics." Pope, "Scientific and natural law analyses of homosexuality," 90.

[14] Paragraph 2359. Here is the Latin *editio typica* text of that paragraph published five years after the first edition of the catechism appeared simultaneously in French and Italian: "Personae homosexuales ad castitatem vocantur. Ipsae, dominii virtutibus quae libertatem educant interiorem, quandoque amicitiae gratuitae auxilio, oratione et gratia sacramentali, possunt et debent ad perfectionem christainam gradatim at obfirmate appropinquare." *Catechismus Catholicae Ecclesiae* (Città del Vaticano: Libreria Editrice Vaticana, 1997).

The Latin "amicitiae gratuitae auxilio" actually seems to be a softening of language used in the original versions. The Italian offers homosexual persons "il sostegno di un'amicizia disinteressata . . . ." *Catechismo della Chiesa Cattolica* (Città del Vaticano: Libreria Editrice Vaticana, 1992). Though "gratuita" is not precisely "disinteressata" the revised English translation has not been changed with the publication of the Latin text.

[15] Pope, "Scientific and natural law analyses of homosexuality," 120.

[16] MacIntyre, *Whose Justice? Which Rationality?* (Notre Dame, IN: University of Notre Dame Press, 1988), 362.

[17] See William M. McDonough, "On the theoretical demands of real life: A review essay on Alasdair MacIntyre's *Dependent Rational Animals: Why Human Beings Need the Virtues*," in *New Theology Review* (Forthcoming, 2001).

[18] Alasdair MacIntyre, *Dependent Rational Animals: Why Human Beings Need the Virtues* (Chicago, IL: Open Court Press, 1999), x.

[19] The first term is Anne Patrick's in *Liberating Conscience: Feminist Explorations in Catholic Moral Theology* (New York: Continuum, 1996) 58. It has resonances with Jean Porter's view that natural law is an attempt to give a theological interpretation of the "pre-conventional givens" of human life. Jean Porter, *Natural and Divine Law* (Grand Rapids, MI: Wm. B. Eerdmans, 1999), 216.

[20] MacIntyre, *Whose Justice? Which Rationality?,* 357, 251.

[21] *Dependent Rational Animals*, 1. MacIntyre speaks of such "facts" at least four other times in the new book, at pages, 6, 64, 82, 101.

[22] *Dependent Rational Animals*, 1.

[23] *Dependent Rational Animals,* 100, 6.

[24] Porter, *Natural and Divine Law,* 145. It is relevant to notice here that Porter's understanding of natural law theory contains a subtlety missing in Stout's approach. Stout 's "principles" are *sui generis*, where Porter's are "an interpretation." See Stout cited above in note three.

[25] *Dependent Rational Animals, 72, 82.*

[26] *Dependent Rational Animals, 159.*

[27] "(Parents') initial commitment has to be in important respects unconditional." And: "The kind of care that was needed . . . had to be . . . unconditional care for the human being as such." And: "What analysts are sometimes able to provide for those whose early childhood experiences were defective is . . . unqualified trust." *Dependent Rational Animals,* 90, 100, 85.

[28] *Dependent Rational Animals,* 109.

[29] *Dependent Rational Animals,* 5.

[30] *Dependent Rational Animals,* 119, 126-129 (for just generosity), 150-152 (for elementary truthfulness).

[31] *Dependent Rational Animals,* 64.

[32] John Noonan, *Contraception: A History of Its Treatment by the Catholic Theologians and Canonists,* Enlarged edition (Cambridge, MA: Harvard University Press, 1986), 46, 49.

[33] Jean Porter, *Natural and Divine Law,* 191, 199. Porter summarized Stoic natural law as "willing acceptance of one's fate." *Natural and Divine Law,* 141.

I stress Stoicism's fatalism because it is especially evident in Catholic teaching on homosexuality. Stoic fatalism is well summed up by John M. Cooper: "'Living in agreement with nature' as the Stoics understand it involves modeling one's thoughts in deciding on and doing one's actions, on nature's own thought in designing the world (i.e., itself), establishing the physical laws, and causing the events that happen within it . . . . So one has to accept as reasonable, and benevolent, what one often cannot know the reasons for—though, one knows, there *are* reasons. This gives emphasis to the idea that in living virtuously one lives in obedience . . . to the *koinos nomos* or the law of the universe, or universal and right reason. This obedience involves two fundamental things: (1) acting so as to pursue or avoid the things that can be seen *normally* to accord with or go against our physical constitution and the social circumstances that naturally suit beings with the constitution, and (2) pursuing or avoiding them always with the idea that it may turn out that achieving those objectives on that occasion was not after all what we or anyone else truly needed, because it does not fit in with the needs of the whole universe of which we are organic parts." John M. Cooper, "Eudaimonism, the Appeal to Nature and 'Moral Duty' in Stoicism," in *Aristotle, Kant and the Stoics: Rethinking Happiness and Duty,* ed. Stephen Engstrom and Jennifer Whiting (New York: Cambridge University Press, 1996), 277.

[34] See note 26 above.

[35] ". . . il faut ranger les opposants . . . . Le plus précieux est assurément Plutarque." Michel Spanneut, *Permanence du Stoïcisme: De Zénon à* Malraux (Gembloux, Belgium: Editions J. Duculot, 1973), 19.

[36] *Dependent Rational Animals,* 82.

[37] The *Loeb Classical Library Edition* translates the text a little differently, but with the same sense: "To the dolphin alone, beyond all others, nature has granted what the best philosophers seek: friendship for no advantage." Plutarch, *De Sollertia Animalium,* in *Moralia,* vol. 12, trans. Harold Cherniss and William Helmbold. Loeb Classical Library (Cambridge, MA: Harvard University Press, 1968), 473.

The relevant Greek is *to philein aneu chreias uparchei.* Both MacIntyre and the Loeb translators understand Plutarch's "chreia" here to describe a property of friendship; the friendship Plutarch describes here is one without "use, advantage, or service." See Henry George Liddell and Robert Scott, "Chreia," in *A Greek-English Lexicon,* revised with a supplement (Oxford, England: Clarendon Press, 1968), 2002. I am grateful to my colleague Vincent Skemp for help with the Greek text of Plutarch.

[38] Plutarch *De Sollertia Animalium,* in Loeb, vol. 12, 479. Plutarch's translators say: "The real point of the dialogue seems to be... that all animals of whatever provenance are intelligent.... The last small section, while refusing to award first honors in the debate, appears to contain Plutarch's exhortation to his pupils to continue the fight against the Stoics." Cherniss and Helmbold, "Introduction (to Plutarch's *De Sollertia Animalium*)," in Loeb, vol. 12, 312-313.

[39] MacIntyre, *Dependent Rational Animals,* 82.

[40] Plutarch, *Bruta animalia ratione uti,* in *Moralia,* Loeb, vol. 12, 529.

[41]Spanneut says three dialogues of Plutarch are especially important for their anti-Stoicism: *De Stoicorum repugnantius, De communibus notitiis adversus Stoicos,* and *Stoicos absurdiora petis dicere.* See Spannuet, 123-124. I do not claim expertise in either Plutarch or Stoicism, and remain open to correction of my brief summary statements here.

[42] ". . . everyone is said to have had his fill of arguments against the Stoic paradoxes concerning those who alone are opulent and fair and alone are kings, citizens, and judges and these notions are dismissed as 'stale goods.'" Harold Cherniss and O'Neil, "Introduction *to Compendium argumenti Stoicos Absurdia Poetis Ducere,* in Plutarch's *Moralia* volume 13.2. trans. Cherniss and O'Neil. Loeb Classical Library (Cambridge, MA: Harvard University Press, 1976), 608. Plutarch's dialogue *Against the Stoics on Common Conceptions* begins with a declaration that the Stoics offer "stale and wilted goods." Plutarch, *De communibus notitiis adversus Stoicos* , in Loeb, vol. 13.2, 671.

[43] Plutarch, *De communibus notitiis adversus Stoicos,* in Loeb, vol.13.2, 693-695.

[44] Plutarch, *De communibus notitiis adversus Stoicos,* in Loeb, vol. 13.2, 673-675. The text in parentheses is inserted from Plutarch's previous sentence.

[45] Plutarch, *De communibus notitiis adversus Stoicos,* in Loeb, vol. 13.2, 743.

[46]Plutarch, *De communibus notitiis adversus Stoicos,* in Loeb, vol. 13.2, 742.

[47] MacIntyre, *Dependent Rational Animals,* 119.

[48] In his study of monastic friendship, Brian Patrick McGuire paints a picture parallel to MacIntyre's view of "blandly generalized benevolence": "For Seneca as for his Christian

descendants, human bonds must not become too pressing or immediate. Distance must be maintained. The Christian must be self-sufficient in the sense that he shows love to other people but does not become dependent on them for their love in return. Charity is required but friendship is not desired, except as a one-way street, a mode of practicing charity." McGuire, *Friendship and Community: The Monastic Experience, 350-1250.* Kalamazoo, MI: Cistercian Publications, 1988), 414-415.

[49] See Kevin Kelly, "Review of *The Sexual Creators* by André Guindon." *The Heythrop Journal* 30 (1989), 491.

[50] "La prima (nostra impostazione) è quella di mostrare il criterio magisteriale che si potrebbe chiamare 'progresso nella continuità' . . . . (I)l matrimonio è un stato di sanctificazione." Giuseppe Baldanza, *La grazia del sacramento del matrimonio. Contribuito per la riflessione teologica* (Rome, Italy: Centro Liturgico Vincensiano, 1993), 9, 78.

[51] ". . . occorreva infatti superare una prospettiva prevalentemente giuridico-morale, consolidata e diffusa da vari secoli." Baldanza, *La grazia del sacramento del matrimonio*, 301.

[52] Trent offered "una visione serena e positiva del matrimonio e della sessualità." But ". . . . il testo tridentino . . . avrebbe potuto far pensare ad una concezione estrinsecistica della grazia nei confronti della natura." Baldanza, *La grazia del sacramento del matrimonio*, 57, 238.

[53] See Baldanza, *La grazia del sacramento del matrimonio*, 299. Baldanza is quoting paragraph 24 of the encyclical. Here is its text in English: "This mutual moulding of husband and wife, this determined effort to perfect each other, can in a very real sense . . . be said to be the chief reason and purpose of matrimony, provided matrimony be looked at not in the restricted sense as instituted for the proper conception and education of children, but more widely as the blending of life as a whole and the mutual interchange and sharing thereof (*sed latius ut totius vitae communio, consuetudo, societas accipiatur*)." From Claudia Carlen, *The Papal Encyclicals, 1903-1939.* (Raleigh, NC: McGrath Publishing Company, 1981), 395.The relevant Latin text is found in *Acta Apostolicae Sedis* 22 (1930), 549.

[54] Paragraph 42 of *Casti connubii* puts it this way: "The parties, . . through their spirit and manner of life (*mentem et mores*), may be and remain always the living image of that most fruitful union of Christ with the Church, which is to be venerated as the sacred token of most perfect love." Carlen, *The Papal Encyclicals, 1903-1939,* 398. Baldanza comments: "Il testo dell'Enciclica si presenta molto ricco. La parola *mores* ingloba anche la vita affetivo-sessuale." Baldanza, *La grazia del sacramento del matrimonio*, 75.

[55] "Qui la *Casti connubii* segna un progresso rispetto alla teologia scolastica ed alla manualistica. Esaminado infatti l'una e l'altra, si potrebbe rilevare, in modo generale, la presenza di una distinzione tra matrimonio come stato e gli atti coniugali come esercizio del matrimonio. Ciò anche a causa del fatto che il matrimonio nella sua struttura concreta è condizionato dal peccato originale.... S. Tommaso accetta I tre *bona* di cui parla S. Agostino, ma precisa che essi sono scusanti perché portano equilibrio nell'atto coniugale: vi è infatti una *iactura* nell'atto coniugale dopo il peccato....Pertanto gil atti sessuali venivano considerati in se stessi e ritenuti anche meritori, se compiuti in stato di grazia e secondo la legge divina; essi, tuttavia, non venivano inglobati nella significazione." Baldanza, *La grazia del sacramento del matrimonio*,75. Augustine's three goods of marriage (offspring, fidelity, stability) are summarized by John Noonan in *Contraception*, 127-128.

[56] "Amor conuigalis . . . assumitur...ut efficatur ad Deum ducant." *Gaudium et spes,* par. 48. Cited by Baldanza, *La grazia del sacramento del matrimonio*, 238.

[57] ". . . il raffronto tra la prospettiva tradizionale e quella della *Gaudium et spes* può essere così sintetizzato: nella prima, l'azione divina è a sanare, potenziare, elevare l'amore degli sposi, a cocedere loro gli aiuti spirituali in vista dei diversi compiti matrimoniali. Nella seconda, senza escludere tutto ciò, si parte anzitutto da Cristo che va verso gli sposi per incontrarli, *per assumere il loro amore nel suo amore sponsale verso la Chiesa*. E ciò in forza dell'incarnazione e del mistero pasquale che costituisce la nuova ed eterna alleanza, che è alleanza di comunione e di salvezza per tutti." Baldanza, *La grazia del sacramento del matrimonio*, 283. The emphasis is mine.

[58] I acknowledge that I am not giving a full description of the theology of marriage of Vatican II. Sean O'Riordan, for example, summarizes the Council this way: "La *dilectio* coniugale non è più una cosa supplementare, anche se molto necessaria, nell'insieme del matrimonio cristiano: è proprio 'l'essenza concreta' del matrimonio stesso. Però, accanto a questa essenza vi è, in un certo senso, un'altra essenza—quella che deriva della 'finalità oggettiva' del matrimonio, ovvero dalla sua ordinazione alla procreazione ed educazione della prole. Come abbiamo visto, il Concilio congiunge questi due concetti dell'essenza del matrimonio senza farne una vera sintesi. Notiamo nei testi conciliari una certa tensione tra le due visuali." O'Riordan, *Evoluzione della teologia del matrimonio* (Assisi, Italy: Cittadella Editrice, 1974), 64.

[59] *Gaudium et spes,* par. 50. All English translations of *Gaudium et spes* are from *Vatican II: Constitutions, Decrees, Declarations: A completely Revised Translation in Inclusive Language,* ed. Austin Flannery (Northport, New York: Costello Publishing, 1996).

Here is the Latin text: "Ideo etsi proles, saepius tam optata, deficit, matrimonium ut totius vitae consuetudo et communio perseverat, suumque valorem atque indissolubilitatem servat." *Acta Apostolicae Sedis* 58 (1966): 1072.

[60] Enda McDonagh, "Love," in *The New Dictionary of Theology* (Collegeville, MN: Michael Glazier, 1988), 608, 605.

[61] McDonagh, *Love,* 611. McDonagh's point is spelled out even more in Diana Fritz Cates' recent book: "The way to insure the appropriateness of the overall structure of our own desire and the appropriateness of our consequent perceptions is not to try to extricate ourselves from the pull of desire (which is impossible). Rather, the thing to do is to *feel* the range of our desires and to reflect upon them honestly in light of a well-deliberated vision of the good and an abiding desire for its realization. We ought to engage in empassioned reflection, privately, in conversation with our friend, and in conversation with others friends who are adept at exposing our base selfishness and the self-deceptions that we employ to keep our selfishness from being exposed . . . . In any case, our desiring, our perceiving, and our thinking function together to constitute a unified process of discerning what is most likely in this situation to contribute to the end desired." Cates, *Choosing to Feel: Virtue, Friendship, and Compassion for Friends* (Notre Dame, IN: University of Notre Dame Press, 1997), 174-175.

[62] McDonagh, *Love,* 608-609, 614-615.

[63] A classic statement of the so-called two ends of marriage is in the 1917 *Code of Canon Law,* at canon 1013.1: "Matrimonii finis primarius est procreatio atque educatio prolis, secondarius mutuum adiutorium at remedium concupiscientiae." Cited by O'Riordan, *Evoluzione della teologia del matrimonio,* 28.

It is very significant that Vatican II purposely abandoned this talk of the primary and secondary ends of marriage. The Council says instead: "For God himself is the author of marriage and has endowed it with various values and purposes: all of these have a very important bearing on the continuation of the human race, on the personal development and eternal destiny of every member of the family, on the dignity, stability, peace, and prosperity of the family and of the whole human race." *Gaudium et spes,* par. 48.

Stephen Pope's and Jean Porter's helpful recent works remain more focused on the language of primary and secondary ends of marriage than does the view proposed here. Pope says a "revisionist natural law perspective" on homosexuality honors the procreative purpose of sexual intercourse but "not necessarily (as) a good in each and every concrete situation or even in each particular monogamous bond . . . . (This approach) grounds ethics on an account of the characteristic desires and ends of human nature, the most important of which are taken to be interpersonal and affective." Pope, "Scientific and natural law analyses of homosexuality," 113.

Porter offers reasons for "why procreation as opposed to the promotion of personal love between individuals (should) be privileged" in natural law morality. Porter, *Natural and Divine Law,* 220.

Pope and Porter do not cite the texts of Vatican II on marriage and sexuality in their works. While both are helping dismantle the wall between natural law and narrative moralities, especially by attending to the field of evolutionary psychology, both seem to me to give that field's criterion of "inclusive reproductive fitness" more moral weight than it deserves. Pope's claim that "Homosexuality is apparently biologically futile," (Pope, 99) masks the deeper futility in all (merely physical) reproduction, evident in Porter's admission that "it may be the case that we will either evolve into something else or (more likely) cease to exist altogether" (Porter, 104). Theologically, Vatican II has already made clear that reproduction is not an absolute value in Catholic natural law thinking about sexuality.

[64] McDonagh, *Love*, 611.

[65] Frederick Crowe, SJ. "Complacency and Concern in the Thought of St. Thomas," *Theological Studies* 20 (1959): 3. See Diana Fritz Cates' treatment of complacency both of a self in its own desires and of a self in another, in Cates, *Choosing to Feel*, 93-100.

[66] Porter, *Natural and Divine Law*, 231.

[67] Andrew Sullivan criticizes eroticism on just these grounds: "One typical writer has characterized gay culture as a 'culture of desire.' But this is condescending exaggeration." Sullivan, *Love Undetectable*, 231. Sullivan's unnamed target here seems to be Frank Browning's book, *A Culture of Desire*.

[68] This statement about a positive natural law estimation of homosexual sexuality is found at Porter, *Natural and Divine Law*, 231.

I do not fully understand Porter's natural law analysis here. She suggests that gay eroticism would "represent an alternative construal of human nature that has its own value and integrity but that is nonetheless in tension with fundamental Christian commitments." Porter, *Natural and Divine Law*, 232.

This evaluation fails to reckon with Porter's own position "that the mores of other communities are expressions of the same natural law . . . (and) that human diversity is intelligible as an expression of an underlying nature." Porter, *Natural and Divine Law*, 177.

Is eroticism really to be thought of as an alternative construal of human nature, or is it intelligible as an (incomplete) expression of one and the same human nature? Anne Thurston, speaking here of divorce in heterosexual marriage, suggests the outlines of a fuller natural law construal of eroticism's meaning: "Human relationships reach for permanence, long for communion. There is, or need be, no contradiction between support for this deep human need—life-long commitment to one partner—and the recognition that people fail, that relationships fail . . . . (This is) the gap between what we desire and what we realize. What we long for, what we most deeply desire shapes our lives." Anne Thurston, "Living with Ambiguity," *Doctrine and Life* (1994): 538-539.

[69] J. Michael Clark, *Doing the Work of Love: Men and Commitment in Same-sex Couples* (Harriman, TN: Men's Studies Press, 1999), 6-7.

[70] James Hanigan, *Homosexuality: The Test Case for Christian Ethics* (Mahwah, NJ: Paulist Press, 1988), 97, 103.

[71] See note fifty-eight above. Andrew Sullivan has followed out the logic of the church's teaching here: "What rational distinction can be made, on the Church's own terms, between the position of sterile people and that of homosexual people with regard to sexual relations and sacred union? If there is nothing wrong per se, with the homosexual condition or with homosexual love and self-giving then homosexuals are indeed analogous to those who, by blameless fate, cannot reproduce." Sullivan, "Alone Again, Naturally," 54-55.

[72] Rosemary Haughton, "The Renovation of Old Jerusalem." *New Blackfriars* 47 (1966): 640. The essay is a review of Häring's book *Marriage in the Modern World,* trans. by Geoffrey Stevens (Westminster, MD: Newman Press, 1965).

[73] Rosemary Haughton, *Images for Change: The Transformation of Society* (Mahwah, NJ: Paulist Press, 1997), 160.

[74] Here is the Hennepin County policy on adoption: "We work only with children with special needs who have experienced abuse and/or neglect. These children are under the custody and guardianship of the Commissioner of the State of Minnesota and are called State Wards. Every child in Hennepin County who is legally free for adoption deserves a permanent home. Adoptive parents may be single, married, gay/lesbian, childless, or already parenting other children. These children do not need perfect parents. They need one or two loving parents

willing to face challenges and make a life long commitment." From Hennepin County Adoption Policy. See www.co.hennepin.mn.us. A Minneapolis non-profit group works with gay parents. See www.rainbowfamilies.org.

[75] Sullivan, "Alone Again, Naturally," 55.

[76] *Dependent Rational Animals,* 137.

[77] *Dependent Rational Animals*, 134. The reference is to the opening line of Tolstoy's *Anna Karenina.*

[78] Simone Weil, cited by Anthony Walton, "Simone Weil: Love Bade Me Welcome," in *Martyrs: Contemporary Writers on Modern Lives of Faith*, ed. Susan Bergman. (San Francisco: HarperCollins, 1996), 182.

John Paul II, Michael Novak,
and the Differences Between Them

Todd David Whitmore

Abstract

Unnamed sources have claimed that Michael Novak is "credited with considerable input" into John Paul II's encyclical, *Centesimus annus*, such that the former's thought "is said to be reflected in" the document. However, while John Paul II affirms economic rights, Novak rejects them. In addition, the Pope critiques the gap between rich and poor and the consumerism that drives it; Novak finds them to be morally irrelevant. Following Catholic teaching before him, John Paul places restrictions on the accumulation of private property for one's own use, while Novak identifies no such limits. Finally, while the Pope rejects the affirmation of any one system as a form of "ideology," Novak argues, "We are all capitalists now, even the Pope." Such dramatic differences suggest that the claim that Novak has influenced John Paul's thought is unfounded and that the former's position may even be one of dissent.

"We are all capitalists now, even the Pope."
  – Michael Novak, *The Catholic Ethic and the Spirit of Capitalism*[1]

"We have seen that it is unacceptable to say that the defeat of so-called 'Real Socialism' leaves capitalism as the only model of economic organization."
  – John Paul II, *Centesimus annus*[2]

After the publication of Pope John Paul II's 1991 encyclical *Centesimus annus* various claims were made that Michael Novak's work in theological political economy had a definite and even definitive influence on the writing of the document. *The National Catholic Register*, for instance, states in two separate articles that Novak is "credited with considerable input in the drafting of the encyclical," such that his "thought is said to be reflected in" the document.[3] Such claims, which never cite any specific sources and are generally stated in the passive voice—"is credited with" and "is said to be"—eventually make it into Novak's own *vita*.[4] However, even a cursory reading of Novak's post-encyclical book *The Catholic Ethic and the Spirit of Capitalism*, side by side with *Centesimus annus*, discloses important differences between the Pope and the American neo-conservative (or, more accurately, neo-liberal).[5] Such differences have led Rodger Charles, in writing for Family Publications and Ignatius Press, two publishers known for their attention to orthodoxy, to charge regarding *The Catholic Ethic* that, "many of the aspects of its presentation of the Catholic tradition can be questioned."[6] Charles does not elaborate, and there are no detailed analyses by other authors regarding the divergences between John Paul II and Novak.

The aim of this article is to offer a close reading of the work of these two figures in order to delineate their differences with textual precision. The argument proceeds in three parts. The first section examines the possible textual sources for the claim that Novak has been a key influence on the thought of John Paul II. The next section details a significant difference, namely John Paul II's affirmation and Novak's rejection of economic rights. Novak's refusal to recognize such rights is set within an overall economic theory and moral theology that diverges from Catholic social teaching at several points that the third section of this article details, including the moral significance of the rich-poor gap, the threat of consumerism, the limits on the use of private property, and, perhaps most significantly, even the nature of Catholic social teaching itself as a genre of theology.

Textual Sources for a Claim of Influence

While the persons making the claim of Novak's influence on John Paul II remain unnamed, it is possible to trace the textual sources for the assertion. To do so, it is necessary to go back to Novak's earlier book *The Spirit of Democratic Capitalism*, written nine years before *Centesimus annus*. In a chapter titled "The Bias Against Democratic Capitalism," he charges that even though Catholic social teaching has condemned the philosophical roots of socialism and has "respected some of the fundamental principles of democratic capitalism," it is still "closer to a mild form of socialism than to democratic capitalism." This tendency is, Novak writes, because Catholic social teaching has paid little if any attention to the way in which democratic capitalism produces wealth, and thus has been insufficiently appreciative and overly critical of the latter. Catholic social teaching "has little to say about markets and incentives, the ethics of production, and the habits, disciplines, and organization necessary for the creation of wealth."[7]

Novak's *The Catholic Ethic and the Spirit of Capitalism*, written in 1993, is an expanded commentary on *Centesimus annus* and also an updating of *The Spirit of Democratic Capitalism*. In it, Novak describes the encyclical as a "sonic boom," whereby John Paul II parts with previous teaching, even with his own earlier documents, to become "the Pope of economic enterprise." On this reading, John Paul is the first pope to recognize "economic initiative." This is, "fresh material, indeed."[8] In short, Novak reads the presence of awareness of the role of economic initiative in *Centesimus annus* as signaling a fundamental shift in Catholic social teaching as a whole. The clinching passage is from paragraph forty-two, which he interprets as an endorsement of the economic theory he has espoused since *The Spirit of Democratic Capitalism*. The Pope's words read as follows:

> [C]an it perhaps be said that, after the failure of communism, capitalism is the victorious social system, and that capitalism should be the goal of the countries now making efforts to rebuild their economy and society? . . . The answer is obviously complex. If by *capitalism* is meant an economic system which recognizes the fundamental and positive role of business, the market, private property and the resulting responsibility for the means of production, as well as free human creativity in the economic sector, then the answer is certainly in the affirmative, even though it would perhaps be more appropriate to speak of a *business economy, market economy,* or simply *free economy*. But if by capitalism is meant a system in which freedom in the economic sector is not circumscribed within a strong juridical framework which places it at the service of human freedom in its totality, and which sees it as a particular aspect of that freedom, the core of which is ethical and religious, then the reply is certainly negative (emphases in original).[9]

Novak cites this passage to back the claim, "We are all capitalists now, even the Pope," and that therefore there is "only one form of economics."[10]

There are serious difficulties with this interpretation of Catholic social teaching in general and *Centesimus annus* in particular. First of all, according to Novak the "sonic boom" of *Centesimus annus* is its recognition of the role of economic initiative in the production of wealth. However, earlier documents also discuss the importance of human incentive, initiative, creativity, and the production of wealth. Leo XIII argues in *Rerum novarum* that the ability to reason and so creatively consider the future is what distinguishes humans from other animals. Through work, a person, "leaves, as it were, the impress of his own personality" on nature. Under socialism, "the sources of wealth would themselves run dry, for no one would have any interest in exerting his talents or his industry." Pius XI, in *Quadragesimo anno*, critiques Mussolini's corporatism, arguing that, "the state is substituting itself in the place of private initiative, instead of limiting itself to necessary and sufficient help and assistance."[11] Although John XXIII receives little mention in *The Catholic Ethic*, the pontiff is noteworthy for the number of times and the force with which he discusses human initiative in the economic sphere. This is particularly the case in *Mater et magistra*. For instance, John writes, "At the outset it should be affirmed that in economic affairs first place be given to the private initiative of individual men who, either working by themselves, or with others in one fashion or another, pursue their common interests."[12] There is no drop in the accent on personal initiative and the reasons for it in the writings of Paul VI. In *Populorum Progressio*, he is unblinking: "The introduction of industry is a necessity for economic growth and human progress; it is also a sign of development and contributes to it. By persistent work and use of his intelligence man gradually wrests nature's secrets from her and finds a better application for her riches. As his self-mastery increases, he develops a taste for research and discovery, an ability to take a calculated risk, boldness in enterprises."[13]

It is clear, then, that recognition of economic initiative and its import for the production of wealth did not start with John Paul II and *Centesimus annus*. Given the evidence to the contrary, it is also clear that the presence of such a recognition in *Centesimus annus* does not imply any influence of Novak's writings on John Paul II. The Pope had other sources—namely, previous popes—and is in continuity with them.

There is one key difference between Novak and Catholic social teaching in the referents of the appeal to initiative. In Catholic social teaching, the appeal refers to everyone in the economic sphere; in Novak it is limited to entrepreneurs and the owners of capital. John Paul II is on point in *Laborem exercens* when he notes that much of Catholic social teaching since *Rerum novarum* has been in response to an economic system that has denied the initiative of workers: "This state of affairs was favored by the liberal socio-political system, which in accordance with its 'economistic' premises, strengthened and safeguarded economic initiative by the possessors of capital alone, but did not pay sufficient attention to the rights of workers, on the grounds that human work is solely an instrument of production, and that capital is the basis, efficient factor, and purpose of production."[14] This oversight on the part of economistic capitalism has led to repeated emphasis in Catholic social teaching—including *Centesimus annus*—on the right of the non-owning worker to exercise initiative in the workplace through participation in decision-making and even by becoming an owner in co-operative arrangements with other workers.[15] References to initiative on the part of non-owning workers or to worker-owned co-operatives are virtually non-existent in Novak's work— one passing mention in the 334 pages of *The Catholic Ethic*—and are never discussed in a positive manner. Therefore, the stronger textual case is that Novak's reference to initiative is narrower than that in Catholic social teaching, both before and after *Centesimus annus*.

As indicated before, Novak draws on the claim that recognition of economic initiative is new to support the reading that paragraph forty-two means "We are all capitalists now, even the Pope," and that there is "only one form of economics." However, this too runs against the textual evidence. John Paul II insists in *Centesimus annus* that "it is unacceptable to say that the defeat of so-called 'Real Socialism' leaves capitalism as the only model of economic organization." Indeed, the Pope is careful to point out that "Western countries," in particular, "run the risk of seeing this collapse as a one-sided victory of their own economic system, and thereby failing to make necessary corrections in that system." John Paul indicates as many as eight times in the document that there is no such victory, once in the very paragraph that Novak cites to support his contrary claim.[16]

These sections of *Censtesimus annus* indicate that it is best read in line with the earlier *Laborem exercens*. In this 1981 document, John Paul II defines the free or market economy as a market economy which is situated in a comprehensive society such that there is recognition of the primacy of the whole person over simple material well-being and of the common good over individual interest. Capitalism, by definition, reverses the priorities. "Precisely this reversal of order, whatever the program or name under which it occurs, should rightly be called 'capitalism.'" John Paul then continues this usage in *Centesiumus annus* when answering the question of whether the collapse of communism in 1989 constitutes a victory for capitalism. This is why when he speaks in paragraph forty-two of an economy that is "circumscribed within a strong juridical framework," he states that it is "more appropriate to speak of a business economy, market economy or simply free economy" than of "capitalism." It is also why, elsewhere in *Centesimus annus*, he continues this understanding of capitalism as an economic system where things come before people, and does so in a way that makes clear that advocates of such a system ought not to claim victory—and certainly not moral victory. "In spite of the great changes which have taken place in the more advanced societies, the human inadequacies of capitalism and the resulting domination of things over people are far from disappearing."[17]

What is at stake is not mere semantics for John Paul, but a normative distinction that must be upheld if there is to be any clarity in economic thought from a moral perspective. The relationship between the juridically circumscribed market economy, on the one hand, and the priorities of the whole person over solely material well-being and of the common good over individual interest, on the other, is this: it is precisely when the market overruns its boundaries and invades other areas of social life that materialism and individualism become predominant. Drawing a term from Paul VI, John Paul II calls such a phenomenon, the "consumer society."[18]

Only if one accepts the distinction between the free market and capitalism can one understand John Paul's claim, in one paragraph, both that the "church acknowledges the legitimate role of profit" and that it is "unacceptable to say that the defeat of so called 'Real Socialism' leaves capitalism as the only model of economic organization."[19] Novak, however, rejects the distinction and instead equates the Pope's understanding of capitalism with a bypassed "early" or "primitive" capitalism. In so doing, he dismisses John Paul's distinction between capitalism and the free market as "ironic." The differences between John Paul and Novak, according to the latter, then, are merely terminological. The capitalism/free market distinction is "probably because of European emotional resistance to the word 'capitalism.'"[20] Novak's rejection of the capitalism/free market distinction results in an economic worldview that is binary, even dualistic: there are only two models, capitalism and socialism. It is this that allows Novak to claim, despite textual evidence to the contrary, that *Centesimus annus* holds that the defeat of "Real Socialism" means that capitalism is victorious.

We have seen thus far, then, that the assertion that Novak influenced the writing of *Centesimus annus* does not stand up to scrutiny. The twin claims that recognition of economic initiative is new with this document and that such recognition indicates that "We are all capitalists now, even the Pope" do not find textual support. We have also seen indications of real differences between Novak and the Pope. One key difference comes to light when we inquire as to the substantive content of the "strong juridical framework" that John Paul highlights in paragraph forty-two as necessary for a market economy to be "at the service of human freedom in its totality." A primary element of that framework is economic rights.

The Differences Between Them
I: Economic Rights

Catholic teaching has, from *Rerum novarum*'s support of a just wage to the present, stressed the importance of claims most often described under the rubric of social and economic rights. In present iterations, this category includes, for instance, the right to work, food, clothing, housing, and health care.[21] Catholic teaching has also affirmed the claims traditionally described as political and civil rights, for instance, the right to be secure in one's person and property, to assembly and speech, and more recently, to religious freedom. John Paul II makes clear in *Centesimus annus* that he is a continuation of these views. He calls for "explicit recognition" of human rights[22] and cites his *Redemptor hominis*. In *Redemptor hominis* he writes in support of the United Nations, which affirms both political and economic rights in its Universal Declaration on Human Rights. He states, "We cannot fail to recall at this point, with esteem and profound hope for the future, the magnificent effort made to give life to the United Nations

Organization, an effort conducive to the definition and establishment of man's objective and inviolable rights . . . . There is no need for the Church to confirm how closely this problem is linked with her mission in the modern world. Indeed it is at the very basis of social and international peace, as has been declared by John XXIII, the Second Vatican Council, and later Paul VI, in detailed documents."[23]

Novak's presentation on rights, in contrast, is at best equivocal on economic rights. His account tends to use different rhetorical strategies. The first is silence. His writing, as exemplified in *The Catholic Ethic and the Spirit of Capitalism*, simply leaves economic rights unmentioned in any account he offers of rights in Catholic social doctrine.[24] The uninformed reader is left to assume that Catholic teaching does not recognize the existence of, let alone strongly affirm, economic rights.

The second stage of Novak's treatment of economic rights in Catholic social teaching occurs when he is presented with textual evidence of such rights. He responds, as he does in a 1986 article, that the texts "do not support the weight" that those who affirm economic rights want to place on them.[25] This reading is problematic not only for Catholic social teaching in general, but also for the documents of John Paul II in particular. We have already seen that the Pope supports the full set of rights delineated in the United Nations Declaration on Human Rights. *Centesimus annus* clearly states elsewhere that "the material goods which sustain human life, satisfy people's needs" are "an object of their rights."[26]

Subsequent documents by John Paul II reinforce his emphasis on the full range of rights, including economic rights. In a 1997 address to the Pontifical Academy of Social Science, he notes his continuity with Paul VI's *Populorum Progressio*, written thirty years earlier, and calls for "ethical and juridical regulation of the market" in line with "the model of the social state." If this regulation is carried out "moderately" then it can avoid the problem of providing assistance that stifles initiative on the part of the poor. In a global setting, the provision of any assistance is difficult, so when he discusses specific agencies, he writes, "I am thinking in particular of the United Nations and of its various agencies providing social assistance" to help embody a "culture of rules" which "takes charge, through reliable juridical tools, of the protection of human rights in all parts of the world." Participation in a democratic polity that is protected by civil and political rights is indeed important, the Pope insists and then adds, "But how can someone who is not properly protected at the economic level and even lacks the basic necessities be guaranteed participation in democratic life?"[27]

The Pope's 1999 message on the World Day of Peace is even more emphatic in its support of the full range of human rights. After setting out the *imago Dei* doctrine as the theological basis for a transcendent human dignity, John Paul proceeds to argue that this unified theological and anthropological center backs the objective "universality and indivisibility of human rights." The Pope elaborates:

> Human rights are traditionally grouped into two broad categories, including on the one hand civil and political rights and on the other economic, social, and cultural rights . . . . All human rights are in fact closely connected, being an expression of different dimensions of a single subject, the human person. The integral promotion of every category of human rights is the true guarantee of full respect of any individual right.[28]

It is difficult to deny the force of the above statements. It is also worth mentioning that John Paul cites *Centesimus annus* repeatedly in both documents. When this sort of textual evidence is presented, Novak's tack is to equivocate. Here, there is acknowledgment of a sort that official doctrine in general and John Paul II in particular support economic rights, but also the insistence, made in a newspaper column, that economic rights have, in Novak's words, an "essentially different meaning" than civil and political rights. The former "requires others, as a last resort, to do something for those in need," while the latter "warns others not to interfere in the subject's natural, legitimate actions."[29] It is difficult to discern the intended force of the claim concerning this "essentially different meaning." These understandings of rights are standard, with the exception that Catholic social doctrine does not teach that persons are to hold back their support of others until the "last resort." Given this fact, one has to look elsewhere to try to understand what might be the intended force of Novak's claim, and it is perhaps less in his explication of the different actions required by the rights than in his insistence that the two kinds of rights are "essentially" different. This term suggests that what is at stake is more than the pragmatics of how to protect and promote each kind of right. It appears that Novak, in keeping with classical and neo-liberal thought generally, is claiming, albeit in an equivocal way, that in the end social and economic claims are not rights at all.

Novak's article, "The Future of 'Economic Rights,'" bears out this interpretation of his work. Again, economic rights include, for instance, the right to work, a just wage, food, housing, and health care. Political rights include the right to religious freedom, assembly, and security in one's property. It is important to note that traditionally the right to private property has been considered a civil and political right, rather than an economic right. This may seem odd given that property appears to be an economic concern. Why it traditionally is called a civil and political right seems to have at least two bases. First, historically, persons needed to have private property in order to participate in the political sphere as citizens. The right to private property protected political participation. The second basis is a judgment about the role of the state. Classical liberal political thought allows for the role of the state to protect private property as a right, but does not want the state involved in the economic sphere for other reasons. What get classified as civil and political rights, then, are those areas of social life where traditional liberal political thought seeks state protection (such as Locke's "life, liberty, and property"). This association of civil and political rights with traditional liberalism gains accent with the rise of Marxist thought and its prioritization of economic over political rights. John Paul follows this usage of the terms economic and political rights and then adds that the two types of rights are deeply interrelated and made universal by their grounding in human dignity.

In "The Future of 'Economic Rights,'" Novak claims to "accept 'economic rights' in the Catholic sense." However, he then says that "'economic rights' properly so called" do not include those rights traditionally called economic rights, but only those rights "already recognized in the U.S. Constitution," such as the right to private property. All other rights traditionally included under the rubric of economic rights are better termed "welfare rights," and are really "not 'rights' in the full sense" but are rather "better to be described in terms of objectives, ends, goals." In Novak's view, to call "rights" those claims that are traditionally termed economic rights is "Marxist," whereas to reserve the term economic rights to rights such as private property is "Catholic (and American.)" [parenthesis in original].[30] In short, Novak takes those claims that John Paul includes and affirms under the rubric of economic rights, places them under the term "welfare rights," and states that they are not rights "properly so called." He then re-ascribes the term economic rights to cover, for instance, the right of private property— traditionally and in John Paul's discussion of the Universal Declaration held to be a political right—and re-describes this view as "the Catholic" view. If we understand the terms as John Paul explicates them, then we see that Novak does indeed reject as rights the claims that the Pope and Catholic doctrine include under the rubric of economic rights.

The Differences Between Them
II: Economic Theory

When there is disagreement on a point as basic as that of economic rights, it suggests that there are other divergences as well, and this appears to be the case with regard to Novak and John Paul II. What is at issue is not a single point of disagreement, then, but an array of claims that underpin Novak's economic theory as a whole. In this section, I will set out key differences regarding 1) the significance of the gap between rich and poor, 2) the threat of consumerism, 3) the limits on the use of private property, and 4) the nature of Catholic social teaching as a genre of moral theology.

Novak claims that the gap between rich and poor is not morally relevant as long as the poor are materially better off than in previous arrangements. He writes, "This 'gap' is not the moral point, but the need for rapid improvement of the lot of the poor." In *Toward the Future: Catholic Social Thought and the U.S. Economy*, a document he drafted for the self-appointed "Lay Commission on Catholic Social Teaching and the U.S. Economy," Novak goes even further to say that it is "improper to concentrate on 'the gap' alleged to exist between rich and poor countries."[31] John Paul, however, does claim that there is just such a gap, and he focuses on it quite intensely. In *Dives in misericordia*, he emphasizes both the fact and the moral importance of the widening gap: "This fact is universally known. The state of inequality between individuals and between nations not only still exists; it is increasing. It still happens that side by side with those who are wealthy and living in plenty there exist those living in want, suffering misery...This is why moral uneasiness is destined to become more acute." He elaborates on the issue at several points in *Sollicitudo rei socialis* and comments, "The word *gap* returns spontaneously to mind" (emphasis in text).[32] In *Centesimus annus* John Paul expands the concern to include the gap in education and training that contributes to economic inequality.[33] It would seem, then, that Novak would have to charge that John Paul's focus on the rich-poor gap is "improper." However, he attempts to explain away the difference by claiming that John Paul refers to the gap only "metaphorically."[34]

The Catholic Ethic goes on to chide those "who too glibly denigrate 'consumerism.'"[35] For Novak, following Adam Smith, the gap between rich and poor is morally insignificant as long as the poor are materially better off. Capitalism produces more overall wealth than other economic systems to such an extent that even with a wide rich-poor gap, the poor are indeed materially better off. What helps drive the production of goods is consumer demand. In short, consumerism is the activity that inspires and enables businesses to produce more goods and thus wealth. The result is that *The Catholic Ethic* offers no critique of consumerism at all.

What is not adequately addressed by Novak in *The Catholic Ethic* is that the seemingly unending quest for more and more of ever more specialized and refined items and services in a consumer society is a spiritual and moral malady. Recall John Paul's definition of capitalism—distinct from the free economy—as that form of market economy that places material well-being before the whole person and individual self-interest before the common good. A consumer society is that society where the market ethos expands to every area of life, overtaking other orders of value so that the only value is material gain for the self.

The Pope describes such a society quite forcefully at several points. In *Redemptor hominis*, he links consumer society to the rich-poor gap. John Paul writes, "Indeed everyone is familiar with the picture of the consumer civilization, which consists in a certain surplus of goods necessary for man and for entire societies—and we are now dealing with the rich highly developed societies—while the remaining societies—at least broad sectors of them—are suffering from hunger, with many people dying each day of starvation and malnutrition."[36] It is in *Sollicitudo rei socialis* that John Paul identifies consumerism not only as a key component of the material problem of the rich-poor gap but also as a spiritual blight. The "civilization of 'consumption' or 'consumerism'" consists of "the excessive availability of every kind of material good for the benefit of certain social groups." Such "superdevelopment" is "contrary to what is good and true to happiness," because it leads to "a radical dissatisfaction" where "the more one possesses the more one wants, while deeper aspirations remain unsatisfied and perhaps even stifled."[37]

On the basis of this spiritual lack, linked to the gap between rich and poor inherent in capitalism, the Pope makes a distinction between "being" and "having." If people have a sense of value—of "being"—that resists being subsumed under the quest for material possession—"having"—then there is hope that the gap between rich and poor will lessen. As it is, "there are some people— the few who possess much—who do not really succeed in 'being' because, through a reversal of the hierarchy of values [recall that capitalism reverses the correct order of values], they are hindered by the cult of 'having'; and there are others—the many who have little or nothing—who do not succeed in realizing their basic human vocation because they are deprived of essential goods."[38]

Novak cites John Paul II's primacy of "being" over "having," but does not link it to the gap between rich and poor. Instead, he reduces the emphasis on "being" to a passing sense of wonder towards the goods one has accumulated and gratitude for having been able to accumulate them. Careful reading discloses that this emphasis purely on interior affect does have the concrete consequence of reinforcing the rich-poor gap, because the gratitude suggests that there is no problem with possession of large quantities of goods; indeed God created such persons to be wealthy, or "to be where we are." To give priority to "being," according to Novak, is "to be overcome (momentarily) by wonder. The habit of making such moments more frequent during one's days is a habit important to Catholic life . . . . The insight into being draws attention to what is truly central in life, uniquely and ultimately important, one's responsibility for saying 'yes' to life, *to the will of God who created us to be where we are* and to achieve all that we are capable of . . . ." (emphasis added).[39]

The issue of economic rights ties into consumerism because, by insisting that there are limits to what people can do to others on behalf of profit, such rights remind the well-off that there is an order of values that is not subsumed under the market. In sum, economic rights serve not only to protect the poor from the well-off, but also, when attended to, to protect the well-off from themselves. The neo-liberal denial of economic rights is of a piece with the lack of adequate awareness that the wealthy are, according to John Paul, in deep moral and spiritual peril. To address this, Catholic social doctrine holds that not only must the Church help the poor become somewhat better off in material goods, it must also help the well-off become, in concrete and not just spiritual ways, poorer.

In other words, in Catholic social doctrine, there is a moral limit to the use of private property. In contrast, although Novak claims that there are moral limits to the private use of wealth, such claims turn out to be empty. We can begin to see how this is the case in terms of the source upon which he draws, John Locke. The latter sets out natural law limits to the possession of private property, and Novak claims that these limits find strong parallels with Catholic teaching. Close examination of Locke's theory of property, however, indicates that while he was likely sincere in his efforts to place natural limits on the use of private property, the limits are empty. In the early stages of Locke's "state of nature," there are three limitations to the accumulation of property. The first we can call the "spoilage constraint." A person can rightfully appropriate only as much property as will not spoil or go to waste. Spoilage is against the fundamental law of nature because it wastes that which is intended by God to help preserve humankind. Second, there is what we can call an "industry constraint." One can claim only as much property as one can mix with one's labor. Finally, in light of the fundamental law of nature, there is a "preservation constraint." One can appropriate only as much as still allows for the preservation of others.[40]

However, Locke allows the introduction of money prior to the social contract, and this permits persons to appropriate "larger Possessions, and a Right to them." Money bypasses the spoilage constraint because, simply put, gold and silver do not rot. A person may "heap up as much of these durable things as he pleased." Money also enlarges the industry constraint, as it allows one to purchase another's labor for wages. Finally, the introduction of money allows Locke to reinterpret the preservation constraint. Prior to money, one has to leave enough and "as good" for others "at least where there is enough." Although the introduction of money makes land scarce, because the private appropriation of land produces so much more than land left undeveloped, even those who are left without property by the introduction of money will be better off. In Locke's words, "A King of a large and fruitful Territory [in America] feeds, lodges, and is clad worse than a day Laborer in England." There appear, therefore, to be no substantive limits to the right of private property.[41]

The pattern is similar in Novak's thought: any limits appear to be in name only. While he does cite the teaching on the universal destination of created goods and the distinction between the right to private property and the legitimate use of that property, he nowhere works out what this might mean substantively. On the contrary, his claim that in a capitalist economy the dynamic production of wealth renders the rich-poor gap morally moot also entails that any natural law limits on the private use of wealth are beside the point as long as the less well-off are faring better than in the other economic alternatives identified by Novak as presently possible. This is why Novak can reduce the distinction between "being" and "having" to a sense of "wonder" towards the goods one has accumulated and gratitude "to the will of God who created us to be where we are."

Official Catholic teaching has a very different interpretation of dynamic capitalism and its implications. Traditional teaching has held that there are three levels or classes of material goods or possessions. The first consists of the basic necessities of life: food, work, shelter, health care, and so forth. These necessities are what is generally included under the title of "economic rights" in Catholic doctrine. The second level or class of goods are those things that are common or typical for a person of a particular social class. The third level of goods are those which are not required to maintain one's social position. The three levels of material goods can be understood as the levels of 1) necessity, 2) substance, and 3) superfluity.[42]

The first effect of dynamic capitalism has been to erase the distinction between what is required for one's position in society and what is superfluous. This is because one's position in society is never set; therefore one can always gain more and not have it be too much. There is no such thing as accumulating too many goods for oneself and one's lifestyle. The second effect of dynamic capitalism, as we have seen, is to deny that the basic necessities—the first level of material goods—are rights. The poor have no strict claim on the wealthy; they can only hope for the latter's generosity, which may or may not be forthcoming.

Catholic teaching on the limits to private property has developed over the past century in response to these effects of capitalism. The earlier documents still hold to the three-level understanding of material goods and state that one is to give out of one's superfluity. Writing *Rerum novarum* in 1891, for instance, Leo XIII has yet to discern any profound erasure of the distinction between what is called for by one's station in life and what is superfluous. He draws on the key Catholic concepts, quoting Thomas Aquinas that, "Man should not consider his outward possessions his own, but as common to all," and argues that "it is one thing to have a right to a possession of money, and another to have a right to use money as one pleases." Yet, he concludes that one is to give "that which is left over" once one has established "one's position fairly considered." Pius XI's 1931 document *Quadragesimo anno* puts increased stress on the common end of private property and elaborates in some detail on the distinction between the right to and correct use of private property, but does not make any major change in Leo's view of the three levels of material goods and the obligations that follow.[43]

Greater awareness that the gap between rich and poor is increasing and of the fact that the well-off have been not not giving adequately begins with the pontificate of John XXIII and the Second Vatican Council. This awareness leads the Council in *Gaudium et spes* to emphasize persons' obligation to give "not merely out of their superfluous goods." In short, the Council's view is that if capitalism is going to erase the distinction between what is required for one's station in life and what is superfluous, then "the universal purpose for which created goods are meant" implies that we are to give out of our substance. We see here that in response to the erasure of the superfluity/substance distinction, official Catholic teaching moves in the *opposite* direction of Novak, away from the neo-liberal removal of any real requirement to give and towards making that requirement more strict.

Gaudium et spes goes on to cite the implication that Aquinas himself draws from the teaching on property, an implication that Leo XIII and Pius XI fail to mention: "If a person is in extreme necessity, he has the right to take from the riches of others what he himself needs." Leo and Pius say to give out of our superfluity. *Gaudium et spes* says that we are to give out of our substance. But in quoting Aquinas, it goes even further to argue that what the person in need takes from us is in fact not really ours to begin with. It is a common good, and to the extent that a person lives in a state of necessity and we do not, his or her taking it from us does not constitute theft in the moral sense. In the 1967 document, *Populorum Progressio*, Paul VI quotes Ambrose to make the point explicit: "You are not making a gift of your possessions to the poor person. You are handing over to him what is his. For what has been given in common for the use of all, you have arrogated to yourself." In other words, "you" are the thief.[44]

Catholic teaching, then, has moved from stating that we must give out of our superfluity to requiring that we give out our substance, to pointing out that that substance is not really ours in the first place. John Paul II confirms and furthers this development. In *Sollicitudo rei socialis*, he writes that private property is "under 'social mortgage,'" which means that it has an intrinsically social function, based upon and justified precisely by the principle of the universal destination of goods." This requires even the church to give more than simply out of its "abundance." Like the recent Popes and Council before him, John Paul II, in response to capitalism, moves in the opposite direction of neo-liberal economics. Where he goes beyond the earlier documents is in his awareness that meeting the requirement involves much more than an individual change of heart. In *Centesimus annus* he writes, "it is not enough to draw on the surplus goods which in fact our world abundantly produces; it requires above all a change of lifestyles, of models of production and consumption, and of established structures of power which today govern societies."[45] Such requirements for concrete personal and structural change in John Paul's writings reveal the lack of substance in Novak's claim to set natural law limits on the use of private property.

We have seen, thus far, that, if we read him correctly, Novak rejects John Paul's capitalism/free market distinction as being unrealistically and irrationally "emotional," considers the Pope's emphasis on economic rights as traditionally understood to be "Marxist" rather than Catholic, regards the emphasis on the gap between rich and poor to be "improper," chides the concern over consumerism, and sets no real moral limits on the accumulation of property for one's own use. However, the most fundamental difference between Novak and John Paul II may well be in their understanding of Catholic social teaching itself.

Again, Novak reads *Centesimus annus* as affirming that "there is only one form of economics" acceptable, and that "We are all capitalists now, even the Pope." These are not isolated statements standing free, but rather are backed by Novak's own use of scripture and tradition to make his case. In *Toward the Future,* he draws upon passages from Matthew 25—in particular, the parable of the talents coupled with the injunctions to feed the poor—to argue that scripture supports only capitalism. Novak points out that the person who buried the talents is chastised because he did not invest the money and thus produce more wealth. If we as a society invest our talents, he argues, then there will be enough wealth so that those who are better off will give to the charitable organizations that aid the poor. The latter will thus be fed and clothed. The parable of the talents "details the terrible punishments which lie in store for those who do not produce new wealth from the talents." Investment of capital, moreover, is the way to aid the poor:

> From before the time of Jesus multitudes have lived in poverty and under tyranny. To further their liberation, our [American] forefathers designed an order of political economy in which the poor and needy might routinely raise themselves out of poverty by methods economically wise and conducive to unparalleled economic creativity. In short, such passages as Matthew 25 have not only personal but also systematic applications.[46]

In *The Catholic Ethic*, Novak couples this scriptural argument for capitalism with a form of natural law argument. Human beings are created in the image of God, and as such have, in an analogous way, some of the capacities of God. Among these are certain capacities for rationality—in a traditional version of natural law thought, the natural law is God's eternal law imprinted on the mind of human persons—and creativity. Novak links these capacities directly and exclusively to capitalism. "Capitalism is a system rooted in the mind, and in this respect goes beyond all preceding economic systems." He even suggests that there is an etymological link between capitalism and the imprint of God's natural law on the human mind. Capitalism "suggests the Latin *caput* (head), the human seat of that very creativity, invention, initiative the Pope sees in 'creative subjectivity.'"[47]

The problem with Novak's interpretation is that John Paul never draws upon the *imago Dei* doctrine to back a capitalist political economy. To do so would be to treat Catholic social teaching as ideology, not theology. The Pope makes this clear in *Sollicitudo rei socialis*: "For the Church does not propose economic political systems or programs, nor does she show preference for one or the other, provided that human dignity is properly respected and promoted." The Church's social doctrine, "belongs to the field, not of ideology, but of theology, and particularly moral theology. The teaching and spreading of her social doctrine are part of the Church's evangelizing mission." In short, the aim of the social doctrine is to draw upon moral and theological concepts to critique all systems in light of whether they promote or obstruct the concrete realization of transcendent human dignity. Support for any specific system, therefore, is always conditional and made on prudential grounds rather than argued directly from scripture or natural law. When the Pope does draw on the *imago Dei* doctrine in *Laborem exercens* and elsewhere, it is to make the general point about the priority of the whole person—including the human creative capacity—over material well-being, not to back a specific system of political economy. Novak does offer scattered disclaimers that Scripture and Catholic social doctrine back no one system, but his *systematic* argument, as we have seen, indicates another approach altogether; he does the very thing he disclaims.

Remaining Questions

It is clear by now, then, that there are significant differences between Novak and John Paul II. Three questions remain for any further inquiry into these differences. The first is whether such differences constitute formal dissent on Novak's part. I believe that they do, but making the case would require a more extended argument than I can take up here. The next question is whether, if it is dissent, this fact should place Novak's views beyond the pale of ecclesially acceptable conversation. I do not think that it should, given that dissent has played a positive role in the development of doctrine before—the case of religious freedom being the most recent. Finally, it must be investigated whether Catholic social teaching ought to develop in the direction that Novak seeks to take it. Here I must side with John Paul II for reasons that he and Catholic social teaching in general make clear: economic rights as traditionally understood are a key component of the strong cultural and juridical framework that must restrain the market and the private use of property if the market and private property are to support the common good rather than a consumerist desire that increases the gap between rich and poor. Such a theologically grounded framework can accommodate a number of economic models, but it is evident that, at present, the official texts do not support the case that what Novak puts forward is one of them, let alone the only one.

NOTES

[1] Michael Novak, *The Catholic Ethic and the Spirit of Capitalism* (The Free Press, 1993): 101; cf. also note 13.

[2] John Paul II, *Centesimus annus*, 35. Unless otherwise noted, all quotations from official documents of the Catholic church are from David J. O'Brien and Thomas A. Shannon, eds., *Catholic Social Thought: The Documentary Heritage* (Maryknoll, New York: Orbis Books, 1992). Citations refer to the official paragraph numbers.

[3] Josh Koopman, "*Centesimus Annus*," *National Catholic Register* (March 2-8, 1997): 6; Tracy Early, "Liberalism and *Centesimus Annus*," *National Catholic Register* (March, 2-8, 1997): 8.

[4] Michael Novak, *Awakening from Nihilism*, edited by Derek Cross and Brian Anderson ([no location given]:Crisis Books, 1995): 75.

[5] In an interesting twist on terms, what the wider economic literature calls "neo-liberal," Catholic writings term "neo-conservative." I will use the former term because what we are addressing is Novak's economic theory and not whether he is a social conservative or not. Many social conservatives—for instance, on issues such as homosexuality—espouse neo-liberal eco-

nomic theory. Neo-liberal economic theory emphasizes a minimum of government involvement in trade other than the protection of private property.

[6] Rodger Charles, S.J., *An Introduction to Catholic Social Teaching* (Oxford: Family Publications/San Francisco: Ignatius Press, 1999): 100.

[7] Michael Novak, *The Spirit of Democratic Capitalism* (New York: Simon and Schuster, 1982): 201.

[8] Novak, *The Catholic Ethic and the Spirit of Capitalism*, 114 ("sonic boom"), 118 (the claim that John Paul II parts with his own earlier teaching), 106 ("the pope of economic enterprise"), 92 (first to emphasize "economic initiative"; cf. also 60), 128 (economic initiative second only to religious liberty), and 88 ("fresh material, indeed").

[9] John Paul II, *Centesimus annus*, 42.

[10] Novak, *The Catholic Ethic*, 101, 101 note 13, 103, and 118.

[11] Leo XIII, *Rerum novarum*, 5, 7, and 12; Pius XI, *Quadragesimo anno*, 95 (cf. also 79-80 and *Divini redemptoris*, 69).

[12] John XXIII, *Mater et magistra*, 51, 57. Cf. also 55, 57, 62, 82-84, 150, 152, 165, 173, and *Pacem in terris*, 34 and 65.

[13] Paul VI, *Populorum progressio* 25; cf. also 27, 30, and *Octogesima adveniens*, 19 and 33.

[14] John Paul II, *Laborem exercens*, 8.

[15] For the call for worker sharing in profits, decision-making, and even ownership, see, for instance, Pius XI, *Quadragesimo anno*, 54-57, 61, 65; John XXIII, *Mater et magistra*, 32, 75-77, 82-103; Second Vatican Council, *Gaudium et spes*, 68; John Paul II, *Laborem exercens*, 8, 13-15; *Centesimus annus*, 15, 35, and 43.

[16] John Paul II, *Centesimus annus*, 35, 56, and 42. Cf. also 8, 10, 26, 33, and 43.

[17] John Paul II, *Laborem exercens*, 7; *Centesimus annus*, 33.

[18] John Paul II, *Centesimus annus*, 19; cf. also 33, 36, and 39.

[19] Ibid, 35.

[20] Novak, *The Catholic Ethic*, 133-135 and 18.

[21] See, for instance, John XXIII, *Pacem in terris*, 11.

[22] John Paul II, *Centesimus annus*, 47.

[23] John Paul II, *Redemptor hominis*, 17.

[24] Novak, *The Catholic Ethic*, 81.

[25] Michael Novak, "The Option for the Poor: Clarifications," *Saint Louis University Public Law Review*, 5 (1986): 321.

[26] John Paul II, *Centesimus annus*, 31.

[27] John Paul II, "Toward a Balanced, Well-Regulated World Market," *Origins*, 27, no. 3 (June 5, 1997): pars 2, 4, 6, and 7.

[28] John Paul II, "Message of His Holiness Pope John Paul II for the Celebration of the World Day of Peace," http://www.vatican.va/holy_father/john_p...21998_xxxii-world-day-for-peace_en.shtml (January 1, 1999): par. 3.

[29] Michael Novak, "Catholic Social Thought, the Pope, and Me," *The Observer* (April 8, 1999): 8.

[30] Michael Novak, "The Future of 'Economic Rights,'" in James Finn, ed., *Private Virtue and Public Policy: Catholic Thought and Economic Life* (New Brunswick/London: Transaction Publishers, 1990): 76 and 80.

[31] Novak, *The Catholic Ethic*, 153; Lay Commission on Catholic Social Teaching and the U.S. Economy, *Toward the Future: Catholic Social Thought and the U.S. Economy* (New York: Lay Commission on Catholic Social Teaching and the U.S. Economy, 1984): 49.

[32] John Paul II, *Dives in misericordia*, 11; *Sollicitudo rei socialis*, 14; cf. also 9, 12-16, 28, 39, 42, and 44-45.

[33] John Paul II, *Centesimus annus*, 33.

[34] Novak, *The Catholic Ethic*, 152.

[35] Ibid., 102.

[36] John Paul II, *Redemptor hominis*, 16.

[37] John Paul II, *Sollicitudo rei socialis*, 28.

[38] Ibid. For the issue of consumerism, see also *Centesimus annus* 28, 29, 33, 36, and 41.

[39] Novak, *The Catholic Ethic*, 204.

[40] John Locke, *Second Treatise on Government*, sects. 31, 36-38, and 27; cf also 33.

[41] Ibid, sect. 36-37, 46, and 50 for how money bypasses the spoilage constraint; sect. 85 assumes the ability to purchase labor. See sect. 45 and 36 for how the introduction of money leaves land scarce, and 41 for how development of land allows greater productivity anyway.

[42] Cf. Kenneth Himes, "The Inextricable Link of Charity and Discipleship," *Origins* (February 20, 1997): 578.

[43] Leo XIII, *Rerum novarum*, 19; Pius XI, 45-49 and 56.

[44] Second Vatican Council, *Gaudium et spes*, 69; Paul VI, *Populorum progressio*, 23.

[45] John Paul II, *Sollicitudo rei socialis*, 31 and 42; *Centesimus annus*, 58. John Paul also makes clear elsewhere in *Centesimus annus* that his emphasis on the universal destination of created goods and on the distinction between the right to private property and the legitimate use of that property has the force of requirement. He writes that "the church teaches that the possession of material goods is not an absolute right, and that its limits are inscribed in its very nature as a human right"(par. 30). He then draws on the concept of the universal destination of goods (par. 31) to argue, "It is a strict duty of justice and truth not to allow fundamental human needs to remain unsatisfied, and not to allow those burdened by such needs to perish" (par. 34).

[46] Lay Commission, *Toward the Future*, x-xi.

[47] Novak, *The Catholic Ethic*, 59 and 128.

Tragedy and the Ethics of Hans Urs von Balthasar[1]

Christopher Steck, S.J.

Abstract

The goodness in many people's lives is often obscured by the limitations and brokenness which mark those same lives. The saint as moral icon, in which the moral beauty of the individual is clearly visible to all, cannot be the exclusive paradigm of Christian holiness. The kind of obscurity effected by limitation and human imperfection can be described as tragic—events and circumstances beyond the agent's control seem to determine the agent's moral fate. I argue that von Balthasar's theological aesthetics helps illuminate the tragic features of Christ's own life and can, in turn, help us understand the tragic dimension present in varying degrees in every Christian life. In tragic situations, where the brokenness and sin of the human condition threaten to undermine human love, the Christian's moral response, like Christ's own, will be inspired more by a hopeful fidelity to God's call than by a confident expectation of the fruitfulness of her love.

The recent case in England of the two twins joined to one another served as a reminder of the tragic character of medicine. No course of action could be undertaken which would avoid the deeply disturbing loss of some important goods. The loss of these goods was disquieting enough that many felt at some instinctual level that there was no right answer, that any response would be inadequate and morally tainted in some way. Such cases exemplify a tragic dimension which is characteristic not just of medical practice but of Christian existence in general.[2] Our moral lives are tragic because we are limited and sinful creatures, facing moral claims in a world whose needs are virtually limitless and acting within a web of relationships distorted in numerous ways by sin.

The tragic dimension of the moral life has been an important topic of conversation among ethicists over the last several decades. Much of the discussion among moral philosophers has focused on the issue of "moral luck," that is, whether and how one's moral character is vulnerable to contingent events.[3] The issues for the Christian are a little different since God's judgment of our moral lives looks not at the vagaries of human existence but the deep movements of the human heart. Furthermore, the commitment to monotheism softens the severity of seemingly irresolvable dilemmas; God's demands, we can assume, do not conflict. I accept then the view of many Christian ethicists, particularly those of the Catholic tradition, that regardless of the situation there is always one course of action available to the agent that is good. The rationalism found in much of Christian ethics (in both Aristotelian and Kantian forms) supports this conviction. While we might be disturbed on an emotional level by the grave loss of important goods in some tragic choices, our practical reason, which must prevail in these matters, helps us see those choices as right and good.

Nonetheless, I believe that tragedy is an important moral category for Christian ethics because, as I hope to show, it illuminates features of moral goodness and agency which an exclusively rational approach can obscure. In making this argument, I focus on a particular meaning of tragedy. In common usage the term has come to refer to any situation where people undergo dramatic reversals of fortune through events and circumstances beyond their control. But the tragedy of the classical Greek tradition often focused on choices made with good intent yet within "no-win" situations where any action promised loss of something greatly valued. The loss was significant enough that it threatened to obscure whatever good was achieved. And because the choices of the agent contributed in some disturbing way to this tragic end, the goodness of the agent herself was thrown into question.

In exploring tragedy from a Christian standpoint, I will use a general, broad version of this classical understanding. Tragedy occurs whenever the goodness of a moral act is severely obscured or hidden from the agent herself and from those who behold her action because of the sinful and broken context in which it takes place. While the action can, by some measure at least, be described as good, it might not look or feel good because of the loss of significant goods, and in that sense can be described as tragic.

The obscurity of goodness in such tragic situations can take two forms. The moral ambiguity of some tragic cases is such that it does not touch upon the moral character of the agent herself. In the case of the conjoined twins, for example, the grave consequences of whatever decision is made can be attributed to the unfortunate circumstances instead of being blamed on those who actually bring about those consequences. But sometimes the limitations of the agent herself contribute to the obscurity of the action's goodness. Take the example of the parent who, with good intentions, tries to practice "tough love" on a problem child but fails because of personal limitations (e.g., her lack of insight, immaturity, insecurity, misreading of the situation). The attempt backfires, pushing the child instead toward a self-destructive life. The kind of limitations which often contribute to these tragedies are morally ambiguous; it is impossible to distinguish in them the effects of personal sin from the givenness of one's life (who or what precisely is to blame for immaturity?). Such ambiguous limitations cause the "evil" of the consequences to redound upon the agent herself. In this paper, I am primarily concerned with how a Christian should understand this second type of tragedy, that is, the tragedy which arises because of human limitation, brokenness, and sin.

The theology of Hans Urs von Balthasar provides a framework for understanding this tragic dimension of the Christian life. His ethical theory is constructed around the idea that moral action flows out of our perception of the world; good, right action follows upon seeing the world rightly. Ultimately, this perception will for the Christian be tutored by her attentive consideration of revelation, particularly the life of Jesus Christ. This saving story, as we will see, is tragic for von Balthasar. And thus as the Christian perceives her own tragic situation and the choices she makes within them, she will do so in accord with the tragic form which appears in the life of Christ. Regrettably, von Balthasar limits the practical implications of his approach by his tendency to rely on one, rather constricted, understanding of tragedy, that is, Jesus as the tragic hero. I will argue that we can expand this understanding in a way that is both faithful to his general approach and also yields a theory applicable to a broader range of human moral experience.

The paper is divided into three parts. In the first I briefly introduce von Balthasar's ethical theory as it is suggested in *The Glory of the Lord*. This will be an interpretation since von Balthasar does not offer any adequate systematic presentation of ethics. I suggest that it is an ethics that can be described as aesthetic insofar as it centers on a way of perceiving the world. Then I turn to von Balthasar's interpretation of the Christ event to see in what way he believes it can be described as tragic. Finally, I explore the implications of this theology for the Christian moral life, further developing his ideas. Specifically, I examine how the perception of Christ's life illuminates the tragic quality of Christian life and elicits a particular response which I call "hopeful fidelity."

Part I: Von Balthasar's Aesthetic Ethics[4]

For von Balthasar, the dynamic life of creation in general, and human agency and moral response in particular, is shaped by the fact that its Creator is triune. God's triuneness stamps everything. But it is a particular type of triuneness, one informed much more by the personalist emphasis of the Greek tradition than by the stress on unity found in the Latin. While recognizing the inadequacy of all language and metaphors dealing with God's triune oneness, von Balthasar suggests that the persons of the Trinity engage one another, face one another in encounter, and even affect one another in their interchange. Thus von Balthasar speaks of the "joys of expectation, of hope and fulfillment, the joys of giving and receiving," of "mutual acknowledgment and adoration," among the triune persons.[5] Von Balthasar agrees with those who argue that only narrative forms can convey the richness and complexity of God's saving act and its existential significance for our lives. However, he adds that the dramatic and narrative character of revelation is not simply a dimension of divine action which arises only with its involvement in human history. The deeper "why" of the inescapable narrative dimension of God's saving act lies in the fact that the interchange of triune persons is itself dramatic. And while von Balthasar suggests that this triune drama is evidenced throughout the Old and New Testaments,[6] its clearest manifestation occurs in the obedience of the Son to the Father as he drinks from the cup he had wished to avoid.

For von Balthasar, the trinitarian imprint is found in the fact that all creation is oriented toward the dialogical. Just as the Father expresses himself in the Son, so also every creature in some way speaks a "word" which expresses what it is to the other.[7] And in the case of the intelligent creature, the encountered manifestation of the other elicits another movement: the *ek-static* reception of the other's address. The triune God who created us imprinted in us a *conatus* toward free, creative engagements with the other. And thus the earthly image of God appears not only in the individual person or in the wonder and beauty of creation—locations very familiar to the Christian tradition—but also, and perhaps especially, in any encounter, any exchange where the expression of the other is given and received. The fullness of the divine, trinitarian image is manifested in the event of interpersonal love.

All interpersonal encounters are to reflect the unity in mutuality of triune life, and thus the creaturely *conatus* toward expression of self and reception of the other has a normative orientation. But for von Balthasar, we experience this moral claim within the encounter aesthetically, and we do so in two senses of the word—that is, we experience the moral claim through our *perception* and as linked with *beauty*. The term "aesthetics" carries both meanings for von Balthasar. When we perceive the other's self-expression to us, we are moved by a radiance that lies therein. Every expression of a creature's being, who or what it is, is marked not only by truth (e.g., it is an adequate expression, it correctly expresses what this creature is), but also by a kind of form that attracts (in being faithful to who or what it is, it reflects the beauty of the God who created it). And with the perception of truth and beauty comes the call to respond—that we witness to the truth and beauty of the other by welcoming the other in love.[8] For von Balthasar, the aesthetic appeal of the other gives the perceived truth of the other its existential imperative; it establishes the claim on the beholder that the address of the other be received. Thus the ethical imperative confronting the moral agent in all encounters (human and nonhuman) can be expressed, von Balthasar suggests, as "let [this other] be"—that is, I should allow the other to be by becoming the type of person who fully welcomes and allows the other's self-expression.[9]

In this approach, moral agency is not primarily a matter of active doing before and within a passive world, but rather an active receptivity of the other. Von Balthasar wants to restore the subject/object balance in the moral event against some contemporary tendencies to locate the entirety of moral agency in the will of the subject. The world rightly perceived will awaken our response. It will draw us beyond ourselves, *ek-statically*, because it is a world which reflects the beauty of its divine author.

We should also note that von Balthasar's aesthetic reconfiguration of the moral claim shapes not only how we experience the "ought" within the ethical encounter, but also its content. We experience the "ought" as an aesthetic claim in the sense that it is something attractive which calls us to respond. But also the measure of what constitutes the fulfillment of that ought is aesthetic. That is, the content of the moral demand for von Balthasar is not simply determined by universal reason and logic, but is rather shaped in part by an aesthetic appreciation of what could be, what attractive form and drama could appear within this encounter with our free response (and how our hatred could mar such a form). The address of the other awakens not a mechanical response, but our creativity and freedom. And the goodness which results from our loving response will also be beautiful not because our response has followed the paint-by-numbers of universal laws, but because it expresses the freedom, creativity, and love of the human agent which are in turn a reflection of divine life.

Von Balthasar sees in this aesthetic, moral response not just the earthly analogate of faith but also the very point at which human agency is in grace transformed into the response of faith. Analogous to the encounter with the other, the encounter with Christ draws forth an *ek-static* response in the individual. She finds in this person a truth and beauty that she could not anticipate, but, once perceived, shows itself as commanding and praiseworthy.[10] The human agent's dialogical openness to the other becomes in grace a surrender of faith to the "ever-greaterness" of God. This is what faith is for von Balthasar: not an intellectual or fiduciary act, but a doxological response to the appearing glory of God in Christ.

The link which von Balthasar makes between aesthetics and ethics is problematic insofar as it appears to presume something about our world which no longer seems credible: that the world strikes the beholder with such a radiance or beauty that it can elicit and shape human action. In the desacralized, disenchanted cosmos of the contemporary era, von Balthasar's aesthetic reconfiguration of ethics seems plagued with romantic longings and a naively mystical reading of the world. Von Balthasar is aware of this issue, and he responds to it on several different levels. First, while it may be true that the world in general no longer shares in the radiance of the sacred for most human eyes, von Balthasar, like a number of contemporary philosophers, believes that the human other resists this general, desacralized flattening of the encountered world.[11] At the same time, von Balthasar grants the general criticism that his theological aesthetics involves a way of looking at the world no longer possible for most. As a second approach to the problem, von Balthasar argues along Christian particularist lines. The task of perceiving the world sacramentally, as a beacon of God's beauty and thus a source of moral energy, falls almost exclusively to the Christian. Because the Christian has been given revelation both in its objective and subjective forms (the objective epiphany of divine glory in the Christ event and the subjective gift of the Spirit helping human eyes to see this glory), the Christian has become attuned to the divine labor as it continues in the world. Thus it is not only that the biblical narrative shapes our affect and the way we interpret the world around us. Von Balthasar's claim here is something more provocative than that of many narrative ethicists. The Christian does not just "read" and interpret the passive text of the world before her, but rather encounters something within it. The dual gift of Christ and the Spirit makes possible our genuine and ongoing encounter of God in the world. The same form which God revealed in Christ is the one which the Spirit labors to impress upon the world before us and through us. The Christian looks at a world filled with the laboring presence of the Spirit and resounding with echoes of the call to join in that saving work.

In addition to these two arguments for an aesthetic ethics—that, first, even in our desacralized world the link between aesthetics and ethics is manifested in our encounter with the other and that, second, Christian perception is so tutored that the link between seeing and doing, contemplation and action, becomes an apt characterization of the Christian life—there is a third. The link between aesthetics and ethics, beauty seen and goodness done, is difficult to experience not just because of the lack of a contemplative vision in the contemporary world, but also and perhaps primarily because of the ways sin has marred our world. Von Balthasar, however, suggests that the tragic literary form points us along a path where even with sin this aesthetic link is preserved. For in the tragic form we find an example of a goodness, or better, glory, that can be seen, however indirectly, and thus loved even while being veiled by the disturbing brokenness of the world.

We will turn to this point in the next section. However, before doing so, I note one additional element in von Balthasar's aesthetic ethics. The above themes of "saving narrative" and the labor of the Spirit allude to an important development that von Balthasar makes in his ethical theory as he moves from the first part of his trilogy, *The Glory of the Lord*, to its second part, *Theo-Drama*. Von Balthasar expands his idea of the moral life as *ek-static* response to the beautiful to include the dramatic form, or what he refers to as "theo-drama." The moral life is viewed as a matter of reading the narrative of the world around us and finding the good and appropriate ways in which our story fits in with and develops that story. This development in von Balthasar's theory, of course, shares commonalities with the ideas of narrative ethicists. At the same time, von Balthasar's aesthetic theory governs his narrative approach. The themes which characterize this aesthetic ethics—the *ek-static* encounter, the active receptivity, the moral challenge "to let be" the other, a moral justification which centers on notions of fittingness, aesthetic completion, and beauty over universal reason's dicta—also inform his narrative approach. The dramatic form appeals to our agency. Watching a good play, for example, offers us a pleasure because "we can project ourselves onto an ultimate plane that gives meaning, and thus we are given to ourselves."[12] There is always some existential tug that comes with beholding a good story. It prompts the question of our own identity and opens up possibilities that our own story might share in the features of this story before us.

What I want to call our attention to here is that situating the narrative approach to the moral life within an aesthetic theory effects a kind of thickening of the dimension of agency. We are not simply socialized into the Christian story, passively shaped by the narrative as we hear it proclaimed to us. Rather, we encounter something that invites our freedom, awakens holy desires, and moves us to make a decision about personal identity. The story of Christ draws us to enter it because we are moved by the love which appears in it, and we find in it something which rings true about human existence. It explains and illuminates the disparate desires, moral claims, fears, and limitations which we live out in joy and suffering endurance. For von Balthasar, the attractiveness of the Christian narrative lies not only in its consoling message of love, but also in the story's power to explain and judge our lives in a way that we find authoritative and compelling. Thus von Balthasar's theological aesthetics can be called a "theo-dramatic aesthetics."

Part II: The Tragic Form of the Christ Event

Christians hold that within the biblical narrative can be found a normative vision of what human life should be. This narrative develops through complex interchanges among its characters which take place in circumstances varying greatly over the course of the narrative's history. And thus we should speak not so much of a single normative vision but of normative possibilities, ones which cohere with one another and yet are able to illuminate the limitless variety of situations that Christians occupy. One such situation is found in the experience of the tragic where endeavors to do good and to contribute to human flourishing through acts of love fail in ways that are disheartening and disturbing. Von Balthasar's aesthetic interpretation of Christ's story, that is, his interpretation of this event in terms of the dramatic form it represents, sees in the events which compose the life of Christ a narrative form that can be described as tragic.[13] The story of Christ is tragic not simply because contingent events made it so, but, von Balthasar argues, because of the nature of the Christ event itself. In order to save human existence from within, God had to enter completely into the sinfulness of our world and in doing so God's salvific labor took on a tragic appearance.

For von Balthasar, the Christian story does not overcome tragedy, but rather "recapitulates" it.[14] Tragedy is part of the ordinary reality of the present fallen and broken order. Christ's work does not override that dimension but rather incorporates it and gives it a new Christian meaning. Grace builds upon nature, even upon fallen nature. In recapitulating human existence, Christ respects the present reality—its meaning and autonomy—while restoring God's sovereignty over it. And thus our ordinary lives "where we wrestle with injustice, crime, suffering, death, and so forth" are not simply "overridden by the resurrection." Rather they are taken seriously by God "who, using hieroglyphs of human destiny, writes his own, definitive word."[15] But this action also gives us warrant to begin our reflection not with the tragic drama of Christ's life, but with human reality—fallen, broken and tragic—asking first what it means to say that our moral lives are tragic before exploring how this dimension is recapitulated in Christ.

Some of the issues involved in understanding the tragic dimension of our moral existence are helpfully framed by the late novelist and philosopher Iris Murdoch. On the one hand, her aesthetic ethics has similarities to von Balthasar's own. Good action follows upon seeing rightly, and thus, conversion toward seeing our world correctly is the key moral challenge.[16] At the same time, she offers a more complete reflection on the relationship between ordinary moral existence and tragedy than can be found in von Balthasar.

The tragic literary form can, Murdoch believes, assist us in perceiving our moral horizon correctly. She acknowledges Plato's concern that any art form can be a source of consoling illusion for an ego determined to avoid the hard realities of its moral world.[17] Tragedy, however, breaks this comforting illusion by helping us confront the harshness which the moral life entails.[18] Tragedy presents a moral life stripped of self-interest and the hope of happy conclusions to moral efforts. And yet great art, especially the tragic form, unveils something beyond the surface absurdity of our moral existences. There is a "necessity"—to use Murdoch's term—which appears in the contingent drama of any particular human person. It must be embraced and obeyed and, as obeyed, is the place where the transcendent Good shows itself.[19] The goodness perceived in the human drama—either through its embodiment or violation—does not depend on human willing or any teleology (i.e., on its capacity to bring benefit to the agent herself or others). It is "purposeless"—a term Murdoch uses frequently in her *The Sovereignty of Good*—and cannot be justified in terms of an intraworldly balancing of goods. We both recognize it and yet cannot make it submit to some rationally-deduced principles of behavior. It transcends us and our world and in doing so captures our attention and reverence.

The good—transcendent, attractive, and source of moral energy—is both veiled and revealed in the tragic drama of human lives. It is veiled because it is situated in the lawless confusion and muck of the world. It is revealed in that in the saintly life, interpreted correctly, one perceives the existence of some normative measure which gives the dramatic developments and reversals a meaningfulness and without which these narrative developments would dissipate into a post-modern flux.[20] The existence of a higher law, a transcendent good, is perceived aesthetically, as the underlying shape and form which give this life its fragile coherence.

Because of her emphasis on the chaos and contingency of our moral world, Murdoch is suspicious of clear and bright stories of unambiguous heroes and saints.[21] They distort the hard realities of our moral existence. The stories suggest there is a realm—the moral life—where we can escape the brokenness of our world and achieve some beautiful form of life transparent to moral goodness.[22] She does not deny the goodness of the tragic individual, but believes that her goodness will often be difficult to see because it is displayed in and through messy, morally ambiguous situations. Because the imperfections of the world and of human existence often hide the true reality of moral action, Murdoch believes that the tragic form is a helpful tool for understanding the ways in which the goodness of the agent appears in the world.

There are three insights suggested in Murdoch's reflection on the tragic dimension of human existence which I believe are, with some qualification, consonant with von Balthasar's thought. First, the world is a place of confusing particularity and chaos and whatever good appears in that world will be touched by its confusion. While Murdoch associates this chaos with the contingency of the world, for von Balthasar it also is due to the presence of sin. Second, the moral life can, nonetheless, be lived in such a world, though it will be costly and lacking the straightforward theoretical justification desired by many moral philosophers.[23] Third, while it cannot be directly justified by any set of theoretical principles or propositions, the goodness of a particular moral life can be perceived within the drama of that life by those willing to undertake the challenge of seeing the world truthfully and without the consoling hope of easy harmony among the claims made upon us and the desires which drive us.

The type of tragedy which von Balthasar finds in Christ's life surprisingly aligns more with Murdoch's view of tragedy than with that found in much of contemporary theology. For many theologians the tragic quality of Christ's life is found in that a good person suffers undeserved evils. We find little of the more classical view of tragedy, where goodness is opaque, obscured by its enclosure in a disordered world. Christ's loving action instead appears in sharp and unambiguous contrast to the evils and hatreds which surround him. Von Balthasar would not, of course, deny that a goodness which is direct and transparently clear to the beholder appears, for example, in the public witness of Christ. But he maintains that the saving narrative undergoes a decisive and important shift in the events of Good Friday, Holy Saturday, and Easter Sunday and shows itself to be about something more than doing good for others. For there we see the full depth of God's plan to bring the story of human existence fully into the internal drama of trinitarian life. Through the Cross, God makes the story of human sinfulness God's own and envelops that story through the ever greater love among the triune Persons. And in the Cross, God's saving story becomes tragic.

The sin-filled drama of human existence must be brought into the divine drama in such a way that divine holiness is not violated. The inner-trinitarian life is an eternal procession of love, and it is in this life that the sinful drama of human existence must be included. But how can that happen? Divine love cannot simply reach out to this humanity while ignoring what this human existence is and how counter to divine life its sinfulness is. It cannot draw the human story into its own without some recognition of humanity's ongoing refusal of God and God's own disappointment and anger at that refusal. Like Anselm, von Balthasar believes that there must be some moment in God's saving narrative where the calamity of human rejection is addressed.[24] And, of course, this conviction has made von Balthasar's soteriology controversial. But whereas Anselm resolves the disharmony introduced by human sinfulness through a legal exchange, von Balthasar resolves it aesthetically. The second person takes on sinful human nature, and in so doing comes to suffer the tragic, fallen lot of human existence. Christ's suffering reaches a climax on the Cross where he faces the full consequences of our sinful existence: the rejection and punishing wrath of God. On the surface, this interplay between brokenness, sin, and divine rejection is all one sees in this very human story. But for graced eyes instructed by the entire saving narrative, another drama appears within this drama of an ignoble death. The suffering of punishment has another valence: sacrificial love giving itself up for the sake of another.[25] In the exchange between God the Father and guilty humanity on the cross another law appears before eyes of faith, that of a love which can encompass even human sinfulness. The drama of human sin is re-cyphered, if you will, through the event of the resurrection into a drama of divine love.[26] Love appears to us in this rejected human life as we see in this life God's response to our brokenness and guilt. The human story is now part of the divine story because it has in all its dimensions, even that of sin, been included in the processions of divine love: Jesus, the one who entered into full solidarity with sinful humanity, is welcomed into the eternal embrace of the Father.

The point I want to stress in von Balthasar's approach here is not so much his soteriology, but the appealing idea that the Paschal event is tragic, not just in the common usage of the term but in its more classical sense, because in this event divine love enters fully into the sinfulness of the world and is transformed by it. Thus von Balthasar will refer to the "ugliness" of the cross and its "monstrosity." But what exactly is the nature of this tragedy for von Balthasar? It does not center on an individual whose flaw makes him vulnerable and leads to his moral downfall. Nor does it involve tragic conflict between two deeply valued goods. In his extended reflection on Greek tragedy,[27] von Balthasar focuses how sacrifice and suffering reveal the divine, and this focus provides the key to understanding his view of tragedy.[28] In Greek tragedies the protagonist often foresees his suffering and accepts it for the sake of some higher good. Suffering in such cases reflects the absence of what should be, the prevailing of goodness over evil. And yet by indicating this absence, suffering paradoxically underscores it, making it present in the minds of the audience. Following this line, Jesus is the tragic hero whose goodness and love are illuminated by the suffering inflicted upon him precisely as a result of his fidelity.

But at different points in his writings, von Balthasar suggests something more radical than this interpretation in describing Jesus' life as tragic.[29] And I believe he must if his soteriology is to succeed— if, that is, God is to draw our broken and sinful stories into God's own saving narrative. The story of the tragic hero, pure in his goodness and undefiled by the world's muck, has little to say to most of us except by way of negative critique and edifying exhortation. The narrative richness of the gospel accounts, however, permits an interpretation of the Christ's life that more fruitfully addresses the tragic ambiguity of our moral lives. While von Balthasar does not explicitly develop this interpretation, two ideas point us in its direction.

First, sin affects what God does in the world:

> And yet something more is involved here [in Christ's suffering and death], and it is the fact that [God] who is absolutely free now stands under the destiny (of the sinful world) that surrounds him, and that his sovereign activity is interiorly touched by a contrary force which transforms it into suffering: it is as if God could no longer do what he wants, because his good actions elicit sin. As he acts he must do violence to himself in order still to act divinely even as he acts differently than he would like. This concealment of the divine will is the manifestation of that violence which sin inflicts on God.[30]

The appearance of God's love is obscured, even concealed, by sin when it enters the sphere of human existence. Second, Jesus enters into full solidarity with sinful humanity. While von Balthasar, to my knowledge, never clarifies precisely the idea behind this statement, it is clear that it represents something important in his thought and that he intends by it something radical: to associate Jesus with the sinful human condition as closely as possible without compromising his sinlessness. Thus, von Balthasar rejects, as he must, the idea that Christ identifies "with the actual No of sin itself."[31] At the same time, he maintains that Christ does not "bear the burden [of sin] as something external: he in no way distances himself from those who by right should have to bear it."[32] He will even say that the temptations of Jesus are "an inner experiencing with sinners, of what the attraction of sin is."[33] Christ shares fully in the human condition, which includes being enmeshed in the same fallen order and broken existence that sinful humanity is.

These two considerations help argue for another possible view of Christian tragedy: the story of a work of love which is tragically disrupted and marred because its central characters share personally and collectively in the fallen human condition. Jesus' life ends in failure: his suffering is seen as an expression of divine goodness only when we look beyond the surface discord. As we look at the Paschal mystery itself it is not transparently clear why the events taking place on Good Friday are good in most of the various meanings which that word has come to have: Are they fruitful, beneficial to someone, an expression of a desire to be helpful, a good exercise of the practical judgment? The Christian is, of course, accustomed to reading the Cross as the sign and symbol of God's love because she has been schooled in seeing the Cross in light of the whole Gospel story. But a tragic view of this narrative underscores other elements of the drama: its waste, the loss of dreams, the hatred it evoked, the suffering it demanded of one innocent man, the discouragement it brought about in good people, and the genuine despair it evoked in its central character ("Father, why have you abandoned me"). Because of the world's brokenness and sin, love does not blaze through the surface of this story, however much it is the engine of its drama. The Paschal event is a tragedy in the sense that because of sin, divine love is veiled. Only in the light of the resurrection and with the gift of the Spirit does one see the love that lies within the suffering and failure of the Cross.

By taking on the lot of sinful humanity, Christ experienced our alienation from God. Christ is always the one who does the Father's will, but his dependence on the divine will for guidance grows ever stronger as he enters into solidarity with us and our alienation from God. This alienation reaches a climax on the Cross which is signaled in Christ's experience of forsakeness. Christ is forced to act, not out of his own clear knowledge of what is good and loving, but out of a dark surrender to the Father's will. Again, Christ's surrender to the Father's will does not begin with his experienced alienation from God, but it does reach a new radicality there. We might say, then, that the distortion of the world's sin touches not only the way divine love appears in the world, but also how it is embodied by Christ. In light of von Balthasar's interpretation of the Cross as tragedy, it could be a little misleading to refer to Christ's acts simply as "loving" if by loving we mean beneficent action. In beneficent action the agent aims to achieve some good for another through an act whose causal connection to that good is clear: she sees with some clarity how her action leads to the desired goal. But if Christ's cry of despair on the cross is any indication, it seems unlikely that he was given such a *clear* knowledge of the direct, causal connection between his journey to the cross and his loving desire to save humanity. The lack of such a connection produces one caution about describing this action, in regard to its intention and motivation, as one of beneficent love. However much we might assume there were intimations of such a connection, Jesus' journey to the Cross can be better described, I suggest, as fidelity to the Father's will. This description is not to deny that Christ's action can be described as loving, or that he both intended to love humanity and was motivated by such love. Rather because of the obscurity of sin which became part of the drama of the cross, an appropriate characterization of the intention and motivation of the action is fidelity to the Father.

Part III: Implications for Christian Life

The Christian will experience the call to general humanitarian love, that is, those daily small acts of generosity bestowed on friend and acquaintance. These acts will be unambiguous to her for the most part; she will know them to be good deeds, ones worthy of a disciple of Christ. She will also experience a more comprehensive and challenging call, one that demands a kind of radical self-giving which cannot always be justified by existing norms of commonsense morality. These acts will often be tragic in the everyday sense of the word in that they will be personally costly for the agent.

I want to suggest that the Christian will also experience a deeper kind of tragedy. The creatureliness of the agent and the sinfulness of the world veil the good she seeks to do from herself and from the others around her. Her actions will disappoint, show themselves inadequate, reveal her own mediocrity, limitations, and brokenness. Her gestures of love often become structured by a broken world which twists these gestures unexpectedly in undesired and painful ways. Loving intentions are often made opaque by the world around us. The individual who is responsible for a beloved but infirm parent and who is also struggling to preserve a fragile marriage might find her efforts to provide for all ending in failure. And the individual might find herself disheartened by the haunting idea that if she were a different person—that is, if she were a more talented, more personable, more attractive, more decisive in her decisions—then her problems might have been solved and her attempts at love more successful. Because the imperfections of the attempts to love can be partly traced to our own limitations (which may or may not have sinful overtones), such actions taint our moral character and leave us guilt-ridden. They disempower our moral response for reasons which an aesthetic ethics makes clear: we cannot imagine and see the good that appears within them. We are attracted to nothing, for nothing of beauty is seen in them. This experience points us to a truth: that our expressions of love are often marred, not so much by explicitly sinful responses, but because of our finitude, our lack of some desirable talents and gifts, and because of the way the world around us can distort and pervert attempts to love. The unambiguous, transparent saint cannot be the exclusive paradigm of Christian existence.[34]

Von Balthasar's theological aesthetics provides a framework for understanding the disturbing hiddenness of goodness in tragic situations. Christian tragedy is not beautiful in any ordinary sense of the word. Von Balthasar claims, however, that the saving narrative comes to us with its own power and compelling authority. It transforms the way one looks at the world and sets a new standard for how one judges the world's truth, goodness, and beauty. The broken life of Christ can be called beautiful because it reveals the self-giving glory of triune love to eyes made ready to see it. The divine beauty which appears in this dramatic failure elicits an *ek-static* response from those who behold it: to make this story their story by interpreting their broken lives in its light.

The Gospel story points us to a way of seeing the tragic dimension of our human existence recapitulated in Christ. The tragedy of Christ's own attempt to love is a story that addresses at least some part of every Christian's life. Perceiving the tragic dimensions of this story can awaken in the Christian a surrender of faith as she confronts her own tragic attempts to love. This is the response which von Balthasar's theological aesthetics underscores. The Gospel has an inexhaustible beauty and power to keep drawing the Christian to new ways of surrendering in faith. Thus at times the Christian will be called to continue in some kind of darkness, an unknowing that is illuminated only by occasional pointers that this path is where God is leading her. The world of the Christian, von Balthasar tells us,

> still contains the possibility of the most profound doubt, the greatest failure, suffering and conflict, unbelief, the baffling nature of existence this side of the grave and apparent meaninglessness. The Christian is not automatically an optimist; [she] is exposed to the risk of freedom and hence to the danger of tragic failure.[35]

The Christian walks in fidelity, not always knowing fully why this path is good, but hopeful in the promise of the resurrection that all such acts of faithfulness to God will draw forth fruit in ways not anticipated. In doing so, she gives a Christian meaning to the sin and brokenness which envelop her actions. She endures not just the sin around her, but also her own limitations, weakness of mind, and failure at human greatness, because these are the human realities that God desires to include in the divine drama. These human realities are made part of that drama when they become the means and moment of the Christ-formed response of hopeful fidelity. All these will be part of her surrender of faith. She will be drawn to this response by the same narrative that awakened her faith and which already includes this response as part of its compelling story.

Conclusion

I have suggested that von Balthasar's ethical theory centers on a link between seeing and doing. Our interpretations of the world draw forth responses from us. The introduction of narrative and drama complicates but does not alter this connection. The story of Christ draws forth the Christian's response; we conform ourselves to it in the self-surrender of faith. We "let it be" by becoming people who further the story's plot. This story is open to new possibilities, new futures. What awakens good and holy desires, therefore, is not just that which appears before us in the present situation, but also the possibilities of some new good which lies ahead in it. Thus the hungry and the homeless draw us toward a world where such suffering no longer exists. Strife-torn relationships make us long for reconciliation. Violence leads to the work of peace. In all of these responses to the world around us we are surrendering to the story of Christ, and thus these acts express the basic response of faith.

We are drawn into the story of Christ not by the Cross that is endured, but by the divine love which that Cross manifests. The love which we offer in return will be forced to enter the muck of our world. Ecstatic love for God modulates into faithfulness before the task at hand, but here our share in the mission of Christ only deepens. For in enduring in faithfulness the apparent waste of her actions, the Christian lives out a form of the Cross. She is invited by the love which is at the Gospel's center to bring the tragedy of her life into the tragedy of Christ's story. She need not despair over the meaningless of her acts or regret once again her inadequacies, for these have become the place for her surrender to God. The tragic dimension of her situation remains, but the promise of the resurrection gives hope—not that her action will unexpectedly accomplish some great good, but rather, in some providential way, her hopeful fidelity will serve to bring the drama of her existence and those which her life touches into the drama of triune life.

NOTES

[1] I wish to thank the three anonymous SCE readers for their helpful comments on an earlier version of this essay.

[2] "I think the emphasis on medicine as a tragic profession helps denote the continuity between the kind of issues raised by medicine and the rest of our lives." Stanley Hauerwas, "Medicine as a Tragic Profession," in *Truthfulness and Tragedy: Future Investigations in Christian Ethics* (Notre Dame, Indiana: University of Notre Dame Press, 1977) 186.

[3] Martha Nussbaum's contribution to this conversation is important: *Fragility of Goodness: Luck and Ethics in Greek Tragedy and Philosophy* (Cambridge: Cambridge University Press, 1986). Daniel Statman has collected the main essays on the topic: *Moral Luck* (New York, NY: SUNY Press, 1993).

[4] For a more complete account of von Balthasar's ethics, see Christopher Steck, *The Ethical Thought of Hans Urs von Balthasar*, forthcoming from Crossroad Publishing (Fall 2001).

[5] He concludes: "And since each hypostasis in God possesses the same freedom and omnipotence, we can speak of there being reciprocal petition . . . . Since these acts are eternal, there is no end to their newness, no end to being surprised and overwhelmed by what is essentially immeasurable. The fundamental philosophical act, wonder, need not be banished from the realm of the Absolute." (Hans Urs von Balthasar, *The Dramatis Personae: Man in God*, vol. 2 of *Theo-Drama: Theological Dramatic Theory*, trans. Graham Harrison [San Francisco: Ignatius Press, 1990] 257-8).

⁶ Karl Rahner likewise argues that in the Old Testament we can see indications of the triune activity of God. We "must admit an authentic secret prehistory of the revelation of the Trinity in the Old Testament." Karl Rahner, *The Trinity*, trans. Joseph Doncell (New York: Herder and Herder, 1970) 42.

⁷ Von Balthasar is influenced by Bonaventure here. The "things of the world," suggests Bonaventure, "possess the power to emit an expressive image of themselves . . . they shine and reveal themselves to a potential knowing subject." Hans Urs von Balthasar, *Studies in Theological Style: Clerical Styles*, vol. 2 of *The Glory of the Lord: A Theological Aesthetics*, trans. Andrew Louth, Francis McDonagh and Brian McNeil C.R.V (San Francisco: Ignatius Press, 1984) 346.

⁸ Here we find von Balthasar's appropriation of the transcendentals tradition so important in Aquinas' thought: all reality insofar as it is, is true, good, and beautiful. Von Balthasar, however, is more eager to stress the *circumencessio*, the interpenetration and mutual informing of the transcendentals. Thus: "If the *verum* lacks that *splendor* which for Thomas is the distinctive mark of the beautiful, then the knowledge of truth remains both pragmatic and formalistic . . . . But if the *bonum* lacks the *voluptas* which for Augustine is the mark of its beauty, then the relationship to the good remains both utilitarian and hedonistic: in this case the good will involve merely the satisfaction of a need by means of some value or object, whether it is founded objectively on the thing itself giving satisfaction or subjectively on the person seeking it." (Hans Urs von Balthasar, *Seeing the Form*, vol. 1 of *The Glory of the Lord: A Theological Aesthetics*, trans. Erasmo Leiva-Merikakis [San Francisco: Ignatius Press, 1982] 152).

⁹ Martin Heidegger's idea of truth as disclosure leads him to likewise underscore the need for receiving the other. Cf., "To let be—that is, to let beings be as the beings which they are—means to engage oneself with the open region and its openness into which every being comes to stand, bringing that openness, as it were, along with itself." Martin Heidegger, "On the Essence of Truth," in *Martin Heidegger: Basic Writings*. Ed. David Farrell Krell. (New York: Harper & Row, 1977) 127.

¹⁰ "Theological aesthetics began as a 'coming to see' the form in which God's Word comes to us . . . . In this act of seeing, there already lies the 'rapture': a breaking out from ourselves in the power of our being called and affected, in the power of divine love which draws near to us and enables us to receive itself." Hans Urs von Balthasar, *Theology: The New Covenant*, vol. 7 of *The Glory of the Lord: A Theological Aesthetics*, trans. Brian McNeil C.R.V. (San Francisco: Ignatius Press, 1989) 389.

¹¹ "The metaphysical question, which seemed to be buried for me as far as the cosmos is concerned—to such an extent that what Paul presupposes, viz., that we would 'see' God plainly in his works . . . simply seems no longer to be the case . . .—is always ready to break open in the encounter with the 'Thou.'" Hans Urs von Balthasar, "Forgetfulness of God and Christians" *Creator Spirit*, vol. 3 of *Explorations in Theology* trans. Brian McNeil, C.R.V. (San Francisco: Ignatius Press, 1993) 332.

¹² Hans Urs von Balthasar, *Prolegomena*, vol. 1 of *Theo-Drama: Theological Dramatic Theory*, trans. Graham Harrison (San Francisco: Ignatius Press, 1988) 308.

¹³ Thus he describes Greek tragedy as "the great, valid cypher of the Christ event." Hans Urs von Balthasar, *The Realm of Metaphysics in Antiquity*, vol. 4 of *The Glory of the Lord*, trans. Brian McNeil et al. (San Francisco: Ignatius Press, 1989) 101.

¹⁴ "The drama of Christ is the recapitulation and the end of Greek tragedy." Hans Urs von Balthasar, *The Dramatis Personae: Man in God*, vol. 2 of *Theo-Drama: Theological Dramatic Theory*, trans. Graham Harrison (San Francisco: Ignatius Press, 1990) 49.

¹⁵ *Theo-Drama*, vol. 2, 94.

¹⁶ "If the magnetic field [of our vision] is right our movements within it will tend to be right." Iris Murdoch, "The Darkness of Practical Reason," in *Existentialists and Mystics*, ed Peter Conradi (New York: Penguin Press, 1998) 201. "When moments of decision arrive we see and are attracted by the world we have already (partly) made." "The Darkness of Practical Reason" in *Existentialists and Mystics* 200.

[17] Plato believed that "art hides the true cosmic beauty and the hard real forms of necessity and causality." Iris Murdoch, *The Fire and the Sun: Why Plato Banished the Artists* (Oxford: Oxford University Press, 1977) 66.

[18] Iris Murdoch, *Metaphysics as a Guide to Morals*, (New York: Penguin Books, 1992) 104.

[19] "Our best task is to distinguish in created things between the divine and the necessary cause and seek to understand and conform ourselves to the divine cause, and to seek the necessary cause for the sake of the divine, since we cannot see the divine without the necessary." *The Fire and the Sun*, 57. "The good artist helps us to see the place of necessity in human life, what must be endured, what makes or breaks, and to purify our imagination so as to contemplate the real world." Ibid., 80. "Good art . . . provides a stirring image of a pure transcendent value, a steady visible enduring good . . . ." Ibid., 76.

[20] "Art shows us the only sense in which the permanent and incorruptible is compatible with the transient; and whether representational or not it reveals to us aspects of our world which our ordinary dull dream-consciousness is unable to see. Art pierces the veil and gives sense to the notion of a reality which lies beyond appearance; it exhibits virtue in its true guise in the context of death and chance." Iris Murdoch, *The Sovereignty of Good* (New York: Schocken Books, 1971) 88.

[21] "The *spectacle* of good in other forms, as when we admire good men and heroes, is often, as experience, more mixed and less efficacious." *The Fire and Sun*, 77. The "spectacle" of the good in these "heroes" is less efficacious because it offers the sort of cheap consolations and illusory images which Murdoch believes to be unhelpful to our moral instincts.

[22] Murdoch criticizes Kant's thought on a similar point. In place of the tragic, Kant supposes a moral freedom which aspires "to a universal order consisting of a prefabricated harmony." Iris Murdoch, "The Sublime and the Good," *Existentialists and Mystics*, 216.

[23] "The indefinability of Good is connected with the unsystematic and inexhaustible variety of the world and the pointlessness of virtue." *The Sovereignty of Good*, 99

[24] See von Balthasar's discussion of Anselm's soteriology in Hans Urs von Balthasar, *The Action*, vol. 4 of *Theo-Drama: Theological Dramatic Theory*, trans. Graham Harrison (San Francisco: Ignatius Press, 1994), 255-262.

[25] "Again this is one of the most important themes in this volume: what we see in Christ's forsakenness on the Cross, in ultimate creaturely negativity, is the revelation of the highest positivity of trinitarian love." Hans Urs von Balthasar, *The Last Act*, vol. 5 of *Theo-Drama: Theological Dramatic Theory* (San Francisco: Ignatius Press, 1999) 517.

[26] The "Cross and burial of Christ reveal their significance only in the light of the even of Easter." Hans Urs von Balthasar, *Mysterium Paschale*, trans. Aidan Nichols O.P. (Grand Rapids, Michigan: William B. Eerdmans Publishing Company, 1993) 189.

[27] *The Glory of the Lord*, vol. 4, 101-154

[28] Suffering is "the way of man to god and the revelation of the deep truth of existence." (103) The "divine presence is announced predominantly in heightened suffering." (106) Pain is "the very medium of transcendence." (127)

[29] "Christ's being is of such a kind that it is able to descend into the abyss of all that is tragic." *The Glory of the Lord*, vol. 2, 84. However, "all that is tragic" includes more than the tragedy of the fallen hero.

[30] *The Glory of the Lord*, vol. 1, 519.

[31] *Theo-Drama*, vol 4, 336.

[32] Ibid., 337.

[33] Ibid., 336n9.

[34] Von Balthasar cites, with approval, Jean Pierre de Caussade's view that while God will make grace visible in some saints, "there is a multitude of other saints . . . who remain hidden . . . they spread no sort of light in this life, but live and die in deep darkness." Hans Urs von Balthasar, *The Realm of Metaphysics in the Modern Age*, vol. 5 of *The Glory of the Lord: A Theological Aesthetics*, trans. Oliver Davies, et al. (San Francisco: Ignatius Press, 1991) 138.

The "saint as hero," he says later, is a "mistaken interpretation." *The Glory of the Lord,* vol. 5, 142.

[35] *Theo-Drama*, vol. 1, 428.

HISTORICAL STUDIES IN CHRISTIAN ETHICS

Divine Compassion and the Mystification of Power: The Latitudinarian Divines in the Secularization of Moral Thought

Jennifer A. Herdt

Abstract

William Placher and others have charged seventeenth-century theologians with "domesticating" divine transcendence, with fostering an understanding of God that was clear and comprehensible, but unattractive, unpersuasive, and easily undermined by secular thought. This essay tests that claim by analyzing the discourse of divine compassion which became prominent among post-Restoration Anglican divines. While the second generation of latitudinarians do exemplify the trends Placher traces, the first generation of latitudinarians, notably Cambridge Platonist Benjamin Whichcote, succeeds in finding a way to affirm divine compassion without undermining divine transcendence. Moreover, Whichcote argues that an insistence on divine incomprehensibility fosters a voluntaristic conception of divine power and—contrary to Placher—undermines efforts to promote transformative justice in human society. The present case study suggests that we must reconsider our modes of articulating divine transcendence.

It has long been recognized that the latitudinarian divines of the post-Restoration period in England introduced, as a key element of their repudiation of Puritanism, a new emphasis on the goodness of both divine and human natures.[1] Sermons on avenging divine justice receded in favor of sermons on divine compassion and benevolence, while exhortations to imitate this benevolence displaced reflections on total depravity. In general, preaching took on a practical cast, and moved away from doctrinal minutiae. The latitudinarian emphasis on goodness, benevolence, compassion, and feelingful morality served, via moral sense thinkers such as Shaftesbury and Hutcheson as well as through broader cultural channels of transmission, as an important source for the eighteenth-century cultural movement of sentimentalism.[2] Sentimentalism itself, in its focus on a naturalized rather than on a grace-transformed moral psychology, fostered the emergence of non-religious modes of moral discourse. In particular, human exchanges of compassion were gradually detached from, and in some instances wholly displaced, divine compassion.[3]

Seventeenth-century thinkers have often been accused of handing theology over to philosophy, of turning away from Christ, grace, and scripture, and more generally of having, in William Placher's memorable phrase, "domesticated" divine transcendence.[4] According to Placher, "before the seventeenth century, most Christian theologians were struck by the mystery, the wholly otherness of God, and the inadequacy of any human categories as applied to God . . . . [I]n the seventeenth century philosophers and theologians increasingly thought they could talk clearly about God."[5] Placher draws on Kathryn Tanner's concept of "contrastive transcendence" in order to characterize these new ways of conceiving of God. Seventeenth-century thinkers explained "God's difference from created things by saying that God was transcendent (distant, unaffected) in contrast to immanent (close, engaged)."[6] What they failed to see was that God lies beyond all human categories and modes of contrast, and thus should not be regarded as distant as opposed to close, transcendent as opposed to immanent, and so on. It was this clearly defined, remote, uninvolved God who was first defended and then, from the eighteenth century on, increasingly seen as unattractive and unpersuasive.[7]

The latitudinarian emphasis on divine compassion hardly suggests that God is distant and unaffected as opposed to being close and engaged. But a focus on divine compassion might suggest the opposite—that God's immanence is being affirmed to the denigration of divine transcendence. And indeed Tanner suggests that the fall into contrastive transcendence can take place in opposite directions—either by affirming transcendence at the cost of immanence, or vice versa, by affirming immanence to the exclusion of transcendence.[8] Did the latitudinarian emphasis on divine compassion sacrifice divine transcendence in favor of immanence? Did it lose sight of the "wholly otherness" of God and thereby contribute to the emergence of secular thought? Yes and no, I will argue. In the first section of this paper I discuss the Cambridge Platonist Benjamin Whichcote (1609-83), a representative of the first generation of latitudinarian thought (and founder of the Cambridge Platonists). I argue that Whichcote affirmed divine compassion in ways that corrected Calvinist distortions of divine power while preserving room for the transcendence of an intimate God. Isaac Barrow (1630-77), whom I discuss in the second section of the paper, was, in contrast, typical of the second generation of latitudinarians in understanding divine compassion in ways that contributed both to a naturalization of divine compassion, and, ironically, to a distancing of God. But there is a further twist; Whichcote's emphasis on the "reasonableness" of God's ways, to which I return in the concluding section, may seem disturbing to those, like Placher, who insist that divine transcendence can be preserved only if we insist that all human concepts collapse when applied to God.[9] Yet Whichcote's insistence is best understood, I will argue, not as compromising divine transcendence, but as revealing the way an insistence on divine incomprehensibility can mystify power in ways that serve the human lust for domination. Placher sees the dangers to transformative justice of regarding God as "the most distant, most powerful thing in the world," but he misses the equally grave threat posed by the claim that all human categories—goodness, justice, power—break down when applied to God (182).[10] When the insistence on divine incomprehensibility overtakes the affirmation of divine perfection, mystery can become a cloak for human abuses of power.

Benjamin Whichcote and the Defense of God's Goodness

Atheism and Divine Compassion

Concerns about atheism are what motivate Whichcote's emphasis on divine compassion. Michael Buckley has argued that worries over atheism drove theologians into the arms of philosophy, where, having abandoned properly theological resources, they fed rather than quenched the rise of atheism. But the atheism that most concerned Whichcote was not speculative atheism, in which belief in God loses theoretical plausibility, but rather what we might call practical atheism, an existential rejection of God arising in reaction to the Calvinist doctrines of double predestination and limited atonement.[11] Whichcote believed that such doctrines had contributed to an image of God as a tyrant who rules by power alone. Not surprisingly, some refused to accept the existence of this tyrant, or denied his right to command them. Others, though heartily sorry for their sins, were psychologically immobilized by the fear of damnation.

In responding to this practical atheism, Whichcote did not abandon specifically theological resources, even if he embraced philosophy as well. Scripture, grace, the work of Christ, remain central to his response, which was to emphasize the centrality of the goodness of God, while problematizing power: "take away Goodness and nothing is a Divine Perfection: For, Power and Wit are in the Diabolical State, as well as other-where."[12] It is not that power is not a divine attribute, but that it is not a pure perfection. Thus, talk of divine power must always be governed by divine goodness. For Whichcote, God's goodness is seen first and foremost in compassion, specifically God's compassion for the repentant sinner; "for this is truly Divine, and God-like, to do Good, to relieve, to be compassionate, and on the contrary it is Diabolical, and most opposite to the Divine Nature, to destroy, to grieve, to oppress."[13]

Whichcote insists on divine goodness and compassion not primarily because he sees compassion as a key human virtue, but because Scripture reveals a merciful God with deep compassion for sinful humanity.[14] His focus is theocentric, not anthropocentric. At the same time, he finds the scriptural depiction of God's character to be in accord with reason. Since we were created fallible, he suggests, it is only reasonable to expect that God will pardon our sins:[15] "It is a compassionable Case for him that is Supream and Sovereign, to pitty an unavoidable Necessity and Misery, and to pardon so far as the Case is compassionate. Now we are in the hands of him that is Primarily and Originally Good: And he will certainly commiserate every Case, so far as it is compassionable. Now the Case of a Sinner is compassionable, if he be penitent; because he was never better than finite and fallible."[16] It is not that God is *bound* to forgive us, but that it is in accord with his goodness that he does so, and we can trust that God will always act in accord with that goodness. Goodness as compassion and mercy is here elevated over the strict equity of retaliatory justice.[17]

Although there is no limit to God's compassion and forgiveness, this does not mean for Whichcote that all will be forgiven; those who fail to repent put themselves beyond the reach of God's grace and compassion. Such stubborn sinfulness "is not at all Compassionable. There is an Incapacity in the Recipient: Tho' there be no want of Mercy in God: For, he is infinitely Merciful, and Gracious: but the Subject is altogether incapable."[18] In fact, the unrepentant sinner, far from desiring compassion, despises and spurns it. In this sense, we could say that Whichcote believes that God will forgive all those who accept forgiveness, since it is only the repentant who do in fact accept forgiveness. The unrepentant sinner, in contrast, creates his own hell. Hell is not properly understood as the expression of God's righteous wrath, "Hell is not a Positive Infliction: but the Fewel of it, is the Guiltiness of Mens Consciences, and God's withdrawing, because the Person is uncapable of his Communication."[19]

Reasonableness and the Redefinition of Power

Whichcote's affirmation of God's compassionate goodness is intimately related to his insistence that "the Ways of God are accountable, in Reason." Neither God's forgiveness nor the hell of the unrepentant is beyond human comprehension. Given that affirmations of reason are often seen as coming at the expense of faith or revelation, it is important to note three things concerning Whichcote's appeal to reason here.[20] First, "rational" can for Whichcote mean anything from "following the inner divine light" to "common-sensical." To invoke reason is not to turn to a specific faculty or mode of knowing which is opposed to or clearly distinct from faith. Whichcote defines faith as "receiving something upon Divine Authority," and makes "natural knowledge" antecedent to it, as we cannot receive something on God's authority unless we know there is a God, and this we know through natural knowledge.[21] More broadly, reason and faith cannot be opposed, since there is an aspect of divine self-revelation in all of our knowing; this is what is at work in Whichcote's references to the "candle of the Lord."[22] Second, in this context Whichcote is discussing the reasonableness of the way God acts as revealed in scripture, as well as in the world more generally. So reason and scripture are also not opposed.

Third, and most importantly, the point of Whichcote's insistence on the reasonableness of God's mercy is to block appeals beyond reason that were often, in his context, appeals to unrestrained domination. Calvinism emphasized God's mysterious and incomprehensible sovereignty, but while this voluntarist framework appeared to preserve divine transcendence, in effect it had come— note that I am not necessarily accusing Calvin himself here—to elevate arbitrary power over goodness. God's majesty and sovereignty were understood as God's right to act in ways that, humanly speaking, were arbitrary and cruel, but which were nevertheless to be praised as good. The heart of Whichcote's insistence on God's compassion and the reasonableness of God's ways is a dramatic reconception (in ways that anticipate process thought and feminist theology) of divine sovereignty and power.[23] "It is a Greater Excellency," writes Whichcote, "to win, and reconcile, by Gentleness and Fairness; than to vanquish, and overcome, by Power and Force."[24] In one sense, he concedes, God's power is revealed when he punishes sinners. But the punished sinner chooses to remain alienated from God, and in that sense represents an independent and opposed power to that of God. Mercy, in contrast, unites the sinner to God in love, and so truly "overcomes" the alienated power. So Whichcote notes that "when he pardons, he procures himself Love, and gains the Heart and Soul of his Creature: but, if he punish, the Party endures because God is stronger, and he cannot make resistance. But, when God pardons, the Creature is overcome; the Heart is melted; he deprecates and submits, and thinks himself for ever engag'd to God."[25] Punishment produces stubborn endurance; mercy elicits a "melted" heart. God's true power, the power that is a pure perfection, is not brute force, but is the power to attract and transform the sinner. Thus, divine power is most properly exhibited through mercy.[26]

Whichcote's appeal to reason is an appeal against the mystification of power. The final section of this paper will take up the question of whether this de-mystification constitutes an erosion of divine transcendence. Now, though, before turning to Barrow, we must get clear on the significance, for Whichcote, of creaturely compassion.

Participating in Divine Compassion

For Whichcote, all compassion is simultaneously a revelation of and a participation in God. His discussion even of creaturely compassion is therefore theocentric. There is no reason to regard scripture as our sole source of knowledge of God's goodness and compassion.[27] Whichcote also finds signs of it in the natural world and within human nature in particular; "there are Impressions of Goodness, and Kindness, that God hath stampt throughout the whole Creation."[28] So, for instance, "in Participation of the Universal Benevolence which is in the Superior World (the Intellectual World of Soul and Spirit) you have the Resemblance of this, in the inferiour World (viz.) the Suitableness and Fitness that is in one thing to accommodate another: As you see the whole Creation of God is *mutually beneficial.*"[29] A key example of this is animal care of offspring, so-called "natural affection," the influential Stoic concept of *storgè*.[30] Even the Ostrich, the only apparent exception to this rule, does take the trouble to cover her eggs with sand to keep them warm before abandoning them, notes Whichcote. Human nature is even more deeply stamped with these impressions of Goodness. All of this points us back to God and divine goodness: "where we see Indulgency of Fathers; this Goodness of Disposition in them, is but a Communication from God, a Resemblance of his Affection to his Creatures, in some measure."[31] Signs of compassion in the natural world and in human nature circle back to the revelation and defense of God's good character: "Whatever Perfection is found in any creature, it is primarily, and originally, in God: other where, it is by Derivation and Participation; but it is in God, as in a fountain."[32]

Although Whichcote is challenging Calvinist accounts of total depravity, he is far from suggesting that goodness is natural to human beings in the sense of being automatic, instinctive, or irresistible. "Nature" is still used by Whichcote as a normative rather than a purely descriptive term. The fact that compassion, and goodness more generally, are seen as natural to human beings does not constitute a denial of human fallenness. Quite the contrary—the fact that so few human beings live up to their true nature is for Whichcote a clear sign that we are indeed fallen. It is only if human nature "be right, and be not abus'd"[33] that it is more tender and compassionate than the natures below it.

Whichcote is thus considerably less confident in human than in divine compassion. We should, though, aspire to imitate God's goodness: "If we propose to our selves what God doth in the World, and how he carrieth it in his Family; this Consideration will promote in us, this Disposition and Temper. For He is the Universal Father. It is He whose Family the whole World is."[34]

This imitation of God is made possible through God's grace and the coming of Christ. Moreover, Grace does not simply restore fallen human nature, for since Christ entered into human nature, we are made partakers in the divine nature in a new and deeper way.[35] Whichcote's suggestion that it is reasonable for God to forgive repentant sinners might seem to call in question the need for Christ's coming. This was indeed the logic of Socinian thought which, spreading from Holland into England in the seventeenth century, rejected the Trinity and original sin, and regarded Christ not as atoning for human sin but as offering an example of a perfect moral life. But Whichcote's outlook is less attuned to Socinian than to Greek Patristic thought; he has a robust Christological stance, though one focused not on expiation but on deification.[36] We should "reckon all our Happiness to consist in our Enjoyment of him, our being and living in Communion and Acquaintance" with God, and this is made possible when we partake through Christ in God's goodness and God's compassion.[37]

The Cambridge Platonists are well known for their view that morality is the heart of religion.[38] When Whichcote declared that "the sum of all Religion is Divine Imitation,"[39] he was pointing to the way in which goodness draws one to God, allows one to be caught up more fully in the life of God. He was not simply suggesting that imitating God allows human beings to obtain for themselves attributes which God possesses.[40] For Whichcote, the natural world and human nature reveal God's goodness, but repentance and further grace are needed if we are to participate more fully in God's goodness and hence draw closer to God. The point of talking about compassion, whether human or divine, was therefore to bring humanity into deeper relation with God, not primarily to enhance human morality as such.

Isaac Barrow and Christ's Compassionate Example

Countering Hobbes with a Naturalized Psychology

Turning to Isaac Barrow, we see many of the themes discussed by Whichcote, but with a subtle shift of emphasis. This subtle shift has dramatic implications. While Barrow often expands on the theme of God's compassion, his primary concern is not with challenging Puritan notions of power and sovereignty, nor with bringing humanity into fuller participation in God. Rather, the focus has shifted to human morality; it has become anthropocentric. God's compassion is discussed primarily in order to encourage human compassion and generosity. The significance of "imitating" God has changed.[41]

This shift reflects Barrow's concern about Hobbesian accounts of human nature; countering Hobbes elicits a modulation in the account of nature, which is now closer to representing the instinctive and permanent rather than the ideal and graced.[42] Hobbes naturalized Calvinist accounts of the Fall; it is not fallen human nature which is described as wholly self-interested, but simply human nature as such. Hobbes did not ask who was responsible for this state of human nature, but focused rather on devising an adequate political response to the condition in which we find ourselves. Others, though, perceived his account as casting aspersions on the character of God as designer of human nature. The second generation of latitudinarians sought to vindicate God's character against Hobbes, but they were driven to do so on Hobbesian terms, that is, on the basis of observable human nature, as opposed to a hypothetical perfected nature. Therefore, rather than pointing to the Fall, and thereby placing responsibility for the corruption of human nature on the shoulders of humanity, Barrow and his successors described human beings as naturally generous, compassionate, and responsive.

Along with this descriptive account of human nature came a more developed psychology. The Puritans drew of course on a rich psychology of despair and conversion, and Whichcote had his own Neoplatonic psychology of transformation by the divine Spirit, but in Barrow we see the beginnings of a naturalized psychology, despite the fact that he continues, in a perfunctory way, to insist on human fallenness and the need for grace. Barrow argued, for instance, that the "love of benevolence (which is precedent to these [narrower affections], and more deeply rooted in nature, more ancient, more unconfined, and more immutable), and the duties mentioned consequent on it, are grounded upon the natural constitution, necessary properties, and unalterable condition of humanity."[43] This position counters Hobbes, source of the "monstrous paradox . . . that all men naturally are enemies one to another."[44] Barrow's emphasis on the immutability and unalterability of the benevolent affections strongly suggests that both Fall and Redemption are irrelevant to this discussion.

Compassionate Instincts as Divine Messages

Barrow's account of human nature makes clear that we are obliged to benevolent actions towards all because "the best of our natural inclinations prompt us to the performance of them; especially those of pity and benignity; which are manifestly discernible in all, but most powerful and vigorous in the best natures." Because these inclinations are necessary and unalterable, it strikes Barrow as beyond question that they were "by the most wise and good Author of our beings . . . implanted therein both as monitors to direct, and as spurs to incite us to the performance of our duty. For the same bowels, that, in our want of necessary sustenance, do by a lively sense of pain inform us thereof, and instigate us to provide against it, do in like manner grievously resent the distresses of another, and thereby admonish us of our duty, and provoke us to relieve them."[45] Whichcote had seen the natural world and human nature as participating in the perfection of God; Barrow, in a way typical of later latitudinarian reflection on natural religion and natural law, sees human nature as embedded with signs or messages from God concerning human duty. In this sense, Barrow regards God as distant from, outside of, the world that he uses as a communication tool.[46]

In order to be clearly readable, these signs had to be constant features of human nature; hence Barrow's comparison of hunger and pity, both arising uncontrollably from the bowels (in the eighteenth century, the site of pity came to be the heart, as the Old Testament language of bowels became increasingly remote.) Even fictional tragedies have the power to move us "against the bent of our will, and all resistance of reason."[47] Will and reason are set aside without any qualms, since Barrow's point is not that this instinctive response is morally praiseworthy in us, but rather that it is a message from God about the form our deliberate actions should take; "since by the discipline of our sense she [Nature] instructs us, and by the importunity thereof solicits us to the observance of our duty, let us follow her wise directions, and conspire with her kindly motions."[48] Regardless of how sinful we may become, these signs from God remain in the form of irresistible impulses which overcome us from time to time even if stifled or weakened.

One sign of Barrow's migration toward a descriptive inventory of the benevolent instincts of human nature is his use of the term "sympathy."[49] By the mid-eighteenth century, when it was central to sentimentalist discourse, sympathy was often used as a synonym for pity and compassion, though strictly speaking it had a broader meaning, since it signified fellow feeling with the joys as well as the sorrows of others. Up through the mid-seventeenth century, however, it had a primarily scientific meaning. There was sympathy between the moon and the tides, and between the moon and women's uteri; such mysterious forms of action at a distance were explained by a hidden cognation of natures shared by the distant bodies. Robert Whytt, who made important early contributions to neurophysiology, discussed at length how the sympathy of the nerves united the body, allowing the suffering of one part to be felt in a distant part. Whichcote had suggested that human nature has "a secret sympathy" with Virtue.[50] Barrow, though, was among the first to appeal to sympathy to account for natural pity and compassion; compassion is possible because all human beings are united together by "indissoluble bands of mutual sympathy."[51] Invoking sympathy lent a scientific air to Barrow's account of human nature, and emphasized the naturalistic elements of it. It also indicated that compassion was to be understood as actual fellow-feeling, taking part in the feelings of others, not simply responding to their suffering.

Naturalized Grace: The Pull of Example

Barrow does note, in a sermon on loving our neighbor as ourselves (a Christian duty which he takes to exceed the duties of common humanity), that some may object that our corrupt nature inclines us to selfishness, and "that the duty thus understood is impracticable, nature violently swaying to those degrees of self-love which charity can nowise reach."[52] Barrow's response to this objection is multifaceted; he suggests that there are many examples of love of neighbor from the Bible, that in Christ, who was in our nature, charity triumphed over self-love, and that if we just do our best to love neighbor as self, God will make up the difference in mercy. Moreover, we can train ourselves bit by bit in this ideal charity, simply by cherishing our good natural affections, for "our nature is not so absolutely averse or indisposed to the practice of such charity" as some suppose.[53] Here again our "bowels of compassion" make an appearance. Finally, for good measure, Barrow adds that even if we are unsuccessful in this, "yet we must remember that a subsidiary power is by the divine mercy dispensed, able to control and subdue nature to a compliance, to raise our practice above our natural forces."[54] One cannot help thinking that this depiction of grace as a last resort has somehow missed the point. For Whichcote, God's grace is active in the world from beginning to end; it is seen when the ostrich digs a hole in the sand for her eggs and when one human being reaches out in compassion to another, as well as when Christ enters human nature and allows it to partake of the divine nature. This certainly softened the nature/grace dichotomy of Puritan thought, but it did so by supernaturalizing nature.[55] In Barrow, in contrast, grace is marginalized and nature becomes increasingly autonomous.

It is thus not surprising that Christ is, for Barrow as for the latitudinarian divines more generally, first and foremost an example of loving compassion. This can be seen in the series of sermons Barrow preached on Christ, which begins with "Upon the Passion of Our Blessed Saviour," and then moves on to "Of Doing All in the Name of Christ," "Of Being Imitators of Christ," and "Abiding in Christ to Be Demonstrated by Walking as Christ Did." The effectiveness of Christ's passion resides in its capacity to move us and thus to transform our affections; grace is naturalized within an emerging sentimentalist human psychology. So Barrow suggests that examples are more effective than precepts, since "examples do incite our passions, and impel them to the performance of duty. They raise hope, they inflame courage, they provoke emulation . . . they set in motion all the springs of activity."[56]

In treating Christ's passion, Barrow dwells on the intensity of Christ's sufferings and on the way they express his compassion for humanity. It was necessary for Christ to die as a despised criminal; "thus would our blessed Saviour . . . not only suffer in his body by sore words and bruises, and in his soul by doleful agonies, but in his name also and reputation by the foulest scandals . . . thus meaning by all means thoroughly to express his charity, and exercise his compassion toward us."[57] While a Puritan sermon might dwell on Christ's passion in order to intensify feelings of guilt and despair in listeners, the function of Barrow's rhetorical rehearsal of Christ's agonies is different; it is intended to elicit emulation, not trigger the process of conversion.[58]

It is vital to the function of eliciting emulation that Christ's passion be a spectacle: "the judgment-hall, with all the passages leading him thither, and thence to execution . . . amidst the crowds and clamours of people, were as so many theatres, on which he had opportune convenience, in the full eye of the world, to act divers parts of sublimest virtue."[59] Only this spectacle can rouse our affections, and if it does not do so upon first reflection, we must return to it again and again in order to rouse our affections into response. If consideration "of God's eternal care for our welfare, of his descending to the lowest condition for our souls, of his willingly undertaking and patiently undergoing all kinds of inconvenience, of disgrace, of bitter pain and sorrow for us . . . will not affect us, what can do it? . . . How desperately hard and tough must our hearts be, if such incentives cannot soften and melt them? Is not such an apathy more than stoical, more than stony, which can stand immovable before so mighty inducements to passion?"[60] Barrow's rhetorical appeals, too, can rouse our affections, intensifying the impact of Christ's example.

But if Christ's passion is effective simply through its example, could not other examples of compassionate suffering be similarly effective? This was a question that could undermine Christocentrism and point in the direction of Socinianism, deism, or Humean sentimentalism. The naturalized moral vocabulary of thinkers like Barrow fed these developments.

Ernest Tuveson saw in Barrow's positive depiction of human nature "the germ of the Enlightenment's faith in perfectibility," noting that "the emphasis is on environment—the external influences . . . . The problem is to see that the personality grows along its native lines rather than to cure by supernatural means a spiritual evil."[61] It is not that Barrow ought to have regarded grace as "supernatural" as opposed to "natural," I would suggest. His preoccupation with natural mechanisms of spiritual transformation did, however, imply a shift in attention from seeing such transformation as a gift from God to regarding it as something that is graspable apart from God and thus subject to human manipulation and control. Divine action in the world then becomes increasingly problematic—a form of "outside intervention"—which is therefore invoked only as a last resort when nature fails.

Divine Compassion and Divine Honor

Compassion and pity can be understood as a disposition to help those who are suffering, and may or may not involve "suffering-with" those whose suffering one seeks to relieve. Whichcote never raised the issue of whether divine compassion involves divine passibility. Barrow, in contrast, given his concern with the natural psychology of morality, is insistent that compassion involves passionate suffering. "It is the property of charity," he writes, "to mourn with those that mourn, not coldly, but passionately (for it is to weep with those that weep), resenting every man's case with an affection suitable thereto, and as he doth himself resent it."[62] Barrow dwells on Christ's eminent sensibility: "his complexion was most pure and delicate, his spirit most vivid and apprehensive."[63]

This emphasis on passionate suffering and physical sensibility, though, renders the attribution of compassion to God theologically problematic, since it collides with divine impassibility. Barrow rests in scriptural language: "he is the Father of pities; . . . full of bowels, his bowels are troubled, and do sound . . . of him it is said, that his soul was grieved for the misery of Israel; and that he was afflicted in all the afflictions of his people."[64] He confesses that this is beyond human understanding, but suggests that God is described this way in scripture in order to show us our duty to emulate the divine mercy: "so incredible miracles doth infinite charity work in God, that the impassible God in a manner should suffer with us, that happiness itself should partake in our misery; that grief should spring up in the fountain of joy. How this can be, we thoroughly cannot well apprehend; but surely those expresses are used in condescension to signify the greatly charitable benignity of God, and to show us our duty, that we should be merciful as our heavenly Father is merciful, sympathizing with the miseries and sorrows of our brethren."[65]

The oddity here is that Barrow construes scriptural accounts of God's character as divine instructions for human behavior, just as he reads the natural world and human nature for divine messages—revelation from rather than revelation of God. The implication here is that God is outside the world, not to be directly encountered in scripture or nature. Ironically, then, the affirmation of divine compassion, which would appear to be an assertion of God's nearness, is presented by Barrow in a way that actually emphasizes God's distance from the world. Scripture and nature reveal God's will for us, but neither directly reveal God to us.

Having emphasized both the compassion of God and the compassion of Christ, Barrow finds that in his account of the passion of Christ, he must insert a certain qualification of the divine compassion. Sending his Son to die on the cross required of God "the withdrawing his face and restraining his bowels from his best beloved."[66] This withdrawal of compassion, which intensified Christ's suffering, was necessary because, argued Barrow, God could not simply forgive sinful humanity without an expiation for sin.[67] Christ came in order to satisfy "God's justice by a most patient endurance of pains on our behalf."[68] It is noteworthy that Barrow here appeals to divine justice. Whichcote, like the Eastern church fathers, understood atonement in terms of the recreation of human nature in Christ, and so did not need to scramble to keep satisfaction theory on its feet. Barrow retains the typical Protestant emphasis on a satisfaction theory of atonement, and must therefore reintroduce the priority of justice.[69] It is important to see that what this invocation of justice amounts to is an appeal to the divine majesty. It is the affront to God's honor that requires satisfaction. (We can imagine Whichcote responding that honor and majesty too must be attributed to God only in ways governed by divine goodness.) According to Barrow, a compassionate God withdraws his compassion, intensifying the suffering of his compassionate son, not out of some deeper compassion, but in order to satisfy a violation of honor. Christ's compassionate suffering makes sense within Barrow's thought as an example that rouses us from cold apathy and inflames our compassionate emulation, but tensions emerge when he places this within the traditional Protestant context of sin and expiation.[70]

Transcendence Domesticated?

In a number of ways, then, Barrow's reflections on compassion, human and divine, helped to usher in secularized moral thought. For Barrow, the compassionate Christ is a moral exemplar, not the one who brings us to fuller participation in God. Natural instincts of pity are to be read as instructions from a distant God, rather than as revealing the immanent traces of a transcendent God. Nature is becoming an autonomous realm, with grace increasingly peripheral. Talk of compassion, whether divine or human, is not a way of drawing us to intimacy with God, but a way of bolstering human moral impulses. And, finally, Barrow's psychologizing of compassion renders its attribution to God problematic, and raises the spectre of divine passibility.[71] Whichcote, in contrast, shows us a way to speak of divine compassion that preserves grace and transcendence, while heightening our awareness of God's intimacy, God's Being-with-us.

But what of Whichcote's insistence that God must be compassionate because it is only reasonable for the Creator to have compassion on his finite creatures' ways, that God must be compassionate because only so are God's ways understandable to us? Does this not represent a domestication of divine transcendence just as significant as anything we find in Barrow? It is certainly true that internal theological tensions--tensions between a compassionate God and the eternal punishment that awaited the lost, as well as between divine compassion and the expiation by which the saved were reconciled with God—encouraged over time a radical reconceptualization—and sometimes a rejection—of the doctrine of hell. Some thinkers experienced even a moderate reconceptualization of eternal punishment as a threat to divine transcendence and sovereignty. In response, they drew back from affirmations of divine Compassion, insisting that God is free to exercise either mercy or justice (i.e. punishment) in ways utterly incomprehensible to us.

One man who followed this path was Edward Wigglesworth, Hollis Professor of Divinity at Harvard in the mid-eighteenth century.[72] Attending briefly to Wigglesworth and to a fellow Bostonian of the previous century, John Cotton, will allow us to see how discourse emphasizing divine incomprehensibility serves not so much to protect divine transcendence as to protect unaccountable power. Writing a century after Whichcote, Wigglesworth is alarmed by pamphlets from England that have drawn from the mercy of God the conclusion of universal salvation.[73] Wigglesworth has concluded that such "dangerous Deductions" result from lack of attention to the "Sovereignty of God in exercising his Mercy."[74] God has required human beings always to be benevolent and merciful, but God himself is free to have mercy when and on whom he will; God "is not, nor can he be, otherwise than absolutely free and unconfin'd in his Acts of Grace and Mercy. Mercy and Justice are both alike dear and essential to him."[75] For Wigglesworth, the Atonement displays this most clearly, for there God causes justice and mercy "to meet together and kiss each other, in the most glorious and astonishing manner."[76] God requires a sacrifice in accord with inflexible justice, and "to secure his own Honour," but in his mercy provides the offering himself.[77]

Should Wigglesworth be seen here as striving to restore a non-contrastive divine transcendence, as re-affirming against the likes of Whichcote that all human categories fail when applied to God? Placher writes admiringly of John Cotton, who preached to "the good citizens of seventeenth-century Boston" that "'God doth sometime pour out the spirit of grace upon the most bloody, and most haynous, and most desperate, and most prophane, and most abominable sinners.'" Placher's interpretation is that Cotton was reminding Christians of God's infinite mercy, telling them that the revelation of the God known in Christ "comes not as accusation but as grace."[78] But eighteenth-century Bostonians were reminded by Edward Wigglesworth, in terms that closely echo Cotton's, that God is utterly free to exercise either mercy or justice (that is, punishment) as he sees fit; the point is that God's power is incomprehensible to us. But incomprehensible power is unaccountable power; it is for us simply to obey, not to ask whether such power be devilish or divine.

Whichcote rejected the notion that "merciful" and "compassionate" were categories that broke down when applied to God. He should indeed be seen as mounting an attack on Puritan understandings of divine transcendence which had flourished in England during the Civil War. As we have seen, he regarded these as elevating power over goodness in a way that rendered God a diabolical figure. His worry was that appeals to the "incomprehensibility" of God's nature in fact often serve in effect as a front for the divinizing of naked domination. Placher wants to portray Cotton as issuing a challenge to the established hierarchical social order. He suggests that when Bostonians heard Cotton preach, "they recognized a threat to their civic order. This was not Addison's sort of preaching, which kept 'the country people' in line, but an invitation to challenge authorities and the order they impose."[79] I would suggest, rather, that the logic of Cotton and Wigglesworth reinforces a social order in which power is unaccountable and thus can be challenged, if at all, only through violent revolt, rather than through reasoned appeal.

Placher is surely right to see as problematic a development in which "many theologians came to think of God as one of the entities or agents in the world among the others."[80] The God who creates the world cannot be one more being within the world. In this sense, the "domestication" of transcendence is surely troubling. Also deeply problematic is a tendency to think of God's transcendence in terms of distance and detachment from the world, such that transcendence and immanence become mutually exclusive terms. But understanding divine transcendence, as Placher does, in terms of the breakdown of all human categories, in terms of incomprehensible mystery, has historically allowed the power of the divine to be invoked as a cloak for raw domination.

There is a dynamic quality to our analogical attribution of perfections to God, since, as David Burrell notes, appraisal terms are those "whose syntactic structure leaves them free to be used in ways that outstrip our present settled idiom."[81] When our "present settled idiom" ceases to be settled, when our sense of the true perfection of power, say, is shifting, our characterization of divine perfection will also shift. However stumbling and inadequate our talk of God, divine incomprehensibility must not be invoked as an excuse for giving up on this quest to predicate perfections of God. One who "hungers and thirsts after justice," writes Burrell, "knows what must be denied, has some glimmer of what might be, and withal feels compelled to assert what he knows must be the case, since it embodies his own good and that of the universe."[82] To resist this compulsion to speak of God is to arrest the dynamic quest for perfection, to be content with our present settled idiom. Whichcote's efforts to speak of God's goodness, mercy, and compassion, his refusal to allow that these categories utterly break down when we come to God should not, therefore, be seen as domesticating divine transcendence, as destroying the divine mystery and as sliding toward secularization, but rather as challenging the mystification of power, a mystification which frustrates the longing for perfection and the drive to transformative justice.

Conclusion

If Whichcote truly does represent an alternative possibility within modern theology, one that did not contribute to the emergence of secular moral thought and naturalized theological discourse (or did so only insofar as Whichcote's thought was imperfectly appropriated by later latitudinarians), then we need not only to revise our estimation of a little-known seventeenth-century thinker but also to question more generally our received grand narratives of the history of modern theology. This will in turn transform our sense of the proper path for future theological reflection. What can be said of God without undermining divine transcendence? The widespread contemporary theological emphasis on divine empathy, to focus on just one piece of the puzzle, can be seen as rooted in an ambiguous modern past, for the later latitudinarian embrace of divine compassion typified by Barrow undermined divine transcendence and assisted the naturalization of moral discourse, while the alternative possibility represented by Whichcote was quickly forgotten. Can contemporary advocates of the discourse of divine compassion learn from Whichcote's alternative, or do they stand in danger of repeating the secularizing slide of the later latitudinarians? These are the questions studies like the present one can hope to help us form and begin to address.

NOTES

¹ The hallmarks of the latitudinarian or broad-church movement were creedal orthodoxy, conformity to the Church of England, an advocacy of reason in religion, an Arminian conception of justification, a hope of comprehending dissenters under the umbrella of the Church of England, and an accompanying emphasis on practical morality over doctrinal disputes. For an overview, see Martin I. J. Griffin, Jr., *Latitudinarianism in the Seventeenth-Century Church of England* (Leiden: E.J. Brill, 1992).

² See R. S. Crane, "Suggestions Toward A Genealogy of the 'Man of Feeling'," *English Literary History* 1 (1934): 205-30; Norman S. Fiering, "Irresistible Compassion: An Aspect of Eighteenth-Century Sympathy and Humanitarianism," *Journal of the History of Ideas* 37 (1976): 195-218; Ernest Tuveson, "The Importance of Shaftesbury," *English Literary History* 20 (1953): 267-299.

³This can be clearly seen in David Hume's sentimentalist ethics. For Hume, moral approval can be explained as a natural sentiment elicited by character traits which prove pleasant or useful to human beings in society. Sympathy allows us to grasp the interests of others, and our sense of humanity moves us to respond to their needs. References to God, whether as lawgiver, judge, or compassionate source of forgiveness and transformative grace, were seen by Hume as superfluous to, indeed perversions of, natural human morality. See J. B. Schneewind, *The Invention of Autonomy* (Cambridge: Cambridge University Press, 1998), 354-77.

⁴ William C. Placher, *The Domestication of Transcendence: How Modern Thinking about God Went Wrong* (Louisville, Kentucky: Westminster/John Knox Press, 1996), 187. See also Michael J. Buckley, *At the Origins of Modern Atheism* (New Haven: Yale University Press, 1987), 357.

⁵ Placher, *The Domestication of Transcendence*, 6.

⁶ Ibid., 7.

⁷ Placher does recognize the dangers of a negative theology that leaves us simply in silence. Instead, he counsels a return to scriptural narratives, notably to the Christ we encounter in these narratives as God's self-revelation (Ibid., 185-187). But if he truly desires to affirm that all events—all of nature and all of history--are the result of God's agency, then revelation cannot be limited to Scripture, and it seems inconsistent to rule out all attempts to speak of God but those grounded in biblical narrative (Ibid., 183-192).

⁸ Kathryn Tanner, *God and Creation in Christian Theology* (Oxford: Basil Blackwell, 1988), 40-47.

⁹ Placher, *The Domestication of Transcendence*, 7.

¹⁰ Ibid., 182.

¹¹ See Frederick Beiser, *The Sovereignty of Reason* (Princeton: Princeton University Press, 1996), 142-43, 147-48.

¹² Benjamin Whichcote, *Select Sermons*, ed. Lord Shaftesbury (London: Awnsham and Churchhill, 1698), and C. A. Patrides, ed., *The Cambridge Platonists* (Cambridge, Mass.: Harvard University Press, 1970), 36. Whichcote and the other Cambridge Platonists believed that doctrinal wrangling had contributed to the splintering of the church and to undermining the plausibility of Christian faith. Thus, rather than directly identifying and countering the problematic doctrines, or engaging with specific Calvinist theologians, Whichcote focused on developing his positive alternative.

¹³ Whichcote, *Select Sermons*, 15.

¹⁴ As Schneewind notes of the Cambridge Platonists generally, "they worked out their views in terms of Scripture, and argued, as did most of those whom they addressed, by interpreting biblical texts. Such theory as they presented was offered largely to show the implications of their new way of reading the texts," *Invention of Autonomy*, 195. In "Irresistible Compassion," Norman Fiering argues that the divine authority of natural compassion, the notion

that compassionate feelings were given to humanity by a benevolent God, was "the main innovation in ethics and psychology that allowed unqualified humanitarianism to flower." At the same time, though, he suggests that "the discovery of the benevolent feelings seems to have preceded and forced the change in the understanding of God's will" (208). In the mid-eighteenth century, as a result of humanitarian pressure, God's mercy and justice came into open conflict, and the doctrine of hell was challenged; "if God had in fact given man involuntary compassionate responses, then God must be at least as compassionate as man. Moreover, truly divine teaching could hardly include eternal punishment, since eternal punishment was wholly incompatible with the divine lesson taught to every man by his own instinct for pity and sympathy" (215). In his view, beliefs about human benevolence arose first, were then applied to God, and this in turn created a crisis for theology. Our consideration of Whichcote, however, suggests that Fiering is wrong about human benevolence having introduced divine benevolence onto the scene.

Whichcote's grounds for insisting on divine goodness and compassion are not first and foremost his convictions about human benevolence, but rather scripture and its indication of God's compassion for sinful humanity. Armed with this scriptural knowledge of God's goodness, he is then able to discern how the natural world and human nature participate in divine goodness. Of course, divine compassion has always been a theme within the scriptures. What encouraged Whichcote to dwell on this theme, to make it central to his understanding of God and salvation history, were his worries that Calvinist emphasis on the incomprehensibility of divine power and majesty was serving to alienate people from God. This suggests—contra Fiering—that the affirmation of divine compassion, far from resulting from a capitulation of theology to outside pressures generated by an emphasis on human benevolence, lay at the beginnings of the discussion. Theological crisis and innovation came from within, rather than being imposed on theology by outside forces.

Fiering also looks too late for reconceptualizations of the nature of divine punishment. While he acknowledges that Peter Sterry, who was at Emmanuel College Cambridge at the same time as Whichcote, actually did insist that the supremacy of the divine attribute of love implied universal salvation, he treats Sterry as an anomaly (216). But if Whichcote did not challenge Hell directly, he did reconceptualize it as the suffering intrinsic to the guilty conscience of one who has rejected God's offer of forgiveness. The doctrine of hell began to be rethought three-quarters of a century before Fiering says humanitarian pressure on theology began to mount.

[15] Whichcote, *Select Sermons*, 12.

[16] Ibid., 62.

[17] Ibid., 50. We see in this emphasis on repentance as the sole condition of forgiveness what appears to be Socinian influence on Whichcote's thought, though Whichcote claimed to have very little acquaintance with either Socinian or Arminian thought. See Louis Richard, "The Mystery of the Redemption in Protestantism," in *The Theology of the Atonement*, ed John R. Sheets (Englewood Cliffs, New Jersey: Prentice-Hall, Inc., 1967), 30. The Puritan Antony Tuckney, a teacher and later colleague of Whichcote, was alarmed at what he saw as Socinian and Arminian tendencies within Whichcote's sermons, and accused him of this in 1651. Whichcote replied that these accusations were groundless, and that he had very little acquaintance with Socinian or Arminian authors. *The Cambridge Platonists*, ed. Gerald R. Cragg (New York: Oxford University Press, 1968), 35-6; 42. Certainly, Whichcote rejected a satisfaction theory of the atonement.

[18] Whichcote, *Select Sermons*, 316.

[19] Ibid., 95.

[20] See also Patrides, who, discussing the Cambridge Platonists' commitment to reason, notes that while it may in some general sense have contributed to the rise of deistic rationalism, "they were developments which failed to take into account the importance attached by Whichcote and his disciples to the 'mystery' at the heart of the Christian faith," 17. I am not convinced that mysticism is the best category to invoke, but Patrides is right to see the centrality to Whichcote of community with, participation in, God.

[21] "The Use of Reason in Matters of Religion," Patrides, 47.

[22] "Moral and Religious Aphorisms," Patrides, 334.

[23] See, e.g., Charles Hartshorne, *The Logic of Perfection* (La Salle, Illinois: Open Court, 1962;1991), 230-231; Anne Carr, *Transforming Grace* (San Francisco: Harper & Row, 1988, 151-2; Elizabeth A. Johnson, *She Who Is* (New York: Crossroad, 1994), 269-70. Johnson, for instance, speaks of "power-with," of "empowerment," and of "the liberating power of connectedness."

[24] Whichcote, *Select Sermons*, 318.

[25] Ibid., 313.

[26] Nor is it the case that Whichcote undermines divine freedom by asserting that we can rely on God's mercy and compassion. Rather, he rejects a notion of freedom as arbitrary action in favor of freedom as the spontaneous expression of one's deepest being (Ibid., 306). We should not think "that God hath imposed a Law upon himself, or in any way limited or disabled himself" in faithfully showing mercy to sinners (Ibid., 120). Rather, God thereby freely expresses his nature in so acting. There is no need to protect God's freedom by asserting with Calvinist voluntarists that God's ways are unpredictable and unfathomable.

[27] Placher, after having attacked the application of human concepts to God, turns to scripture for language with which to speak of God (*The Domestication of Transcendence*, 185ff). His point is that we cannot speak of God unless God reveals Godself to us. For Whichcote, however, God's self-revelation permeates all of creation. To use nature to interpret scripture is not to abandon revealed for human categories, therefore, but to seek to be fully receptive to revelation.

[28] Whichcote, *Select Sermons*, 310.

[29] Ibid., 252. Italics in the original.

[30] Ibid., 310. On classical sources for reflections on natural affection and compassion, including *storgè*, see Fiering, 196-97.

[31] Whichcote, *Select Sermons*, 122.

[32] Ibid., 312.

[33] Ibid., 311.

[34] Ibid., 284.

[35] Ibid., 56, 347.

[36] On the influence of the Greek Fathers on the Cambridge Platonists, and on deification, see Patrides, *Cambridge Platonists*, 4-6, 19-21.

[37] Whichcote, *Select Sermons*, 130.

[38] Schneewind, *Invention of Autonomy,* 196.

[39] Whichcote, *Select Sermons*, 284.

[40] The full story is rather more complex. As I discuss in "Community with God and the Loss of Transcendence" (unpublished manuscript), there are moments in which Cambridge Platonist accounts of participation slide in the direction of applying a univocal notion of divinity to both God and human beings.

[41] This is typical of the second generation of latitudinarians. See, for example, William Clagett, *Of the Humanity and Charity of Christians* (London: J. Robinson, 1687), 8-9, Richard Kidder, *Charity Directed* (London: 1676), 6, Edward Pelling, *A Practical Discourse Upon Charity* (London: W. Crooke, 1693), 2, John Tillotson, "Of the Example of Jesus in Doing Good," in *Works*, Vol. II (London: Richard Priestly, 1820), 180.

[42] Although Cambridge Platonists Ralph Cudworth and Henry More dedicated considerable effort to refuting Hobbes, Whichcote rarely mentioned him. See Patrides, 28. Beiser argues that it would be anachronistic to see Hobbes as the original adversary of Cambridge Platonist thought, *Sovereignty of Reason*, 141.

[43] Isaac Barrow, "Of a Peaceable Temper and Carriage," in *Works*, vol. 1 (New York: John C. Riker, 1845), 309; cf. "Motives and Arguments to Charity," ibid., I, 286-7. Likewise John Tillotson, who noted that mercy "is so proper and agreeable to mankind, that we commonly call it humanity; giving it its name from our very nature," "Of the Great Duties of Natural Religion," *The Works of John Tillotson in Ten Volumes* (London: J. F. Dove, 1820), vol. 5, 279.

[44] Barrow, "Motives to Charity," I, 287

[45] Barrow, "Peaceable Temper," I, 310.

[46] A very similar line of thought is found in Clagett, *Humanity and Charity*, 4-5, and in Tillotson, "Of the Great Duties of Natural Religion," *Works,* vol. 5, 281-286, who notes that "there needs nothing more to make any thing a law, than a sufficient declaration that it is the will of God; and this God hath sufficiently signified to mankind by the very frame of our natures, and of those principles and faculties which he hath endued us withal," 286.

[47] Barrow, "Peaceable Temper," I, 310

[48] Ibid., 311.

[49] Barrow, "Peaceable Temper," I, 310, 311, "The Duty and Reward of Bounty to the Poor," 343, 344, "Of the Love of Our Neighbor," 264; "Nature of Charity," 278.

[50] Whichcote, *Select Sermons*, 381.

[51] Barrow, "Peaceable Temper, I, 311.

[52] Barrow, "Love of Neighbor," I, 265.

[53] Ibid., 270.

[54] Ibid.

[55] Patrides suggests that "all that the Cambridge Platonists ever uttered reverts in the end to Whichcote's refusal to oppose the spiritual to the rational, the supernatural to the natural, Grace to Nature," 10.

[56] Barrow, "Imitators of Christ," I, 393; cf. "Walking as Christ," 400. Paradoxically, while this appears to be clearly anti-Stoic rhetoric, Barrow immediately goes on to illustrate the power of example by suggesting that Zeno's embodiment of Stoicism proved that the stoical doctrine was not impossible, as it would otherwise have seemed. Barrow thus suggests that examples, by inciting the passions, could inspire someone to emulate Zeno's Stoicism, which sought to subdue all passions! Barrow seems unaware of the tensions which riddle his appeal to the power of Zeno's example, probably because he identifies Stoicism with "the mortification of *unreasonable* desires" (emphasis added), and thus implies that examples may incite our passions in a reasonable and morally useful way; the passion of emulation "may be subservient to the production of virtue and piety" ("Imitators of Christ," I, 396). Precisely this is what neo-Stoics like Lipsius and Le Grand denied. Justus Lipsius, *Two Books of Constancie,* tr. Sir John Stradling, ed. Rudoph Kirk (New Brunswick, New Jersey; Rutgers University Press, 1939). One of Lipsius' followers, whose work was early on translated into English, was Antoine Le Grand, *Man Without Passion: or the Wise Stoick, According to the Sentiments of Seneca* (London: C. Harper, 1675), 101. Le Grand explicitly critiques compassion as infirmity and effeminacy, 277-278, as does Lipsius, 99.

[57] Barrow, "Upon the Passion," I, 361-2.

[58] Isabel Rivers suggests that the latitudinarians tended to focus on persuading the reason rather than on moving the affections, in contrast to nonconformists and dissenters, even though she thinks that this distinction has been exaggerated in the past; *Reason, Grace, and Sentiment,* vol. I (Cambridge: Cambridge University Press, 1991), 52. But the difference is perhaps more subtle; latitudinarians such as Barrow believed that the affections must be moved, but moved in the service of rational morality. According to Norman Fiering, "in certain decisive respects the sentimentalist movement may be understood as a translation into the secular realm of particular forms of Puritan emotionality," *Moral Philosophy at Seventeenth-Century Harvard* (University of North Carolina Press, 1981), 149. Concepts of sensibility, zeal, and the heart that had been central to Puritan discourse became transformed into the concepts of moral sentiment, disinterested benevolence, and feelingful moral reform (180). But Fiering recognizes that this Puritan impulse was transformed through Cambridge Platonist and later latitudinarian thought as appropriated by Shaftesbury, Hutcheson, and Hume; thus, it was not the dissenters who gave rise to sentimentalism, even if they emphasized the emotions more than did the latitudinarians (195).

[59] Barrow, "Upon the Passion," I, 362.

[60] Barrow, "Of the Love of God," I, 252.

[61] Ernest Lee Tuveson, "The Origins of the Moral Sense," in *The Imagination as a Means of Grace: Locke and the Aesthetics of Romanticism* (Berkeley: University of California Press, 1960), 45.

[62] Barrow, "The Nature, Properties, and Acts of Charity," I, 276.

[63] Barrow, "Upon the Passion," I, 366.

[64] Barrow, "Nature of Charity," I, 278.

[65] Ibid.

[66] Barrow, "Upon the Passion," I, 369.

[67] This notion of the cross as a suspension of the compassion of the Father is reminiscent of Luther's notion of the *Deus absconditus*, as the God who is hidden in his revelation on the cross: "in the one unitary event of revelation in the cross, God's wrath and mercy are revealed simultaneously—but only faith is able to recognize the *opus proprium* as it lies hidden under the *opus alienum*; only faith discerns the merciful intention which underlies the revealed wrath." Alister E. McGrath, *Luther's Theology of the Cross* (Oxford: Basil Blackwell, 1985), 165. The difference is that for Barrow, the *opus alienum*, the withdrawal of compassion, does not hide a deeper compassion, but rather a concern for the divine honor.

[68] Barrow, "Upon the Passion," I, 360.

[69] Anselm was, of course, the first to emphasize satisfaction in atonement. Still, following Luther's understanding of the atonement in the context of a confrontation between divine anger and divine love, satisfaction theory was given a new emphasis, and satisfaction through penal substitution was central to both Lutheran and Calvinist doctrines of atonement; Richard, "The Mystery of the Redemption," 27-29.

[70] Clearly a deep rethinking of Christology was called for, but in the century that was to come, this took place primarily outside of the Anglican church, within the arena of rational dissent and beyond, where Christology tended to melt away and the simpler picture of an ever-compassionate and benevolent deity took center stage. See Timothy Gorringe, *God's Just Vengeance: Crime, Violence, and the Rhetoric of Salvation* (Cambridge: Cambridge University Press, 1996), 191.

[71] Without taking up the subject with the care and precision it demands, I would suggest that the move of affirming divine passibility is likely to undermine divine transcendence, for it suggests that God can only be with us in our suffering if God, too, suffers. The argument is that if God does not suffer with us, then God is somehow cut off from us and our experience. In order to suffer with us, God must be passible. To make this claim, though, is to affirm God's immanence while undermining God's transcendence. But on a non-contrastive understanding of divine transcendence, God's intimacy with us is not predicated on co-suffering. Human beings cannot be with us as we suffer, cannot understand our experience, without sympathetically entering into our suffering. But a radically transcendent God's intimacy and solidarity with us need not be mediated in this way; God the Creator, ground of our existence, is closer to us in our suffering than we can ever be to others by experiencing their suffering; see Thomas G. Weinandy, *Does God Suffer?* (Notre Dame, Ind.: University of Notre Dame Press, 2000). So there is a danger that affirmations of divine compassion and solidarity will threaten to domesticate divine transcendence, but only if divine compassion is understood in a way that implies divine passibility. There was a tendency to move in this direction, not in Whichcote's thought, but in Barrow's thought. Barrow delves into the psychology of compassion and wrestles, if only briefly, with how to understand divine compassion in light of this psychology. So Barrow's thought fostered an understanding of God as distant and of grace as naturalized in a way that Whichcote's did not.

[72] Edward Wigglesworth, *The Sovereignty of God in the Exercises of his Mercy; And how he is said to harden the hearts of men* (Boston: Rogers and Fowle, 1741). Fiering draws attention to this treatise in his essay.

[73] Ibid., 6.

[74] Ibid.

[75] Ibid., 12.

[76] Ibid.

[77] As Randall McGowen shows, debates over the relation between divine mercy and justice continued throughout the eighteenth century and had an important impact on theories of criminal justice. See "The Changing Face of God's Justice: The Debates over Divine and Human Punishment in Eighteenth-Century England," *Criminal Justice History* 9 (1988): 63-98. See also Gorringe, *God's Just Vengeance,* which examines links between theology of the atonement and criminal justice theory from the 17th through the 19th centuries.

[78] Placher, *The Domestication of Transcendence*, 214.

[79] Ibid.

[80] Ibid., 181.

[81] David Burrell, *Analogy and Philosophical Language* (New Haven: Yale University Press, 1973), 168.

[82] Ibid., 169.

Natural Equality: Freedom, Authority and Obedience in Two Medieval Thinkers

Jean Porter

Abstract

The middle ages is commonly seen as an age of inequality, when society was structured by fixed social hierarchies. However, beginning in the late eleventh century and continuing through the thirteenth century, widespread economic and cultural changes, together with a revival of spiritual intensity and widespread concern for religious reforms, transformed the dominant structures of Western European society. These changes did not immediately transform Europe into an egalitarian society, but they did give new saliency to ancient Christian ideals of equality, particularly among scholastic theologians and canon lawyers of the period. In this paper, I focus on the virtue of obedience and its limits as one entrée into the scholastic concept of natural equality, further restricting myself to a comparison of Bonaventure and Aquinas on this topic. I will argue that while both theologians value the virtue of obedience highly, both also place clear limits on the obligation of obedience, limits which point beyond themselves (explicitly, in Aquinas' case, but clearly in Bonaventure's case) to a norm of natural equality which constrains the exercise of authority.

The middle ages is commonly seen as an age of inequality, when society was structured by fixed social hierarchies. There is some truth to this perception, at least as applied to the earlier medieval period, although the structures of medieval society were never as rigid as popular stereotypes would suggest. However, beginning in the late eleventh century and continuing through the thirteenth, widespread economic and cultural changes, together with a revival of spiritual intensity and widespread concern for religious reforms, transformed the dominant structures of Western European society. These changes did not immediately transform Europe into an egalitarian society, but they did give new saliency to ancient Christian ideals of equality. In particular, the meaning of equality became a central issue for scholastic theologians and canon lawyers in this period.[1]

Seen from our perspective, the concept of equality as developed in the twelfth and thirteenth centuries is limited. Even as the scholastics reflected on the practical implications of this concept, they hedged it with all sorts of qualifications and restrictions based on gender, free or unfree status, age, religious standing, and the like. Yet it would be a mistake to dismiss the resultant concept of equality out of hand as either tendentious or irrelevant to our own time. Equality is after all a very general concept which must be translated into a framework of social obligations and liberties in order to be meaningful. Probably no society has succeeded in eliminating every form of inequality, nor is it obvious that such a goal would be attainable or even desirable. None of this suggests that the medieval qualifications on the idea of equality would be acceptable today. Nevertheless, the very fact that the scholastics placed constraints on equality reflects the fact that they took it seriously as a social norm, which must be limited and specified in order to be meaningful.

It would take us well beyond the bounds of one paper to examine all of the ramifications of the scholastic concept of natural equality. In what follows, I will focus on the virtue of obedience and its limits as one entree into this concept, further restricting myself to a comparison of Bonaventure and Aquinas on this topic. It will not be surprising to find that both value the virtue of obedience highly, but at the same time, both also place clear limits on the obligation of obedience, limits which point beyond themselves (explicitly, in Aquinas' case, implicitly but clearly in Bonaventure's case) to a norm of natural equality which constrains the exercise of authority.

However, in order to appreciate the full significance of Bonaventure's and Aquinas' views on equality, it will first of all be necessary to place these views within a wider context. That will be my task in the first section of this paper.

Authority, Freedom, and Equality: Preliminary Considerations

In order fully to appreciate the practical force of the concept of equality as it is understood in a given society, it is necessary to see it within the context of the central institutions and forms of relationships structuring that society. In our case, this task is complicated by the fact that European society was in flux throughout the period we are considering, and the sheer pace of social change was as important for the development of the concept of equality as any one of the particular changes that we might identify. Although I can only briefly indicate the nature and extent of these developments in this paper, some sketch is necessary in order to understand what follows.[2]

Up until the beginning of the twelfth century, European society was largely rural and de-centralized; by and large, social structures were maintained through custom rather than through legislation, and the most effective forms of authority were generally localized and dependent on personal and familial relationships. For these reasons, it is difficult to say just what privileges and obligations were attached to central social relations such as marriage, family, dominion, and servitude, or how far theory diverged from reality in these matters.[3] To a very considerable degree, the extended family made fundamental choices for its members, both male and female, forming marriage alliances and committing children to organized religious life through the practice of offering them as oblates. Family control was limited, however, by the stipulation that both marriage and religious profession required explicit and mature consent on the part of the individuals directly involved, and by reforms of marriage in the late eleventh century which tended to displace control of marriage from the extended family to the church. Within marriage, the wife was subject to the authority of her husband, although this was somewhat mitigated by the insistence that husband and wife have equal rights to sexual gratification within marriage (an obligation charmingly referred to as the "marriage debt"). Women could own and control property, and they could and did exercise secular authority in their own name. We have at least a few examples of women serving as judges.[4] Finally, organized religious life offered considerable freedom and scope for women of the upper class, although not poorer women.

The social relations which offer the hardest problems to students of the early middle ages are those set by relations of authority and power on the one hand, and subjection and servitude on the other.[5] We all "know" that early medieval society was feudal, and yet even the existence of feudalism has been challenged by some scholars.[6] Similarly, the extent of servitude in this period and the exact condition of those in such a state have been widely debated.[7] It appears that the fundamental forms of social authority were in fact structured around relations of personal fealty such as we associate with feudalism, but these did not have any fixed form and were by no means the only forms of power and authority in the early middle ages. Chattel slavery appears to have been replaced by serfdom as a basic economic structure in European society by the beginning of the eleventh century, although chattel slavery did persist in some parts of Europe throughout the medieval period.[8] The status of the serf again is unclear to us, and probably was unclear to the men and women of medieval Europe themselves.[9] On the one hand, serfdom did not involve as many restrictions on personal freedom as did chattel slavery, and on the other hand, free status did not imply freedom from all obligations of service to an overlord. The difference between servile and free had as much to do with the relative value given to the forms of service offered by those in each status; the service of a free person was considered honorable, whereas servile service was not. Moreover, serfdom differed from chattel slavery in another critical respect, insofar as the serf was able to enter into and maintain socially recognized relations of marriage and family. Nonetheless, the serf's freedom was sharply curtailed, and like a slave, the serf could be bought and sold. Finally, dominion and servitude were closely connected to wealth and poverty in the thought and practice of the time, so much so that the status of the *pauper*, the poor individual, was seen as more or less equivalent to a form of servitude as well as dependence, just as the lord, the *dominus*, exercised economic as well as social dominion.[10]

Beginning in the late eleventh century and continuing through the early fourteenth century, a variety of factors came together to transform every aspect of European society. As its population expanded in a period of relative peace and security, Europe became increasingly urban and mobile, and its economy became increasingly mercantile and money-based.[11] For the first time in medieval Europe, we see the emergence of a significant monied urban class which did not fit neatly into the traditional divisions of nobility, churchmen, and peasantry. This urban middle class, in turn, provided much of the impetus for a new spirituality, which emphasized individual piety and the universal call to holiness to a far greater degree than had been the case. At the same time, improved networks of communication and transportation rendered the development of centralized authority and formalized legal codes both possible and necessary. Over the course of the latter eleventh and twelfth centuries, we see the emergence of formalized law-codes and analytic jurisprudence in both civil and canon law; we see for the first time the development of an extensive papal bureaucracy; and we see the beginnings of the modern nation-state. In the thirteenth century, the development of universities, which offered training in theology, law, and medicine, provided access to the expanding civil and church bureaucracies for the newly emergent urban middle class, and sometimes even for the children of the poor.[12]

None of these changes had the effect of producing a society that would be considered egalitarian in our own terms. Older forms of social stratification continued to exist alongside the new class and economic structures. To a significant degree, social roles were inherited, or at least restricted to those possessing particular characteristics; men and women were born into servile, free, or noble status, and women were excluded from clerical orders, which meant that they were prevented from exercising one centrally important form of authority. Furthermore, the status of women actually seems to have become worse in some respects, partly because women at all class levels lost power in the more centralized economy then developing, and partly because the university structure systematically excluded them from access to higher education.[13]

Yet the social and economic changes which Europe experienced in this period did tend to promote social equality in at least one critical respect. That is, they expanded the possibilities for social mobility and changes in status. While persons were still born into servitude, they were not necessarily fated to remain in that condition for the rest of their lives; a serf could buy his or her freedom, and in some regions of Europe, simply living in a city for a year and a day rendered a person free. The existence of large urban centers opened up new possibilities for the free population of Europe as well. Now for the first time since the end of the Roman empire, we see the emergence of an urban class of free persons who are not noble, yet who possess the financial resources and the communal strength to remain relatively independent. The increasing centralization of both civil and church government further reinforced the strength of the urban middle class, because this process inevitably generated bureaucracies, which drew most of their personnel from this class. This process, finally, was supported through the emergent universities, which provided access to positions of leadership in both civil government and the church to those who were neither noble nor wealthy.

How did the social mobility of this period foster ideals of equality? In the first place, in a society in which one's status is normally fixed from birth, it is easy to focus moral and social analysis on the distinctive duties and privileges attached to specific roles. But in a community marked by extensive social mobility, we would expect to find more emphasis on those aspects of a common humanity which persist through all the changes in social status, and that is in fact what we do find in twelfth and thirteenth century moral thought. In this period, theologians and jurists begin to turn from earlier motifs of society as a body, or society understood in terms of the traditional division of three orders of priest, warrior, and peasant— both of which reinforced a hierarchical social organization—and to base their analysis of society on ideas of the natural law, which appealed to a shared humanity as the basis for moral claims.[14] Secondly, the increasing mobility of European society in this period gave rise to a high valuation of personal freedom, understood as the honor and power enjoyed by those of free, not servile status.[15] The high value on freedom, again, tended to reinforce an ideal of equality, because freedom implied a relative—although not absolute—independence from the control of religious or civil authorities.

Ideals of freedom and equality were further reinforced in the twelfth and thirteenth centuries by developments in religious life and thought. This was one of the great periods of reform in organized religious life and church structures. These reforms, in turn, were both inspired by and served to foster widespread aspirations for a deeper, more personal relation with God and Christ and for a way of life more faithful to Christ's teachings and example. It is important to note that these aspirations were prevalent among lay men and women, as well as clergy and religious, particularly among the new urban middle class.[16] As such, the religious aspirations of the time served to consolidate the place of the urban middle class as an alternative to traditional social structures, which were themselves supported by older forms of spirituality.

These religious developments fostered ideals of freedom and equality in a variety of ways. In the first place, they gave new force to earlier Christian ideals of spiritual equality. Furthermore, they reinforced the high value which medieval society placed on personal freedom—the freedom to move from one religious community to another, in spite of long-standing traditions of monastic stability, the freedom to marry or not to marry, to enter into religious life or not, to pursue one's spiritual vision in relative independence of one's immediate community. The ideal of freedom in pursuit of one's vocation was given the force of law through an early twelfth century canon (that is, decree of church law) known as *Duae sunt leges* ("There are two laws"), in which the public law is contrasted with the private law of personal inspiration which may lead someone to pursue a more perfect way of life. Hence, the decree continues, a secular canon can become a monk or a regular canon, positive laws to the contrary notwithstanding. The "private law is more worthy than public law," the decree explains, since it is an expression of the Holy Spirit in the heart of the individual.[17] Finally, the religious aspirations of the time found expression in a number of popular movements which were more or less explicitly egalitarian in their ideals and provided scope for the exercise of authority on the part of women as well as men. Not all of these were sanctioned by official church structures; on the contrary, some of them were harshly persecuted as heretical. Yet all of them, whether sanctioned or not, provided a social embodiment for ideals of spiritual equality, thus serving to indicate that these ideals could have practical force.

Among these popular movements, the most significant for our purposes was the mendicant movement, which began as a lay movement in the late twelfth century, and which gave rise to the Franciscan and Dominican orders in the thirteenth century.[18] While there were differences among the various mendicant movements and communities, they shared a commitment to a closer imitation of Christ through a life of poverty and itinerant preaching. As such, they offered a further embodiment of the ideals of spiritual equality, and one which proved to have far-reaching social consequences. Furthermore, the clerical orders of mendicants considered themselves to have a special mission to the laity, and more particularly to the urban laity from which they themselves recruited most of their members. The sympathy between the mendicant movements and the emergent middle class led theologians from these movements to defend the independent value of marriage and of lay spiritualities. Such defenses were not explicitly defenses of equality, but they did have the effect of equalizing a social situation in which the vast majority of lay men and women had been marginalized within the Christian community. Finally, when the mendicant orders began to dominate the universities in the thirteenth century, they gave rise to generations of scholastics whose religious formation, sense of mission, and (often) social background predisposed them to a positive view of the egalitarian ideals developing at that time. This is particularly significant for us, of course, because both of the authors whom we will be examining, the Franciscan Bonaventure and the Dominican Aquinas, were formed in the matrix of scholasticism and mendicant ideals.

Hence, when we find reflections on equality as an ideal in the early scholastic period, these do not necessarily reflect egalitarian norms of social relations;

indeed, scholastic reflections on equality often take their starting point from the manifest fact of social inequality. Nonetheless, it would also be a mistake to conclude that scholastic reflections on equality did not reflect social realities, or affect them, at all. The critical factor which gave rise to reflection on equality was not the structure of society *per se*, much less any institutionalized expressions of equality as a social norm, but rather the degree to which social structures were in flux and the remarkable degree of personal freedom and social mobility that a rapidly changing society made possible. Moreover, the scholastics were themselves participants in, and often defenders of these social changes. In this context, the egalitarian components of their inherited traditions of social and theological reflection were particularly important to them, and they emphasized and expanded upon these components while down-playing other strands which focused on the organic and hierarchical character of society. In the process, they transformed the traditions they inherited, even while expressing themselves in the familiar language of their forbears.

At the same time, we can only appreciate the full force of scholastic reflections on equality by examining what they have to say about actual social relations. In this paper, I have chosen to focus on one specific question, namely the scope and the limits of the obedience owed by a subordinate to a superior. As we would expect, in this period relations of authority and obedience were pervasive in the family and in religious life; a wife was expected to obey her husband, children (even adult children) were expected to obey their father, and members of a religious community were expected to obey their abbot, abbess, or other superior. Serfs owed obedience to their lord (or lady—feudal authority could be exercised by women), and soldiers owed obedience to their commanders. In addition, a wide range of civic and ecclesiastical obligations could be treated under the rubric of obedience; for example, we find the secular theologian William of Auxerre, writing in the early decades of the thirteenth century, discussing the obligations of a priest to his bishop, and of royal officials to the king, under the rubric of the virtue of obedience (*Summa aurea* III.15.4.2,3).

Whatever specific forms they take, relations of authority and obedience might appear to reflect a social situation which is antithetical to equality. Yet seen from another perspective, social norms governing authority and obedience can provide one of the most significant practical expressions of equality as a social ideal, because these norms will reflect the kinds of constraints on authority and the limits to obedience which are thought to be appropriate in a particular society. These limits and constraints need not be justified in terms of an ideal of equality, but when they are, they offer a window into the embodied meaning of this ideal. And in fact, at least some scholastic authors do appeal to ideals of equality, drawn from the natural law tradition, in order to delimit the boundaries of authority and obedience. In the second half of this paper, I will examine the discussions of obedience offered by two such authors, Bonaventure and Aquinas.

Obedience and Authority in Bonaventure and Aquinas

The Franciscan Bonaventure and the Dominican Aquinas were almost exact contemporaries who were born within five years of each other (Bonaventure in 1221, Aquinas sometime around 1225) and died in the same year, 1274. Both were scholastic theologians who spent a significant part of their adult lives in the University of Paris, although Bonaventure, unlike Aquinas, also held ecclesial office, first assuming leadership of the Franciscans in 1257 as the minister general of the Franciscan order and then assuming the position of cardinal bishop of Albano in 1273.[19]

Contemporary scholarship has emphasized the differences between Bonaventure and Aquinas, and they certainly offer two distinctive theological positions. At the same time, however, they share important points of contact. Most importantly from our standpoint, both are mendicant theologians who are deeply involved in the controversies surrounding the practices and the status of the mendicants in the thirteenth century; both write extensively in defense of the mendicants, and these defenses provide them with occasions for considering, *inter alia*, the significance and limits of the virtue of obedience.[20] Indeed, the theological differences between Bonaventure and Aquinas make their points of contact on these issues all the more interesting. At the same time, the comparison between the two is skewed in one way; that is, Aquinas writes more extensively on obedience than does Bonaventure, considering obedience not only in the context of organized religious life, but also in other social contexts. This difference may partially be due to the fact that Aquinas did more purely academic writing, but it also stems from a difference in their substantive views about the grounds of authority.

In what follows, I will focus on Bonaventure's discussion of obedience in the *Quaestiones disputatae de perfectione evangelica* (hereafter, DPE), and Aquinas' discussions in the *Summa theologiae* (ST).[21] Let us turn first to Bonaventure.

The *De perfectione evangelica*, as its name implies, presents Bonaventure's views on the nature of evangelical perfection. More specifically, it provides a defense of the mendicant movement as one framework for pursuing evangelical perfection, a defense which was occasioned by vitriolic attacks on the mendicant orders by some members of the secular clergy. In the process of explaining and defending the mendicant way of life, Bonaventure takes up specific questions of practice, and for this reason his treatise provides us with a valuable witness to the way in which the ideals of the mendicant movement were given practical force— particularly valuable, since Bonaventure himself assumed leadership of the Franciscans at about the time that it was composed.

This treatise is structured around the three vows which were by now recognized as standard to organized religious life, namely, poverty, chastity, and obedience. The question which concerns us most directly here is the fourth and last question of the treatise, concerning obedience, which is further divided into three articles: 4.1 on the legitimacy of obedience, 4.2 on whether it is legitimate to bind oneself to obey by a vow, and 4.3 on whether it is appropriate for all Christians to obey one supreme authority, that is to say, the Pope.

As this outline indicates, Bonaventure is particularly concerned with the legitimacy of obedience in religious and ecclesial contexts. However, he begins his discussion with the general question, whether obedience is consistent with the natural law. After all, obedience cannot be considered to be a praiseworthy aspect of organized religious life if it turns out to be an illegitimate practice. By raising this question, Bonaventure alerts us to the fact that the understanding of the natural law which he shared with his contemporaries did render authority and obedience problematic for them, and the arguments which he adduces are representative of those which were brought forward in this context. He will ultimately claim that obedience is morally legitimate, but in so doing, he also attempts to preserve key elements of the natural law arguments for the natural equality of all persons.

In the usual scholastic fashion, Bonaventure frames his discussion of the legitimacy of obedience by first reviewing the arguments on each side, beginning with ten arguments in support of the view that obedience is consonant with the natural law, and then proceeding to offer ten arguments that it is not. On the positive side, he first adduces the duty of obedience which children owe to their parents, supported by both natural piety and scriptural injunctions. This claim is developed over the first three arguments; he then sets forth a series of further arguments, most of which take the form of a claim that some aspect of human life in society which is grounded in the natural law, for example, domestic peace, presupposes or implies obedience. We clearly see Augustine's influence here, and his *City of God* is cited twice in support of the fundamental naturalness of a society which incorporates differences of status and grades of authority and subordination (at DPE 4.1 *obj.* 4 and 6). None of these arguments necessarily implies that obedience is a virtue, but they do offer at least indirect support for its legitimacy in terms of the natural law, and suggest strongly that in some circumstances obedience is morally obligatory.

These kinds of arguments reflect a widespread sense of what medieval views on the natural social order would be, and for this reason, it is somewhat surprising to turn to Bonaventure's next set of arguments, to the effect that domination and subordination, and by implication, obedience, are contrary to the natural law (DPE 4. 1 *contra* 1-10). Even more surprisingly, these are remarkably strong and direct arguments, backed up by impressive authorities such as Gregory the Great and even, surprisingly, Augustine himself (at DPE 4.1 *contra* 2 and 4). The first of these sets the tone: It is God's will, we read, that the human person, who is made in the divine image, should be subject only to God (DPE 4. 1 *contra* 1). This is followed by Gregory's uncompromising claim that we are all equal by nature, and by the further claim that inequality among human persons was introduced by sin

(DPE 4.1 *contra* 2, 3). This is followed by an argument, similar to the first, that subordination is inconsistent with the dignity of the divine image (DPE 4.1 *contra* 4). In the fifth argument, Bonaventure quotes what was by now a catch-phrase to the effect that according to the natural law, all persons are equally free, and adds that all persons possess that free judgment which makes freedom possible. The remaining five arguments include the claims that obedience is contrary to charity, and that it presupposes someone in authority, which authority is a temptation to pride—hardly the kinds of considerations which would suggest that obedience is a virtue.

To a contemporary reader, Bonaventure's assembly of twenty natural law arguments, ten of which cancel out the other ten, might well appear to be at best uncritical, at worst simply so much window dressing for a predetermined conclusion. Such a view would be unfair both to Bonaventure and to the scholastic conception of the natural law which he represents.[22] On this view, the expression "natural law" is a kind of short hand for whatever can be considered as a pre-conventional starting point for morality; hence, those instincts which we share with all other animals, rational norms of conduct, and the capacity for moral discernment are all spoken of as forms of natural law. God's will as expressed in Scripture provides the indispensable key for interpreting the natural law and is itself in some sense a form of natural law, although this does not imply that rational discernment and social practice are empty or superfluous in discerning the natural law. When his discussion of obedience is placed in this context, Bonaventure's point in setting forth so many natural law arguments for and against the naturalness of obedience does not appear to be different from the starting point for many contemporary arguments over equality—that is, there are some respects in which persons do seem to be naturally equal, and others in which they are not.

The critical question, of course, is where we go from there. For many of our contemporaries, the ambiguity attaching to claims for natural equality leads to the conclusion that this is a kind of benevolent fiction, something that we assume even if we do not really believe it. Bonaventure, however, presses forward to offer an interpretation of the natural law which will allow him to affirm the legitimacy of some forms of dominion and subordination while still holding on to the claim that by the natural law, all persons are in some sense equal. In order to do so, he once again draws on Augustine, observing that the natural law is the impression within the human soul of God's eternal law. As such, it is permanent and unchangeable in its general principles, but admits of differences of application in accordance with the different conditions of human existence (DPE 4.1 *conclusio*).

As Bonaventure goes on to indicate, the key natural law principle in this context is expressed by Augustine's claim in the *City of God* 19.13 that "Order is an arrangement of equal and unequal things, allocating its place to each." In other words, the key principle of the natural law in this context is the naturalness, the necessity, and the fundamental goodness of order, which in the context of human society implies some framework of authority and subordination, even though this, as we will see, is only a limited and provisional implication.

So far, Bonaventure has shown the possibility of a legitimate form of authority and subordination, but he has not shown that there actually are any such forms, or what shape they might take. Accordingly, he goes on to observe that one person is said to be the superior of another in three respects: as a result of natural origin, or through the power of dominion or presidency, or as a result of the rule of providence. The first form of inequality is exemplified by the relation of parents to their children, and this is indeed the only form of authority and subordination which arises directly from pre-rational nature. The second form of inequality represents the introduction of servitude, which Bonaventure, reflecting the almost universal consensus of this period, considers to be a result of human sinfulness.[23] Finally, the third form of inequality has its proper place in the remedy for sin, that is to say, the life of grace itself, and is expressed through the obedience of subordinates to ecclesiastical authority. Correlatively, since the natural law takes on different expressions in the different conditions of human life, it can be said to prescribe obedience in three ways:

> Hence it is that the natural law prescribes filial obedience whether in accordance with the state of fallen nature, or the state of nature as originally constituted. It prescribes servile obedience, however, not without qualification, but in the state of fallen nature as a punishment of sin, in accordance with a dictate of the law of nations, which proceeds from reason and from an instinct of nature. It prescribes jurisdictional obedience in accordance with the state of nature as capable of being restored, or as restored, and this with respect to the condition of this life...Therefore, in accordance with the threefold differentiation of superiority, there is a threefold mode of obeying: the first, nature prescribes without qualification, because it does so universally and explicitly and with respect to every state; the second and third, however, it prescribes implicitly and in accordance with a specific state (DPE 4.1 *conclusio*).

This certainly amounts to a defense of obedience, and correlatively, to a defense of the naturalness of social structures of inequality, but it is worth underscoring just how limited and conditional this defense is. Only one form of obedience, namely filial obedience, is said to be natural in a straightforward sense; other forms of obedience are only conditionally expressions of the natural law. Furthermore, with the exception of filial obedience, the natural law does not prescribe the specific forms which domination and subordination should take.

Bonaventure does not dwell on the question of which particular social structures might be appropriate, however, because his interests lie elsewhere. He wants to show that the practice of vowing obedience is praiseworthy, and in order to do so, he must first establish that it is consonant with the natural law. Turning in 4.2 to the legitimacy and value of a vow of obedience, he argues that such a vow is particularly praiseworthy, and integral to religious perfection, precisely because it comprises a surrender of that which is most valuable to a person, namely, the individual's capacities for freedom and self-direction. Because it represents the surrender of oneself, obedience represents the greatest form of humility and liberality, and it is particularly appropriate for someone seeking evangelical perfection, since it is one form of the imitation of Christ.

Understood in this way, the practice of vowed obedience represents a more complex set of values than we might at first have assumed. Precisely because it is construed as a surrender of what is valuable, it reflects the high value which this society placed on individual freedom. By the same token, because vowed obedience is freely chosen, it presupposes a fundamental equality between superior and subordinate, which makes the humility and generosity of the latter even more valuable and precious. More tellingly, Bonaventure is not prepared to endorse the idea that obedience requires the complete and unconditional surrender of one's own judgment. In response to an objection that it is an act of rashness to vow obedience to someone whose character and wisdom are unknown quantities, Bonaventure responds that

> if someone were to commit himself [to obey another] in any eventuality, presupposing no law, norm, or rule, without doubt this would be foolish. When, however, someone vows obedience in accordance with an approved form of the rule, there is no danger in this, because certain things are in accordance with the rule, certain things are above the rule, and certain things are contrary to the rule. With respect to the first, he binds himself even apart from the command of a superior; with respect to the second, he binds himself to the command; with respect to the third, however, he is not bound, unless he wills to do it for the sake of perfection, just as the blessed Benedict says, that whoever obeys perfectly ought to submit, even if something impossible is imposed on him. This, however, is not necessary, but pertains to what is supererogatory even for those who are perfect. That however which is contrary to the rule is in no way, by no consideration bound to be observed through obedience, and similarly, whatever is contrary to the law of God, that is, whatever is prejudicial to our salvation or to the divine honor. And thus no one incurs danger by undertaking a vow in accordance with the established mode (DPE 4.2 ad 13).

Hence the obligation of vowed obedience presupposes an established framework of mutual relations, reflecting both the rule of the religious community and a wider network of moral and ecclesial laws. This framework places constraints on the obligations of obedience, not only by ruling out immoral commands, but also delimiting a space, even for religious, in which obedience is praiseworthy but not strictly required. Furthermore, it presupposes the subordinate's own active judgment with respect to the appropriateness of the commands he or she receives, and correlatively, presupposes that the religious has a right or even a duty to refuse some commands. In short, even within the framework of vowed religious life, there is still a recognized place for the exercise of free judgment.

By the same token, Bonaventure's restriction on the scope of the obligation generated by a vow of obedience provides a space for the expression of the natural equality of persons. This implication is not evident from the text we are considering, but when we turn to Bonaventure's other writings, the significance of the restrictions he proposes become clear. In his writings on conscience and the natural law, Bonaventure argues that the basic precepts of the natural law are known to all persons through the operation of reason functioning through the conscience.[24] This innate capacity for moral discernment, together with the fundamental orientation of the will towards goodness which Bonaventure identifies with *synderesis*, is present in all persons. As such, it reflects the most fundamental way in which all persons are equal, namely in the common possession of rationality, in virtue of which all persons are (actually or potentially) capable of rational action, self-direction and moral discernment. Hence, by allowing subordinates in a religious community to exercise discretion in practicing obedience, Bonaventure is in effect acknowledging the natural equality of superior and subordinate with respect to the common possession of a capacity for rational discernment and self-direction.

I have already noted that Aquinas' discussions of obedience do not offer exact parallels to Bonaventure's treatment. The nearest parallels that we find occur in the brief discussions of vowed obedience in the *Contra impugnantes* C.1, the *De perfectione vitae spiritualis* 10, and the relevant questions of the *Summa contra gentiles* (SCG III. 130) and the *Summa theologiae* (ST II-II 186.5). A comparison of these texts with Bonaventure's discussion indicates that Aquinas understands vowed obedience in much the same way as Bonaventure does, and values it for the same reasons: It represents the greatest possible self-surrender and offers a particularly eminent way to the imitation of Christ. However, taken by themselves these texts do not tell us much about the limits of obedience, as Aquinas sees them. For this, we need to turn first to the general discussion of obedience in the ST, II-II 104-105.

These questions occur in the context of Aquinas' discussion of the virtue of justice, comprising questions II-II 57-122 of the ST. Seen within this context, the virtue of obedience is not just a component of evangelical perfection, but a moral duty, and correlatively a virtue, which has a place in every human life. More specifically, obedience is one of those virtues, like piety or gratitude, which are attached to justice even though they do not fully exemplify the equality which is proper to justice per se (ST II-II 80.1 *ad* 3). Obedience is a distinct virtue because it concerns a specific kind of human good, and its object is the express or implied command of a superior (ST II-II 104.2).

Like Bonaventure, Aquinas considers but rejects the claim that relations of authority and subordination are themselves illegitimate. We also find here, even more prominently than in Bonaventure, the argument that God created the human person free, willing that the individual should be governed only by his or her own judgment (this is the first of three objections offered at II-II 104.1, "Whether one person is bound to obey another?") However, he takes a different line than does Bonaventure. Just as lower creatures are moved by higher creatures in the order of natural causality, so in the realm of human action, the will of a subordinate is appropriately moved by the command of superior authority. However, this does not imply that a subordinate surrenders his or her own judgment and will: "God leaves the human person in the hand of his own counsel, not because it is licit for him to do everything he wants, but because he is not bound to that which is to be done by a necessity of nature, as irrational creatures are, but by free choice proceeding from his own deliberation. And just as other things which are to be done must proceed from his own deliberation, so this also, that he obeys his superiors . . . . " (II-II 104.1 *ad* 1).

This qualification suggests that Aquinas, again like Bonaventure, is going to resist any suggestion that the obligations of obedience are absolute and unconditional. When we come to II-II 104.5, "Whether subordinates are bound to obey their superiors in all things?" we find that this is indeed the case. Continuing with his parallel between natural causes and human action, Aquinas first observes that in the realm of human action, as in the interplay of natural causes, it is possible that some intervening consideration can prevent a higher authority or force from acting on a lower. The first of these stems from the interposition of a third, still higher authority, namely God; no one is bound to obey another in contravention of God's law, but is on the contrary positively obliged not to obey such a command. This is hardly surprising, of course.

However, Aquinas goes on to qualify the obligation of obedience in another way. "No inferior is held to obey a superior if he commands something in which [the inferior] is not subordinated" (ST II-II 104.5), and for this reason, no one is obliged to obey another human being with respect to those things which pertain to the inner motions of the will. The scope of human obedience extends only to those things which are done externally through the body, and the parameters of obedience in a given context are further delimited by the rationale for the form of authority in question, such that, for example, a soldier is required to obey in military matters. Furthermore, just as the obligation to obedience is grounded in nature, so nature sets limits on the extent of this obligation:

> With respect to those things which pertain to the nature of the body, a human person is not obliged to obey another human person, but only God, because human persons are equal by nature, for example, in those

things which pertain to the sustaining of the body and the generation of children. Hence, those in a state of servitude are not obliged to obey their lord, nor are children obliged to obey their parents, with respect to contracting matrimony or preserving virginity, or anything else of this sort (ST II-II 104.5).

It should be noted that Aquinas is here commenting on what was still a relatively recent development in church law. The right of those in a state of servitude to marry without the consent of their lord had been contested in the eleventh and twelfth centuries. Gratian, whose compilation of canon law (ca. 1140) became the definitive text for scholastic thought, defended this right, but it was not finally incorporated into church law until an 1155 decree of Hadrian IV, *Dignum est*, which unequivocally affirmed the right of men and women in servile condition to marry without their master's approval.[25] Subsequently, we continue to find serfs appealing to the Holy See for the right to marry without their lord's consent, and the Holy See consistently supported these claims. Aquinas thus offers a theological support for what was by his time the official church position on the freedom to marry, even though this right was almost certainly not always respected in practice.

There is one form of obedience which is conspicuously absent in Aquinas' comprehensive analysis; what about the obedience which a wife owes to her husband? In order to see what Aquinas' views are on this form of obedience, we need to turn to his scripture commentaries, where he takes up the issue in some detail in commenting on the Pauline injunctions to wives to obey their husbands. In commenting on Ephesians 5.22, he remarks that a wife is obliged to obey her husband in all things, excepting of course injunctions which go contrary to the law of God; however, he adds, this is not a servile obedience, because the husband's dominion over his wife (and children) is exercised for the sake of their common utility, and not for his own self-interest (*Ad ephesios* 5. 8). On the face of it, this account of obedience offers a more unlimited and much less nuanced account of the scope of the obligations entailed by obedience than we find in the *Summa*.

However, Aquinas' remarks on obedience in a marital context need to be placed in the context of his remarks elsewhere on the marital debt, that is to say, the obligation of each spouse to provide sexual gratification to the other (*1 Ad Corinthios* 7.1). In this respect, Aquinas says, husband and wife are equal; each of them can ask, and neither can refuse. (Here again, Aquinas' writings reflect contemporary church law; not only was the obligation to render the marital debt considered to oblige on pain of mortal sin, it could be, and was, defended in a court of law.[26]) This does not exactly limit the wife's obligation to obey her husband, but it does mean that in one critical respect, he is equally obligated to obey her. Moreover, this helps to explain why Aquinas does not discuss marital obedience explicitly in the article of the *Summa* just cited. "With respect to those things which pertain to the nature of the body," the equality of husband and wife is preserved through a framework of mutual obedience, and in other matters, the authority of the husband would have the same rationale (and perhaps, the same limits?) as the authority of a parent over a child, namely, "the discipline of life and domestic well-being (*ST* II-II 104.5)."

We are now in a position to compare Bonaventure and Aquinas on the virtue of obedience and the ideal of equality presupposed by that ideal. The first point to emerge from such a comparison is that Bonaventure and Aquinas share the same basic orientation in their approach to these questions. Both place a high value on the virtue of obedience, but at the same time, both also value the capacities for free judgment and self-determination which they take to be fundamental human qualities. So far from these two aspects of their thought being at odds with one another, their analyses of why obedience is a virtue presupposes the goodness of freedom. It is precisely because freedom is so valuable that obedience exemplifies a praiseworthy humility and liberality—a point which is central to Bonaventure's analysis, but which Aquinas also makes. Moreover, both Bonaventure and Aquinas presuppose the goodness of human freedom in their analysis of the scope and limits of a praiseworthy obedience. For both, there are occasions when a subordinate need not obey, or should not obey, and this presupposes that the subordinate continues to exercise judgment and choice in evaluating commands and deciding whether to carry them out. In this respect, superior and subordinate stand on one plane as two persons who are equally capable of free judgment and equally responsible before God for the right use of their freedom; the relation between them does not obviate that fundamental equality, even though it does qualify it.

Yet there are also noteworthy differences between Bonaventure and Aquinas on this subject. Aquinas' analysis is more comprehensive than Bonaventure's, and as a result, he considers aspects of obedience which Bonaventure does not discuss. For this reason, Aquinas' account of the value of obedience places less emphasis on obedience as an exemplary expression of Christian humility and generosity, and more emphasis on obedience as one of those virtues which finds its place in the day to day functioning of human society. In addition, Aquinas makes explicit what Bonaventure only implies, namely, that the natural equality between persons limits the obligations of obedience. Finally, while both Bonaventure and Aquinas hold that we are all equal insofar as we all possess a rational nature and therefore have at least a potential for self-direction, Aquinas also grounds natural equality in commonalities which we share in virtue of our bodily existence.

How are we to account for these differences? The greater comprehensiveness of Aquinas' analysis is only a partial answer, since Bonaventure and Aquinas differ even where their analyses overlap. A more fundamental explanation lies in the difference between them with respect to the nature of political authority. To be more exact, Aquinas defends the possibility of a positive form of political authority which would have existed even in a community of unfallen men and women, whereas Bonaventure does not envision any such possibility. For this reason, Aquinas has both a need for, and the resources to develop, a more comprehensive account of obedience.

As we have seen, Bonaventure recognizes three forms of superiority and subordination: the relation of parents to children, that of masters to their servants or slaves, and that of religious superiors to their subordinates. The first form of authority and obedience appears to him to be straightforward, and the third is understood by him in terms of the dynamics of charity working itself out in the conditions of the present age. So far as this analysis goes, every other form of superiority and subordination falls under the second category. That is, every relation of authority in civil society, excepting only the relation between parents and children, is understood to be a form of servitude, and as such, to be the result of human sinfulness.

Most of the scholastic theologians in the twelfth and thirteenth centuries approached the question of authority in the same was as Bonaventure does, with, of course, considerable variation in detail. They were well aware of the stock phrase from Roman law according to which the natural law prescribes that all possessions be held in common, and that all persons enjoy the same free status.[27] Yet clearly, society is not structured in this way. The scholastics typically deal with the resulting paradox by appealing to another ancient idea, pre-Christian in origin although now interpreted in terms of a Christian doctrine of the fall, according to which both servitude and property were introduced into human society as a result of corruption and sin. This might seem to suggest that inequality can be eliminated once sin is eliminated. In fact, some of the communities of penitents which arose among the devout laity at this time did draw just that conclusion, claiming to have no need for social hierarchies among themselves since they were freed from sin. The scholastics were not so optimistic, however. They held that original sin and its effects would be present until the end of time, and by the same token, so would social inequalities.

Although he shares many aspects of the scholastic approach to property and political authority, Aquinas breaks with this consensus in one critical respect. For him at least some forms of political authority are natural in the sense of stemming from uncorrupted human nature—those, specifically, in which one person governs others for their sake and the sake of their common well-being. This form of authority, he argues, is essential to the proper functioning of any group of people living together, and since it is natural to the human person to live in society, some forms of authority are natural and would have existed even in Paradise *(ST* I 96.4).

This claim is reminiscent of Aristotle's argument for the naturalness of social hierarchies in the *Politics*, and in all likelihood Aquinas' defense of the naturalness of political authority has been inspired by Aristotle. Nonetheless, it should be emphasized that there are critical differences between Aquinas' account of political authority and Aristotle's social analysis. For Aristotle, social hierarchies reflect natural divisions among human persons; only some persons are capable of rational judgment and self-control, whereas others lack this capacity altogether (natural slaves), or else possess capacities for judgment but not self-control (women; see the *Politics* I. 4-5, 12-13). Aquinas, in contrast, consistently denies that human persons are unequal in these fundamental ways. He does say that women are generally less reasonable than men (ST I 92.1 *ad* 2). Yet this is clearly a difference of degree and not kind, since as he repeatedly reminds us, with respect to the fundamental rational nature of the human soul there is no distinction between the sexes (ST I 93.4 *ad* 2, 6 *ad* 2; II-II 177.2); at any rate, the relative superiority of men over women does not apply in every case (ST II-II 177.2). He does not object to women holding secular authority over men (as he says in his commentary on Peter Lombard's *Sentences*, *IV Sent.* 25.2 *ad* 1a), and in fact, one of his treatises, the *De regimine judaeorum*, is addressed to a female ruler.

Similarly, Aquinas reinterprets Aristotle's remarks on natural slaves in such a way as to deny, in effect, that there are any such. It is true, he notes, that someone in a servile or subordinate condition does not exercise prudence *as* a slave or serf; but because every human person possesses capacities for rational judgment and self-direction, it is proper to such persons to exercise prudence, precisely as human beings (ST II-II 47.12). Compare this to Aristotle's claim cited above that a natural slave is constitutionally incapable of exercising prudence. More generally, Aquinas explicitly denies that social inequality is grounded in differences of nature among human beings (ST I 109.2 *ad* 3)—in contrast to the demons, whose hierarchical differences *do* reflect natural differences (as do the hierarchical distinctions among the angels, at least in part; see ST I 108.4). Finally, and most tellingly, Aquinas does not follow Aristotle in saying that servitude, as such, is natural. He agrees with the medieval consensus that servitude, involving dominion over a subordinate for the sake of the master, has only been introduced into human life as a result of sin; his distinctiveness lies rather in the fact that he identifies another form of authority between adults that is not a form of servitude (ST I 96.4).

At any rate, whatever Aquinas' account of political authority owes to Aristotle, it owes at least as much to Augustine. Like Bonaventure, Aquinas takes his key texts for justifying authority and obedience from Augustine's *City of God*, including the critical text in defense of social order which was also central for Bonaventure's analysis (cf. ST I 96.3 *sed contra*, which cites the *City of God* 19.2). Nor is this simply window-dressing; the logic of Aquinas' analysis indicates that he is attempting to draw out the implications of Augustine's claim. If society is natural to the human person, and if a good order sustained by human authority is necessary to human society, then authority must be considered to be an integral part of human life, and not simply an accommodation to sin; this is the logic of his analysis. Bonaventure does not go in this direction. From his own perspective, there was no reason for him to do so. He is interested in authority and obedience within the church, and within that context, different issues arise.

As their shared dependence on Augustine would suggest, the views of authority and obedience put forth by Bonaventure and Aquinas are in some respects quite similar. They agree that servitude is a consequence of sin which would not have existed without the Fall. Moreover, they agree on the fundamental value of an orderly society and on the necessity for structures of authority and obedience to sustain that social order. Seen from this perspective, the difference between Bonaventure and Aquinas is not great; for Bonaventure, authority and obedience are conditionally natural, that is to say, appropriate expressions of the natural law in less than ideal circumstances, whereas for Aquinas there are at least some forms of authority between adults which are natural to the human person without qualification.

Furthermore, to the extent that Bonaventure and Aquinas do differ, it might appear that it is Bonaventure who takes the more radically egalitarian position. After all, on Aquinas' view, there are at least some forms of authority between adults which are fundamentally natural and positive. Bonaventure does not admit this. For him, secular authority between adults always reflects a departure from the ideal that would have obtained in a pre-lapsarian society. Furthermore, Aquinas is more prepared than Bonaventure, or most of his other contemporaries and immediate successors, to discuss the ways in which persons are naturally unequal; even in Paradise, he says, we would have found differences of sex, age, ability, attainment, and holiness (ST I 96.3).

Yet paradoxically, Aquinas is able to develop a more comprehensive account of natural equality, precisely because he considers some forms of authority to be natural, in the sense of stemming from uncorrupted human nature. Bonaventure shares in the widespread scholastic view that human persons are naturally equal without qualification, and therefore the inequalities which we find in secular society, at least those outside the ambit of family relationships, are the results of sin. Since this is the case, it is difficult to develop criteria for determining the limits and the scope of political authority. To the extent that civil authority is seen as either punitive in character, or at best as an accommodation to a sinful society, it is difficult to identify criteria for better and worse, more or less appropriate ways of exercising that authority. This tendency should not be exaggerated; the scholastics did recognize limits to political authority, set by God's law and for some, at least, also set by the obligations of the civil authorities to dispense justice. But they found it difficult to offer a systematic rationale for these limits. The difficulty does not stem from a general sense that obedience should not be unconditional, as Bonaventure's strong words about the stupidity of such a vow indicate. However, it does reflect the practical limitations of what would seem at first to be a radically egalitarian view.

In contrast, Aquinas' analysis of the natural origins of authority, while it appears on the surface to be the less radical position, offers greater resources for developing an account of natural equality which has normative force. Because the origins of political authority are natural, the scope and the limits of authority can likewise be determined through an intelligent reflection on nature. This analysis offers a set of parameters which can then be applied even to forms of authority which are not grounded in primitive human nature, that is to say, forms of servitude, on the general principle that the determinations of human law cannot override natural and divine law (cf. ST II-II 66.7). By the same token, Aquinas is able to identify respects in which we are all equal by nature, precisely because he acknowledges that there are some respects in which we are not equal by nature. What appears at first to be a straightforward assertion of natural inequality turns out on closer inspection to be a nuanced account of the different respects in which human beings are equal and unequal by nature. Aquinas' account of natural equality is carefully limited, but for that very reason, he is able to offer a plausible case for a sense of natural equality which has real normative force.

Some Concluding Observations

While it might seem strange to turn to medieval discussions of obedience for insights into the ideal of equality as we understand it and try to live it out today, I hope that I have shown that these discussions do have something to offer us. Let me suggest three lessons that we can draw from them.

First, as the comparison between Bonaventure and Aquinas indicates, there is no necessary inconsistency between defending a norm of equality and admitting that there are some senses in which persons are naturally unequal. On the contrary, a serious defense of natural equality, taken as a basis for a normative ideal of equality, presupposes that we take seriously the manifest fact that persons are unequal in so many ways. For this reason, both Bonaventure and Aquinas do so, although Aquinas' account is more developed than Bonaventure's. Bonaventure takes the starting point for his analysis from the inequality between parents and children, and Aquinas notes multiple inequalities of sex, age, and ability. These observations provide a framework within which to identify the commonalities which underlie these differences, commonalities which make it possible to speak of a human identity that is more basic than human differences. This human identity, in turn, provides the basis for an account of equality which is both descriptive and normative. For both Bonaventure and Aquinas, all persons are at least potentially capable of judgment and self-direction, and all persons should exercise these capacities, even in the very act of rendering obedience to another. Aquinas adds to this the observation that all persons are equal with respect to that which pertains to the human body; we all have bodies with certain characteristic needs and capacities (although the latter may be only potentially present in some cases), and this fact about us places constraints on what one person can demand of another.

These examples suggest that it is not so hard as some modern theorists suggest to identify some respects in which persons really are equal by nature. Certainly, we are unequal in all sorts of respects, but there are also some respects in which we are fundamentally alike. For both Aquinas and Bonaventure, equality is grounded in key capacities or features of existence which we all share, even if we possess them in differing degrees; we are all capable of judgment, even though some persons are better at it than others, and we all have animal bodies with basic needs and capacities, even though we differ widely with respect to both our needs and our physical capacities.

At the same time, this line of analysis does not presuppose that natural equality is a "fact of nature" which can be read off from observation, prior to any theoretical commitments. For both Bonaventure and Aquinas, norms of equality are not derived from pre-theoretical observations of human nature; rather, they represent interpretations of that nature which are informed both by a normative commitment to equality and by a wider set of theoretical commitments. Does this imply that the scholastic ideal of equality represents nothing more than an ideological construct imposed on the indifferent facts of observation? Is there any real sense in which this represents a norm of natural equality, a norm given by nature, as opposed to a norm that we impose on nature?

These questions raise some of the most basic and controversial issues in contemporary social theory, and I am not going to try to settle them now. Yet I would suggest, with all due tentativeness, that the accounts of equality that we have been examining are not just projections onto experience, but interpretations of aspects of human existence which are genuinely there. If we are going to allow for the possibility of any realistic description of human nature at all, then Bonaventure and Aquinas have identified what certainly seem to be plausible candidates for such descriptions: we are characteristically capable of self-direction, we are likewise characteristically capable of reproducing ourselves and we have certain needs as physical, bodily creatures. (Characteristically, even if not always actually; this reflects one of the most fundamental theoretical commitments of all, to the reality of a species-specific nature the essential elements of which are potentially present in each member of the species, even if they are not always actualized. This is why neither Bonaventure nor Aquinas has much of a theoretical problem with infants and the handicapped; they are included within the scope of our regard in virtue of their participation in a common nature.)

What Bonaventure and Aquinas bring to their observations about human nature is a normative and theoretical framework within which to interpret characteristic features of our existence. Most importantly, this framework leads them to give more weight to those respects in which we are similar, than to those in which we are diverse. In this, they reflect their milieu, since the experiences of the twelfth and thirteenth centuries gave salience to the capacities for freedom, self-determination, and spiritual aspiration. At the same time, however, the facts of human existence shape the interpretative framework, which would have no plausibility unless we did share certain basic needs and capacities.

This brings me to a final point. The scholastic accounts of equality which we have been examining represent one plausible construal of human nature, but this is of course not the only possible construal; we might, for example, construe equality in utilitarian terms as equality of capacities for pleasure or suffering. As this example suggests, it is at best highly misleading to speak of one norm of equality, or much less to identify this as a universal principle of morality. A general ideal of equality has very little meaning without some account of just how it is that we are equal and why it matters. And this account cannot be derived from reflection on the concept of equality by itself; it calls for both theory and social practice.

If this is so, then a further question arises. That is, I have emphasized the distinctiveness and the social specificity of the scholastic concept of equality; but do not these very aspects of the concept render it irrelevant to our own times? After all, our society is very different from that of the thirteenth century, and so it would seem that concepts of equality developed in that society can have very little relevance to our own society.

Here again it will not be possible in this paper to settle the complex and much-debated issues that this question raises. Let me simply offer two observations. First, we need to distinguish understanding a concept from appropriating it. Certainly, we cannot fully understand a moral or social concept without seeing it in the context out of which it emerged. Yet this fuller comprehension of a moral concept does not at all prevent us from going on to reformulate it for application in our own period. We might question whether, at the end of this process of reformulation, what we have is still the same concept, but this ambiguity does not call into question either the validity of the initial interpretation, or the legitimacy of the subsequent appropriation. Secondly, the distance between the medieval world and our own, while very real, should not be exaggerated. To a very considerable extent, the institutions which structure modern western society are descended from twelfth and thirteenth century antecedents, and by the same token the social ideals of our own day are in part late developments of medieval social ideals.

At any rate, we need not fear that an affirmation of equality as a Christian norm will compromise the distinctively theological character of our Christian ethic. Equality as understood within a Christian context will not look the same as equality interpreted from within the framework of, say, a full-bodied utilitarianism. If Christian defenses of equality sometimes seem to resemble secular ideals, I would suggest that this has as much to do with the theological origins of what we think of today as secular liberalism, as with any supposed secularization of Christian theology. But that is a topic for another day.[28]

NOTES

[1] I argue for the centrality of the concept of equality to scholastic natural law thought in more detail in *Natural and Divine Law: Reclaiming the Tradition for Christian Ethics* (Ottawa: Novalis Press and Grand Rapids: Eerdmans, 1999).

[2] In addition to the specific sources cited below, in this section I rely on the following: Giles Constable, *The Reformation of the Twelfth Century* (Cambridge: Cambridge University Press, 1996); C. H. Lawrence, *The Friars: The Impact of the Early Mendicant Movement on Western Society* (London: Longman, 1994); Lester K. Little, *Religious Poverty and the Profit Economy in Medieval Europe* (Ithaca, NY: Cornell University Press, 1978); Orlando Patterson, *Freedom in the Making of Western Culture* (New York: Basic Books, 1991); R. W. Southern, *Scholastic Humanism and the Unification of Europe, Vol. I: Foundations* (Oxford: Blackwell, 1995); and Hendrik Spruyt, *The Sovereign State and Its Competitors* (Princeton, NJ: Princeton University Press, 1994), 59-150. For a very helpful brief discussion of medieval political thought seen in its social and institutional context, see Janet Coleman, *A History of Political Thought from the Middle Ages to the Renaissance* (Oxford: Blackwell, 2000), 5-80.

[3] For further information on family structures in medieval times, see David Herlihy, *Medieval Households* (Cambridge, MA: Harvard University Press, 1985); the material covered in chapters 3 and 4, 56-111, is most relevant to this paper. In addition, for a good discussion which gives special attention to the status of women, see Penelope D. Johnson, *Equal in Monastic Profession: Religious Women in Medieval France* (Chicago: Chicago University Press, 1991), 13-61; the book as a whole contains much helpful information on organized religious life in the period at hand. Finally, James Brundage provides an exhaustive account of medieval social and institutional practices of marriage and sexual activity, with special attention to the eleventh and twelfth century reforms and their aftermath, in his *Law, Sex, and Christian Society in Medieval Europe* (Chicago: Chicago University Press, 1987); in particular, see 176-228.

[4] See Johnson, *Equal in Monastic Profession* 201-205 for details.

[5] Although some details of his work have since been questioned, Marc Bloch offers what is still the best overview of the structures of feudalism in *Feudal Society*, in two volumes, L. A. Manyon, translator (The University of Chicago Press, 1961)

[6] See Barbara Reynolds, *Fiefs and Vassals: The Medieval Evidence Reinterpreted* (Oxford University Press, 1994).

[7] This appears to be the current scholarly consensus, at any rate; for a good summary of the relevant arguments, see Pierre Bonnassie, *From Slavery to Feudalism in South-Western Europe*, Jean Birrell, translator (Cambridge: Cambridge University Press, 1991), 25-32.

[8] Over the past century, there has been considerable debate over when, and indeed whether chattel slavery was eliminated in Western Europe. I here follow Bonnassie, *From Slavery to Feudalism* 1-59. However, some have argued that chattel slavery was more common in medieval Europe than he recognizes; see for example, Patterson, *Freedom in the Making of Western Culture*, 347-352.

[9] In addition to Bloch, *Feudal Society*, Vol. 1, 255-274, see William Chester Jordan, *From Servitude to freedom: Manumission in the Sénonais in the Thirteenth Century* (Philadelphia: University of Pennsylvania Press, 1986) 19-34; for a framework within which to distinguish a slave from a serf, I rely on Orlando Patterson, *Slavery and Social Death: A Comparative Study* (Cambridge, MA: Harvard University Press, 1982), 172-208.

[10] Janet Coleman, "Property and Poverty," 607-648 in *The Cambridge History of Medieval Political Thought: c.350-c.1450*, J. H. Burns, editor (Cambridge University Press, 1988).

[11] All the authors mentioned above in note 2 advert to these developments, but they are central for Little, *Religious Poverty and the Profit Economy in Medieval Europe*, and he offers a particularly helpful analysis of the way in which these economic and social changes gave rise to the mendicant movement, with its own distinctive approach to social thought; see 171-217. For a similar analysis, see Lawrence, *The Friars* 1-25, 102-126.

[12] See in particular Southern, *Scholastic Humanism and the Unification of Europe* 134-144, 198-234.

[13] On the former point, see Herlihy, *Medieval Households* 100-101; on the latter, see M.T. Clanchy, *Abelard: A Medieval Life* (Oxford: Blackwell, 1997), 43-47.

[14] I argue for this in more detail in my *Natural and Divine Law*, 41-53. In addition, see Brian Tierney, *The Idea of Natural Rights: Studies on Natural Rights, Natural Law, and Church Law 1150-1625* (Atlanta: Scholars Press, 1997), 43-77.

[15] This point is particularly emphasized by Patterson, *Freedom in the Making of Western Culture*, 347-401.

[16] For further information on lay spiritual movements and their impact, see Little, *Religious Poverty and the Profit Economy in Medieval Europe*, 97-170, Lawrence, *The Friars*, 1-25 and Andre Vauchez, *Les laïcs au Moyen Age: Pratiques et expériences religieuses* (Paris: Cerf, 1987), especially 95-112 and 133-144.

[17] For further information, see Giles Constable, *The Reformation of the Twelfth Century* 262-263; the quote is taken from 262. In this paragraph, I rely largely on Constable 257-295.

[18] Again, this point is especially emphasized by Little, *Religious Poverty and the Profit Economy in Medieval Europe*, 97-170, and Lawrence, *The Friars*, 1-25.

[19] For helpful brief introductions to the life and thought of Bonaventure and Aquinas, see Michael Robson, "Saint Bonaventure," and Fergus Kerr, "Thomas Aquinas," 187-200 and 201-220 respectively in *The Medieval Theologians: An Introduction to Theology in the Medieval Period*, G.R. Evans, editor (Oxford: Blackwell, 2001).

[20] For further information on the controversies surrounding the mendicant movements and the responses of Franciscan and Dominican theologians to attacks by the secular clergy, see Lawrence, *The Friars* 152-165.

[21] It is difficult to determine the exact date of the DPE, but its place in the controversies over the mendicant movement suggests a date of about 1260. The ST was written between 1268 and 1273. In order to avoid further burdening the text with notes, all references to the texts of Aquinas and Bonaventure are incorporated into the body of the article. All translations are my own. The reader may consult any critical edition for the originals.

[22] I develop this interpretation of the scholastic concept of the natural law in more detail in *Natural and Divine Law*; see 48-53 for a summary statement of what I understand this concept to be.

[23] For a more detailed account of this position, with detailed documentation, see Rudolf Weigand, *Die Naturrechtslehre der Legisten und Dekretisten von Irnerius bis Accursius and und von Gratian bis Johannes Teutonicus* (Munich, Germany: Max Hueber, 1967), 259-282, 307-360. Note, however, that Weigand's study only includes the scholars of civil and canon law.

[24] See in particular Bonaventure's discussion of conscience in his commentary on the *Sentences* of Peter Lombard, *In II Sent.* 39.1.2. J.F. Quinn provides a detailed account of Bonaventure's treatment of the term in "St. Bonaventure's Fundamental Conception of Natural Law," 517-98 in *S. Bonaventura 1274-1974*, vol. 3 (Rome: College of St. Bonaventure, 1974).

[25] On this and other church legislation on the marriage of unfree persons, together with further information on subsequent challenges to this position, see Antonia Bocarius Sahaydachcy, "The Marriage of Unfree Persons: Twelfth Century Decretals and Letters," 483-506 in *De Jure Canonico Medii: Festschrift fur Rudolf Weigand, Studia Gratiana* XXVII (1996).

[26] Believe it or not; see Brundage, *Law, Sex, and Christian Society in Medieval Europe* 358-360.

[27] For further details, see *Natural and Divine Law* 247-259.

[28] This paper was originally given at the 2000 meeting of the Society of Christian Ethics, and I would like to thank those present for their comments and questions; I would also like to thank three anonymous referees of the *Annual of the Society of Christian Ethics* for their very helpful comments. Finally, I would like to acknowledge the support of the Institute for

Scholarship in the Liberal Arts of the College of Arts and Letters, the University of Notre Dame, which supported my work on this paper through a research grant for the summer of 2000.

JUDAISM AND BIOETHICS

Panel

Is There a Unique Jewish Bioethics?

Is There a Unique Jewish Ethics?
The Role of Law in Jewish Bioethics

Elliot N. Dorff

The direct answer to the question in the title of this essay is: "Yes and No." No, in that Jews are in many respects human beings like all other human beings, with the same pressures, sorrows, and joys, and, like people all over the world, Jews seek to do the good as they understand it. Thus some of the moral norms of Judaism are identical to those of many other traditions—norms, for example, requiring aid to the needy and prohibiting murder and theft. Moreover, Jewish ethics uses many resources, as do other religions and secular systems, to know the good, teach it, and motivate people to do the good. In these ways, then, Jewish ethics is like other moral systems of thought and practice.

There are many ways, however, in which Jewish ethics is indeed unique. The Jewish vision of the ideal person and society is a different picture from that in Christianity and most other religions and secular philosophies. Indeed, of the religions of the world, Islam may be the closest to Judaism, given the strong emphasis the two of them place on family and community and on improving life in this world. The varying perspectives in the world's religions and secular philosophies about "what is" and "what ought to be" produce, in turn, varying concrete moral norms. While I shall mention two of these at the end of this paper as illustrations of how Judaism differs in *content* from Christianity and from American secularism, the thrust of this paper will be instead on the differing *methodologies* Judaism employs to discern the good and motivate good behavior. Even there I will concentrate on one method that Judaism uses more than most other moral systems, and perhaps more than any other—namely, law.

Some of the Major Moral Methodologies of Judaism

Jews use many resources to know and motivate the good. These include:

1. *Stories.* For example, the core Jewish story—the Exodus from Egypt, the revelation at Mount Sinai, and the trek to the Promised Land—loudly proclaims that we can and must work together with God to redeem ourselves and others from slavery of all sorts. It also says that we must live our lives in accordance with revealed norms, and that we must continue to hope and work for the Promised Land of the Messianic age. (The State of Israel's anthem is *Hatikvah*, "The Hope.")

2. *History.* No nation that has gone through the exile and persecution endured by Jews can possibly have an idealistic picture of human beings; the evil that people have foisted on each other must be part of the Jewish perception of reality. This is, of course, all the more true after the Holocaust, which, among other things, makes Jews very wary of medical research on human subjects.

3. *Maxims and theories.* The biblical Book of Proverbs and the tractate of the Mishnah entitled *Ethics of the Fathers (Pirke Avot)* are two important reservoirs of moral maxims by which Jews are supposed to live their lives, and medieval and modern Jewish theories of morality (e.g., Maimonides' rationalism; Israel Salanter's nineteenth-century *Musar* movement) produced their own recipes for living a moral life.

4. *Theology.* All of Jewish morality is based, ultimately, on the biblical command that we should seek to be holy as God is holy (Leviticus 19:2). That has meant, in the Jewish tradition, that we must model ourselves after God: "As God clothes the naked, so should we . . . . As God visited the sick, so should we . . . . As God comforted those who mourned, so should we . . . . As God buried the dead, so should we . . . ."[1] Moreover, the revelation at Sinai made clear that we must seek to do what God wants of us, that moral action is commanded by God.

5. *General moral values.* The Torah announces some general moral values that should inform all our actions—values like formal and substantive justice, saving lives, caring for the needy, respect for parents and elders, honesty in business and in personal relations, truth telling, and education of children and adults. The Rabbis who created the Mishnah (c. 200 C.E.) and Talmud (c. 500 C.E.), the primary repositories of the Jewish Oral Torah, expanded on those and applied them to concrete circumstances. These general values continue to inform specific Jewish moral norms.

6. *Laws.* This is the methodology employed by Judaism on which I shall concentrate in this essay, and I will leave it to my colleagues on this panel to explore some of the other methods and content of the Jewish tradition.

I have chosen to discuss law for two reasons. First, Judaism puts a great deal of emphasis on law as a moral tool—more, I think, than any other tradition. The extent to which Judaism uses law for moral purposes is, I would argue, one important factor that makes Jewish ethics unique.

Second, classical Christian texts have a very negative view of law. The Gospels' view of the Pharisees as legalistic, especially in Matthew, sets the tone for seeing Jews as concerned only with details of rules and not with the broader aims that they have. Paul's description of law as leading people to sin and as the exact opposite of life lived by the Spirit is another major source of Christians' negative views of the law. Society may need laws as long as we live in Augustine's City of Man, but law is not, for Christian writers, the way to know what is right and good. So both the importance of law within Judaism and the disparaging attitude toward it within Christianity motivate me to focus on the role of law in Jewish morality.

The Problems with Using Law for Moral Purposes

Matthew and Paul were not altogether wrong. There are indeed problems in using law to discern moral norms and motivate moral behavior, just as there are problems in using every other method to accomplish those ends. No method—an authority figure (such as the Pope), individual conscience, popular will, a utilitarian calculus, principlism, fundamentalism vis-a-vis some text (such as the Bible or the Qur'an)—is free of problems, and any reasoned belief in a moral system must take into account both the advantages and disadvantages of the proposed moral method. I plan to do that here for law, and I would encourage all others to do the same for their preferred moral method.

What, then, are some of the problems in using law to know what is moral and to induce people to behave accordingly? Here are some of the most serious:

1. *The danger of becoming legalistic.* This was Matthew's concern. When law is used to define morality, some people can become so caught up in the details of the law that they lose sight of the goals of the law in the first place. This is indeed a fault that one must avoid. One can and should take a *legal* approach to moral matters–that is, one can apply laws and legal reasoning to moral questions– without becoming *legalistic* about it–that is, without becoming blind to the larger aims of the laws themselves. Indeed, a proper legal approach does precisely the opposite: it interprets specific laws with the larger convictions and values of the tradition in mind.

2. *The danger of producing sin.* This was Paul's worry:

> Except through the law I should never have become acquainted with sin. For example, I should never have known what it was to covet if the law had not said, "Thou shalt not covet." Through that commandment sin found its opportunity, and produced in me all kinds of wrong desires. In the absence of law, sin is a dead thing.[2]

There is, of course, truth to that claim: law can function to teach you how to rebel against moral norms and maybe even to tempt you to do that. I must say that in my experience law usually functions in the opposite way—that is, it teaches you how to carry out your good intentions in morally murky waters—and that those who want to act immorally do not need the definitions of the law to teach them how to do that. Still, if there were no norms, then sin would be impossible.[3]

3. *The danger of becoming too inflexible.* Since law functions to establish norms and to define them, laws may make it difficult, if not impossible, for people to respond appropriately to the need to revise norms when that is necessary. That is, law may make us too conservative and perhaps even reactionary if it is understood incorrectly as fixed rather than as a genre that permits and actually requires continual updating. To take one obvious example, laws permitting and even protecting slavery in the American South—reinforced by some of the laws of the Bible itself—added to other social and economic factors in making it hard to overturn that practice in this country.

The Advantages in Using Law for Moral Purposes

While fully understanding and acknowledging those problems in using law to define moral norms and motivate moral behavior, I now want to point out its advantages. This will hopefully explain why Judaism places so much store in law as one vehicle to instill moral knowledge and desire.[4]

1. *Law establishes a moral bottom line, a minimum standard of practice.* Because many moral values depend on the mutual action of a number of people, a minimum moral standard enforced as law enables a society to secure the cooperation necessary for such moral attainment. Furthermore, a beneficent act, whether done for the right reason or not, has its own objective value.

2. *Law translates moral goals into concrete rules.* It is not just on a minimal level that law is important for morality; at every level of moral aspiration law translates moral insight and fervor into modes of daily action. Without that translation, our moral vision and courage lose their meaning and influence.

So, for example, it is easy to call up a passionate affirmation of values like love and justice, but what does that mean in specific circumstances? For example, Deuteronomy 22:1-3 demands that when I come across any object that appears to have been lost, I must not ignore it but rather take steps to return it, even bringing it into my house until the owner comes for it. But how exactly am I supposed to carry out that biblical demand which combines concerns of love and justice? Suppose that when I announce that I have found the object, ten people claim it. How do I identify the real owner? What if I cannot? Suppose instead that nobody comes to claim it. Then, according to the Torah, I am required to take it into my house until the owner comes to claim it. How much effort must I expend to announce the fact that I have it? How much money must I spend in taking care of it? May I use it in the meantime? What if it is an animal (the biblical verse specifically mentions a wondering ox or sheep): at whose expense do I feed it? May I use the ox in plowing my field or shear the sheep's wool and sell it? What if it is a cat and I am allergic to cats? When, if ever, does the object become mine? The relatively simple moral command to return a lost object quickly becomes quite complex, and only if I know the answers to those questions can I carry out this demand for love and justice. It is exactly for that reason that the Rabbis spent an entire chapter of the Mishnah and Talmud—chapter two of *Bava Mezia*—to spell out what I must do to fulfill this demand and—just as importantly—what I am not required to do. If that is necessary even for a clear and direct command like returning a lost object, how much the more is this kind of detailed, legal analysis required to define the obligations of more complicated moral demands, as, for example, the demand to honor parents.

3. *Law helps us to decide among conflicting moral goals.* When moral values conflict, law provides a method for determining which value will take precedence over others, and under what circumstances. When a person is dying of a terminal illness, for example, when does my duty to do what I can to keep people alive cease and my duty not to delay the dying process with its attendant pain begin? Non-legal systems commonly rely on the sensitivity and analytic ability of the individual or an authority figure to do that; law enlists the minds and hearts of legislators, judges, and the public at large. Although such a process does not guarantee wisdom, it does at least provide a greater measure of objectivity and experience, hence a more thorough consideration of relevant elements.

4. *Law enables us to appreciate the reality, nuances, and immediacy of moral issues.* In contrast to moral treatises, which are usually general and non-directive, judicial decisions respond to concrete cases in which judges must ultimately make decisions. Thus in contrast to many "ivory-towerish" moral treatises, legal precedents respond to reality in all its complexity and provide specific instructions for action. Much of the classical Rabbis' sheer wisdom, in truth, can be attributed to the fact that they served as judges as well as scholars and teachers. Thus, the legal context adds a sense of immediacy, nuance, and reality to moral deliberation.

5. *Law helps to clarify and preserve the integrity of our moral intentions.* Law brings our motives into the arena of action, where we can see them clearly and work to change them if necessary. It is easy to deceive oneself into thinking that I always want the good thing, that I am, indeed, a good person. If I must demonstrate that character in concrete actions demanded by law, however, I discover exactly how good a person I actually am. Law thus helps to identify the depth of our moral intentions and to preserve their integrity, clarifying and verifying them in action.

6. *Law enables us to balance continuity with flexibility in defining the substance of moral norms.* Because law operates on the basis of precedent, it preserves a strong sense of continuity in a moral tradition. On the other hand,

through legal techniques like differentiation of the present case from previous ones, limiting the scope of previous cases, finding other analogous cases in the tradition that lead to a different conclusion, redefining some of the critical terms involved, or, ultimately, issuing a *takkanah*, that is, a "fixing" or changing of the law, law preserves a reasonable amount of flexibility and adaptability. Since, in the Jewish tradition, this process is in the hands of rabbis, whose ordination signifies that they are both committed to the tradition and schooled in it, such changes will not happen cavalierly—especially if any one rabbi's decision enters into a larger discussion among many rabbis—but will instead enable appropriate change to take place over time.

7. *Law preserves the coherence of a moral system.* If authorized judges in each generation—in the Jewish case, rabbis—are entrusted with the task of legal interpretation for their communities, then even if there is disagreement among them, we learn from their deliberations what counts as a legitimate approach to a given issue within the particular moral system—namely, a norm formulated in the judicial line of precedents within the system. This is all the more true if the judges have a communal method of setting parameters for legitimate dissent among them; the Sanhedrin did that for Jewish law in times past, and the Conservative Movement's Committee on Jewish Law and Standards functions in that way for the Conservative Movement now.[5] To achieve a measure of coherence, even Judaism's Reform movement, which puts so much emphasis on individual autonomy, has shown renewed interest and creativity in developing its own legal response to moral issues by creating a Committee on Halakhic [Jewish legal] Inquiry and by publishing books of rabbinic rulings.[6]

8. *Law establishes and preserves the authority of moral norms.* Jews have historically adopted legal methods primarily because they believed that this was the only way to preserve the divine authority of the tradition. Rabbinic authority ultimately rests on Deuteronomy 17:8-13, which provides that in each generation questions about the law (and hence about what God wants) should be addressed to the judge of that generation. One may not, as the Rabbis warn us, complain that this generation's judges pale by comparison to those of previous generations; instead, one must accept that "Jephtah in his generation is like Moses in his." Thus divine authority—and indeed continuing divine revelation—takes place in the form of judicial decisions throughout the generations.[7]

9. *Law is a vehicle to teach morality.* The law serves as a tool for moral education as well. Although theories of education are many and diverse, the Jewish tradition has a clear methodology for teaching morality:

> Rav Judah said in Rav's name: A person should always occupy himself/herself with Torah and good deeds, even if it is not for their own sake, for out of [doing good] with an ulterior motive the person will come to [do good] for its own sake.[8]

Study of the tradition complements this largely behavioristic approach to moral education. On balance, however, the emphasis is on action:

> An excellent thing is the study of Torah combined with some worldly occupation, for the labor demanded by both of them causes sinful inclinations to be forgotten. All study of the Torah without work must in the end be futile and become the cause of sin.[9]

The same educational theory is applied to moral degeneracy and repentance:

> Once a man has committed a sin and repeated it, it appears to him as if it were permitted.

> Run to fulfill even a minor precept and flee from the slightest transgression; for precept draws precept in its train, and transgression draws transgression.

> If [the opportunity for] a transgression comes to a person a first and second time and the person does not sin, he or she is immune from the sin.[10]

Formulating moral norms in terms of law is thus very important educationally; for by so doing people are *required* to act in accord with moral rules as a step in teaching them how to do the right thing for the right reason.

Beyond the Letter of the Law

In all of these ways, and undoubtedly in others, law contributes to our moral sensitivity and behavior. Still, the Jewish tradition, for all of its faith in law as a vehicle to define moral substance and engender moral behavior, understood that law cannot encompass all moral norms. The Rabbis therefore spoke of norms beyond the letter of the law (*lifnim mi-shurat ha-din*).

They stressed the importance of such norms in a variety of ways. First, they saw such norms as demanded by the Torah itself, specifically, by God's requirement that we "Do what is right and good in the sight of the Lord" (Deuteronomy 6:18).[11] Nahmanides (1194-1270) later spells this out explicitly:

> The intent of this [Deuteronomy 6:18] is that initially [in Deuteronomy 6:17] He had said that you should observe the laws and statutes that He had commanded you. Now He says that, with respect to what He has not commanded, you should likewise take heed to do the right and the good in His eyes, for He loves the good and the right. This is a great matter,

> for it is impossible to mention in the Torah all of a person's actions toward his neighbors and acquaintances, all of his commercial activity, and all social and political institutions. So, after He had mentioned many of them . . . He continues to say generally that one should do the right and the good in all matters through compromise and conduct beyond the letter of the law.[12]

Moreover, one talmudic source maintains that the Second Temple was destroyed because people did not abide by the norms beyond the letter of the law.[13]

Thus the Rabbis had a keen awareness of the limits of the law as a moral device as much as they put their faith in it to accomplish most moral ends. Indeed, they used moral norms to shape the very substance of the law in their ongoing interpretation and application of it. Thus, for them, as for the later Jewish tradition, the law informs morality as much as morality informs Jewish law.[14] The *interaction* between them improves both, especially when they are both put into the larger contexts of the other sources of Jewish morality mentioned above.

Substance: Two Examples of Unique Jewish Moral Stances

My claim is that Jewish ethics, while overlapping other moral systems in some ways, is unique in others in both methodology and in substance. It would take us beyond the scope of a paper like this to compare the Jewish ideal vision to those of other religions and philosophies or even to describe it itself in proper detail. I will, though, provide two illustrations of how Jewish law, the subject of this essay, affects the substance of Jewish morals in a way that is characteristic of Judaism and possibly even unique to it.

1. *Abortion.* The official Catholic stance sees the fertilized egg as already a full human being, and therefore abortion for any reason constitutes murder. At the other end of the spectrum, American secular thought, as encased in the Supreme Court's decisions from *Roe v. Wade* (1973) to our own day, sees the fetus as a part of the mother, and therefore, at least until the child can live independently outside the womb, abortion is solely a matter of the mother's choice. Protestant views vary, but ultimately it is the individual's conscience that governs on this matter as it does generally in Protestant thought. The Jewish tradition treats abortion, like most other things, as a legal matter, and its conclusions based on that method differ from all three of those other moral systems.

First, the Torah (Exodus 21:22-25) says the following:

> When men fight, and one of them pushes a pregnant woman and a miscarriage results, but no other damage ensues, the one responsible shall be fined according as the woman's husband may exact from him, the payment to be based on reckoning [or as the judges determine]. But

if other damage ensues, the penalty shall be life for life, eye for eye, tooth for tooth, hand for hand, foot for foot, burn for burn, wound for wound, bruise for bruise.

From a legal point of view, there are many issues that have to be defined in this passage. For example, what if women fight and cause the miscarriage? What criteria are to be used to determine the fine? Does the last clause mean retribution, as it seems to mean, or monetary compensation, as the Rabbis understood it? What is clear, however, is that this passage draws a definite distinction between the status of the fetus, where only a fine is due to the victim (actually, her husband), in contrast to the woman, where the remedy is "life for life, eye for eye, etc." Thus the fetus does not have the same status as a full human being; it is rather something less than that, as the lesser remedy indicates. At the same time, this passage announces that there are penalties for killing or injuring others.

With this passage as their foundation, the Rabbis spell out the status of the fetus. They understand it developmentally. Specifically, during the first forty days of gestation, the fetus is "as if it were merely water." The Rabbis clearly knew that it is not merely water, for left alone the fertilized egg may well become a human being. They were saying, however, that rationales to abort the fetus at that stage need not be as stringent as they are in the next stage of pregnancy, between the forty-first day of gestation and birth—specifically when the head emerges or, in a breach birth, when the shoulders emerge. During that period the fetus is "like the thigh of its mother." What is the status of a thigh? Neither a man nor a woman may have their thigh amputated on a whim because we are not allowed to injure our bodies unnecessarily. That is because, legally, the Rabbis extended the prohibition in our passage from Exodus to proscribe harming ourselves as well.[15] (Genesis 9:5 already forbids suicide.) Theologically, we may not harm ourselves because God own our body, very much contrary to the assumption underlying American secular ethics. As a result, abortion is generally prohibited according to Jewish law, not as an act of murder (the fetus is not a full-fledged person), but as an act of self-injury.

On the other hand, if one's thigh had become gangrenous, and if the person were likely to die if the leg were not cut off, then amputation of the leg would not only be permitted, but required, for we have the duty to preserve our life and God's body. Similarly, if the fetus poses a clear threat to the mother's life or health, including her mental health (that is, she will go insane if she carries the baby to term), then an abortion is required, even if she herself does not want the abortion.

Finally, there is a middle case, where abortion is permitted but not required. That occurs when there is a greater threat to the mother's life or health than normal pregnancy poses but not so much of a threat as to constitute a clear and present danger to her. That would occur, for example, if the woman has diabetes, but the diabetes is under control. Then, with her doctor's concurrence and care, she may choose to undertake the risks of pregnancy and carry the fetus to term, or she may choose to abort. Similarly, most Conservative and Reform rabbis, and some Orthodox rabbis, would permit the woman to abort a fetus that has a terminal genetic disease like Tay-Sachs or is grossly malformed (e.g., anencephalic) as a function of the mother's mental health, and some would even extend that permission to a finding of Downs' syndrome if the parents cannot bear the thought of raising such a child. In most cases, though, abortion is prohibited, in some cases it is required, and only in a minority of circumstances is it permitted but not required.

The Jewish treatment of abortion, then, illustrates some of the Jewish tradition's uniqueness in both method and substance. Methodologically, the stance is based primarily on legal precedents and reasoning while taking into account theological doctrines and, in this case, contemporary science. Substantively, Judaism takes a position somewhere in between the Catholic and American secular positions, and it makes this a matter of shared, public law rather than individual conscience.

2. *Poverty.* Elsewhere I have written at some length about Jewish approaches to poverty and their legal, moral, and theological foundations.[16] For our purposes, it is sufficient to say that the Jewish tradition treats aid to the poor not as charity—that is, not as a gift that someone may give in a supererogatory way—but rather as a legal duty. Hence the Hebrew word that we translate "charity" is *zedakkah*, which comes from the Hebrew root meaning justice. (Here, as often, English, a language created by Christians and still spoken as a native language primarily by Christians, misstates Jewish moral and theological terms.)

In other words, providing for the poor is not only the response of genuinely nice people acting beyond the call of duty; Jews caring for the poor may indeed be nice, but they also may not be, for in Judaism all Jews have the *obligation* to care for the poor, whether they feel humanitarian impulses or not.

Still, Jewish law recognizes the importance of engendering humanitarian feelings in donors, and it places great emphasis on preserving the dignity of recipients. Thus Maimonides (1135-1204) outlines eight levels of assistance to the poor, the lowest being giving an insufficient amount directly to the poor person with a pained expression. Even though this is far from the ideal, it is still a form of assistance, despite the patent unwillingness of the donor and the indignity suffered by the receiver in being identified as a person in need. At the other end of the spectrum, the second-highest form of giving is one who gives money to the poor anonymously, with neither the donor nor the recipient knowing the identity of the other. The very highest form of assistance is enabling the poor to provide for themselves, either through a loan or a job or through teaching them a trade.[17]

Other traditions' treatment of poverty may differ completely—until the nineteenth century, England considered poverty a crime and put the poor in debtors' prisons—or in part. The important point for our purposes is that the Jewish tradition sees assisting the poor as a legal duty in a way that few other traditions do. Although many Jews do not consider themselves to be very religious, this norm of Judaism, as Jacob Neusner has argued, has remained, becoming one of the chief ways in which Jews identify as Jews.[18]

Epilogue

Judaism has gone further than most other religious or secular systems of ethics in trying to deal with morality in legal terms. It is therefore not surprising that contemporary decisions in Jewish ethics flow out of the continuing *interactions* among Jewish religious thought, stories, values, and law. To isolate any one of these perspectives is to distort Jewish tradition. Yet Jewish law is central to the Jewish moral system, and the degree to which Judaism uses law makes it unique as a moral system. That methodology has implications for the substance of Jewish morality as well, as illustrated above with regard to abortion and poverty. Still, to see and apply the many resources of the Jewish tradition to frame its moral stance requires knowledge of, and a commitment to, them all in addition to a developed moral and legal sense and the capacity for sound judgment, compassion, and wisdom.

NOTES

[1] B. *Sotah* 14a.

[2] *Romans* 7:7-9

[3] Even Paul maintains that we are subject to the law of God and that law *per se* does not disappear even after Jesus has died to the law for us. It is just that our physical desires, in his view, make it impossible for us to obey the law, and so if we are held accountable to it, only punishment and death can follow. God, in His grace, has therefore, through the death of Jesus, redeemed us from the punishment prescribed for disobeying its demands, but we nevertheless can and should fulfill God's intentions in prescribing the law by living by the Spirit of God directly which still prescribes behavior in accordance with God's law:

> "In my inmost self I delight in the law of God, but I perceive that there is in my bodily members a different law, fighting against the law that my reason approves and making me a prisoner under the law that is in my members, the law of sin. Miserable creature that I am, who is there to rescue me out of this body doomed to death? God alone, through Jesus Christ our Lord! Thanks be to God! In a word then, I myself, subject to God's law as a rational being am yet, in my unspiritual nature, a slave to the law of sin. The conclusion of the matter is this: there is no condemnation for those who are united with Christ Jesus, because in Christ Jesus the life-giving law of the Spirit has set you free from the law of sin and death (*Romans* 7:22-26; 8:1)."

This makes Paul's claim against the law less clear since it seems that he is not arguing that the advent of Jesus voids God's law altogether; it only nullifies the punishment entailed for disobeying it and the desire to disobey it in the first place. But then God's law still defines good and bad behavior and still, presumably, teaches people how to rebel—even if, hopefully, God's Spirit infused in people will prevent them from wanting to do that. But if that is true, then I, as a Jew, would say that we can and should be infused with God's Spirit even without Jesus and that that spirit should lead us not only to follow God's law, but to want to do so.

⁴ This section is adapted from the Appendix to my book, *Matters of Life and Death: A Jewish Approach to Modern Medical Ethics* (Philadelphia: Jewish Publication Society, 1998), 401-404.

⁵ There is no equivalent body among North American Orthodox Jews, who are badly splintered and who tend to follow a particular rabbi revered by their particular segment of the Orthodox community. Thus, until their deaths during the last decade, Rabbis Dov Baer Soloveitchik, Moshe Feinstein, and Menachem Mendel Schneirsohn served in the capacity of ultimate authority for the modern Orthodox, Agudat Yisrael, and Lubavitch portions of the Orthodox community, respectively. The Israeli Orthodox community has a Sephardic and an Ashkenazic Chief Rabbinate, but that office does not deter sharp criticism from other Orthodox rabbis, even of the same stripe, as, for example, the roundly maligned decision of the Ashkenazic Chief Rabbi to allow heart transplants. See *Assia* 14:1-2 (August, 1994) (Hebrew), where ten rabbis take issue with Rabbi Abraham Kahana-Shapira's decision to permit heart transplants. The three American rabbis mentioned above were rarely, if ever, subjected to such open rebellion.

The Central Conference of American Rabbis (Reform) has constituted a Committee on Halakhic Inquiry, and its Chair, Rabbi Walter Jacob, has edited three books of Reform responsa, namely *American Reform Responsa* (New York: Central Conference of American Rabbis, 1983), *Contemporary American Reform Responsa* (New York: Central Conference of American Rabbis, 1987), and *Questions and Reform Jewish Answers: New American Reform Responsa* (New York: Central Conference of American Rabbis, 1992). Since Reform ideology champions the individual autonomy of each Jew to make religious decisions, however, these responsa function exclusively in an advisory capacity for Reform Jews. For two Reform theories on how that process should work, see the articles by Eugene B. Borowitz and David Ellenson in *Contemporary Jewish Ethics and Morality: A Reader*, Elliot N. Dorff and Louis E Newman, eds. (New York: Oxford University Press, 1995), 106-117 and 129-139. In the end, even a policy against intermarriage, overwhelmingly approved by the delegates to the 1985 convention of the Central Conference of American Rabbis, could not become binding on individual Reform rabbi, and in the intervening years it has actually become hard for Reform rabbis to refuse to perform intermarriages.

The Conservative Movement tries to balance the authority of the individual rabbi for his/her community with communal norms. The Committee on Jewish Law and Standards validates acceptable options on issues which individual rabbis raise; if a responsum (a rabbinic ruling) attains six votes or more (out of 25), it becomes a validated option within the movement. If two or more rulings are validated, individual rabbis may use their own discretion as to which to follow. Even if only one option is validated, individual rabbis may choose to do otherwise. Three "standards" of the movement, however, have been adopted -- forbidding intermarriage, requiring a Jewish writ of divorce (a *get*) for remarriage, and defining Jewish identity through birth to a Jewish mother or conversion according to the standards and rituals of Jewish law -- and no Conservative rabbi or synagogue may violate those standards on pain of expulsion. For more on this, see Elliot N. Dorff, *Conservative Judaism: Our Ancestors to Our Descendants* (New York: United Synagogue of Conservative Judaism, 1996), 152-162. This structure makes for plural practices within the movement within a given framework.

⁶ Three sets of books come especially to mind: the many books of responsa (rabbinic rulings) by Solomon Freehof, published by the Central Conference of American [Reform] Rabbis; the three books of new responsa which have already been published by that same body under the editorship of Walter Jacob (see note 5 above); and the books published by the Freehof Institute of Progressive Halakhah, edited by Walter Jacob and Moshe Zemer.

⁷ For a thorough discussion of how this line of divine authority is understood in the biblical and rabbinic sources, see Elliot N. Dorff and Arthur Rosett, *A Living Tree: The Roots and Growth of Jewish Law* (Albany, NY: State University of New York Press, 1988), 123-133, 187-198, and 213-245. The specific sources mentioned in this paragraph are these: the Torah's attempts to differentiate true from false revelation: Deuteronomy 13:2-6; 18:9-22; examples of problems with false prophets: Jeremiah 23:16-40; that prophecy ceased after the Haggai,

Zechariah, and Malachi died: B. *Sanhedrin* 11a; that interpretation (*midrash*) took the place of prophecy: B. *Bava Batra* 12a; the comparative lenses through which Moses and other prophets see: *Leviticus Rabbah* 1:14; Jephtah in his generation is like Moses in his: T. *Rosh Hashanah* 1:18; B. *Rosh Hashanah* 25a-25b.

[8] B. *Pesahim* 50b, *et al.*

[9] M. *Avot* 2:1.

[10] B. *Yoma* 86b; M. *Avot* 4:2; B. *Yoma* 38b.

[11] The Talmud makes several legal rulings on the basis of the requirement to act beyond the letter of the law: B. *Ketubbot* 97a; B. *Bava Kamma* 99b-100a; B. *Bava Mezia* 24b. God Himself acts beyond the letter of the law and is thus a model for us of such behavior: B. *Berakhot* 7a; B. *Avodah Zarah* 4b. Other talmudic phrases that similarly describe expectations beyond the letter of the law are *middat hasidut* (a measure of piety) in B. *Bava Mezia* 52b, B. *Hullin* 130b, etc. and *ru'ah hahamim nohah heimenu* (the spirit of the Sages takes pleasure in him," as in M. *Shevi'it* 10:9. Conversely, talmudic phrases that describe a person's failure to respond to such requirements include that the spirit of the Sages is displeased with him) (e.g., B. *Bava Mezia* 48a), *minhag ramaut* (the behavior of a cheat, as in B. *Kiddushin* 59a) and *yesh bahem mishum mehusarai emunah* (they are untrustworthy, dishonest, as in B. *Bava Mezia* 49a and B. *Bekhorot* 13b). Talmudic passages invoking Deuteronomy 6:18 as the basis for expected behavior: B. *Bava Mezia* 16b; 38a; 108a-108b.

[12] Nahmanides, *Commentary to the Torah*, on Deuteronomy 6:18.

[13] B. *Bava Mezia* 30b.

[14] Cf. Elliot N. Dorff, "The Interaction of Jewish Law with Morality," *Judaism* 26:4 (Fall, 1977), 455-466.

[15] M. *Bava Kamma*, 8:6.

[16] Cf. Elliot N. Dorff, *"You Shall Strengthen Them" (Leviticus 25:35): A Rabbinic Letter on the Poor* (New York: Rabbinical Assembly, 1999), 60 pages. In a somewhat revised form, this will be one of the chapters in my forthcoming book, tentatively titled *Doing the Right and the Good: A Jewish Approach to Social Ethics*, to be published by the Jewish Publication Society in February, 2002.

[17] M.T. *Laws of Gifts to the Poor* 10:7-14.

[18] Jacob Neusner, *Tzedakah: Can Jewish Philanthropy Buy Jewish Survival?* (Chappaqua, NY: Rossel Books, 1982).

Is There a Unique Jewish Bioethics
of Human Reproduction?

Aaron L. Mackler

Introduction

I recall when I was a child growing up in Chicago area, I was a frequent visitor to the Field Museum of Natural History. There was a dramatically lit glass display case, which housed a stuffed gorilla that had lived at the Lincoln Park Zoo. On the case was an inscription that was simple, but somehow struck me as a child, and has stayed with me. It read:

> Every person is in some ways like every other person,
> In some ways like some other persons,
> And in some ways like no other person.[1]

I thought of that quotation when I was asked to address the topic, "Is There a Unique Jewish Bioethics of Human Reproduction?" My general answer would be that, in some ways there is. Jewish bioethics on this topic is in some ways like all other religious ethical approaches, in some ways like some other approaches, and in some ways like no other approach.

Comparing Jewish bioethics with the bioethics of other faith traditions is a complex matter. There are many differences as well as similarities among Jewish bioethical approaches to reproductive technologies. Also, many similarities as well as differences may be found in comparing Jewish approaches as a group with those of other traditions. Having said this, I believe that there are some distinctive (though on the whole not unique) characteristics that tend to establish a family

Annual of the Society of Christian Ethics, 21 (2001): 319-323

resemblance among Jewish approaches in this area. I will briefly consider some general characteristics, looking first at general sources of guidance and methodology in Jewish ethics; then at some prominent values that guide ethical deliberation in the area of reproduction; and finally at some particular positions commonly articulated by Jewish writers in this area.

Sources and Methodological Concerns

At the most general level, Jewish approaches as a class are distinctive in the centrality they accord to texts of the tradition. Painting in the broadest of strokes, one can look at the role of three general sources of moral knowledge: Scripture, tradition, and reason.[2] Jewish approaches tend to give primacy to tradition, supplemented by reason, with Scripture foundational in principle but less directly appealed to. This may be compared to Roman Catholicism, in which there is a tendency for reason (especially in the form of natural law) to be most prominent, supplemented by tradition, with Scripture again in the background. Among Protestant approaches, reason and Scripture are generally primary.[3] For Judaism classically, normative analysis of specific issues, such as those posed by reproductive technologies, centers on *halakhah*, or Jewish law. A writer typically will cite earlier sources and draw analogies with precedents. The model is one of applying the tradition's guidance to the case at hand; or, in unusual cases, showing how modification of accepted practice is appropriate based on principles of the tradition itself. The use of reason is clearly present, and ethical judgments are informed by human experience. Still, these influences are often implicit. Tradition is privileged, and even claims that may seem to an outside observer to be motivated by reason and experience may well be ascribed to tradition.[4]

Within contemporary Jewish ethics, diverse approaches continue to look to the Talmud and traditional sources of *halakhah* as providing the basis and framework for analysis of ethical concerns. Starting from this framework, vigorous debate may be found among Jewish thinkers. One general point of controversy concerns the legitimacy of change and the development of tradition over time. For example, women have not in the past served as rabbis or led prayer services; could it be legitimate to start authorizing them to do so, based on values inherent in the tradition, as well as the reflections of human reason and experience? This issue tends to divide Conservative (centrist) and Reform (left-wing) Jewish authors, who value development and growth as a sign of a living tradition, from their Orthodox (right-wing) colleagues, who tend to emphasize the unchanging truth of Torah (teaching) and Jewish law. Jewish writers also exhibit differences concerning the appropriate weight to be given to individual autonomy and subjective authority, relative to the objective guidance of the tradition. Writers within the Reform movement generally find autonomy to be decisive, while

Orthodox and (to a lesser extent) Conservative writers focus on the objective normative guidance of the tradition.[5]

Values

In examining the Jewish bioethics of reproduction, four guiding values are prominent: respect for persons, procreation, human stewardship, and healing.[6]

The value of respect for persons flows from the Bible's teaching that humans are created in God's image. This concept powerfully expresses the intrinsic value and dignity of each human being. Traditional and contemporary sources appropriately emphasize the importance of respect for persons (*kevod habriyot*).

A second general value concerns procreation and the family. Judaism values children as a blessing for their parents and for the broader community. For those able to do so, having children represents the fulfillment of a religious responsibility, or *mitzvah*, one that can be traced back to God's charge to "be fruitful and multiply" in the biblical account of creation (Gen. 1:28).

A third general value involves the responsibility of human stewardship, and reverent but active partnership with God in completing the works of creation and improving the world. An important corollary of the value of active stewardship is what has been termed "the mandate to heal." While the Bible depicts God as both providing healing, and purposefully causing illness (as well as famine and other forms of human suffering), the overwhelming consensus of the tradition is that God has entrusted humans with the power and responsibility to and heal the sick.[7] Traditional sources have associated this mandate with biblical injunctions to heal the injured; to restore that which has been lost (construed to include lost health and function); not to stand idly by the blood of one's neighbor; and to love one's neighbor as oneself.[8]

None of these values is unique to Judaism. Still, looking broadly at the tradition, there is a distinctive element in the strength of Judaism's endorsement for the legitimacy of, and need for, human activity; in particular, the powerful support accorded the provision of medical care. With regard to reproduction, an especially noteworthy element is the extent to which Jewish writers include the use of reproductive technologies within the paradigm of healing.

Specific Positions

Jewish thinkers overwhelmingly have applied the values noted above to authorize the use of reproductive technologies, at least in principle. For the tradition, procreation normatively occurs within marriage and, ideally, conception arises from marital intercourse. Still, this ideal scenario does not represent an absolute requirement. Infertility is understood as a disease, one that often entails human suffering. Medical responses are supported by the mandate to heal, as well as by the value of children, and a sense of compassion for individuals seeking to have a child. Some writers will express concern with technical issues, such as the manner in which sperm is obtained from the husband. Many will note the need to consider medical risks, as well as the burdens and uncertainties of many procedures. As with all medical procedures, prudential judgments are called for on the use of particular reproductive technologies in particular cases. Nonetheless, general support for the legitimacy of the procedures remains strong.

In accord with the values of the tradition, artificial insemination with a husband's sperm, for example, is almost universally accepted, by very traditionalist Orthodox authorities as well as by more liberal thinkers. In vitro fertilization, using a couple's own genetic materials, similarly enjoys wide acceptance. Most thinkers recognize the use of donated sperm or eggs to be more problematic. Some see the use of donor gametes as impinging on the exclusivity of the marital relationship. More general concerns include the impact on the relationship of the child with his or her parents, in light of genetic asymmetry; the risk of consanguinity in future generation; and the corrosive dangers of the secrecy that often accompanies the use of donor gametes. Still, even the use of donor sperm or eggs is accepted by some Orthodox authorities in selected cases, and more broadly among other Jewish thinkers.[9]

In general, Jewish bioethics tends to take an activist stance toward the use of reproductive technologies, supported by values of healing, procreation, and compassion. The strength of support for these activities is, if not unique, a distinctive characteristic of Jewish bioethics of human reproduction.

NOTES

[1] I have replaced the word "man" in the original quotation with "person."

[2] See, e.g., Charles E. Curran, *The Catholic Moral Tradition Today: A Synthesis* (Washington, D.C.: Georgetown University Press, 1999), 47-55; James P. Hanigan, *As I Have Loved You: The Challenge of Christian Ethics* (Mahwah, N.J.: Paulist, 1986), 19.

[3] See Aaron L. Mackler, "Jewish and Roman Catholic Approaches to Bioethics: Convergence and Divergence in Method and Substance," *Louvain Studies* 25 (2000): 6-9; James M. Gustafson, *Protestant and Roman Catholic Ethics: Prospects for Rapprochement* (Chicago: University of Chicago Press, 1978).

[4] See similarly Mackler, 7.

[5] For a somewhat fuller sketch of the movements, see Aaron L. Mackler, "Introduction," in *Life and Death Responsibilities in Jewish Biomedical Ethics*, ed. Aaron L. Mackler (New York: Jewish Theological Seminary Press and Finkelstein Institute, 2000), 6-8.

[6] This list is adapted from a listing of three guiding values in my "An Expanded Partnership with God? In Vitro Fertilization in Jewish Ethics," *Journal of Religious Ethics* 25 (1997): 279-81.

[7] David M. Feldman, *Health and Medicine in the Jewish Tradition* (New York: Crossroad, 1986), 15-21. One classical narrative depicts two rabbis as offering medical advice, only to have the patient accuse them of interfering with God's will of making the patient ill. The rabbis asked the man, a farmer, why he interfered with the God-given state of his vineyard by fertilizing and

weeding. When he responded that crops would not grow well without human care, the rabbis replied: "Just as plants, if not weeded, fertilized, and plowed, will not grow and bring forth fruits, so with the human body. The fertilizer is the medicine and the means of healing, and the tiller of the earth is the physician" (*Midrash Temurah*, translation based on Feldman, 16).

[8] Ex. 21:19; Deut. 22:2; Lev. 19:16, 19:18.

[9] See essays by Elliot N. Dorff and Aaron L. Mackler in *Life and Death Responsibilities in Jewish Biomedical Ethics*, ed. Mackler, 15-122.

Nursing Fathers and Nursing Mothers: Notes toward a Distinctive Jewish View of Reproductive Ethics

Laurie Zoloth

Introduction

Of all the debates in the field of bioethics, perhaps there is none as contentious as that surrounding the ethics of human reproduction. For it is precisely at this locus—in the contended dramas of love, loss, sex, birth, blood, genetics, women, status, control, property, and family (although, given modern medicine, in no particular order)—that we find every possible disagreement in American life. It is also here that the particularities of tradition have been most fully developed. To be sure, upon reflection, one can see clearly how a position both adheres to tradition, while resisting and rewriting that tradition, as faith and history collide over the body-in-culture. An awareness of a religion's position on abortion, adoption, and sexual practice allows a robust consideration of the sources, assumptions, and practices of both the tradition and its dissenters. Moreover, a comprehension and respect for the depth of various positions can shape policy and public discourse.

Consider, for example, the Catholic stand against the destruction of any embryo—regardless of its locale—after conception has occurred. We all have to contend with and respectfully acknowledge the Catholic view that the destruction of an early embryo is a kind of killing. What will this mean? How will this alter us? How does the argument that every single life, from the very first instant of its being, deserves the highest respect from us help us to understand something fundamentally true about our shared existence? Is the moral appeal justifiable and not merely admissible?

In the debate over human genetics, the clear opposition of Catholic moral theology to any use of embryos forces us to suspend the debate while we collectively consider the argument. As one with a distinctive and different view, I have found this suspension critical. The Catholic voice has enabled a deliberate consideration of the *gravitas* of our actions in a way that may not have happened without this clarity. The Catholic concern reminds us, lest we forget in the dazzle of technology and the seduction of the future, of all that is great and all that is Babel in these structures which we are building "over the abyss." They are not unimportant, these pieces, these cells, these genetic portions, which are too easily treated as "things," as commodities, and as "spare" parts. Each of these embryos is a miraculous event, and ending the narrative course of any—even for the good of our science—exacts a high price that we must be willing to pay. Without the insistence of Catholics, we might too easily forget to count the cost accurately.

A second and equally difficult example is the understanding found in Islamic texts that the State, rather than being distinct from religion, ought to be guided by religious precepts and laws, and led by authorities who hold such faith commitments. Clearly, much work needs to be done to offer more clarity to those outside of specific religious traditions, about which substantive arguments are worth fighting for in the common place that bioethics is creating. In that spirit, let me now turn to my tradition of Jewish thought and practice.

Pharisees and Peculiarities: The Jews at the Table of Discourse

Currently there is considerable contention in the arena of public policy, American democracy, and morality. What role should the Jewish voice play in the secular discourse about public policy? I would argue that, rather than retreating from contention or muting its ethical and moral argument, the Jewish voice needs to be raised clearly and distinctively. Too often theologians and religious studies academicians shrink from the frankly prophetic voice out of a fear of being thought "fanatic." Forgetting that the knife edge of alarm is part of the religious imperative, these scholars too often overlook the fact that a commitment to culture, faith, and text can offer a critical alternative claim to ongoing debates.

For the Jewish community, this avoidance is sociologically understandable. The standards of immigrant politeness and a careful attention to the separation of Church and State as a defense against persecution by Christians have led Jewish scholars to two distinct responses to participation in civic discourse. The first response is a limited entrance into the comity of the liberal tradition. In this case, Jews are a part of a larger coalition seeking to find unity and common purpose around moderate stands. Since the emphasis is on commonality, the particularity of any single tradition is de-emphasized. The second response of the Jewish community has been to proceed with the intricacies of the ethical debate, but with increasing insularity, as if the larger world were only tangentially relevant. Neither response is a uniquely American phenomenon; both mirror the stances taken by the Jewish community toward modernity in general, for example, when the Enlightenment drove Jews toward assimilation or internalized debate.

Let me propose a few answers to the question of how religion—and Jewish thought in particular—can play a critical role in public life. In what follows, I will suggest issues in which Jewish ethics can make a distinctive contribution (and about which I believe that my colleagues may agree.) Then I will discuss two specific arenas in which my colleagues may disagree, but which would also be within the traditional norm.

Words Matter

All we have to offer one another in the public realm and in the discourse of bioethics is the power of the word.[1] This seems little when placed against the heavy artillery of the marketplace or the inducements of, say, the pharmaceutical industry. But for bioethics to provide justice or meaning, we must rely on the potency of our words to change the world. It is only the potency of my argument that can convince the powerful that there is a place for justice beyond the merely expedient, that there is a call for the possible beyond the moral horizon of *mitzrayim*, the narrow place of slavery. Without opinion polls or financial influence, we bioethicists have only the curious power of the outsider who utilizes a set of texts, certain procedures for argument, and a set of discursive conventions.

Jewish tradition insists on the method of critique and argument. For the Pharisaic tradition to work, a case must be argued aloud within a conversational circle in which the voice of the minority is also heard. This tradition is not a fundamentalist one, but is based on the idea that a source text, a history of case law, and the arguments to support, compare, and contrast the moral appeals of the text and the cases can shape response.[2] In this tradition, Jewish texts offer a specific method—an argumentative, midrashic method in which we fill in the textual story with what we know. Case stories function, then, in much the same way as classic narratives do: they tell us much by design and inference, and they allow us to write in moral possibilities and arguments. Hence, the possibility of permeability and inclusion enlivens the form, allowing it to move beyond narrative ethics toward something more like an interruptive narrative, a multivocal conversation in which there is overlapping assent, dissent and more tales.

History Matters

But it is not only the strength of the conversation that is key in this approach to bioethics. Beyond this model of procedural democracy are important substantive stances as well, stances which require preferring some values and narratives over others. In medicine, for example—a field in which we often weigh the teachings of tradition against the values of innovation—a Jewish approach insists on a careful consideration of both previously accepted arguments and previously experienced history. This approach is especially difficult in American civic discourse, which is so enamored with the new. But Jewish tradition insists that the lessons of history, particularly the Holocaust and the attendant perils of state violence, be honored and studied carefully. Such an attention allows for a cautionary and skeptical voice against the hegemony of medicine, a stance often needed in the clinical setting.

Community Matters

The subject of autonomy creates a sharp distinction between the values of secular life and those of Jewish thought. Autonomy needs to be challenged vigorously in our secular society in which the self, the body, and the personal are at the center of all conversations in medicine. In Jewish thought, by contrast, an encounter with the Other must be at the heart of all public policy. From talmudic discussions on how much a community may impoverish itself to free captives to the postmodern contributions of Emmanuel Levinas, Judaism constructs the self as a "self-in-relationship," that is, a self which is commanded to meet the difficult obligation of caring for the Other. Indeed, it is the burdened one, the "nursing father," who is the hero of the Exodus story: Moses is overwhelmed with the children he carries, insistent that they must make it to the Promised Land.

Against the central claims of autonomy, the Jewish worldview posits the claims of justice, fostering an awareness of the needs of a circle far larger than the self. Ethical limits, whether to the power of desire or to the conduct of medicine, must be established by a larger system of faith and law which has been instituted to protect and maintain not only individual human life but also the community that makes this life possible.

Linked to this concern is the importance of compassion, as seen, for example, in the obligations of *birkur holimm*—the duty to visit and to care for the needs of the ill. Judaism is not an abstract principle: rabbinic commandments are tangible and detailed. One cannot simply claim Jewish values as a possession—one must do something to actuate the values: the vulnerable must be cared for, and their needs privileged over the calls of the marketplace. The ill one who stands at the gate in front of the marble pillars, the bandaged one who lingers in the corridors of the hospital—this person is more likely to be the Messiah who has come to this unredeemed world. Our redemption is linked to our willingness to care for him. [3]

The Family Matters

Even given the recurrent history of catastrophe, there exists a distinctive voice in Jewish thought that argues for a reproductive ethics in which the moral position of a woman and her family takes precedence over the moral status of the embryo. Nowhere is this clearer than in the texts that provide infants with a prolonged period of nursing and rearing, and which allow for birth control during this entire time. "The Bariata of the Three Women,"[4] for instance, is a central text which is repeated in five different places in the Talmud[5] and once, with a few changes, in the later commentary called the *Tosefta*. In this work, the rabbis discuss the times when women must or may use a birth control device to prevent pregnancies.[6]

> R. Bebai recited before R. Nahman: Three (categories of) women use a *mokh* in marital intercourse: a minor, a pregnant women, and a nursing mother. The minor, because she might become pregnant and die. A pregnant woman, because she might cause her fetus to become a *sandal* [flattened or crushed by a second pregnancy]. A nursing woman because she might have to wean her child prematurely and the child would die.[7]

What is occurring in this text? The rabbis set a requirement for birth control using a device called a *mokh*, a soft cotton pad worn internally against the cervix.[8] It may have been worn during coitus, or it might have been used afterwards as a kind of absorbent—these details are left unanswered. The text is concerned with women for whom pregnancy might carry additional risks and, thus, must be avoided. In these cases, the male obligation to procreate must be forestalled in order to protect the woman and, as importantly, to protect her child. In the first case, the rabbinic understanding that married minors (girls under the age of twelve years and a day) are at higher risk should they become pregnant is straightforward.[9] In the second, the rabbis, who at this point debate whether superfetation (second pregnancy) is biologically possible, are concerned primarily that the fetus might be compromised by intercourse.

The Centrality of the Nursing Mother—Reclaiming a Core Text

The same protective spirit animates the final category of women who must use birth control to avoid pregnancy—nursing mothers. Nursing, which was believed to suppress pregnancy, was expected to be a prolonged period of two to three years.[10] During the entire two-year period established by Rabbinic texts for nursing,[11] pregnancy was forbidden. Indeed in several Talmudic texts, the threat of another pregnancy to the health of the nursing child was considered so grave that a divorcee or widow who was nursing, or who was pregnant (and would be nursing soon) could not marry until her child was two years old. This is even a stronger prohibition than that which applies to the first marriage, since, in the case of a non-related child, the rabbis feared that birth control might not be used as diligently.

The violation of this law carries severe punishment: if a couple cannot abstain from unprotected sex, the couple must divorce and cannot remarry before the full twenty-four month period. This law assures family planning and a space of at least thirty-three months between each child. Over the following centuries this law would be debated vigorously. When the question arose about the reason for the ruling, later *responsa* tried to sort this out and understand how to apply the ruling in the societies in which Jews found themselves. What follows from this "*Bariata* of the Three Women" is a long and complex argument by those who would use the cases in as expansive a way as possible, permitting both a widening circle of cases in which contraception could be used and the clear use of barrier methods of birth control.

In the eleventh century, R. Hai Gaon, citing the risk that a pregnancy might impair the nursing mother's milk, explored the argument that pregnancy could be permitted if the nursing child's diet was supplemented with milk to avoid this risk. He then *rejected* this argument in favor of the *mokh*: the latter method was more reliable in avoiding pregnancy altogether. He argued that this method was consistent with the biological plan; birth control was to be understood as a supplement to the natural protection against pregnancy that nursing provides. Indeed, the belief that a second pregnancy should be prevented until the child was fully weaned was so strongly held by some rabbis that R. Y'hudah Ayyes (in early eighteenth-century Italy) wrote a *responsa* allowing an abortion for a nursing mother so that her nursing child might be protected.[12]

By the nineteenth century, however—just as birth rates were rising in Europe and, interestingly enough, Jewish culture was beginning to feel the growing pressure to re-examine woman's position in society—textual arguments seem to have changed. Later rabbinic *responsa*, to explain this shift, offered what would become a idiosyncratic argument of *responsa* literature: namely, human biology has "changed" since the Talmudic era and thus, earlier rulings and justifications are no longer binding. Proponents of this view clearly believed that it was easier to change human physiology than to declare canonical texts incorrect. R.Y. L. Don Yahya, one such proponent, is representative of a large group of later commentators who entered this debate:

> (Though the rabbis of the Talmud) required a *mokh* during the nursing period, I suspect that natures have changed in this matter, . . . for in our times we see many women wean (before the 24 month period) and their children live and thrive. Perhaps then the permission of contraception is not applicable today . . . . Nevertheless, in questions of physical health we cannot depend on such reasoning because perhaps the majority of (such infants) live, while a very small number become thereby weak and die young.[13]

This text is intriguing in two ways. First, it is one of several *responsa* that allow radical changes in interpretation based upon the new understandings of science and biology. Second, while acknowledging this flexibility in interpretation, the text nevertheless offers an opinion that protects the minority group which is still at risk.

Later *responsa* debated this point. Some suggested that, since lactation itself reduces the risk of pregnancy (although not reliably), the *mokh* is only a supplement. As the argument developed over time, however, those with a more restrictive view come to the fore, confining the use of contraception to ever-narrowing categories of women, and providing for further limitations (such as describing the *mokh* as a post-coital "absorbent" only).

No less an authority than the sixteenth-century R. Solomon Luria supports the use of the *mokh*: "Precoital *mokh* is assumed, and it is not improper [during the entire nursing period]."[14] But despite this clear support of birth control for women during the nursing period, stricter views prevailed; for instance, the restriction of birth control devices to those cases in which the health of the mother is in peril. Correspondingly, this led to decreasing intervals between pregnancies. Lost was the premise of protection of the nursing infant and, hence, lost were the cultural practices that this might have suggested.[15] This loss was caused, in part, by a lack of knowledge of Luria's opinion, but it was also reflective of the nineteenth-century faith in medicine and the prevailing social norm, during this era, of larger families. In the end, the carefully-reasoned prohibition against a second pregnancy during the two year nursing period was essentially lost; indeed, it is barely mentioned in contemporary texts.[16] This once central obligation has been replaced by calls for rapid fecundity and newly stated social responsibilities.

But the philosophic point that was made by the prohibition of conception during nursing still provides a key insight for our exploration into those things which may be reclaimed from Jewish texts on reproductive practice. What matters in the "*Bariata* of the Three Women" are the health of each woman, the value of each pregnancy, and the careful nurturing of each child. What is at stake is the family itself.

Justice Matters

Yet compassion is not enough. While the Pharisaic tradition is oriented toward praxis, the rabbinic culture it shaped is deeply prophetic as well: the calls for justice in policy-making are heard in every text of Judaism. It is here, I would suggest, that we discover Judaism's single most important contribution to the discourse of bioethics—as significant as the Catholic insistence on the respect for life. It is the insistence on the relentless pursuit of justice: the courage to insist—despite the inexpedient, unpolitical nature of the demand—on the need for universal access to health care services. Certainly there are texts which teach us that, for a city to be justly habitable, it must have a basic level of services, including a physician, public hygiene, and a school.[17] But beyond this is a vision which insists that the very structure of production must take into account the needs of justice. The Sinaitic commands link healing with justice; the prophetic tradition scorns the community that abandons the poor. In a society in which care is doled out, managed, and curtailed to protect the bottom line, one might do well to invite a Jeremiah to the table of discourse. He would remind us of the top line, speak truth to the powerful, and encourage us to persist beyond politeness.

Justice as Tzedakah, Tzedakah as Sacrifice

In a *New York Times Magazine* article, bioethicist Peter Singer spoke of a classic philosophical problem: how much charity ought one to give?[18] He used a classic Jewish ethical method, that of the *mashal* or parable (although this is an old philosophy trick as well).

Imagine that a retired professional has put all of his life savings into a fancy car. As its worth appreciates, he plans on selling it as an investment for his declining years. Driving the car around one day, he finds himself on an old railway spur. Suddenly he notices that an oncoming train is racing out of control toward an innocent child who is toddling toward his inevitable death—inevitable unless the professional switches the train to the track his car is on. He can do this, and it will save the child's life, but it will mean that the car will be destroyed along with his life savings. In the *mashal* as written, the man does not rescue the child; instead, he protects his car and drives away cheerfully rich. At first, we are meant to be appalled by this evil man: "Arrest that guy!" And then the philosopher can point out to us that we who live in the West, with our pensions and air-conditioned lives, are just like the man in his car, refusing to rescue children with our charity. To illustrate this, the article points out that every $200 sent to Oxfam or UNICEF can feed, house, and school one child for one year, and it can immunize that child till adolescence. By not giving to others, and by eating out, seeing movies, or buying a book or two instead—we are like that man, driving off scot-free. This article has attracted a great deal of attention.

While Singer is a Jewish ethicist, his solution to the *mashal* is distinctive rather than pharisaic, and by examining where Singer goes wrong, we may have a vivid encounter with core Jewish texts on justice. [19] I would argue that the response of justice is not simply a social response, that is, a reflection of the rabbinic understanding of social ethics as a key enactment of the cultural/political system for which religious leadership was responsible. Rather, in a fundamental way, *justice is prayer* or, to put it another way, the moral gesture is literally how one speaks. [20]

Hence Singer, who tells us that we should give away not only the $200, but all that we have above $50,000 a year until poverty in the world is eliminated, has actually given us a diminished moral gesture. The problem is not that what Singer is asking is so hard that no one would do it;[21] to the contrary, it is too easy. To give money to someone whom we will never see, to a theoretical child whom we can completely abstract or (worse yet) romanticize, actually requires far too little. What the Jewish law on justice asks for instead is tithing, a full 10% of one's money, one's time, one's work, and most importantly, one's self to the Other. But the difficulty in this principle (and why it is linked to both social justice and spiritual quest) lies in discerning the precise perimeters of the self. Moreover, one must accept that the constancy of the call of the Other is precisely that which makes us human in the first place, and gives us the ability and courage to ask anything in faith at all.

It is the cycle of the harvest that teaches us best about tithing, but the stories about the harvest are never far from issues of justice within families, or from the dramas of reproductive duty. In the commentaries on Ruth and Leviticus, the farmer-readers of the Biblical text are reminded that the harvest is always more abundant than can be gathered into one's own hands, that the field's corners are always out of reach of the plow, and that the grain will always fall behind you as you gather it in. This is not clumsiness; it is simply the way that humans and the natural world are constructed, with error, loss, and remnants left behind. We are made as persons much like the Torah text is written, with gaps and silences needing to be filled in with talk. Every human work is like this. When we tithe the crop, it is because not all of it belongs to us in the first place; it is simply held by us in keeping for the poor. In this deepest sense then, there is a part of any gesture you make—whether the gesture of medicine or the gesture of moral philosophy— that is simply not yours: it is kept and stored for the moment when the poor come to call for it.

Consider what this might really mean in your daily life. If 100% of the time you work as a professor, then for 10% of that time, you must teach for free, you must write for the poor, you must walk into a nursing home or a literacy center and say, "Let me teach someone to read. *Here I am.*" It does not matter how poor you are in this most Jewish of systems, for the point of tithing is that each has the obligation to tithe. The poorest person still must give *tzedakah* and tithe from his portion.

Teaching in the wake of the destruction of the Temple, Rabbi Johannon b. Zakkai considered what he should do in exile in Yavnah, hiding out from the Roman authorities. At issue was how Jews were to exist without the centrality of sacrifice. Without the moaning of the animals, the pools of blood, and the loss of the most perfect lamb; without the priest dipping his hands in the blood and the blood on the gold of the Temple; without the expiation of the scapegoat, how could one be religious? How could one live as a faithful Jew while walking ever more deeply into Diaspora outside the walls of Jerusalem, into the new Roman Empire with its glitzy road projects and military might? The rabbis tell us simply that the answer is "giving *tzedakah*." Giving *tzedakah* is elevated to the level of Temple service and the reception of the Divine Presence.[22] This serious understanding of the new parameters of the human is an ontological issue. It is where one asks, "Who am I?", and not simply, "What do I do?"

According to the French talmudist Emmanuel Levinas, *Who you are* is the one who must respond, "I am the one who will come up with what you need, naked, hungry stranger. I will find in myself the resources that you need." Like Johannan b. Zakkai, Levinas makes the "inconvertible demand for justice the equivalent of the spirituality of the Spirit and the proximity of God."[23] Levinas reminds us that the central text of Isaiah 58, read in the liturgy of Yom Kippur, is about this point precisely: The pious ones ask of God, "Why have we fasted, and why have we humbled ourselves, and thou takest no knowledge of it?" Levinas teaches us that the answer of the prophet is clear: the ordinary economic life, with its brutality and domination, must in some way be broken, not only by faith expressed in ritual, but by something far harder—by interrupting one's life with the ethical. One must yield to the risky demands to share one's bread with the hungry, to bring the homeless poor into one's own house, to see nakedness as one's own nakedness. Then and only then can the healing of justice begin. The language of the vision is one of a curious reversal. If this is done,

> Your righteousness (*tzaddik*) shall go before you, and the glory of the Lord shall be your rear guard. Then you shall call, and the Lord will answer you; you shall cry, and he will say "Here I am." (Isaiah 58)

Who I am is tied to what I must do, for the self is incomplete as a self as long as it is wrapped and clothed in itself. One needs the nakedness of the Other to know the nakedness of the self. If the great theme of the Torah is God's search for a person who can finally answer, "*Hineni*, Here I am," and if, after Adam, Chava, Cain, and Noah failed in this, Abraham finally *can* answer in this way in the *Akedah* itself, then the great reversal in this verse is even more striking. Your own deeds of justice must go first, then the self, and then the Lord in the rearguard. Then when you cry out, it will be God who answers "*Hinini*"—a response and a presence which is only possible once the obligation to the other is met, that is, if you hear and answer the cry of the Other first.

In truth, the point of reproduction and its corresponding ethical demands are finally awakened at night by a child who is hungry. At its best, this teaches all of us (especially ethicists) how to live, answering what Levinas might call the ceaseless cry of the other. Families encourage us to think of *tzedakah* as a part of us, to understand that we overlap one another like the leaves of the palm fronds Jews place over Sukkahs built for the holiday which follows the Day of Atonement. Like those fronds, we are tightly bound and intertwined, with a piece of each of us given over to the others. When we tithe in this way as a bound community, we are assured that no one's child is wandering around on the train tracks, that thought will be given on how to build fences around dangerous things. But we will also make sure that no one is terrorized into selfishness because he is afraid of age and abandonment, another concern that Jewish thought would ask of the philosopher's story.

Taking this approach seriously means insisting that our ideas on the ethics of reproduction should not be separated from the problems of justice. It would also mean that we must build acts of sacrifice and tithing of the self into our understanding of health care, not out of pity, but out of our desire to live in an authentic way. For Jews, this means to live under inescapable obligations. Taking this seriously means that, in our debates on stem cell research and genetic medicine, the issues of justice, equal access to health care, and the uninsured should never be obscured by the dazzle of the new. It also means insisting that biotechnology always be discussed in light of the poor of one's own city. Jewish bioethicists should insist on this in the same sober way that our Catholic colleagues insist on respect for life. By living in this way, we will be wakened by the immensity of the need, but unlike the man on the tracks with no one to turn to, we will understand that we are never alone if we make justice an intrinsic part of our practice and theory of bioethics.

So the appeal to justice—where "appeal" means entreaty, petition, invocation, prayer—is the first act of speech in the conversation of ethics. To live ethically is to call and to invoke, and that means to pray. None of us are alone in either the speech act or the moral gesture of justice. As we call, desperate to hear the reassurance of "*Hinini*," we know that we need to answer first. We know that the first act of this calling, which we identify as covenant, is to be present, to understand that part of us is owned by and owed to the other. That piece, a constant part of our very being, is to be kept until the poor come for it.

In the final analysis, the attention to procedural issues, the rabbinical discursive method, and an awareness of the substantive issues of community, justice and history—each of these can help to shift the language of the secular debate in bioethics in a powerful way. The clearer Jews are about our own texts, tradition, and history, the more articulately we can join conversations in the medical commons. And the more clearly we understand what Judaism brings to that discussion, the more we will understand why turning the talk firmly toward justice—why interrupting with the unruly story of the stranger—is an obligation for which we are responsible.

Intending our Imaginations into Being

In this brief outline, I have made two large claims beyond the usual skirmish over Judaism and bioethics. First, I have suggested that the substantive and particular assertions of religious thought can, if they are convincing (as in the primacy of the nursing mother), be incorporated in the emerging canon. Second, I have argued that the Jewish insistence on justice as an ontological and normative category makes such a claim. But what if I have failed to convince you? Then it would seem that I, like all theologians, must take stock of what remains, whether that be in the public discourse about a state we fear has taken a wrong turn, or in a field that has made a fundamental error. "How can we be both civil and disobedient?"—this is a question of the utmost seriousness for scholars of religion, and like all religious questions, it must be answered from significantly different texts and histories. But learning to be part of a dissonant, interruptive minority may be turn out to be the familiar, critical task.

There is hope of another way; that we might take the time to teach one another about that which animates our moral imagination so thoroughly that we are shaped and made whole by it. Perhaps the greatest hope for all participants begins the moment after we cease speaking. It is in this moment when we carefully begin to listen, and when we begin to see the passion of the Other who is showing us the deepest meaning of her world.[24]

NOTES

[1] Many sources expand on this point. See for example, David Ellenson, "Preface" to Rachel Adler's *Engendering Judaism* (Philadelphia: Jewish Publication Society, 1998).

[2] Elliot Dorff, *Matters of Life and Death: A Jewish Approach it Modern Medical Ethics* (Philadelphia: Jewish Publication Society, 1998). See "Appendix."

[3] Or her, as the case may be.

[4] The bariata is a textual argument not written in the Mishnah, but debated in the Gemora as part of the oral tradition of the Mishnah.

[5] Yevamot, 12b and 100b, Ketubot 39a, Niddah 45a, Nedarim 35b.

[6] There is a long argument about whether the term is "must" use birth control or "may" use birth control, and another about the type, placement and timing of the devices. The details of this are important, but lie outside the scope of this chapter. It is my intent to note only the intense concern with the problem of the nursing child, and the intent to both protect that child's infancy, and to allow for sexuality during the space between procreative sex.

[7] Yevamot, 12b, Ketubot 39c.

[8] The actual description is obscure.

[9] Even today, the risk of maternal morbidity in women between 12 and 17 is higher.

[10] Weaning ceremonies that re-enact the Biblical narrative in which Sarah weans Isaac at three were commemorated in European tradition by deferring the first haircut to age three. This practice, the *upsharin*, is still observed in many communities today.

[11] Yevamot 34b; Tosefta Niddah Chapter 2, with emendation of Gaon of Vilna, as cited by David Feldman in *Birth Control in Jewish Law; Marital Relations, Contraception, and Abortion as Set Forth in the Classic Texts Of Jewish Law* (New York: New York University Press, 1968).

[12] Feldman, *Birth Control in Jewish Law*; R. Y. L. Don Yahya, *Responsa* Bikkurei Y'Hudah. II, 121. Also see Magen Avaraham, by Abraham Gumbiner in his 17th century commentary on the Shulkan Arukh, Responsum Shem MiShim'on, No. 7, Yad, Eliyahu, P'sakim No. 70, Mosheh Shick in Responsum Maharam Schick, Hoshen Mishpat No. 54. One sees this argument even in the Lubavitcher Rebbe Menahem Shneirson in the late 19th century, Rep. Tzemah Tzedek, (Ha-hadshot), Even HaEzer Vol. I, No. 89. All as cited in Feldman, *Birth Control in Jewish Law*, 190.

[13] Feldman, *Birth Control in Jewish Law* 190

[14] Ibid., 191.

[15] Far more research is called for to explore what these practices of childrearing and prolonged nursing might have been.

[16] Indeed, one can see this with a review of contemporary Orthodox marriage manuals, popular texts, etc.

[17] Sanhedrin 17b, Talmud Balvi, Soncino Press, London.

[18] Peter Singer, "The Singer Solution to World Poverty," *New York Times Magazine* (September 5, 1999): 60-63.

[19] Although it can be argued that the most Jewish thing about this at all it the way that Singer and I will argue fiercely within the tradition itself.

[20] When I struggling to write this piece, we were in the very middle of the Jewish holiday season, and I was asked at the same time by my synagogue president to give the Yom Kippur sermon, which includes a charity appeal to my Orthodox congregation. I will tell you that I did not want to give this talk, and why I then did give the sermon, the place where in my childhood, the most serious man, serious in both senses of that term, a serious man and a serious *man* told you to buy Israeli Bonds, in a way that as a child I thought a big distraction from the real prayer of this day. I did not want to give this talk because I was too busy. When the shul president stopped me in the lettuce aisle erev Rosh Hashana, I was frantic to accomplish the detail of the holiday, food, candles, challah, laundry. So I told her to ask someone else. There were good reasons, but mostly, I thought that I had too much to do, what with all the time it takes to write articles, and prepare classes telling people how to be ethical, which is what I get paid to do. It was in the writing of the sermon that I realized that I had finally articulated what it was about justice that I could bring to the bioethics discourse, and for this, I am deeply indebted to the small shul that makes me enact my theories.

[21] Or even, as a clever letter writer to the *Times* pointed out (October 2, 1999) that the best course of action would be to let the train hit the child, and then sell the car, and save dozens and dozens of children with the cash. Thus the fallacy of pure utilitarianism.

[22] Ephraim Urbach, *The Sages* (Cambridge: Harvard University Press, 1987), 348.

[23] Emmanuel Levinas, "Demanding Judaism," *Beyond the Verse* (Bloomington: Indiana University Press, 1982), 4-6.

[24] The ideas expressed in this essay are ones I have been working with for some time. For elaboration of the material concerning the laws of the nursing mother, interested readers may consult "Each One a World," an essay scheduled to appear next year in a volume edited by Daniel McGuire. On charity in Jewish law, please see my book *Health Care and the Ethics of Encounter: A Jewish Discussion of Social Justice* (Chapel Hill: University of North Carolina Press, 1999). Some of my notions of justice were utilized in the development of the project that issued in *Christianity in Jewish Terms*, ed. Peter Ochs and Tikva Frymer-Kensky (Boulder: Westview, 2000).

ETHICS IN INTERNATIONAL CONTEXT

Doing Ethics in the Pacific Islands: Interpreting Moral Dimensions of Prose Narrative

Jack Hill

Abstract

Given the current interest in globalization, this paper seeks to identify and explicate some of the distinctive moral perspectives of Pacific Islanders. Drawing on the narrative approach of Nussbaum, within a broader hermeneutical perspective, the author seeks to interpret moral orientations in legends from Fiji and the Cook Islands. It is argued that these orientations provide a fresh understanding of contemporary political events and social relations in the islands. The paper concludes by discussing issues raised by this type of narrative ethical analysis for the field of comparative religious ethics.

Introduction

One of the anomalies of the current interest in globalization is that many of our neighbors in far reaches of the globe are suspicious of the idea. Academics in the Two-Thirds World have expressed the fear that the language of globalization is yet another manifestation of the North's dominance of the South. They argue that efforts to promote a monolithic globalization process will swallow up and run rough shod over particular contexts and displace or denigrate indigenous value systems.[1]

I want to take this suspicion seriously by doing ethics in a way that is not only sensitive to specific cultural contexts, but that also avoids unduly abstracting ethical discourse from lived experience. In this article, I argue that traditional prose narratives[2] represent significant terrains of moral experience, especially in

Annual of the Society of Christian Ethics, 21 (2001): 341-360

cultural contexts where narrative traditions are particularly vibrant. For example, it is illuminating to do research in a region such as the South Pacific Islands, where story telling, singing and speech making are still primary modes of communication.[3] Even though videos and recently, television, are becoming increasingly popular, a majority of islanders still spend enormous amounts of time in traditional and pseudo-traditional informal gatherings where narratives flourish. For the sake of argument, let us assume that the oral narrative traditions that are generated in such contexts mediate value meanings that reflect the concrete moral experience of the people who tell the narratives.

If moral orientations can be accessed through in-depth, contextual analyses of oral traditions, the question arises as to how such analyses can be related to ethical discourse in the North American context. In an essay devoted to pedagogical approaches in comparative religious ethics, Sumner Twiss outlines a useful typology of interpretive paradigms.[4] My approach has affinities with what Twiss labels "hermeneutical-dialogical comparison."[5] This paradigm stresses receptivity to the moral world of the other, presupposes a capacity to translate from one world to another, and entails a constructive effort to address normative questions about our lives.[6] It can be contrasted with what Twiss calls the "formalist-conceptual" paradigm, which approaches all moral experience as an expression of "patterns of rationality identified in the light of Western philosophical reflection."[7] My concern here is not to isolate and analyze principles, rules and action-guides, but to explore nuances of human action in relation to taken-for-granted norms and values in the culture in question. Rather than viewing "morality" as a species of a formal rationality, I conceive of it as a complex psychosocial orientation regarding the needs, wants and desires of particular actors, as dynamic cultural agents in particular contexts.

My approach can also be distinguished from the "historical-comparative" paradigm,[8] with its focus on depicting the nature of entire traditions and providing holistic descriptions of worldviews. Also, rather than investigating traditional types of socio-moral problems (such as war, abortion or economic injustice), I focus on the prior task of discerning the subjective meaning content of social actions within a specific cultural tradition. The primary aim is to ascertain the nature of moral predispositions, motivations and proclivities at play in everyday life.[9] Finally, because historians indigenous to the region have been extremely critical of the way the history of the South Pacific has been written,[10] I focus on indigenous oral traditions in order to provide a fresh way of illuminating the heart and soul of moral experience in the region.

This paper is thus an attempt to demonstrate some of the merits of a hermeneutical approach for unearthing islander moral experience by focusing on two legends from different sub-regions of the South Pacific.[11] It represents the initial phase of a broader project aimed at interpreting a variety of South Pacific narrative forms, including contemporary oral performances, sermons and popular fiction, as resources for articulating different ethical traditions in the region.[12] Let us now consider some of the more salient methodological issues, proceed to the analysis of moral orientations in two legends, and then consider implications for comparative studies in ethics.

Hermeneutical Issues

Pacific islanders love to make speeches and tell stories. During my seven years in Fiji, teaching at a regional theological college,[13] I heard countless stories and tales, usually in connection with rituals of farewell, welcome, mourning, reconciliation, twenty-first birthdays and varieties of ethnic group celebrations. At nearly all of these rituals, there is a great deal of story telling associated with the ancient ritual of drinking kava. Kava is a drink made from steeping the pulped fresh root of a local plant (also called kava), or its powdered or dried equivalent, in water.[14] Consumed steadily in moderate amounts over several hours, it has a mildly sedative effect. One's mouth and tongue may feel slightly numb, and one's body as a whole feels very relaxed. Although this calming influence may induce drowsiness, more often than not, it facilitates a smooth flow of dialogue and lively social interaction. It can entail extensive ceremonial elaboration. And when islanders drink kava, they tell their stories.

Although there is not space here to provide ethnographic accounts of the contexts in which these stories arise, it is important to acknowledge the senses in which they are the social constructions of particular persons who are situated in specific cultural traditions.[15] In this paper, I draw on a variety of social scientific accounts of cultural life in the region.[16] I also draw on first-hand experiences of teaching and interacting informally with islanders from many different parts of the Pacific. I first heard the stories I will introduce below late at night, at festive occasions around the kava bowl at an ecumenical theological college in Fiji. They were told in English by those who grew up hearing the stories in their native idioms to staff and students from various cultures in the South Pacific and beyond. Although the somewhat artificial social setting of a theological college represents a context that is several steps removed from the indigenous cultural locations in which the stories originated, the many evening festivities provided opportunities for informal social interaction in which story tellers and listeners could relax and re-create a way of being present for one another in which they felt "at home." To the degree that every telling of a story is a "construction" in its own right, there is no question that some indigenous material and references were deleted, altered or embellished when the stories were re-told in such a pluralistic, overtly Christian setting with non-Pacific Island professors in ear shot! In this regard, it is not only important to read other versions of the same stories, transcribed by those who heard them told at similar occasions in their indigenous contexts, but also to talk to persons from the contexts in question about the variations they perceive.

As an ethicist, I am interested in these stories for several reasons. With every telling, they "re-present" storehouses of moral insight that have stood the test of time. They also constitute the moral reservoirs of persons who have been either demeaned or ignored in discussions of cross-cultural ethics. Islanders are still largely portrayed as happy-go-lucky, carefree children in paradise, or, as savage cannibals who have no identifiable or coherent moral traditions.[17] One searches in vain for substantive treatments of the religious ethics of Pacific Islanders. In addition, because these stories are rooted in what are essentially oral rather than literary cultures, they have a compelling reality sense.[18] That is, they may be useful in understanding what is actually occurring in social and political life in the region. And finally, given centuries of cross-fertilization in the Pacific, these stories express moral orientations that may have broad cross-cultural applicability in the region.[19]

But since there are thousands of such narratives, and they vary in type and function, the question arises, "How do we decide which stories to investigate?" Moreover, which versions will be of particular interest? Furthermore, how does one "read" these stories, let alone interpret the ethical dimensions within them? In this paper, I focus on only two stories, but select them from different islands in two of the three major sub-regions: the Melanesian island of Taveuni in Fiji and the Polynesian island of Atiu in the Cook Islands.[20] Although I first heard these myths around the kava bowl, I later asked the storytellers to write them down in connection with research projects they were working on at the College.[21]

I selected these particular stories for several reasons. First, it was clear that the Pacific Islanders who told them, as well as the students who listened to them around the kava bowl and later in class, regarded them as interesting, amusing and in some way significant as expressions of who they were as a people. Second, I wanted to select stories that expressly dealt with situations of conflict. While myths of origin, journeys of epic heroes and amusing anecdotes can be significant for moral inquiry, we can enter a people's moral universe at a more profound level by focusing on narratives that deal with self-deception and ruptures in the social fabric. Third, I am especially interested in stories that give voice to the marginalized in a culture.[22] In this connection it is instructive to focus on elements of what Edward Schillebeeckx has called, "negative contrast experiences."[23] Such experiences refer to a people's "complaints" and point to the ground of their discontents. This ground represents an implicit moral terrain because it entails attitudes, judgments and values that are being threatened or compromised. We gain access to a people's moral imagination by interpreting how the major figures in such stories deal with the fallout from broken or unjust relationships involving marginal persons.

Where different versions of the same narrative are concerned, there is no way to avoid a more or less arbitrary decision regarding the choice of a version. In each case below, I have selected a version that persons familiar with the cultural heritage accept as a reasonably plausible telling of the story. To a great extent, like the islanders themselves, I have simply "come across" this or that version in the course of my experience in the region and as a result of subsequent research.

Perhaps the most important issue is how we are to "read" the version we come across, especially as cultural outsiders. We all bring a point of view to a text, and we are all predisposed to "see" what we are expecting to see. The trick is to somehow allow the text to speak for itself. In his work on biblical narrative, Christian ethicist Stanley Hauerwas approaches this task by paying careful attention to the plot line the story tells.[24] But this approach tends to direct our attention away from the particularity of the text. As John Barton argues, "Hauerwas' approach invites us to generalize from the narratives we read, and to extract from them the basic framework that holds them together."[25] While this approach is useful up to a point, Martha Nussbaum's focus on the particulars of the text is especially well suited to working with Pacific oral tradition.[26] It is frequently in the detail, in changes of colors, forms or shapes, or in references to nuances of gaze, gesture or tone, that an ethical insight is disclosed. Nussbaum stresses the complexity of moral experience—the interplay of benevolent and malevolent intentions, mistakes, misdeeds and chance occurrences.[27] Once such moral details in the "human theater" become more apparent, the ethicist can go deeper into the moral world of the story by viewing these details in relation to more general cultural perceptions of virtues and vices. The story teller's moral wisdom is thus revealed in the way the main characters are seen to interact with one another and the cosmos in relation to general sets of value meanings. Nussbaum's approach may also be helpful to the extent that its focus on particularity may facilitate a discerning of the voices of the marginalized.

Appropriating Nussbaum's perspective, I assume that all humans seek to do the good, however they perceive it, in the midst of power struggles, encumbered with layers of self-deception, and in relation to unexpected responses to their actions. It is by examining the way agents handle this complex of factors, in relation to general moral values and perspectives, that we gain practical moral insight. As a social ethicist, I read narratives in a way that is attentive to background ethical categories of the self, community, good and evil. But as a comparativist, I also seek to discern the way these categories are configured in the narratives themselves. Let us now turn to a consideration of moral orientations in two legends from different sub-regions of the South Pacific: a story of conflict between father and daughter in Fiji, and a tale of a marital dispute in the Cook Islands.

Discerning Moral Orientations

The Legend of Tagimoucia[28]

The ancient Fijian narrative, The Legend of Tagimoucia,[29] is a story centered on Adi Perena,[30] the beautiful daughter of a chief. Adi falls in love with Taitusi, a poor commoner, and promises to marry him. The main plot develops when Adi's father declares publicly his decision that she should marry an old man of another powerful family in the community. Adi is grief stricken and runs away from the village. After lamenting on an isolated beach by the sea, she flees to the forests and ascends mountains until she collapses beside a waterfall. Adi weeps, and her tears turn into the beautiful flower, Tagimoucia.[31] In the meantime, her father has set out to search for her. When he finds her, he is profoundly moved by her suffering. He sees in the color and shape of the Tagimoucia how passionately Adi loved Taitusi. He then reverses his earlier decision and gives his consent for her to marry the commoner. Adi and Taitusi have a traditional wedding, celebrated with full honor.

Viewed within the cultural context of the eastern Fijian islands, the legend depicts at least three surprising developments. First, it is important to note that there is a strong, hierarchical, chiefly social system in the eastern Fiji group. Traditionally, the daughter of a chief would not, as a rule, publicly express romantic sentiments for a commoner. And yet we are told that Adi does not hide her feelings, but "glances" at Taitusi in public, goes "near" him while he is drinking kava with the men, and plays a traditional group game of flirtation (*vakagigi moli*), in which boys show their affection for girls by rolling lemons along the ground toward them.[32] We learn that she takes the further step of "promising" her love to Taitusi, and that their feelings for each other were common knowledge in the village.

Second, a chief's daughter would normally be obliged to obey her father's wishes regarding a suitable marriage partner. His authority was virtually absolute. But again, we see that Adi resists. We are told that she pleads to her mother with her eyes and that her mother sees her misery, but does not interfere. Adi broods at the beach and then decides to run away before dawn the next morning, rather than marry the old man. Third, a chief would almost never reverse a decision, especially when he had made his will known in a public setting. In Fiji, marriages have traditionally represented unions between large extended families, and chiefly marriages could entail hundreds of relatives in festivities with major economic and political significance. We are not told the extent of the marriage arrangements which the chief had undertaken, but he stood to loose considerable face and perhaps economic and political leverage by changing his mind. In addition, by resolving that Adi should marry Taitusi, he overrides the usual paramount importance of rank in deference to his daughter's wishes.

Let us examine these surprises in turn. Adi's strikingly public displays of affection suggest a degree of self-regard we might miss if we interpret her flirtatious behavior as merely willful, disobedient misconduct. She is after all, the daughter of a chief, and therefore has a certain elevated status vis-à-vis non-chiefly women. Her love for Taitusi is certainly passionate, and perhaps deep and far-reaching. We are told that her eyes "sparkled" and that her face "glowed" with happiness. And so, in following her heart, we might argue that she refrains from ignoring a basic need for intimacy, as well as refraining from breaking a "promise" she has made to Taitusi.

At the same time, however, she also indirectly honors a need for order and security within the traditional Fijian worldview. That is, she does not cause a scene in front of her father. She pleads with her eyes to her mother, but does not verbalize her disappointment or otherwise entreat her mother to join in her protest.[33] Rather than flaunting her feelings in public at this stage, Adi retreats to the beach. Taitusi watches her from afar. This may be more of his own choosing, but clearly he is not being given a signal from Adi that further contact is either desirable or permissible given her father's decision. Finally, Adi flees the village before dawn in a quiet, clandestine fashion. She resists by taking herself out of the picture rather than by overtly challenging her father.

In retrospect, Adi's course of action suggests a moral tension between self-regard and obedience to the *vakaturaga* (meaning, "the chiefly manner").[34] It implies that in the Fijian moral universe, there is ample space for individual self-assertion against the collectivity of the group as institutionalized in the *vakaturaga*. Here such self-assertion takes the form of attending to a need for intimacy—to be known by another person and to be affirmed and accepted for who she is. Consequently, an honoring of the rank order system of authority does not necessarily entail the suppression of individual preference.[35] Adi's love for a commoner implies a flexibility in attitudes toward the social structure that is not usually reflected in structural analyses of Polynesian cultures.[36] Indeed, she is allowed to flirt openly with Taitusi.

The symbol of Adi's flight has additional moral significance. It suggests that, in situations of conflict, it is crucial to find creative ways to demonstrate one's opposition. Adi could have run off with Taitusi. She could have publicly protested. She might well have "gone through the motions" of marrying the old man, and, by adopting a lack luster attitude, expressed unhappiness with her father's decision. But instead, by retreating to the beach, forest, mountains and lake, Adi creates a liminal space apart from the ordinary, everyday context of village life.

The flight to a liminal arena has several implications. First, it gives one's family, social class or allies an opportunity to recognize the depths, and ponder the roots, of one's opposition. Second, it creates time so that an outcome is not found too quickly. Third, and perhaps most significantly, it reaffirms the sense in which our relationship to the land can be a resource for liberation.[37] In the myth, it is from the womb of the earth that new life in the form of the flower springs forth in response to Adi's yearning. The Tongan theologian Keiti Ann Kanongata'a has stressed the metaphor of "birthing" as an apt symbol for what is occurring in the region, especially in terms of the emergence of a women's movement.[38] Perhaps Adi's flight represents a deeply rooted sense of a primordial birthing motif in traditional culture. It certainly enables her to give birth to something new.

From the standpoint of our relationship with the environment, Adi's seeking refuge in nature not only suggests the therapeutic value of re-connecting with the eco-system, but also the transformative power which is latent in such reconnection. Here the earth becomes a salvific agent. When the land births her tears into the delicately shaped white and red flower of the Tagimoucia, it creates a multi-vocal symbol of love, despair, passion, beauty and reconciliation.

The earth is not only a source of liberation for Adi. It becomes a liberating element for her father as well. When he sees Adi's tears in the shape and color of the Tagimoucia plant, he has a change of heart. He realizes how dearly Adi loves Taitusi. The narrative informs us that, because he is a chief, he "knew the truth of things when he saw them." He becomes reconciled with his daughter and also agrees to embrace the commoner, Taitusi, as his future son-in-law. The climax of the plot points to the profound significance of reconciliation as a forgiveness of willful acts of separation from community life. In this case, the reconciliation takes precedence over all sorts of other traditional values, not the least of which are the ranking system and the chief's decision-making prerogatives. It suggests that there is an extraordinary range of give and take in interpersonal relations, and a willingness to set aside cultural norms in the interest of a fuller and deeper sense of what constitutes right social relationships in practice.

Before moving to an analysis of a parallel legend from the Cook Islands, let us consider three implications of this interpretation of moral experience in the Legend of Tagimoucia for interpreting the recent political upheaval in Fiji. First, the assertion of self-regard and individual preference, in the context of an allegiance to the *vakaturaga*, may help explain the way in which many Fijians appear to embrace both the *vakaturaga* and modern, democratic institutions at the same time. The continued co-existence of the traditional hierarchical chiefly system alongside modern democratic institutions of government has often baffled Western commentators and researchers.[39] The human rights assumptions of the latter are often viewed as being in contradiction with the authoritarian strictures of the former. Western observers shake their heads in disbelief when western educated Fijians, who celebrate individual liberties, continue to extol the merits of the *vakaturaga* and the *vanua*. Yet many Fijians appear to juggle, if not move comfortably, between the two value systems.

Second, my interpretation of the moral tension between self-regard and the chiefly manner suggests that the military coups of 1987 were more a matter of a collusion between charismatic and traditional authority and less a rejection of democratic principles than Western observers have previously thought.[40] Or at the very least, this tension implies that moral action is not to be solely equated with action in accordance with either democratic models or the chiefly manner. This insight may shed light upon how the coup maker and commoner, Sitiveni Rabuka, could command such popular support, both before and after, the military takeovers.

In May 1987, as a result of a democratic election in Fiji, the first non-chief, Timothy Bavadra, was catapulted into the position of Prime Minister.[41] This was a major affront to the *vakataraga*. In the minds of traditionalists, it may even have implied disrespect of the *vanua*. Even though Bavadra was a Fijian who was respectful of Fijian cultural traditions; he was supported by labor union, Indo-Fijian,[42] and left-wing university activists who were not particularly sympathetic to the vakaturaga. To many western observers, democracy had simply won out over the traditional chiefly system. In this light, Rabuka's military overthrow of the Bavadra government was viewed as a tyrannical blow to democracy. And yet, Rabuka had an uneasy relationship with the chiefs. It was only after several approaches to the Great Council of Chiefs, the highest body of chiefly authority in Fiji, that he was able to gain the support of traditional leaders.

The above analysis of Fijian moral experience in the Tagimoucia legend suggests a fresh interpretation. Bavadra's election tilted the balance between the chiefly way and democratic aspirations in favor of the latter. What Rabuka did, in asserting a charismatic authority, was bring the traditional and democratic worldviews back into a kind of equilibrium. In fact, Rabuka himself later became an embodiment of democratic principles as a political party leader and prime minister. It is particularly interesting to note that virtually all of the political commentators in the region predicted that Rabuka would not succeed in the election.[43] This was because he was viewed as having run rough shod over democratic principles on the one hand, and as having offended leading paramount chiefs, and by extension, their constituents, on the other hand. But if Fijians are understood, in the light of our analysis, as embracing both a respect for *vakaturaga* and for the dignity of individual human aspirations, it is not surprising that they would rally behind a charismatic figure like Rabuka, who shows deference to the *vanua* while simultaneously acting as an autonomous agent who fights for his own perception of justice.

Given the traditional respect for the chiefly way, it is also not surprising that the 1999 elections, resulting in the ascendancy of Mahendra Chaudhry, the first Indo-Fijian Prime Minister, would be followed by yet another military coup. Clearly, the 2000 coup, like the 1987 coups, constitutes a complex social event, related to a host of factors, including class struggles, inter-tribal rivalries, racism, ethnocentrism, international alliances and rapid economic changes. But it also is important to consider the sense in which it too can be interpreted as representing a moral predisposition toward restoring the tension between an affirmation of individual autonomy and loyalty to the chiefly system.

Third, the centrality of moral values, such as reconciliation and forgiveness, in the Tagimoucia legend help explain the way in which these coups were conducted, as well as their aftermath. Western commentators have marveled at the so-called "bloodless" character of the 1987 coups and the amicable, if protracted, series of negotiations leading to a settlement of the 2000 coup.[44] In 1987, there were no lives lost in the take-over. In the 2000 coup, there was less control of the situation. Two lives were taken. Parliamentarians were held hostage for a longer period of time. Properties were burned and looted, and there were isolated incidents of assault and physical intimidation. But Indian and Fijian hostages, though separated in captivity, were unharmed. Some Fijian hostages were allowed to leave to attend funerals or to seek health treatments. Indian hostages were photographed embracing their captors on the day they were released. The interim military government made various efforts to include the coup makers in negotiations regarding the establishment of a new government, even though they opposed some of their positions and rejected their means. This inclusion of the rebels in decisions that also involved the Great Council of Chiefs is indicative of the saliency of the moral predisposition toward reconciliation identified in the Tagimoucia legend.[45] Let us now consider a second story of conflict and flight.

The Legend of Te Ana Taki Taki[46]

The narrative of Te Ana Takitaki is a Polynesian story from the island of Atiu, north of Rarotonga in the Cook Islands.[47] Atiu, also known as "Tauranga" and "Enuamara," is a locus of sacred power. Cook Island creation myths speak of inhabitants of Atiu as springing from the ancestor *Atiu-Mua*, whose father was the supreme divinity *Tangaroa*. All people on Atiu are related to one another because they are descended from *Tangaroa*. The title of the legend, "Te Ana Takitaki," roughly translates, "the cave to which one is led," and signals the centrality of both a leading by the spirit world and the cave as key symbols in the narrative. The main protagonists in the legend are Inutoto and Pararo, a young married couple. The story begins at a time of heightened ritual activity. A special dance, the Moonlight Dance, is being held during the night of the full moon.[48]

Inutoto is described as a beautiful, graceful woman who loved dancing and is looking forward to this special occasion. The plot develops when Pararo forbids her to attend the dance. Pararo then goes fishing but does not catch anything and wonders why the sea seems empty of fish. He senses that the gods are against him. Inutoto eventually gives in to her desire to go dancing, puts a red hibiscus flower in her hair and, swaying seductively, joins the dancers. When Pararo returns home and discovers his wife missing, he assumes she has gone to the dance and sets out for her. He finds her at the dance, forcibly drags her away and curses her for disobeying him.

That night in their hut, Inutoto lays awake feeling hurt by what she perceives as the injustice of Pararo's anger and the humiliation of being dragged off in front of her friends. She then slips out of bed and runs away while Pararo is sleeping. Initially, Pararo discounts her absence because she has run away before and always come back after a cooling off period at the home of her brother, Ngarue. However, when he realizes that she did not go to Ngarue's home as expected, he becomes alarmed and both he and Ngarue set out to find her. After a long unsuccessful search over several days, Pararo finally, in desperation, prays to the gods for help. At that moment, a kingfisher bird appears and leads Pararo into the secret heart of an awe-inspiring cave. He calls to Inutoto and she comes to him out of the darkness of the depths of the caverns. They embrace and forgive each other, and Pararo leads her out of the cave.

Viewed from a Western perspective, in the light of feminist thought and from the vantage point of a human rights culture, it might appear that Inutoto is the victim of an authoritarian husband. She therefore justifiably flees a context of spouse abuse. It seems outrageous that Pararo "forbids" her to go to a communal ceremony and forcibly drags her home. It is disturbing, at the very least, that the legend concludes with a statement that they "forgave each other" as if Inutoto had also wronged Pararo, or as if her wrongdoing should be viewed as equivalent to his.

But such a reading not only ignores the context of the story, it also leads us away from some of the central moral features evoked in the narrative. First of all, Inutoto's desire to go to the dance is certainly not wrong in the traditional setting. As a communal activity of celebration and recreation with links to the regenerative power of Atiu-Mua and Tangaroa, the dance would represent a significant context for enacting and expressing right social relationships.[49] What makes her attendance at the dance problematic is not the erotic character of the dance itself, but the fact that in this case it represents an act of disobedience to her husband. In disobeying his express command, Inutoto not only wounds her husband, but she also undermines the larger social fabric in which wives are supposed to obey husbands.[50] In this traditional island context, Pararo has every reason to be furious with her behavior.

At the same time, all is not well with Pararo. One of the anomalies of the legend is Pararo's insistence on going fishing on the night of a full moon. It seems to be common knowledge in the islands that fish do not bite during the full moon.[51] Either Pararo is out of his mind, he is doing something intentionally irreverent, or he is setting his wife up to disobey him. In any event, we are told that while fishing he also heard the drums and felt "uneasy." He was surprised that the sea seemed "empty of fish" and felt that "the gods were against him." It is as if he is driven by some irrational desire to push against and defy the boundaries and limits of the cosmic order of things. Yet he still paddles across the sea to other areas in a futile attempt to get a catch.

Viewed in the context of everyday life in the islands, it is also surprising that Pararo is apparently fishing all by himself. Traditionally, fishing is a group activity. The image of Pararo drifting alone in his canoe, while a sizable group of relatives are dancing and celebrating within earshot, suggests that he is isolating himself from community life. As some Pacific Islanders have indicated to the author, it would have been appropriate for him to accompany his wife to the dance. In all likelihood, it was a communal event involving men and women, married and unmarried, young and old. One wonders why Pararo is not participating.

Consequently, a contextual reading of the narrative discloses a husband who is dangerously disregarding the relational character of the cosmic and communal order. Pararo acts as if he does not rely on the gods for support and presumes that, full moon or not, he can defy the odds and catch fish anyway. Inutoto's willful disobedience is thus matched by Pararo's own willful self-assertion against communal expectations and the gods. Moreover, although Pararo would have been expected to assert his familial authority over a disobedient wife in the traditional context, his extremely aggressive public display of anger may well have crossed the line.[52] It would certainly have highlighted the fact that he had not accompanied his wife in the first place. It would also have injected an angry note into an otherwise celebratory occasion and disturbed the cosmic harmony symbolized by the unity of drum, dance and moon.

It is instructive to note that Inutoto, like Adi Perena, flees rather than self-destructs, seeking refuge in nature. It was not uncommon, according to Cook Islanders, for women to either grudgingly submit to their husbands or, in extreme cases, to commit suicide. Further, her entry into the cave symbolizes a journey back into the depths of creation, such that her emergence evokes a sense of re-birth as well as reconciliation and reunion. It is as if Inutoto knows on some deep level that Pararo would never have found her without the kind of change of heart that entailed a re-establishing of links with the gods. And it is remarkable that as soon as Pararo reached out, the kingfisher bird immediately comes to his aid. Pararo has been humbled. Perhaps the new Pararo will be more likely to freely enter into community. Perhaps Inutoto will develop a deeper regard for Pararo's newfound integrity. Or, perhaps she will not. But the story leaves open the possibility of interpersonal transformation within the norms of the traditional social and religious context.

One implication for social ethics in the Pacific is that morality is integrally related to religion. Right social relationships in the human community are grounded in proper relationships with the spirit world. One cannot ignore prevalent understandings of the intentionality of the gods. Again, the title of the legend, "Te Ana Taki Taki" (meaning, "the cave to which one is led"), suggests the importance of attending to the directionality that is operative in the spirit world. Pararo is led to the cave. And this raises a second point. A key feature of his moral experience is an ordeal of suffering. In the narrative, as Pararo is led to the cave, he "stumbles down" into a depression, climbs over "sharp coral" and enters "great gloomy chambers." Rather than leading, he has to follow, and the path trodden is a rugged one. All the while he fears that he will not find Inutoto. He almost does not find her. She answers only when he asked "one last time."

In addition to the interrelationship of morality with religion and the element of suffering, the legend highlights the centrality of forgiveness. Just as Adi Perena's father readily forgives Adi's disobedience when he "sees the truth of things," so the gods forgive and assist Pararo when he sincerely prays to them. Inutoto forgives Pararo for humiliating her at the dance, and Pararo forgives Inutoto for disobeying his command. The climax of the plot in both this narrative and the Tagimoucia legend is thus centered in reciprocal acts of forgiveness.

An understanding of such acts is crucial if we are to move beyond the two basic stereotypes perpetrated in the bulk of expatriate literature about the South Pacific—as either romantic primeval paradise or fearful enclave of cannibals and savages.[53] In particular, the legend of Te Ana Taki Taki suggests that the roots of moral discord or rupture may lie in a profound alienation from our destinies, the leading of the spirits and the social fabric as a whole. As both legends disclose, island moral experience represents distinctive cultural responses to deep-seated conflicts. It stresses the environment, participation in community rituals and situational flexibility.[54] Let us now turn to a brief consideration of a few implications of this way of doing ethics for scholarship in comparative religious ethics.

Implications for the Cross-Cultural Study of Ethics

I began this article by noting how our colleagues in the Two-Thirds world are suspicious of globalization discourse. In order to be more receptive to the moral worlds of these colleagues, I have attempted to utilize a hermeneutical approach that facilitates, as much as possible, a non-reductionistic, deep-level understanding of other cultural traditions and values. Although I am aware of the inescapability of my social location as a North American ethicist, I have sought to avoid some of the more obvious ethnocentric assumptions and preoccupations associated with doing ethics in Western academic circles. For example, I have tried to avoid the preoccupation with patterns of moral reasoning that is associated with the formalist-conceptual paradigm. I have not presupposed that there is a relative epistemological autonomy between moral understanding and religious belief. Indeed, given the above discussion of the relation of religion and morality in the legend of Te Ana Taki Taki, the boundaries between religious and moral ways of attending to the world may not be as clear cut as they appear to be in the formalist-conceptual paradigm.[55]

I have also sought to explore the senses in which the imaginative, empathetic understanding of "the other" in this type of hermeneutical approach resonates with Nussbaum's focus on attending to the idiosyncrasies and particularities of a text. In this respect, my approach has affinities with a "historical-comparativist" perspective, in the sense that, like Nussbaum, I view actors as conditioned by culturally specific, concrete, historical factors, and subject to a wide range of external forces beyond their control. Although Nussbaum focuses specifically on human action in Greek tragedy, she assumes that various courses of action in one culture may well share family resemblances with courses of action in another culture, simply because the actions in question are human actions. That is, the different ways humans deal with existential struggles, fears, triumphs and failures can be recognized as in some way familiar to peoples of widely differing cultural contexts. This is why, for example, Greek myths and Hindu epics still speak to us today. Indeed, a comparativist perspective is possible because a salient narrative contains elements that touch basic human sensibilities that are expressed wherever human beings, to borrow a motif from Alfred Schutz, "gear into the world."[56]

However, any attempt at comparison begs the question of our capacity to translate from one world to another. While the hermeneutical-dialogical paradigm is expressly concerned with a fusion of horizons between the moral world of the scholar and the moral world of the tradition under analysis, the nature of such a "fusion" is fraught with theoretical difficulties. In fact, I think it is not so much a question of a fusion as it is of a provisional "interface" with one another as we move in and out of our own orbits of experience.[57] Beyond the formidable problem of translating a dialect in one language into an effective equivalent in another language, there are a whole range of epistemological problems with translating between different ways of attending to different worldviews. In the West, our understanding of interpersonal dynamics associated with Adi Perena's flight is necessarily tempered by themes of "romantic love," which predispose us to read the legend in ways that are not completely congruent with the original text.[58] For example, her disappointment is rooted in a reaction against an entire node of social relationships, not just to her father as a patriarchal figure. At the same time, by utilizing culturally familiar images with great care, it is possible to shift a legend from an alien culture into a context which is meaningful for readers in their own cultural worlds, without necessarily distorting the meaning of the text in its original setting.[59] For example, by viewing the Tagimoucia legend in relation to a notion of the therapeutic value of re-connecting with the environment, North Americans can appreciate something of the power and significance of the *vanua* in the Fijian worldview.

Beyond the issue of translating from one world to another is the issue of translating between provinces of meaning within the same lifeworld. One advantage of doing culture-specific narrative ethics in oral traditional contexts may be that it is particularly conducive to the articulation of the interrelationship of moral experience with other activities in everyday life, such as politics. While I am not expressly concerned with establishing causal hypotheses between moral activity and events in everyday life, my approach does seek to establish affinities between moral and non-moral ways of attending to the world. In this article, I have argued that, viewed from an insider perspective, the military coups in Fiji were related to enduring moral predispositions. This claim represents a novel way of viewing events that were almost universally condemned in the Western media as immoral, or, in the regional press, interpreted as essentially amoral developments.

Finally, since my major focus is on interpreting narrative themes and symbols that are embedded in texts, I think it is important to keep the dialogical dimension of the "hermeneutical-dialogical paradigm" subservient to the hermeneutical one. To a certain extent, I dialogue with the text as I encounter it, and I certainly valorize speaking with persons in the tradition about what the text means to them. But the dialogue is understood as facilitating the hermeneutical task, rather than as a transformative exercise in its own right. Nevertheless, it is also clear that dialogue generates new sets of lenses for the interpretive task. Consequently, it is critical to that task. Without it, we also run the risk of missing and misconstruing major nuances in the text.

In summation, I propose to do narrative ethics by interpreting the moral dimensions of oral narratives in cultural contexts where oral traditional expression is alive and well. I aim for a deeper understanding of the moral experience of the persons in question and seek to relate that understanding to events in everyday life. Finally, I strive to prepare the groundwork for cross-cultural comparisons between ethnic groups within multi-ethnic and multi-racial regions, such as the South Pacific. In my analysis of the legend of Te Ana Taki Taki, I identified core motifs of suffering, forgiveness and reconciliation. To the extent that such motifs are also found in, or presupposed by, narratives in other sub-regions (such as in the Legend of Tagimoucia in Melanesia), I envision the possibility that these motifs may be useful for facilitating common moral discourse in the South Pacific region as a whole.

NOTES

[1]This argument is increasingly voiced in church publications and international consultations on globalization. See Godwin Hlatshwayo, "The Global Commons," *GEAR* [Global Education and Advocacy Resource—A publication of the UCC & Christian Church] (April 1998): 20-23, 25; and Liberato Bautista, "Subversive Globalization," *GEAR* (April 1998): 9-15. In 1999, the Fiji Council of Churches and the South Pacific Association of Theological Schools hosted workshops and international gatherings on globalization. A critical perspective on the issue was highlighted in several papers at the Consultation on Globalization and Partnership held at Deuba, Fiji, July 7-11. See especially the unpublished papers of Njoroge Nyambura, "Women in Ecumenical Theological Education and Ministry in the Age of Globalization," and Sevati Tuwere, "Affirming the Faith of the Church in the Process of Globalization," available at the South Pacific Association of Theological Schools, Suva, Fiji.

[2]"Prose narrative" is a generic folklorist term for a broad category of oral traditions that includes myths, legends and folk tales. Technically, "myths" are narratives that are considered by the storytellers to be true accounts of what happened in the remote past. This article focuses on "legends," or "narratives which, like myths, are regarded as true by the narrator and his audience, but...are set in a period considerably less remote, when the world was much as it is

today." See William Bascom, "The Forms of Folklore: Prose Narratives," in Alan Dundes, ed., *Sacred Narrative: Readings in the Theory of Myth* (Berkeley: University of California Press, 1984), 9.

[3]The region's premier novelist, Albert Wendt, notes that many of the region's writers continue to draw on oral traditions and utilize techniques of oral storytelling. He asserts that oral narratives "are still our richest literatures even though most of them have not been recorded." Wendt, "Introduction," in *Nuanua: Pacific Writing in English Since 1980*, ed. Albert Wendt (Honolulu: University of Hawaii Press, 1995), 5.

[4]"Four Paradigms in Teaching Comparative Religious Ethics," in *Explorations in Global Ethics: Comparative Religious Ethics and Interreligious Dialogue*, ed. Sumner B. Twiss and Bruce Grelle (Boulder: Westview Press, 1998), 11-33.

[5]For examples of this perspective see my own appropriation of the dialogical interpretive approach of Ada Maria Isasi-Diaz, *En La Lucha/In the Struggle: A Hispanic Women's Liberation Theology* (Minneapolis: Fortress, 1993) in *Seeds of Transformation: Discerning the Ethics of a New Generation* (Pietermaritzburg: Cluster Publications in Association with the Centre for Constructive Theology, 1998). See also, Lee H. Yearly, "Education and the Intellectual Virtues, in *Beyond the Classics? Essays in Religious Studies and Liberal Education*, ed. Frank I. Reynolds and Sheryl L. Burkhalter (Atlanta: Scholars Press, 1990), 89-105.

[6]Twiss, 17.

[7]Twiss, 13. The "formalist-conceptual" paradigm is exemplified in the seminal work in the field, Sumner B. Twiss and David Little, *Comparative Religious Ethics: A New Method* (New York: Harper & Row, 1978).

[8]This paradigm represents, to a certain extent, a development of the Weberian interpretive tradition and is exemplified in *Cosmogony and Ethical Order: New Studies in Comparative Ethics*, ed. Robin W. Lovin and Frank E. Reynolds (Chicago: University of Chicago Press, 1985).

[9]One assumption, however, is that a basic understanding of moral predispositions will better equip the ethicist to interpret ambiguities and anomalies which arise in moral reflection on social problems.

[10]Gananath Obeyesekere has revived a long-standing debate about historical methodologies and the role of foreign scholars in the Pacific. See his *The Apotheosis of Captain Cook: European Mythmaking in the Pacific* (Honolulu: Bernice P. Bishop Museum, 1992).

[11]The South Pacific is usually divided into three sub-regions: Polynesia, Melanesia and Micronesia. From a geographic standpoint, Polynesia includes virtually all of the islands within a triangle ranging from New Zealand eastward to Easter Island, and then north to the Hawaii group, including Tonga, Samoa, Tahiti, and the Cook Islands. Melanesia refers to the islands west of Polynesia, including Fiji, New Caledonia, Vanuatu, the Solomon Islands and Papua New Guinea. Micronesia encompasses the smaller islands north of Melanesia and west of Polynesia, including Kiribati, the Federated States of Micronesia, the Marshall Islands, the Marianas and Guam. Technically, Fiji represents a blend of Polynesian cultural traditions and Melanesian ethnic and racial characteristics. The eastern Fijian islands, which lie in close proximity to the Tongan group, share the hierarchical chiefly social system usually associated with Polynesian cultures.

[12]The author will be gathering data in the South Pacific during the summer of 2001, for a book on ethics in the region. One of the goals of this research will be to explore the possibilities for common moral discourse in the region by examining the moral underpinnings of what islanders call, "the Pacific Way." See Ron Crocombe, *The Pacific Way: An Emerging Identity* (Suva: Lotu Pasifika Productions, 1976).

[13]I was the Lecturer in Church and Society and Chair of the Department of Theology and Ethics at the Pacific Theological College (PTC), in Suva, Fiji, from 1989-93 & 1998-99, respectively. PTC is the major ecumenical, degree-granting seminary in the South Pacific region.

[14]In Fijian, kava is called, *yagona*. The term, "*yagona*," refers both to the drink and to the green plant, *piper methysticum,* from which the drink is derived. Kava is consumed in a

leisurely fashion, often outdoors, in small groups where participants are seated in a circle around a large bowl (called a *tanoa*). Although kava drinking was formerly associated more with chiefly festivities and sacred observances, today it is widespread among commoners. For a description of its use and significance in traditional ritual, see Asesela Ravuvu, *The Fijian Ethos* (Suva: Institute of Pacific Studies, University of the South Pacific, 1987), 25-26.

[15]For a classic description of this perspective see Peter Berger and Thomas Luckmann, *The Social Construction of Reality: A Treatise in the Sociology of Knowledge* (New York: Doubleday, 1966). Clifford Geertz's ethnographic approach to worldview analysis exemplifies my concern for contextuality in *The Interpretation of Cultures* (New York: Basic Books, 1973).

[16]There is no way to avoid utilizing "ideal types" of social, moral and religious experience, with all the epistemological problems that the use of such types entails. See especially the essays by Vijay Naidu, Wadan Narsey, George Bertram, Ray Waters, Asesela Ravuvu and Epeli Hau'ofa in *Class and Culture in the South Pacific*, ed. Anthony Hooper (Auckland: Centre for Pacific Studies, University of Auckland, 1987).

[17]The Indo-Fijian scholar, Subramani, presents a trenchant critique of the "negative influence" of European fiction about Pacific Islanders in *South Pacific Literature: From Myth to Fabulation*, rev. ed. (Suva: Institute of Pacific Studies, University of the South Pacific, 1992), 75-94. The critical literature regarding Margaret Mead's classic work, *Growing Up in Samoa: A Psychological Study of Primitive Youth for Western Civilization* (New York: Blue Ribbon Books, 1928), demonstrates that anthropologists were also not immune to romantic stereotypes.

[18]In utilizing oral as opposed to literary constructions, we seek to avoid some of the problems of moral disorientation associated with the "objectification," and concomitant abstraction, of indigenous knowledge from concrete contexts. For an introduction to some of the issues at stake in this ongoing debate see Walter Ong, *Orality and Literacy: The Technologizing of the Word* (London: Methuen, 1982). Murray Jardine has argued that persons who dwell in literary cultures have particular difficulties linking the objects evoked by literary meaning constructions to particular contexts of concrete practices or narrative traditions (see his "Sight, Sound and Epistemology: The Experiential Sources of Ethical Concepts," *Journal of the American Academy of Religion* 64.1 [Spring 1996]: 1-22).

[19]There was a great deal of cross-cultural interaction among South Pacific islanders prior to the advent of western colonization. Some historians have argued that ocean voyages in outrigger canoes by Islanders may have been more frequent and averaged greater distances than parallel ocean voyages in ships by European sailors during the late Middle Ages. The question of cross-cultural applicability raises the possibility that there may be common moral elements within sub-regions and even between different sub-regions in the South Pacific as a whole.

[20]Due to the range and scope of the British colonial legacy in the South Pacific, English is the *lingua franca* of the majority of islands. Although formidable problems in translation and transcription must be taken into account, many of the popular, well known texts of prose narratives are written in English.

[21]The myths were then discussed and interpreted in my course, Contextual Theology and Ethics, taught during the third trimester of the 1998 academic year at the Pacific Theological College.

[22]The argument is not that we attribute any epistemological privilege to the voices of the marginalized, but rather that it is in how themes which are important to the marginalized are dealt with that we glimpse something of the deeper moral tenor of a people. For a critique of the valorization of the epistemological vantage point of the marginalized, see Dennis McCann, "Commentary on Part Two," in Twiss and Grelle, 325-330.

[23]*God the Future of Man*, trs. N.D. Smith (London: Sheed and Ward, 1969), 136, 149-164, 191.

[24]*The Peaceable Kingdom* (Notre Dame & London: University of Notre Dame Press, 1983).

[25]*Ethics in the Old Testament* (Harrisburg, PA.: Trinity Press, 1998), 22.

[26]See *Love's Knowledge: Essays on Philosophy and Literature* (New York: Oxford University Press, 1990).

[27] It is important to note that Nussbaum is expressly concerned with tragedy, especially in *The Fragility of Goodness: Luck and Ethics in Greek Tragedy and Philosophy* (Cambridge: Cambridge University Press, 1986). While the two stories that I interpret in this article are clearly not tragic in the sense of plot development, there are underlying tragic dimensions interwoven in the myths. My argument is that Nussbaum's approach facilitates an exploration of these particularities. However, in so far as the stories do provide means for reconciliation they also reflect a distinctive thrust in the Pacific Islands regarding the centrality of reconciliation in everyday life. Traditionally, this emphasis has been dramatically illustrated in countless specific types of reconciliation rituals. For detailed descriptions of some of these rituals, see Ravuvu, *The Fijian Ethos*.

[28] *Tagimoucia*, a delicate, bright red flower, with multiple petals and white centers, is one of the world's rarest wild flowers. It can only survive at higher elevations and is only found on one of the three hundred plus Fiji islands, Taveuni. It is the national flower.

[29] For purposes of analysis, I am drawing primarily on a version of the myth as told to me by a Fijian student, Marama Savaki, a native of Taveuni, in 1998. For an abbreviated account of this commonly accepted version, see Nadine Amadio, *Pacifica: Myth, Magic and Traditional Wisdom from the South Pacific Islands (Sydney: Angus and Robinson, 1993)*, 56-57. For an alternative version, see A. W. Reed and Inez Hames, *Myths and Legends of Fiji and Rotuma* (Auckland: Reed Books, 1967), 200.

[30] In Fijian, "Adi" is a term of honor used with reference to high-ranking women in a hierarchical chiefly social system.

[31] In Fijian, "Tagimoucia" means "tears of despair."

[32] The above quotations, and all the quotations from the myth below, are taken from the version that appears in Amadio, *Pacifica*, 56-57. Traditionally, in public settings, the drinking of kava would often have been an exclusively male activity. For a young unmarried woman to pass nearby in this context would have signaled, among other things, an extreme demonstration of affection.

[33] This is significant because eye contact is a rich and complex form of social interaction in the islands. A slightly raised eyebrow can communicate a world of sentiment, allegiance, disdain or solidarity, depending on the agents and context involved. We can only conjecture what transpired between mother and daughter in this emotionally laden, non-verbal exchange, but perhaps the mother is signaling her daughter to follow her gut instincts. Or, on the contrary, she may be signaling her to give it up and resign herself to her father's expectations. Or, what is perhaps more likely, the mother may be conveying a complex, ambiguous set of feelings involving grief, regret, remorse, hope and rebellion.

[34] *Vakaturaga* refers to actions and personal characteristics that are associated with a person of high status, and evokes respect, deference, compliance, humility, loyalty and honesty, among other virtues. For a detailed discussion, see Ravuvu, *The Fijian Ethos*, 18-19.

[35] Depending on the antiquity of the myth, it could be argued that this moral tension already existed prior to western impact, or at least prior to missionary Christian influences. Jocelyn Linnekin and Lin Poyer stress the tenacity of indigenous notions of identity and morality even in the face of major political and economic changes in "Introduction" to *Cultural Identity and Ethnicity in the Pacific*, ed. Jocelyn Linnekin and Lin Poyer (Honolulu: University of Hawaii Press, 1990), 9.

[36] Representative examples of such analyses include Patrick Kirch, *The Evolution of Polynesian Chiefdoms* (Cambridge: Cambridge University Press, 1984); and Peter Bellwood, *The Polynesians: Prehistory of an Island People* (New York: Thames and Hudson, 1987).

[37] In Fijian, the word for land is *vanua*. The *vanua* denotes not only land, but also sea and air. Furthermore, the *vanua* includes all the persons and ancestors associated with the geographical area, all the natural and humanly constructed artifacts rooted in the land, and all the traditions and rituals that give expression to the basic value of the land. For a detailed description of the *vanua*, see Ravuvu, 14-15.

[38] "A Pacific Women's Theology of Birthing and Liberation," *Pacific Journal of Theology* 2.7 (1992): 3-11.

[39] This puzzlement is apparent in Donald Heinz's article on recent political developments in Fiji. See "The Sabbath in Fiji as Guerrilla Theatre," *Journal of the American Academy of Religion* 61.3: 415-442.

[40] On May 14, 1987, five weeks after a coalition of the Indian National Federation Party and the Fijian Labor Party had unexpectedly won election, the first coup in modern Pacific history took place in Fiji. It was led by the then Brigadier Sitiveni Rabuka. Rabuka seized parliament with eighteen masked soldiers and held parliamentarians hostage until he facilitated the appointment of an interim government. Then, fearing the direction in which the interim government was moving, Rabuka staged a second coup four months later, on September 25. In May 1992, he successfully led his political party, the Soqosoqo ni Vakavulewa ni Taukei (SVT) to victory and became Prime Minister. For a condemnation of the coups as an affront to democratic principles, see Hugh Tinker, et al., "Fiji," Minority Rights Group Report No. 75, London (October 1987): 3-15. For detailed accounts, see Robert Robertson and Akosita Tamanisau, *Fiji: Shattered Coups* (Leichhardt, New South Wales: Pluto Press, 1988); and Kenneth Bain, *Treason at Ten: Fiji at the Crossroads* (Auckland: Hodder & Stoughton, 1989).

[41] See the collection of speeches and writings in 'Atu Bain and Tupeni Baba, *Bavadra: Prime Minister, Statesman, Man of the People* (Nadi, Fiji: Sunrise Press, 1990).

[42] Approximately 46% of the population of Fiji is comprised of the descendants of sugar cane workers who were brought to Fiji in the nineteenth century, as well as descendants of Indian merchants and professionals who later immigrated. This segment of the populace is referred to as "Indo-Fijian" to distinguish them from the indigenous "ethnic Fijians" who were native to the islands prior to the waves of immigration from India. Ethnic Fijians make up approximately 49% of the population. See "Background Notes: Fiji, May 1996," U.S. Department of State, Bureau of East Asian and Pacific Affairs (Washington, D.C., 1996 [cited 12/10/00]); available from www.state.gov/www/background_notes/fiji_0596_bgn.html.

[43] As a case in point, see Robert Keith-Reid, "The Major-General's Losing Battle to Succeed Ratu Mara," *Islands Business Pacific*, April 1992, 20-25.

[44] A Fijian businessman, George Speight, staged the May 19, 2000 coup. After Speight's raid on parliament, the Fijian army gave in to most of his demands, including the throwing out of the 1997 multiracial constitution. While this coup entails a number of different elements than the 1987 coups, and the author does not condone the racist dimensions of the take-over, the argument is that once the army finally won control of the situation, they sought to become reconciled with the coup makers. Although there have been numerous reports of assaults on Indian activists and rapes of Indian women, it is certainly not clear that the vast majority of Fijians would condone such acts.

[45] It is frequently the case, in contested appointments in church life or the private sector, for the defeated opponent to be offered a major position as a conciliatory gesture.

[46] The late Tua Tome Tapurau, a Cook Island student at the Pacific Theological College, related this myth to the author during the first trimester of 1999. Tua's account is very similar to the version provided in Amadio, *Pacifica*, 60-61. Quotations from the myth that are cited in the text are taken from Amadio's version.

[47] Ernst Beaglehole's *Social Change in the South Pacific: Rarotonga and Aitutaki* (New York: Macmillan, 1957) is a classic ethnographic study of social change processes in the Cook Islands.

[48] Although we are not given specifics about the dance in the myth, Cook Islanders reported to the author that the moonlight dance is probably a reference to a particularly erotic dance, known in the local idiom as *Urupiana*. The early missionaries especially despised Urupiana, which was often a prelude to lovemaking. Generally, a full moon is also associated with a longer period of informal talking among villagers in the evening, and thus may serve as a catalyst for social contact. See Beaglehole, 162.

[49] Community dances are an important component of Cook Island village activities and represent a pervasive orientation toward physical, interpersonal contact in the culture. See Beaglehole, 172-174.

[50]According to Cook Island customs, marriage is patrilocal and descent is patrilineal. See Beaglehole, 177.

[51] I did uncover dissenting opinions on this point. However, the majority view of Pacific Island men from Polynesian areas was that it was not a good idea to go fishing during the time of a full moon. Speculation ranged from the idea that the additional light on the surface of the water frightened the fish away to lower depths, to a belief that it was taboo to fish during this time because it was perceived as disrespectful to the gods, whom one should be attending to rather than fishing for one's own needs.

[52] Although, traditionally, it would not have been uncommon for a husband to beat his wife, especially if the wife refuses to obey a command from her husband. See Beaglehole, 179.

[53]The Samoan novelist Albert Wendt presents a thoroughgoing critique of Western stereotypes, in "Novelists and Historians and the Art of Remembering," in *Class and Culture in the South Pacific*, 78-92.

[54]Linnekin and Poyer emphasize that these and similar elements are much more formative for Pacific Islander identity in general then factors such as descent, innate characteristics or unchanging social and cultural boundaries. See *Cultural Identity*, 1-16.

[55]A phenomenology of religions perspective regarding the nature of religious and moral experience is particularly helpful in this connection. See my application of Alfred Schutz's description of different finite provinces of meaning to the conceptualization of a religious mode of awareness in Jack Johnson-Hill, *I-Sight: The World of Rastafari—An Interpretive Sociological Account of Rastafarian Ethics* (Lanham, Md., & London: American Theological Library Association and Scarecrow Press, 1995), 121-37.

[56]See Alfred Schutz, *The Phenomenology of the Social World* (Evanston: Northwestern University Press, 1967).

[57]In discussing problems of translation between cultural worlds, Daniel Stempel says that, "East and West do not meet, they do not collide, they pass each other with at best a friendly wave, proceeding in different directions." See Cornelia N. Moore and Raymond A. Moody, eds., *Comparative Literature: East and West: Traditions and Trends: Selected Conference Papers* (Honolulu: College of Language, Linguistics and Literature, University of Hawaii and the East-West Center, 1989), 9-10.

[58]See a demonstration of this point with respect to how Japanese readers were inclined to interpret a western poem in terms of conventional Japanese images of "autumn" in Jean Y. Toyama, "Intertextuality and the Problem of Translation: A Study of Two Translations of Verlaire's 'Chanson d'Automne,'" in *Comparative Literature*, 65-70.

[59]Nakajima Atsushi's fictional biography of Robert Louis Stevenson uses the image of the silkworm spinning its cocoon and its transformation into a butterfly to describe Stevenson's struggle to complete his work before his death. See Nobuko Miyama Ochner, "Robert Louis Stevenson through a Japanese Eye: The Silkworm Image in *Light, Wind and Dreams*," in *Comparative Literature*, 58-64.

On Keeping Theological Ethics Theological in Africa: The Quest for a (Southern) African Theological Ethics

R. Neville Richardson

Abstract

What is the direction of South African theological ethics as that country moves out of the apartheid era into a new democratic future? Following its struggle against apartheid, how will theology respond to the new challenge of making clear its distinctive stance in a democratic, multi-faith society with a secular constitution? A danger, similar to that previously discussed in the United States, exists in South Africa as theology evolves from a mode of resistance to that of compliance and accommodation, especially under the guise of "nation-building." The essay plots a trajectory by means of a consideration of four works representing nonracial liberationist theology which emerged at key points in the past fifteen years—the *Kairos* Document (1985), and works by Albert Nolan (1988), Charles Villla-Vicencio (1992), and James Cochrane (1999). For all their contextual sensitivity and strength, these works appear to offer little of a distinctively theological nature, and little of Christian substance to church and society. The way lies open for the development of an African Christian ethics.

South African Christian theological ethics has been faced with many sharp challenges during the past twenty years. The most recent and ongoing challenge is its encounter with the totally new socio-political context following the inauguration in 1994 of the new, democratic South Africa with its new president, Nelson Mandela. What does it mean to "speak theologically" in the new national context? How adequate are recent theological statements, and what are the prospects for South African theological ethics into the twenty-first century? South African theological writing seldom explicitly calls itself theological ethics, but most of it has been thoroughly ethical in its motivation, concern, and application. Given the context of the apartheid cauldron that boiled for the second half of the twentieth century, and the involvement of the church both for and against apartheid, it is small wonder that almost all theological writing relates in some way to apartheid and the massive social problems associated with it.

In the context of a ruthless and oppressive political system it was appropriate for South African theology to respond by using the method known as "contextual." The church tended to separate itself into at least three streams: churches supporting apartheid; compliant, uncaring forms of Christianity;[1] and relatively small pockets of Christians intensely committed to respond to the overwhelming social evil of apartheid. It was with this latter group that contextual theology was institutionally associated. The dramatic change in political context, however, now challenges theology to move beyond the abnormality of the apartheid context and to clarify its Christian and unequivocally theological stance in a multi-faith society with a secular constitution. Unless it meets that challenge it runs the serious risk of having nothing specific to say and no distinctive contribution to make to post-apartheid South Africa. The precise form which theological ethics should take is beyond the scope of this paper, but it seems important that it should remain contextual in nature, taking account of cultural as well as political factors, and in so doing uniting the concerns of both a theology of enculturation and a theology of liberation. That these two concerns should ever have been separated is an indication of an inadequate understanding of our context, for surely that context comprises both concerns inseparably and interactively. To separate them would be to be guilty of abstraction under the influence of a Western and decidedly most un-African dualism.

In a very different social context the challenge of "saying something theological" became the occasion for Stanley Hauerwas's well-known 1985 article "On Keeping Theological Ethics Theological."[2] There Hauerwas traces the development of Christian ethics in the United States and argues that, largely through the social gospel and the influential work of Reinhold Niebuhr, theological ethics came to address itself to the task of serving society by developing social strategies which could be adopted by all people of goodwill, whether Christian or not. He accepts that the motivation for this development is understandable in an increasingly secularized society in which Christianity was being marginalized from the public arena. The irony is that the more successful this approach became, the more it rendered itself unnecessary:

> For as that society increasingly becomes secular, Christians, insofar as they endeavour to remain political actors, must attempt to translate their convictions into a nontheological idiom. But once such a translation is

accomplished, it becomes very unclear why the theological idiom is needed at all.[3]

The work of Christian ethics, in Hauerwas's diagnosis, developed from that of revision to one of accommodation, with the subsequent danger of becoming discarded as uninteresting and unimportant.[4] That danger in its very different South African setting takes the form of a change from a mode of resistance to one of compliance and accommodation, especially in response to the perceived social imperative of "nation-building."

Works of contextual theology, all of a strongly political and liberationist nature, have developed in two main directions in South Africa—that of non-racial liberationist theology, and of specifically Black Theology. The concern of this paper is the direction in which South Africa's ethically inclined theology is headed at the start of the twenty-first century. It seems that the trajectory that is developing to the point of being representative is one described above as "non-racial liberationist" theology.[5]

The trajectory to be focused on starts with the *Kairos Document* and may be plotted according to three main works by Albert Nolan, Charles Villa-Vicencio, and James Cochrane, respectively. These works are social-ethical beacons in the dramatic period of transition from the dark night of apartheid to the dawn of the new democratic South Africa and as such they are works not lightly criticized. The scrutiny given here will become increasingly detailed in chronological order, for the more recent the work the more it should be of current interest, and also less likely to have already received critical comment. All of the works are powerful and unequivocal statements against political and economic oppression. For this feature, especially given the extremity of the South African social context, they are all to be commended and admired. Indeed, one criticizes them with profound reluctance, and in the realization that one runs the risk of appearing socially and politically insensitive, even possibly reactionary or downright immoral. One might easily be taken to be an advocate for an unethical theology and an uncaring church. I therefore proceed with some trepidation.

The Kairos Challenge

The *Kairos Document* was not the first expression of liberation theology in South Africa, but it marks a major step in the development of such a theology. True to its name, it emerged at a highly sensitive moment in 1985, a strategically vital time in the winding down of the tragedy of apartheid. Subtitled "Challenge to the Churches," the document distinguishes two churches in South Africa under apartheid, the church of the oppressor and the church of the oppressed. It outlines three types of theology: "state theology" and "church theology," both of which are condemned, and "prophetic theology," which is strongly advocated. I have reflected on this approach in a previous work and therefore will not repeat myself here.[6] Suffice to say that, however appropriate in its immediate context (it may even claim to have generated some of the international pressure that caused the demise of apartheid), its understanding of the church leaves much to be desired. True, its criticisms of a particularly infamous instance of church apathy and even complicity are accurate, valid, and needed to be expressed, but (as will be seen in Cochrane's work) theology which gains significance in one particular situation tends to become universalized. Given the generally weak ecclesiology of our time, the teaching of *Kairos* on the church is theologically dangerous. For theology which becomes, for whatever reason, too closely identified with a particular set of circumstances has great difficulty in rediscovering its identity when those circumstances change. The ecclesiological problem generated by *Kairos* is that it sees the church as constituted by oppressed people and the church's agenda as set by the leaders of the political struggle. No effort is made to distinguish the people of God among the suffering and oppressed masses. *Kairos* is a brief statement, roughhewn for extremely rough times, but its impact is still felt in the very different context of the new South Africa, and its theological legacy is the concern of this paper.

Gospel for the Poor and Oppressed

Albert Nolan's *God in South Africa (1988)* is set in the last few years of apartheid.[7] The cracks are showing, but the end is not yet in sight and there are instances of the brutal security system winding itself up to desperate, manic levels to counter the perceived "total onslaught." The book is subtitled *The Challenge of the Gospel,* an accurate description of what it sets out to do. For Nolan, the meaning of the gospel as good news is taken seriously and literally. If there is to be good news, it must have a directly practical applicability of a kind that brings joy. "There is something radically wrong if the message we preach cannot be welcomed spontaneously and immediately as good news."[8] It cannot be some general pronouncement, but must have the sharp particularity of the offer of genuine deliverance in the face of an urgent need:

> If we simply repeat the formulas of the past, our words may have the character of doctrine and dogma but they will not have the character of good news. We may be preaching perfectly orthodox doctrine but it is not *the gospel for us today.* We must take the idea of good news seriously. If our message does not take the form of good news, it is simply not the Christian gospel.[9]

Nolan then makes an important social distinction as to the applicability of the gospel. While Jesus, he says, intended his message to be good news to all the people of his time, it was primarily good news to the poor. The implication for the understanding of the gospel in apartheid South Africa is clear—it is first literally good news to the poor and oppressed, and it is a challenge to the rest. The fact that the subtitle emphasizes the challenge aspect indicates that Nolan expects the bulk of his readership to come from the non-oppressed group.

Nolan then unfolds the logic of this understanding of gospel in thoroughly theological terms, taking detailed note of Biblical sources, yet grounding all of them in the concrete realities of the experience of the suffering people of South Africa. He begins with an account of sin, in order to set the scene for an understanding of salvation as the announcement of the coming reign of God, as Jesus announced it in his time, "but on the basis of our experience of the work of God in South Africa today."[10] The work is a skillful intertwining of basic theological concepts such as sin, guilt, original sin, the cross, salvation, faith, hope, and the reign of God, with such features of the South African experience as "the system," unemployment, homelessness, punishment, alienation, participation, labor organization, and people's education. Nolan leaves no room for doubt that he deals thoroughly with the context. There can also be little doubt that this is a work of Christian theology. It is in respect of this latter point that I must disagree with my colleague Tony Balcomb who, while acknowledging the brilliance of Nolan's reinterpretation of fundamental aspects of the Christian faith, criticizes him on the grounds that "the reinterpreted version bore such little resemblance to the commonly accepted version that few could recognize it as the Christian gospel in the first place."[11] Balcomb claims to write from the perspective of "the ordinary people of God" for whom this would be an "emasculated" gospel, but one wonders precisely which people he has in mind. One cannot gauge the merit of a work by its reception—after all, the message of Jesus himself was not enthusiastically received by all.

I agree with Balcomb's estimation of Nolan's book as "one of the few, if not the only, definitive pieces of [South African] liberation theology coming out of the struggle years."[12] The main weakness of the work, in my view, is, like that of *Kairos,* ecclesiological. It is significant in a book whose structure follows a tight logical scheme that the chapter on the church is the last in the book and that in the penultimate chapter, the gospel is seen to challenge individualism; yet the church is not put forward as a Christian solution. The problem seems to lie in Nolan's radical disjunction between the church as institution and as the people.[13] While he acknowledges the necessity of the institutional aspect "to bring God into the picture," he sees that picture as political and excludes that institutional church from direct involvement in the political, public realm. It is here that the church as people must be involved, but he seems to have in mind Christians as individuals only. He seems to overlook the importance of the church's own political life, both within itself and as a community of witness in the public arena. It is true that he sees God's saving power as finding embodiment in structures of power. Among these structures he notes church communities alongside political organizations:

> Structures of true power are structures that embody the right use of
> power: the power of service, the power of sharing, the power of
> solidarity and love, the power of faith and commitment, the power of
> hope. In the name of justice and freedom it is these embodiments of
> God's saving power that will confront the systems of sin and evil.
> Victory is certain.[14]

What is Nolan's source of knowledge of these social embodiments if not the
church? Where is his certainty of victory grounded if not in the eschatological
community? Unfortunately Nolan's brief, passing insight into the church as a
communal structure remains undeveloped.[15]

Nation-Building Theology

Charles Villa-Vicencio's *A Theology of Reconstruction* has a special place in
our trajectory because it is a response to the transitional phase between the old and
the new dispensations in South Africa. Its historical setting is the heady days of
the sweeping away of political logjams, not only in South Africa, but also in
Eastern Europe.[16] His guiding metaphor is appropriately that of ancient Israel's
post-exilic experience of reconstruction in which new forms of national life had to
be developed. It is a metaphor for the discontinuity of the new from the old and
has obvious affinities to the South African transition. Villa-Vicencio's central
concern is that in South Africa immediately following the demise of apartheid, the
embryonic process of developing the laws and constitution for the new
dispensation should proceed according to the author's religiously informed vision
of human rights. Recognizing that church and theology previously played an
important role in criticizing and condemning the old dispensation, Villa-Vicencio
is concerned that this negative role should in the future become a more positive,
constructive role:

> The challenge now facing the church is different. The complex options
> for a new South Africa require more than resistance. The church is
> obliged to begin the difficult task of saying "Yes" to the unfolding
> process of what could culminate in a democratic, just and kinder social
> order.[17]

Such a change of roles is a daunting challenge, however, and he observes that a
"theology useful in resistance does not easily become a useful instrument in the
period of reconstruction":[18]

Bluntly stated, theology works well in combating political abuse, but can become a dangerous device in the arena of power. The concern has legitimately resulted in a hesitation by theologians to move beyond what they regard as legitimate forms of liberation theology to a theology of nation-building.[19]

Villa-Vicencio's justified fear is that theology and church will not adapt to the demands of the new national context. He recalls analogous situations, such as the Cuban revolution, in which the church did not play a positive role in the process of change, indeed it impeded change. "As such it surrendered the moral right to provide a prophetic critique of the new society."[20] He does not want to see the same situation developing in South Africa, and points to ways in which theology may play a nation-building role by interacting to positive effect with national discussions of law, human rights, economy, and communal structures.

He would agree with Nolan that it is not the business of theology and church to become a political policy or party or to identify itself too closely with one or other political movement. He also warns against the opposite danger of an uncaring relativism in which one party or policy is as good as any other. The role he urges is that of empowering and guiding the process of national reconstruction:

Nation-building theology has a special obligation to enable and empower the nation to realise the highest ideals which may be enshrined within a new society. And, given its theological bias in favour of the poor and dispossessed, it is to facilitate the emergence of a social force that specifically empowers the poor and marginalised people of society. For this to happen those who are oppressed are, without being parochial or isolationist, obliged to look to their own resources and discern the spirit of the Lord within their own culture, history and identity.[21]

It must be noticed that a phrase such as "the highest ideals" sounds fine, but is lacking in content and therefore devoid of any power to guide. The role of the oppressed is foregrounded, but what is that role to be? They are limply encouraged to "look to their own resources." What are those resources? Do they have any relation to Christian faith? And if people are to "discern the Spirit of the Lord," how and in terms of what is this to be done? Which Lord is referred to and how is his Spirit known? If theology is being put forward as vital to the nation-building process, the theology presented here is unfortunately vague. Most, if not all, of the poor and marginalized who are addressed here would be Christian and would respond to Biblically related guidance, but this guidance is not forthcoming. In spite of the early prominence given to the Biblical metaphor of post-exilic national reconstruction, this metaphor is not developed, and the work as a whole is disappointingly lacking in Biblical reference.

Another obviously weak aspect of Villa-Vicencio's theology is ecclesiology. The historical, institutional church is brought into the reckoning of the book mainly to be confronted and condemned. The proposed theology of reconstruction is addressed *to* the church rather than discussed *with* the church. There is no sense in these pages of the church itself speaking, and one is led to recall Paul Ramsey's concern at the deliberations of the 1966 Geneva conference on Church and Society and the title question of his critical reflections, *Who Speaks for the Church?*[22] Certainly Villa-Vicencio confronts the church with social obligations, but it is difficult to see any real, concrete church of a kind that may have any chance of fulfilling these or any other social obligations. Indeed, when it comes to the institutional church, he is relentlessly negative. Just one among many indicators is this:

> Despite the theological opportunity to begin anew that has come with every major political or ecclesial revolution, the church has never succeeded in exercising a positive, liberating, and prophetic role within the structures of power. It has been either essentially excluded from the political decision-making process, or used as an instrument of ideological self-legitimation.[23]

The implication of this thoroughgoing dismissal of every social role the church has ever played in situations of national transition seems to be that, if his vision of theology's positive role is to succeed in the South African case, it will be a historic first for the church. Another possibility, of course, is that he is operating with a church-less theology. Some of the criticisms of the institutional church could be taken as suggesting that the church per se is an anachronism to be superseded by a church-free theology that will somehow work like some mysterious leaven in the national lump. In any case, it should not be the church that sets the agenda of theology, but "ordinary people."[24] It is instructive to note that Villa-Vicencio seems to distinguish sharply between ecclesiology and the historical institutional church. Nowhere is this distinction openly discussed, but it certainly seems to characterize Villa-Vicencio's ecclesiological thinking. How else could he be so negatively inclined, to the point of being dismissive of the historical social role of the church, yet continue to operate throughout the work in the hope that the church will make a positive contribution to the development of key aspects of the new South Africa? In any case, it is clear that whatever the church means for Villa-Vicencio, its primary function is that of a religious means to a national end. It may be concluded that the communal locus of faith and religious insight for Villa-Vicencio is not the church but the nation. As Hauerwas says of America in relation to the ecclesiology of Reinhold Niebuhr, the new South Africa is Villa-Vicencio's church.[25]

In his generally appreciative review, James Cochrane also singles out ecclesiology as a major weakness of Villa-Vicencio's work. The first deficiency he points to is that the South African church is assumed to be homogeneous and able to take a uniform position in the great areas of national debate. This is a far cry from the church riven with differences not only doctrinal and denominational, but also of race, class, and ideology. He sees Villa-Vicencio to be working with "a universal ideal of the church rather than a situated analysis of it."[26] Such an ecclesial abstraction will rob the church of the ability to engage with society in the energetic, decisive way Villa-Vicencio hopes it will, especially since the institutional church is in fact very well placed to make a significant social impact. As Cochrane points out:

> [T]he Church is probably the only social organisation in South Africa which reaches into every democratically identifiable type of community and which has the infrastructure to connect even the most marginalised groups of people to the patterns of discourse at the centres of power and influence where national decisions are made.[27]

More telling still is the question of how the church will address society at large. We may agree that laws should be value-based rather than constructed by a process of legal positivism, but the natural law basis to which Villa-Vicencio points can hardly be held up as a distinctive theological contribution to the process. The social-ethical method which Villa-Vicencio recommends and with which the book culminates is that of middle axioms. A feature of the ecumenical social thought of the first half of the twentieth century, middle axioms are medium-term arrangements by which theological principles may be brought to bear on practical problems and strategic goals. In this method, the theological element becomes relegated to one component in an ethical calculation alongside other contextually-related factors, and an abstract element at that. Most telling of all, however, is the question of what the church will say in its dialogue with the secular society. Villa-Vicencio is so eager to develop a dialogue between theology and the social sciences that he seems prepared to sacrifice distinctive theological language in order to facilitate the dialogue.

> Unless the church is able . . . to translate the values of the gospel into practice, and proclaim its beliefs in a language that makes sense even to those who are no longer interested in its views, it may well have no significant role to play in the period of reconstruction.[28]

Here is precisely the no-win situation to which Hauerwas points in the case of American social ethics.[29] The effect will surely be to render the church incapable of making any distinctive contribution to the very nation-building process that is Villa-Vicencio's concern. Cochrane's response is precisely correct:

On what basis does the Church have anything at all to say if it is not on the basis of its inherited tradition, specifically of those images, symbols, concepts and narratives which give it its identity? . . . Will it not be left only with the task of speaking in the idiom of others (e.g. legal philosophers), surreptitiously supporting perspectives which are consonant with its values without ever admitting to the foundations upon which those values are built?[30]

A face-value understanding of the title of the book would be that it is theology before it is anything else and, at various points in the book, Villa-Vicencio declares himself to be a theologian. Whatever the author's self-understanding and intention, however, and despite his vision of liberation theology's new role in helping to shape post-apartheid South Africa, it seems that his approach has the effect of sidelining theology. In its concept, the book is timely and important, but its contents seem better described by the subtitle "Nation-building and Human Rights" than by a title which gives preeminence to theology.

Radical Localism

James Cochrane's *Circles of Dignity: Community Wisdom and Theological Reflection*[31] is broadly similar in intention to Villa-Vicencio's work, in that it sees the need for the church to develop a socially relevant prophetic vision for the future and to move beyond the protest mode of the *Kairos Document* to a more constructive engagement in society.[32] Alternatively, it could be seen to be offering a corrective to Villa-Vicencio's method of approach. Having criticized Villa-Vicencio for not taking account of the church at local level, especially among the poor and marginalized communities where the physical need for the work of national reconstruction is greatest, Cochrane sets out to do precisely this. Where Villa-Vicencio takes the "high road" of dialogue with lawmakers, economists, and constitutional experts, Cochrane takes the "low road" of focusing on one particular rural community, and emphasizing that the spatial-temporal location of that community is vital to the theological process he seeks to explore. That community is the rural settlement of Amawoti, north of Durban. Cochrane's work is more recent than the works cited above and should therefore be more pertinent to the national context which has evolved since the inauguration of President Mandela in 1994 and the enactment of the Constitution in 1996, a context which *Kairos* may have despaired of ever seeing, Nolan could only hope for in eschatological fashion, and Villa-Vicencio could only dimly envisage as a possible future waiting to be given its legal and communal shape.

Cochrane's motivating concern is that the theological enterprise should genuinely engage, interact, and dialogue with the poor and marginalized, and that the people not normally heard or seen, because they are located beyond the boundary of the "denominational churches," be listened to in a receptive and responsive way. He believes that such a dialogue should take place not only because it is the right thing to do but also because "the interpretative activity of the church and its theologians needs the wisdom of specific local Christian communities if it is to be both ecumenically and pastorally valid."[33] In agreement with Per Frostin, he regards local knowledge as "epistemologically privileged" and having the potential to provide insight into what otherwise remains hidden, not only about others but also about ourselves.[34] It is clear that his intended audience consists of trained theologians. In a number of places he identifies himself as a theologian,[35] so there can be no doubt that this is intended as a work of Christian theology—of a theologian addressing theologians. The aim is to "to force respect and attention" for those on the margins and to encourage them to make their contribution to theological discussion. The means by which Cochrane hopes to achieve this is "to draw from an interpretation of the readings of one local community a set of theoretical perspectives that may be meaningfully placed before the church at large."[36] He claims that what emerges is "not a system of theological thinking or reflection, but a growing sense of a complex process of communicative action,"[37] and that out of this process arises what he calls "incipient theology."

Cochrane's approach is theoretically sophisticated, and he draws on the work of a number of social theorists in order both to diagnose the difficulties inherent in establishing the depth of dialogue he seeks and to establish the means of realizing the task. For instance, in his discussion of the interplay of universals and particulars in our understanding, he points to Paul Ricoeur's view of knowledge as polysemic. This view implies that we can never have certainty, and should be humble about the theological knowledge garnered in connection with our uncertain, ongoing journey. On this journey we most certainly cannot take refuge in the "servile application" of past tradition; indeed the entire book is "a challenge to the servile application of the Christian tradition, and a plea for a calculated deviation from those paradigms."[38] Cochrane also recognizes "the asymmetries of power" in the engagement between theology and the marginalized community, employing the work of Michel Foucault, Jean and John Comaroff, and James Scott to address these. He finds their respective categories of "networks of micro-power," of "small-scale resistance" to hegemony, and of "hidden transcripts" to be highly appropriate in his reflections on the Amawoti community. Similarly, in the necessary business of foregrounding the experience of the poor and understanding it in their terms rather than, as is usually the case, in the terms of the dominant and powerful, he draws on Gayatri Spivak and Elizabeth Schüssler Fiorenza. It is Paul Ricoeur's idea of the self as constituted not by but *with the other* that provides Cochrane with the theoretical means of hearing the voice of the other. There is, however, never a symmetry of power—the hope for such a symmetry is a matter of eschatology.[39] It is in this context of thought that Cochrane introduces the Christian notion of discipleship, for he sees in an authentic listening relationship with the other the ongoing and often painful necessity of transformation in ourselves. Such reciprocity between the self and others, for Cochrane (following Ricoeur), is not only ethical but spiritual.[40] One senses here that one has reached the depths of Cochrane's theology, "the theological foundation for engaging with the marginalised other, as represented by the Amawoti BEC in this case."[41]

Having thoroughly diagnosed the difficulties in theological dialogue with the poor and marginalized community, it is to Jürgen Habermas that Cochrane turns for the therapeutic solution, a solution in which the tension between personal and private is resolved. For Habermas, the communal process of "knowing how" is more important than the "knowing that" of knowledge already attained. Cochrane sees in the Amawoti community's Bible study method of relating the Bible stories to their own struggles and needs, the development of "communicative action":

> The Bible study process of the BEC clearly was the basis of its communicative action: it was acknowledged by members and observers to be the key to their capacity to empower themselves and those around them, and to organise themselves effectively around a number of needs and struggles in the broader community, encompassing educational, civic, political, and developmental (economic) spheres of their life world.[42]

The therapeutic method pursued here is by no means seen as being for the particular community of Amawoti alone—Amawoti is merely the starting point, and to start there is "to start in Galilee."[43] Cochrane believes that by thus starting at the socio-political margins and then making the findings more widely available a form of communal knowing is made possible in which the post-Cartesian disjunction of either objectivism or relativism is overcome.[44] Herein lies Cochrane's proposal for an entirely new ecclesiology:

> If we are to develop a schema for the reconstruction of ecclesiology, it must be done by focusing on specific local communities that embody, or seek to embody, the values proposed in the model of communicative action as they reinterpret and reconstruct their faith understanding according to practical life in their context.[45]

By contrast with Villa-Vicencio's abstract church, Cochrane has done well to ground his work in the life of one particular historically and geographically located community. It is therefore rather strange and disappointing that we are told so little of that community's life and thinking. Apart from the insertion of a few extracts from Bible study transcripts, the sketchily described Good Friday marches, the noting of the efforts of some women to establish vegetable gardens, and the call for the university's School of Theology to provide training for the conducting of funerals, very little else is said about the thinking and action of the poor and marginalized group supposedly at the center of this entire study. Where these instances do occur, they are not presented as significant events in their own right, but usually as passing illustrations in some lengthy theoretical argument. It is as though the author on rare occasions pauses for a moment in his discussion of theory and says, "O, by the way, that reminds me of . . . . " It is true that the community is located historically and geographically early in the work, but that is done in a mere three paragraphs[46] and would seem to be sociologically inadequate. It would be good to know, for instance, how many people make up the Bible study group, sometimes called a Base Ecclesial Community (BEC), which plays the central and essential "agentive" role in its contextual reflection; what is the gender and age composition of the group; and how it interacts with the social structures and the "needs and struggles"[47] of the wider Amawoti community. Not knowing such empirical details makes for a rather blurred picture, and the communal life of the focus group whose life and thought is ostensibly at the heart of this study remains something of an abstraction.[48]

The social theory on which Cochrane draws raises salutary points for the church. One is left with no doubt as to the difficulty of authentic communication, especially where major differences of class, culture, and race are involved. Indeed one might even be driven to despair over the possibility of such communication ever being achieved, but the main impact of the work is to say that the church should be engaged in precisely this kind of dialogue, armed with all the sensitivities which the social theories show to be necessary. It seems that the author's main aim is to challenge the church to reconstruct its ecclesiology.[49] Of course, the social theory itself could be relevant to any organization or group. One might ask why the church should pay special attention to the theories selected for this study. Could the church not just as well look into its own traditions and find there many instances of the gospel engaging poor and needy communities, such as those which heard Jesus gladly?[50] At the least it should be shown how the theories might interact with Christian theology.

As noted, the work sets out to be theological, but it is in fact a work of social theory. It is intended to be relevant and challenging social theory for church and theology in post-apartheid South Africa. In my view it is indeed relevant, but it is not itself theology. To be theological requires more than the inclusion of a few passing metaphors, such as "starting in Galilee"[51] and the "conversion" and "discipleship" required in being a self with and for others,[52] without any specification of who those others might be or for what the open dialogue is intended. Perhaps the closest we are brought to theology in the midst of social theory is the reference to McGaughey about the spiritual nature of the self's relation to the other: "Spirituality is the self transcending itself for the sake of the self and, by implication, the other."[53] This may be so, and it could be taken to include Christian theology, but it is not itself Christian theology. It has an affinity to John's Gospel, "The greatest love a person can have for his friends is to give his life for them" (John 15:13), but that saying has its theological significance not in its general meaning, but in where it is recorded, to whom it was said, and especially by whom it was said.

Having held up the Amawoti Bible studies as the main resource for his theological reflection, Cochrane admits: "One cannot draw too many conclusions from a limited set of Bible studies."[54] What he does find affirmed is his methodological preference for "praxis over theory." One of the few submissions of theological content shows that the group prefers to see Jesus as human and "tricky" in his interaction with others. When this view is set alongside the accompanying observation of the group that "God is undemocratic," it clearly issues in a problem for Christology and trinitology. Of course, Cochrane would insist that the group is entitled to read the Bible its way, and at least this "incipient theology" could be the catalyst for a lively debate with Christian tradition! Is the descriptive "incipient," however, not just a convenient escape route for avoiding the theological task? Even if what is presented indeed has the makings of a more fully developed Christian theology, there is still the glaring fact that the author is presenting someone else's incipient theology and not his own.

The book closes by referring to theology (this theology?) as a journey which is not ending, but only beginning. That journey, we are told, must be marked by "the creative impulse that marks us as human beings," yet this describes any human quest, not only a theological quest and certainly not only a Christian theological quest. For Cochrane, however, it is enough that "we join in the unending pilgrimage that is our lot and our hope—we who, for better or worse, have been made in the image of God."[55] One wonders, however, where the author learns that "we have been made in the image of God"—certainly not from the human creative impulse alone.

It seems clear that this is a work not of theology, but of social theory, and as such even its relevance for theology is not self-evident. Although Cochrane makes it very clear that he regards himself as a theologian and that he is trained as a theologian, he may well agree that his project is a work of social theory rather than of theology, and point out that he puts it forward in the hope that it will in fact be taken up as a challenge by church and theology. As it stands, it falls short of being theology. It is representative of the approach criticized by Tony Balcomb in his article mentioned above, "Is God still in South Africa or are we still clearing our throats?" The article draws its title from a comment by Jeffery Stout about theology being concerned with nothing but method and thereby losing its audience. Should anyone insist that this work be seen as theology, then from what we have seen, it can only be sociology masquerading as theology. It is one thing for theology to engage the social sciences, as with the social gospel in the United States. It is another thing entirely when a Christian ethicist becomes "but a social scientist with a religious interest."[56]

A final question needs to be asked about the theological status of the Amawoti group. Nowhere is it explained that they see themselves as a church. They are referred to at times as a Base Ecclesial Community after the fashion of the Brazilian BECs, but who constituted them as a BEC? Marcello Azevedo has pointed out that the Brazilian BEC's, while operating with relative independence of the church, were nevertheless started with the blessing of the Roman Catholic church.[57] Indeed they were part of a strategy to match the growth of other Christian groupings. In what sense is the Amawoti bible study group a BEC, or linked to the institutional church in any way? If it is a BEC only in the mind of the author and his researchers, then has Cochrane in fact been successful in his corrective response to Villa-Vicencio's abstract ecclesiology? Is his chosen group perhaps so local and so small that it is not the church at all?

The Journey Ahead

Our consideration of an important trajectory of theological ethics in South Africa in the last fifteen years of the twentieth century—that of nonracial liberationist theology—seems to indicate that it is ecclesiologically defective, has little to say of a distinctively theological nature, therefore little of Christian substance to contribute to church and society, and, in the case of the latter two works, not theology at all. Is the theological road ahead as bleak a prospect as it may seem? As we have noted, the Black Theology which flourished in the 1970s and 1980s faces an uncertain future. The forms of Christianity which are burgeoning from the encounter between Western Christianity and African religions are creative, energetic, and impressive in their growth and dynamism. Theological reflection on this phenomenon, as distinct from anthropological accounts, however, has yet to develop in any great proportion and depth. It must therefore be said that African Christian ethics is embryonic in form, not yet even in its infancy.

What shape might that new theological ethics take? Tinyiko Maluleke is representative of sophisticated younger African scholars who see Black Theology in South Africa as being in crisis, but not without vitality and potential.[58] Significant points made by Maluleke are that the old division between Black and African theologies must go. It is both a false division and an un-African way of seeing the world. Maluleke therefore speaks characteristically of "Black and African Theologies." His perception of this combination of approaches, however, is far from the comparatively innocent view of Desmond Tutu and others. What Maluleke requires is that the Marxian hermeneutic of much South African Black Theology interrogate even the concept of African culture and tradition. His hermeneutic of suspicion demands that Black and African theologians "go it alone" and develop their own theology, "to drink from our own wells."[59] It seems that his proposed theology with its probing and problematizing function is not quite the same as African Christianity, for he speaks of his theology as having to link up with African Christianity, something that in his mind has yet to happen.

But if his theology is not yet linked up with African Christianity, then is it linked with Christian theology at all? Do we have yet another case of theological ethics whose theology is questionable? Much depends, of course, on what Maluleke finds in his African wells. What will be interesting to see is whether Maluleke identifies the product of this process as Christian, and what criteria he uses to justify the claim.

But this concluding observation is to begin to explore another trajectory in South African theological ethics, one in which this writer accepts his status as a resident alien, and merely a "student,"[60] looking to others to lead the way. It is to be expected that concepts like "holism" and "communalism" will guide this trajectory in its development. Whether or not it turns out to be Christian and theological, only the future will tell.

NOTES

[1] David Walker identifies and theologically analyses this form of South African Christianity in his *Challenging Evangelicalism: Prophetic Witness and Theological Renewal* (Pietermaritzburg: Cluster Publications, 1993).

[2] Stanley Hauerwas, *Against the Nations: War and Survival in a Liberal Society* (Minneapolis: Winston Press, 1985), 23-50.

[3] Ibid., 38.

[4] William Meyer's excellent critique of Hauerwas's article affirms its diagnosis, but claims that the more serious theological accommodation, of which he argues Hauerwas is also guilty, is the "widespread acceptance of the modern denial of metaphysics." (William Meyer, "On Keeping Theological Ethics Theological: An Alternative to Hauerwas's Diagnosis and Prescription," *Annual of the Society of Christian Ethics* 19 (1999): 21-45). That a fifteen year old article should be taken with such seriousness is indicative of the significance of the Hauerwas article. Meyer's point is not to be taken lightly, but in South Africa's socio-political context it seems unimportant, and given the holism of traditional African thought forms it would not be entertained by theological studies on enculturation.

[5] It is fascinating to consider what has happened to the once burgeoning Black Theology industry. Basil Moore, one of the movement's early facilitators, seems to believe that the movement's future is in jeopardy. See his "Black Theology Revisited" in *Bulletin for Contextual Theology* 1 (1994): 7-19. At the very least it can be said that there seem to be no obvious latter-day descendants of Mofokeng, Mosala, Boesak, Maimela, Buthelezi, et al. The nearest, perhaps, would be Tinyiko Maluleke, who commits what would have been a near heresy in the eyes of earlier Black Theologians by calling for theology to be as concerned with African culture as it is with African politics, in the process developing a sharply critical new direction.

[6] R. Neville Richardson, "The Struggle for Social Justice in South Africa and the Need for an Ethic of Christian Community," *The Annual of the Society of Christian Ethics* (1988): 55-75.

[7] Albert Nolan, *God in South Africa: The Challenge of the Gospel* (Cape Town: David Philip & Grand Rapids: Eerdmans, 1988).

[8] Ibid., 9.

[9] Ibid., 10. Italics in the original.

[10] Ibid., 133.

[11] Anthony O. Balcomb, "Is God still in South Africa or are we still clearing our throats?" (Unpublished manuscript, 2000), 3.

[12] Ibid., 2.

[13] Nolan, A. *God in South Africa*, 216.

[14] Ibid., 115-116.

[15] Ibid., 115.

[16] Charles Villa-Vicencio, *A Theology of Reconstruction: Nation-Building and Human Rights* (Cape Town: David Philip & Cambridge: Cambridge University Press, 1992).

[17] Ibid., 7.

[18] Ibid., 34.

[19] Ibid., 21.

[20] Ibid., 33.

[21] Ibid., 43.

[22] Paul Ramsey, *Who Speaks for the Church?* (Edinburgh: St. Andrew's Press, 1969)

[23] Villa-Vicencio, *A Theology of Reconstruction*, 20.

[24] Ibid., 40.

[25] Hauerwas, *Against the Nations*, 47, n.22.

[26] James R. Cochrane, "A Critical Review of Charles Villa-Vincencio's *A Theology of Reconstruction*," *Journal for the Study of Religion* 8/1 (March 1995): 89.

[27] Ibid., 90.

[28] Villa-Vicencio, *A Theology of Reconstruction*, 4.

[29] Hauerwas, *Against the Nations*, 40.

[30] Cochrane, "A Critical Review of Charles Villa-Vincencio's *A Theology of Reconstruction*," 88.

[31] James R. Cochrane, *Circles of Dignity: Community Wisdom and Theological Reflection* (Minneapolis Fortress Press, 1999).

[32] Ibid., 124.

[33] Ibid., 5.

[34] Ibid., 22.

[35] Ibid., xx, 144.

[36] Ibid., xxvi.

[37] Ibid., 5.

[38] Ibid., 67.

[39] Ibid., 110-111.

[40] Ibid., 116.

[41] Ibid., 117.

[42] Ibid., 129.

[43] Ibid., 132ff.

[44] Ibid., 134.

[45] Ibid., 135.

[46] Ibid., 8.

[47] Ibid., 129.

[48] Strangely, apart from the opening story of the book, there is no reference in the body of the text to the democratic election or to any other effects of the setting up of the new political infrastructures of post-1994 South Africa. One would have imagined that the interaction of the Amawoti community with the new national and regional political process would have been of paramount concern to such an avowedly contextual study.

[49] Cochrane, *Circles of Dignity*, 135.

[50] John Wesley in eighteenth century England and the growth of much Third World Pentecostalism today are other obvious examples.

[51] Cochrane, *Circles of Dignity*, 132.

[52] Ibid., 109.

[53] Ibid., 117.

[54] Ibid., 38.

[55] Ibid., 169.

[56] Hauerwas, *Against the Nations*, 28. A good example of interaction between sociology and theology in which the difference is made very clear is James Gustafson's early work

Treasure in Earthen Vessels in which he shows the relevance of sociology for ecclesiology. James M. Gustafson, *Treasure in Earthen Vessels: The Church as a Human Community* (New York: Harper & Brothers, 1961), 99ff.

[57] Marcello Azevedo, M. *Basic Ecclesial Communities in Brazil* (Washington, D.C.: Georgetown University Press, 1987), 214..

[58] Tinyiko Maluleke, "Black Theology Lives! On a Permanent Crisis," *Journal of Black Theology* 9/1 (May 1995): 1-30

[59] Tinyiko Maluleke, "Black and African Theologies in the New World Order: A Time to Drink from Our Own Wells," *Journal of Theology for South Africa* 96 (November 1996): 17.

[60] Maluleke, "Black Theology Lives!": 10, n. 8.

Contributors

Mary Jo Bane is professor of public policy and management at Harvard University's Kennedy School of Government. She was Assistant Secretary of Health and Human Services for Children and Families, with responsibility for welfare programs, in the first Clinton administration; she resigned that post after President Clinton signed the welfare reform law.

Harlan Beckley directs the Shepherd Program for the Interdisciplinary Study of Poverty at Washington and Lee University where he is the Fletcher Otey Thomas Professor of Religion. He is also the author of "Capability as Opportunity: How Amartya Sen Revises Equality of Opportunity," which will appear soon in *The Journal of Religious Ethics*.

John R. Bowlin is associate professor of religious ethics at the University of Tulsa. He is the author of *Contingency and Fortune in Aquinas's Ethics* (Cambridge: Cambridge University Press, 1999) and numerous essays and reviews. He is currently at work on a book entitled *Toleration and Forbearance*.

William T. Cavanaugh is assistant professor of theology at the University of St. Thomas in St. Paul, MN. His books include *Torture and Eucharist: Theology, Politics and the Body of Christ* (Malden, MA: Blackwell Publishers, 1998) and *Eucharistie et Mondialisation: Theopolitique d'une resistance* (Geneva: Ad Solem, 2001).

Rabbi Elliot N. Dorff is Rector and Distinguished Professor of Philosophy at the University of Judaism in Los Angeles. Author of over 150 articles, he is also the author or editor of eight books, two of which deal with ethics: *Contemporary Jewish Ethics and Morality: A Reader*, edited with Louis E. Newman (New York: Oxford University Press, 1995); and *Matters of Life and Death: A Jewish Approach to Modern Medical Ethics* (Philadelphia: Jewish Publication Society, 1998). His book, *Doing the Right and the Good:*

A Jewish Approach to Social Ethics, is due to be published by the Jewish Publication Society in February, 2002.

Jean Bethke Elshtain is the Laura Spelman Rockefeller Professor of Social and Political Ethics at the University of Chicago and the author of many books, most recently *Who are We?: Critical Reflections, Hopeful Possibilities* (Grand Rapids: Eerdmans, 2000). She is the recipient of the Theologos Award for the best book of 2000, presented by the American Theological Booksellers Association.

Eric Gregory teaches in the Religion Department at Princeton University. After studying theology as a Rhodes Scholar at Oxford University, he began his doctoral work in religious studies at Yale University. He is completing a dissertation in the area of Augustinianism and the ethics of liberalism.

Jennifer A. Herdt is assistant professor of theology at the University of Notre Dame. She is the author of *Religion and Faction in Hume's Moral Philosophy* (Cambridge: Cambridge University Press, 1997), and served as guest co-editor of a recent "Focus" on Eighteenth-Century Ethics in the *Journal of Religious Ethics* (Summer 2000).

Douglas A. Hicks is assistant professor of leadership studies and religion at the Jepson School of Leadership Studies, University of Richmond. He is the author of *Inequality and Christian Ethics* (Cambridge: Cambridge University Press, 2000).

Jack Hill is assistant professor of social ethics in the Department of Religion at Texas Christian University. He is the author of *Seeds of Transformation: Discerning the Ethics of a New Generation* (Pietermaritzburg: Cluster Publications, 1998) and *I-Sight—The World of Rastafari: An Interpretive Sociological Account of Rastafarian Ethics* (Metuchen, NJ: Scarecrow Press, 1995).

Christine Firer Hinze is associate professor of Christian ethics at Marquette University. Her recent research and writing focuses on economic ethics, in particular questions surrounding relations between wage and domestic economies, wages and livelihood, and consumerism. She is currently completing a book project tentatively entitled *A Good Living: U. S. Catholics, the Family Wage, and a Transformative Feminist Agenda.*

Aline H. Kalbian is assistant professor in the Department of Religion at Florida State University. Her research interests include gender and Roman

Catholic moral theology, and issues in bioethics related to human reproduction.

Aaron L. Mackler is associate professor of theology at Duquesne University in Pittsburgh, and teaches in Duquesne's doctoral program in Health Care Ethics. He is the editor of *Life and Death Responsibilities in Jewish Biomedical Ethics* (New York: Jewish Theological Seminary Press, 2000). Current projects include a book comparing Roman Catholic and Jewish approaches to bioethics, to be published by Georgetown University Press.

William McDonough is assistant professor of theology at the College of St. Catherine in St. Paul, MN. His main area of teaching is Catholic moral theology, and his scholarship has focused on moral epistemology. His most recent published work is a review essay in *New Theology Review* (forthcoming, fall, 2001) on Alasdair MacIntyre's book *Dependent Rational Animals*.

Charles T. Mathewes is assistant professor of religious ethics in the Department of Religious Studies at the University of Virginia. His research and teaching focus upon historical and contemporary theological ethics, moral psychology, and theology of culture. He is the author of *Evil and the Augustinian Tradition* (Cambridge: Cambridge University Press), and is currently writing a book entitled *During the World: A Theology of Public Life*.

Jean Porter is currently the John A. O'Brien Professor of Theological Ethics at the University of Notre Dame. Her research interests include foundational moral theology and the history of moral thought, especially in the medieval period. Her most recent book is *Natural and Divine Law: Reclaiming the Tradition for Christian Ethics* (Ottawa: Novalis and Grand Rapids: Eerdmans, 1999).

Christopher Steck, S.J., is assistant professor of Christian ethics in the Theology Department at Georgetown University. He is author of *The Ethical Thought of Hans Urs von Balthasar: Missioned in Christ*, to be published by Crossroad in Fall 2001.

Emilie Townes is Professor of Christian Ethics at Union Theological Seminary. She is editor of two collections of essays: *A Troubling in My Soul: Womanist Perspectives on Evil and Suffering* (Maryknoll, NY: Orbis Books, 1993) and *Embracing the Spirit: Womanist Perspectives on Hope, Salvation, and Transformation* (Maryknoll, NY: Orbis Books, 1997). She has also authored

382 *The Annual of the Society of Christian Ethics*

Womanist Ethics, Womanist Hope (Atlanta: Scholars Press, 1993), *In a Blaze of Glory: Womanist Spirituality as Social Witness* (Nashville: Abingdon Press, 1995), and *Breaking the Fine Rain of Death: African American Health Issues and a Womanist Ethic of Care* (New York: Continuum, 1998). Her current writing project considers the interrelationship between culture and evil.

Todd David Whitmore is associate professor of Christian ethics, Department of Theology, and Director of the Program in Catholic Social Tradition at the University of Notre Dame. Recent publications include, "Practicing the Common Good: The Pedagogical Implications of Catholic Social Teaching," in *Teaching Theology and Religion,* and "Teaching and Living Practical Reasoning: The Role of Catholic Social Thought in a Catholic University Curriculum," in *The Journal of Peace and Justice Studies.* Professor Whitmore has been named a 2001-2002 Carnegie Scholar for his project, "Practical Reasoning and the Catholic University."

Laurie Zoloth is professor of social ethics and Jewish philosophy, and Chair of the Jewish Studies Program at San Francisco State University. She is president of the American Society for Bioethics and Humanities and a founding member of the Society for Jewish Ethics. Her primary research interest is in bioethics and post-modern Jewish philosophy. She serves on the National Advisory Board for NASA and on the Howard Hughes Medical Institute's Ethics Advisory Board. She is the author of *Health Care and the Ethics of Encounter: a Jewish Discussion of Social Justice* (Chapel Hill: University of North Carolina Press, 1999) and co-editor (with Karen Lebacqz and Suzanne Holland) of a recent volume on human embryonic stem cells.

NEW IN PAPERBACK

WHO COUNT AS PERSONS?
Human Identity and the Ethics of Killing
John F. Kavanaugh, S.J.

*"Fr. Kavanaugh remembers what too many
philosophers forget—that philosophy begins with
the human person. . . . His book is challenging,
moving, and provocative."*—Jean Bethke Elshtain,
Laura Spelman Rockefeller Professor of Social and
Political Ethics, The University of Chicago

240 pp., paper, $24.95

CLAIMING POWER OVER LIFE
Religion and Biotechnology Policy
Mark J. Hanson, Editor

Eight contributors challenge policymakers to
recognize the value of religious views on
biotechnology and discuss how best to
integrate the Christian and Jewish traditions
into public policy debates.

Hastings Center Studies in Ethics
192 pp., cloth, $44.95

NEW IN PAPERBACK

SCIENCE AND RELIGION IN SEARCH OF COSMIC PURPOSE
John F. Haught, Editor

*"John Haught has very successfully managed to
bring together a remarkable group of scientists and
religious scholars, and the result is a challenging
diversity of perspectives that are readable, persuasive and thought-provoking. . . . The authors also
. . . broaden this interdisciplinary dialogue to
intercultural and interreligious conversation in the
best sense of the word."*—Wentzel van Huyssteen,
James I. McCord Professor of Theology and Science,
Princeton Theological Seminary

156 pp., paper, $16.95

ETHICS AND ECONOMICS OF ASSISTED REPRODUCTION
The Cost of Longing
Maura A. Ryan

*"[The author] demonstrates the folly of
approaching assisted reproduction exclusively
in terms of the procreative liberty. . . . Argued
with exceptional care, this book is a singular
contribution to the literature."*
—Paul Lauritzen, John Carroll University

Moral Traditions series
192 pp., cloth, $44.95

NEW IN PAPERBACK

BURYING THE PAST
*Making Peace and Doing Justice
after Civil Conflict*
Nigel Biggar, Editor

Examining the legal, political, social, and
psychological processes of burying the past after
civil conflict, contributors such as Donald Shriver,
Charles Villa-Vicencio, and Jean Bethke Elshtain
explore ethical concepts such as justice, retribution, forgiveness, and reconciliation.

304 pp., cloth, $45.00

JEWISH AND CATHOLIC BIOETHICS
An Ecumenical Dialogue
**Edmund D. Pellegrino and
Alan I. Faden, Editors**

*"Begins an important dialogue on common
issues of concern to both Jewish and Catholic
ethicists today."*—Choice

Moral Traditions series
256 pp., paper, $22.95

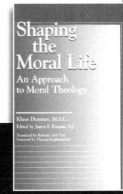